shit
magnet

one man's miraculous ability
to absorb the world's guilt

jim goad

The following is a work of nonfiction. The autobiographical and historical information contained herein is based on the author's recollection and other documentary sources. In addition, this book contains the personal opinions of the author, which are his alone and do not necessarily reflect the views of Feral House.

ISBN: 0-922915-77-6

FERAL HOUSE
P.O. BOX 13067
LOS ANGELES, CA 90013

WWW.FERALHOUSE.COM
INFO@FERALHOUSE.COM

10 9 8 7 6 5 4 3 2 1

written behind bars

5/31/98 - 10/23/00

Overture: Drowning in Shit

I **WAS STANDING** on the stairs, my oversized Tweety Bird head sticking out of fuzzy pajamas. I was three. And I was crying.

Please, Mommy, I don't wanna say it anymore—let me watch TV!

"SAY it!"

Shit...shit...shit...shit...wahhh! PLEASE!

"SAY it!"

Shit...shit...shit...shit...shit...shit...

My mother was forcing me to say the word "shit" over and over for a solid half-hour, ensuring that I'd miss my favorite TV program, *The Dick Van Dyke Show*. The stairs faced away from the television while the show aired, making my torture that much worse. I was being punished.

My crime?

I had said the word "shit."

I probably had overheard my parents say it and was only mimicking them, but no matter—I was to bear the full weight of my sin. Because "shit" had slipped from my tongue once, mom demanded that I chant it a thousand times.

These days I'm wondering whether my thirty-minute shit mantra was a magical incantation or some sort of fecal rain dance, because ever since that night, the gods have been emptying their bowels on me.

Take a whiff.

You know that smell. It's unmistakable. Enough to make you gag. And there's no getting away from it. I'm surrounded by it. A vast shitscape. Dung-heaps piled high as landfills. I'm smothered under a crapalanche. A gooey, oozing, pulsating poop mountain. I inhabit a colossal brown loaf. I am cocooned in shit, a turd-coated larva.

All sewer pipes lead to me. I'm tainted. Defiled. Infected. Soiled. A human septic tank. A black hole. A toilet bowl. When the shit goes down...when it hits the fan...it winds up sticking to me.

My life is a maelstrom of violence and morbidity. A tragedy. An absurdist farce. A slasher film. A triage center where I struggle to stop the bleeding. My life has gone way past the point where it ceases to be thrilling and sexy and funny...and becomes scary and ugly and sad.

A year ago I was on national television, plugging a hardcover book from a major publisher.

Now I'm in prison, writing on loose-leaf. And my pen's almost out of ink.

I lost my house, my car, my wife, even my dog.

I guess it could be worse. I could be on Death Row. I could have a terminal illness. I could be blind or hopelessly crippled.

Worst of all, I could be ordinary.

I knew almost from infancy that I wouldn't have a normal life.

At three or four years old, I was stricken with a waking nightmare which now seems prophetic. I sat screaming in our bathtub with all the water drained down, my pruny pink body shivering. My mother asked what was wrong. I said that I knew—I just *knew*—that I had already lived this life, and that it had ended in acute violence. And for some reason, God had rewound the movie and was forcing me to relive everything, motion for identical motion. I was headed straight for disaster, and there was nothing I could do to stop it.

Quite precocious. Little boys are supposed to be made of snips 'n' snails 'n' puppy dog's tails. I was made of shit and teardrops and visions of my own demise.

Physicists struggle with the question of why things break. My great scientific inquiry is the matter of why my life resembles a jet-plane explosion. I'm searching for the black box.

Again, I was three or four—a time in my life filled with black magic— and I drove with my parents from our suburban Philly home to a furniture store in south Jersey. While loading their purchase into the trunk, they gave me the car keys and told me to hold onto them. As dad was slamming the trunk closed, I purposely tossed in the keys, leaving us all helpless and stranded.

From then onward, whenever there's been a trunk slamming, I've thrown in the keys. I really see no other way. I keep painting myself into a corner for the sick pleasure of finding a way out. I'll roll that boulder almost all the way up the hill, just to let it tumble down again. Like Harry Houdini, I'll wrap myself inside ropes, chains, and a locking trunk, then get dropped in the ocean for no other reason than to see if I can avoid drowning.

Place something good in front of me, and I'll smash it to pieces.

I sat there with my coloring book at age four or five, blithely using crayons on an anthropomorphized cartoon carrot. "Here, mommy," I asked with feigned innocence, "do you like the way I colored this picture?" Leaning over my shoulder and swallowing the bait, mom said, "Yes, Jimmy, that's very nice." With that, I savagely defaced the page, violently slashing across Mr. Carrot with bold, fat strokes from a black crayon.

I destroyed what had been nice.

It was pure instinct.

I don't like nice things.

I never wanted an easy life. Never craved for serenity or wealth or popularity. I wanted trouble. I was very careful what I wished for.

Many people talk about going to extremes but really aren't serious about it. They surely don't want to risk anything. But I know the crucial difference between shouting "Fire!" in a crowded theater and *setting* a fire in a crowded theater.

And I have a pack full of matches in my hand.

Drama queen. Crisis junkie. Shit Magnet. I am the black sheep of the global village. The Bermuda Triangle on two legs. A living, breathing stigma. I've cornered the market on bad karma. My negative vibes set off every seismograph along the West Coast. They say I'm #1 in the Dead Pool, the next micro-celeb to die. A lot of people want me dead. Or silenced.

Ha, ha—I'm alive. And still chanting the word "shit." I've faked my own death just so I'm twice as scary when I return.

Yet for all the human waste caked onto my torso, I don't feel half as guilty as they say I am. It's just that once you start getting into trouble, they typecast you.

My birth wasn't…intended. I was an accident, and my parents blamed me for forcing them to stay together. They also blamed me for mom's health problems.

The nuns at school told me I was going to hell. I often got blamed for things which weren't my fault, things which other kids had done.

My ex-wife has cancer, and she blames me for it.

My ex-mistress is violent, suicidal, and psychotic, and she blames me for it.

An ex-soldier shoots at the White House, and I get blamed.

Three British tourists blow their brains out, and I get blamed.

JFK's assassination? The Oklahoma City bombing? Hiroshima? The Wreck of the Edmund Fitzgerald?

I did 'em all.

Blame me for everything from world famine to the Ebola virus to the Holocaust to Christ's crucifixion. Blame me for all of your measly dissatisfactions with life. But please, blame me for that annoying voice in your head that tells you I'm right. Blame me when you wonder whether it'll be a car crash or a bad biopsy or a rusty blade which finally brings you down...down...down alongside me.

Your new cellmate.

You want a piece of me?

Come into my lair, said the spider to the fly. If you think you can get some of this, slink on down this web I've woven. I've warned you before to stay away, but since you refused, come a little closer. See the dewy beads as they hang from each steely strand. Watch how they trap and refract the sunlight, how they hold a tiny rainbow before dripping down into bottomless darkness. And watch your step, for you might scuttle over a corpse or two, the brittle husks of insects who thought they could invade my domain without suffering, without writhing in final, fatal seconds of remorse, without losing their souls in the game. This time, well, it won't be like the other times. I thought you were smarter, but I was wrong. So come on down, little fly—I have something for you.

The story of my shit-stained life. My literary autopsy. My premature auto-obituary.

The court papers list my name as James Thaddeus Goad. The "Thaddeus," my mother would always remind me, was an homage to St. Jude Thaddeus, patron saint of hopeless causes.

Mom had big plans for me.

2

The Lingering Effects of Prenatal Violence

HERE I AM. I bring you blood. I bring you droplets and puddles and buckets and oceans of blood. Spurting like cum shots. Falling like rain. Slashed bellies and severed limbs. Brains just blasted all over the walls and carpet and furniture, gooey strawberry-swirl chunks sticking to lampshades.

You want it.

Need it.

It's why you came here.

Don't lie to me. We both know why you came.

You need that violent jolt, that sense of mastery over the chaos. You fucking cowardly spectator. You voyeuristic rubbernecking hypocrite, watching the gladiators through binoculars. You want bad news and dead bodies, but from a distance. You crave cinematic blood, the kind safely encased within a TV screen. Oh, isn't that horrible—I hope they show it in close-up. It's awful what he did to that little girl, and they're going to show the autopsy photos after the next commercial.

Really, they can't give you enough blood. You sop it all up with a dinner roll, and while talking with your mouth full, you beg for more. The professional dream-weavers struggle to keep pace with your appetite. Writers and film makers serve you sumptuously gory buffets, but honestly, what do they know about it?

How many of them have been convicted of assault?

They bring you red food coloring.

I bring you real blood.

Some of it flows from my victims.

Some of it's dripping out of me.

My face has been cut open and stitched up so many times, it's like getting my teeth cleaned. I've been peeled apart and sewn back up like a rag doll. Stitches have crisscrossed my mug like train tracks. My nose has been smashed so many times, I had it fixed. I have chipped teeth. A broken toe. Scars on every limb.

I've been bitten. Kicked. Punched. Smacked with blunt instruments.

Never been stabbed or shot, although the night is young.

My face has been swollen like a multicolored beach ball. Like a bloody pink pumpkin. I've had painful knots all over my skull. Hair matted in blood. Scabby red latticework covering my face.

I know the process so well. First the swelling. Then the bruising. Then the pain, so acute that it hurts to talk.

Bandages and ointments. Icepacks and hot washcloths. Cotton balls and hydrogen peroxide. Antiseptic creams and about ten aspirin to kill the headache.

The purples and magentas and reds fade to browns and greens and yellows. The scabs shrink, dry, and fall off. The stitches sting a little when they pull them out, but not too bad.

And then you're fine again. The pain never lasts. It's no big deal.

I've endured so many brain-loosening head shots, it's a miracle I can spell my name. A wonder I don't see cuckoo birds and exclamation points spinning around my head continuously. I haven't seen stars, I've seen constellations.

Sometimes I repeat myself and don't even realize it.

Sometimes I repeat myself and don't even realize it.

I'm not particularly strong. Not especially quick. Not even six feet tall.

But my skull is made of brick. I've never been knocked out. Or even knocked down. Never been punched so hard that it knocked all the bad memories out of my head.

And physical pain doesn't scare me.

So if you wanna go, let's go.

On flick my brain cells like stadium floodlights. Each blood cell is a flashing red siren. Plasmatic excitement. Sweet adrenaline. Hyperventilation. Rapid pulse. Throbbing head. Buzzing ears. My vital signs are all more elevated than during sex. There's no greater high.

Fuck, yeah. I love it. I enjoy it. It turns me on. I'm ready to smash. Ready to win. Ready to defend myself. Ready to prove I'm alive.

I've knocked people unconscious. I've broken noses. Caused skull fractures. Bruised ribs. Loosened teeth. Forced an ambulance to be called more than once. I've provided great business for emergency rooms from coast to coast.

I'd love to slam your eyeball so hard that it's a bloody glob crawling down your face like lava-lamp jelly.

I'd love to punch your kidney so hard that you'll piss blood into a catheter from a wheelchair the rest of your life.

I'd love to crack your ribs so hard that they pierce your lungs like popped balloons.

I'd love for you to be swallowing your own teeth while telling me you're sorry.

I love violence. It's a universal language. It has a purity which words can't approach. There is no ambiguity. No danger of misinterpretation. The shortest distance between two points is a fist to the face. A black eye speaks for itself. Blood doesn't lie.

Some would like to pretend that violence is unnatural.

Idiots.

Violence is not an aberration, it's a rule. It governs big things and small ones.

Astronomers theorize that all the matter in this universe was compacted onto a pinhead before exploding in a divine orgasm of almost inconceivable violence. From the Big Bang onward, violence has been a constant. Predatory black holes swallow galaxies. Asteroids vaporize planets. Supernovas blaze and destroy. Violent, violent cosmos.

Gravity chains us to a violent earth with an angry molten core. The earth's howling, shifting crust raised mountains and opened valleys in staggering strokes of violence.

The animals which cling to this earth for life are relentlessly, remorselessly, deliciously violent. Violence brings life—for the violent. It brings death for the victims, but that's *their* problem.

Zoom in on high-magnification footage of an insect killing and eating another insect. Watch the triumphant insect in full battle armor suck the life from the smaller, weaker bug. Watch its mandibles rip into its prey. Watch the victim helplessly twist, turn, and finally collapse.

Is remorse involved? Or is it strictly a matter of survival?

There's a balletic beauty when a great white shark tears into a smaller fish...see how the red blood softly billows into blue seawater.

But from the smaller fish's perspective, it's an ugly scene, man.

The animal predator exults in its own life, not its victim's death. Violence is more closely linked to self-preservation than to the destruction of others.

You, too, are an animal. You have teeth with which to bite and hands with which to strangle. You piss and shit and breathe and fuck like all other animals. You bleed, like all "higher" animals do.

You are also something more than an animal, but your nervous system is encoded with all of evolution's harsh lessons. You don't have one brain, you have a layered series of nerve clusters with different evolutionary instincts and priorities. Part of you has evolved beyond the reptiles, and part of you is right down there with them. Your brain has not evolved beyond the need to crush and smash and dominate. And that brain fantasizes about the death of your enemies. Don't even try to deny it.

Violence is inside you. It cannot be created, only awakened or suppressed. You were born violent and had to be taught otherwise. You had to be spanked, or at least punished, before you stopped hitting other creatures.

Homo sapiens. King Carnivore. Human beings did not invent violence, they merely perfected it. We did not ascend to the top of the animal kingdom through charm and diplomacy. Our dictatorship over other animals was not accomplished with prayer beads and drum circles.

Violence never solved anything? HA! It solves *everything!* It always has. Violence makes the world go 'round. It is an inescapable historical principle. There isn't a nation on earth that wasn't built on its enemies' corpses. Each word in every history book is written in the losers' blood.

Torture dungeons and gas chambers and hot molten lead poured down heretics' throats. Firing lines and death squads and masked guerrillas pouring down from the mountains. Mustard gas and Agent Orange and little vials of anthrax. Ethnic cleansing. Ideological purging. And pure holy pillaging. Barbarian hordes crushing everything in their path. Draining life from the victims and injecting it into the conquerors.

Violence is only "senseless" to the losers. To the winners, it makes perfect sense. It gives them life. Societies only condemn violence when it threatens their own safety. And they applaud whatever violence alleviates the threat. Kill the killers. Assault the assaulters. Rape the rapists.

It isn't wrong when *we* do it. It's wrong when *you* do it.

There are two types of blood: mine and yours. Ours and theirs. The good kind and the bad kind.

That's why Christianity has such perennial appeal—someone *else's* blood purchasing your eternal life.

We are all born covered in our mother's blood.

I was one of the few who managed to *stay* covered in blood.

My parents gave me life and then tried their best to snuff it out of me.

My childhood's defining moment came before I was even born. There I am, Jimmy the Fetus, enjoying the lightless quietude between zygote and infant. Little pink stumps of hands and feet. Tiny pepper-speck eyes. More like a sea shrimp than a person. Yet a cloudy, jelly-fishlike web of veins is building me into a human being.

And as I'm happily curled in a ball within that warm amniotic sac, dad hauls off and punches mom in the stomach.

Since then, things just haven't been the same.

While I don't consciously recall the incident—my brother told me about it—I sense I retain it on a much deeper level. I'm sure it rustled my placenta. I had to have felt it in some way.

While mom's umbilicus is feeding me all the nutrients necessary to build skin and bone, that blood-filled computer cable of hers is also sending me distress signals:

YOU'RE UNDER ATTACK
YOU'RE SOMETHING TO BE DESTROYED

I'm unable to defend myself. To hit back. I'm under siege and help-less. My sanctuary is a killing zone. My safe place is a torture cham-ber. I'm backed-up against mom's uterus like a cornered rat. If you can't hide in the womb, where can you hide?

Dad's punch partially aborts me. It kills whatever sense of safety I had. His fist shatters my infant reverie. He sprays graffiti on the altar of my innocence. My "childhood" was the wormy, embryonic spate of quiescent darkness preceding that punch.

After that, I'm no longer a child. Dad put a black eye on my soul.

There's something intensely deliberate about a punch to a pregnant woman's belly. Was he punching my mother...or me?

My parents had been together for eighteen years before I started swelling up inside mom's guts, and my arrival meant they'd be forced together for another eighteen. This was in the days when Catholics didn't get abortions and divorces.

Feel dad's misery as he cocks his fist to strike. Another unplanned fetus. Another squalling mouth to feed. Another reason to drink. Another reason to tense up and get violent. He's mad at mom's unex-pected fertility. Mad at the lump of protein growing inside her. Mad at himself for not jacking off and shooting me down the drain. And so I become the fetal shock absorber for his resentment.

Prior to my arrival, dad's favorite punching bag was my brother Bucky, who was seventeen years older than me. Bucky was a spindly, bespectacled, emotionally tortured deaf mute. The old man made certain that Bucky knew *he* was an unwanted annoyance, too.

Less than a week after my birth, my father and Bucky brawl near my crib. As dad's pummeling his disabled son, Bucky grabs an ashtray and smashes it in dad's face, raining glass fragments all over me.

It's a fractured lullaby. Just when I should be hearing the tinkling music-box sounds of a mobile whirligig spinning over my crib, I hear a violent shower of glass and angry barking men.

My sleek, shiny nerves probably writhe as if poisoned. I'm sure I cry. When you're an infant, crying's easy. Not so much anymore.

I'm baptized in broken glass. After that, I never see the glass as half-empty or half-full—it's shattered to pieces.

Bucky runs out of the room, out of our house, and never lives there again. Dad follows him out of the room, his face cut-up and bleeding.

Once out of our house, Bucky runs straight into trouble. Violence is his only inheritance. He drifts in and out of prisons in the South. He languishes for fourteen months in a Florida jail facing attempted-murder charges which are finally dropped. He spends over a year in a Texas prison, where he is raped. Back in Pennsylvania in the late 1960s, he plows into a man with his car, killing him. It is ruled an accident.

Bucky usually dresses like an undertaker in a black suit, white shirt, and skinny black tie. In 1969, he takes a vacation to Paris. The morning after his arrival, his corpse is found in a ditch a hundred yards from his rent-a-car. He had been stabbed over thirty times and strangled with his own belt.

Imagine the horrid last moments when you realize your vacation is turning into your murder. As a deaf man, was Bucky able to hear his own screams? Did his killer remind him of our father?

Early on I learn that families are groups of humans who bruise each other and draw blood from each other and scream like foamy-mouthed dogs at each other. I watch my father kick my sister as she lies in the fetal position on the floor, crying. Dad likes to hit the fetuses he's created. I see blood drip from my sister's mouth into the toilet and how she blames it on my father. I watch each red drop dissolve into the water just like it does when a shark attacks a smaller fish.

By the time I'm six, my siblings have grown up and fled our cozy gingerbread house. So it's just me, mom, and dad.

My parents are a pair of mass-produced, infantile, working-class nobodies caught in the mousetrap. Dad is a raging, drunken werewolf with slicked-back hair and stained work clothes. Mom is a shrieking, coldly sadistic opossum who counts on her fingers and stares warily behind thick glasses.

Dad is fire. Mom's ice. And I'm wedged in between them.

Mom slaps me while driving and scolds me in supermarkets and tells me I'm the Bad Seed.

Dad teases me until I cry, scalds my wrist with hot teaspoons, and tells me I have no heart.

Your parents are supposed to keep you safe from the monsters who chase you and hurt you. They aren't supposed to chase and hurt you themselves.

Oh, the helpless feeling of running from your towering, Tyrannosauric progenitors.

I'm seven or eight and alone with dad in the house on a bright Saturday afternoon. He chases me down into the basement and wallops me with his hairy backhand, giving me a bloody lip. After he walks upstairs, I grab a sheet of paper and spit my blood onto it. I mark the date on the paper with a pen, figuring I'll need this evidence at trial.

It isn't the first time dad has made me bleed. It isn't the second or third time. It's happening so much, I fear I'll wind up in court over it.

Around the same time, mom shuffles me off to a psychiatrist because, well, I've been acting a little weird, and my behavior must be *my* problem rather than a response to my surroundings.

The headshrinker gives me a little game to play.

"Here's a picture of a room in a house. Let's say it's your house. Here are some little stick-on figures of family members. Let's say it's your family. I want you to use these figures and make a family scene for me."

And so I do.

What does the scene show, Jimmy?

It's a mommy and her little boy. They're walking in through the front door. Daddy is lying on the floor in a pool of blood. Somebody killed him with a machine gun.

I'm only seven or eight, and no family portrait would be complete without some blood.

Then I'm a little bit older and much more rebellious—probably twelve, although I still have no pubes. I come home late from school after my parents had warned me not to dilly-dally. Dad tackles me on the stairs and pins down my ankles with his knees. He takes off his belt and begins whipping me. As I'm trying to wriggle loose and run upstairs into my room, mom yells at him to pin me down tighter. I'm howling in pain while dad keeps thrashing me and mom keeps encouraging him. Dad's snarling, mom's screaming, and I'm crying. It's a deliberate, prolonged beating, not just one frustrated blow. It's lash after lash after lash, mother and father ganging up to whip and destroy the little boy they'd created.

The bruising on my left outer thigh is so extensive that my thigh is more purple than white. Just a big, ugly, meatloaf-sized bruise. Down in the basement bathroom of the church hall where my Boy Scout meetings are held, I drop my pants and show the bruise to the other Scouts.

The oddest thing is that I feel entirely normal while showing it to them. This is how it is for everyone, isn't it? You defy your parents, they beat your legs another color, and you show your friends. This is the way life is. This is what families do. Family life is a bad thing, but bad things are normal.

As I'm cruising through suburban Philly with mom at about age twelve, Barbra Streisand chirps on the radio about how we choose to forget the pain and remember the laughter. I tell mom that I'm the opposite—I remember the bad things.

I feel the bad things more deeply. They sink further into my skin.

There's a joke about how beauty is only skin deep, but ugliness cuts to the bone. Same goes with tenderness and violence. Pain cuts deeper. It *weighs* more. Trauma lasts longer than euphoria. Intense pain is always more extreme than intense pleasure. Love is a feather; hatred is a hammer. The sound of a bomb exploding drowns out a symphony. The smell of shit overpowers the smell of roses.

Love should be something you feel, shouldn't it?

I didn't feel it from my parents.

When my dog licked my face, I felt love.

But on the rare occasions when dad hugged me, all I felt was his coarse stubble like little black cactus needles.

When mom would hug me, she'd pat me on the back as if she was uncomfortable and couldn't wait for it to be over. There was a stilted insincerity to her hugs.

But she hit me like she meant it.

All the nice things of my childhood, all my books about dinosaurs and saber-toothed tigers, my stamp and coin and rock collections, my pet hamster Itchy, the baseball cards and Hank Aaron's autograph, my World Book Encyclopedia and science-fair trophies, the Quisp cereal and Zotz! candy, the Silly Sand and Sea Monkeys, the Fuzzy Wuzzy Bear soap that grew "hair" after you used it, the boxes of Mr. Bubble, the Candyland and Operation games, the plastic soldiers for Christmas and Aunt Jemima costume for Halloween, all of it seems drowned and smashed and overwhelmed by the blood and bruises and screaming.

I remember dreaming about how a little plastic toy I'd bought from a gumball machine grew into a giant plastic monster that started strangling me.

My parents wrapped a tight splint around my emotions and made them grow a certain way. Early traumas hard-wired my neurological motherboard for violence. Every nerve cell generated in my body since infancy has retained those memories. Trauma is a unwanted guest that never leaves me. My brain holds those memories in tiny little jail cells. The dark corridors of my mind are haunted with screams and kicks and bloodshed. Violence is woven into my identity. Welded into my physiology. Imprinted on my character. Rubber-stamped on each neuron. Intracellular. Ingrained. Indelible.

Perhaps it's just an epileptic fluke, some easily explained neurological affliction cured with a scalpel, electrodes, and a barrel full of pills. Perhaps it's dad's black leather belt or mom's plastic lavender enema bag or my brother's murder or the nuns smacking me in the face.

You can talk all you want about free will and ethics, but I swear on my life that my parents placed a violent force within me that all the *Ubermenschian* ass-clenching I can summon hasn't eradicated. They planted something in me that grew along with my muscles and bones.

No, it's just a coincidence that my parents were violent to me and I became violent.

Just a coincidence that molestation victims are fucked-up about sex.

Just a coincidence that adopted kids tend to float through adulthood feeling disconnected.

Just a coincidence that drunks breed drunks and junkies breed junkies.

I have a nagging feeling that I'd look at life differently if my parents didn't want me dead.

My death instinct and life instinct are arrayed against each other like black and white chess pieces. Life and death struggle for primacy within me, waging a custody battle over my soul. Tectonic plates of self-preservation and self-destruction grind against each other, giving off sparks. The clash of these primal instincts has lent my personality a seismic intensity. I suffer from an internal energy of a magnitude that is by turns homicidal and suicidal, but never both. I have become obsessed with my own survival and destruction to the point where I view life as something to be won or lost, not merely lived. I feel that if I'm not constantly vigilant, death will win.

So I will confront death and subdue it. I will run into the darkness and call death by name. I will show no fear, because fear is capitulation to the forces that want me destroyed.

Either implode or explode. Either succumb to your destruction or fight back. This massive destructive force inside me has to be aimed in some direction, either inwardly or outwardly. It won't just leak out casually. It won't melt. I've tried relaxing—it doesn't work.

There I am, very young—pre-kindergarten, definitely—and I chance upon some other kids in our back alley. They begin taunting me.

I flex my string-bean biceps and boldly proclaim that I'm Superman, so they can't hurt me.

They laugh at me like I'm crazy and walk away. But they didn't hurt me.

And so I became Superman because that's what it would take to overcome not being loved. I would become my own superhero, the one who would lift myself by the scruff of the neck and fly over all the adversity. I would rise above it all, that's what I'd do.

A boy lets his parents beat him.

A man hits them back.

A boy cries over his wounds.

A man wounds others.

Becoming a man meant scaring away potential predators. It meant, as Nikita Khrushchev said, kicking off the head of whoever slapped me on the cheek. It meant never backing down. Never. Even if you got beaten into unrecognizability, you don't back down.

Something more than my body is at stake here—self-defense means that I'm fighting in defense of my very self, of my whole existence.

I can fight the death inside me. The only way to win is by fighting it. So I will approach life as a military campaign. To live is to fight against those who want me dead. To live is to never forget what they've done to me, to never let it happen again.

Polishing my boots. Oiling and buffing my leather jacket. Cutting my hair military-short. Lifting weights so I can form the mighty exoskeleton of the insect warrior.

I will show no weakness.

I will not let you crack this shell.

To protect myself from ever being hurt again, I will erect a wall of angry fire around myself. Anger is more dignified than suffering. Anger is a reaction. A battle plan. A way of assuming control.

In a choice between open wounds and scars, I'll take the scars.

So rage became my mother's milk. You become addicted to the poison. You go with what you know.

It is easier for me to punch you than to cry in front of you. To yell at you than to hug you. To insult you than to ask you for what I need.

But I'm not a rude person. In fact, part of my problem may be that I'm too polite. I don't fuck with people. I keep to myself.

I don't get in people's faces. I wait until they get in mine.

I don't go hunting. I set traps.

I don't start things. I finish them.

I'm very respectful of others' boundaries. I don't go anywhere I'm not wanted and don't even go half of the places where I'm wanted.

But sooner or later, somebody tries to step inside my oxygen tent.

When I bump into someone, I say, "excuse me." But not everyone is so courteous.

Once they've trespassed that invisible force field I've constructed around myself, they're in trouble. I feel as if they've entered my amniotic sac and have to be banished through violence.

If you are foolish enough to wrong me in some way, I will get more than even, don't you worry. I will hold a grudge and clutch onto the idea of vengeance like an oyster wraps around a grain of sand and turns it into a pearl. I won't forgive you. I can't. I can't "let go" when there's a score to settle. When the account isn't balanced. I will never forget what you did to me. Never. Never. Never. You may think you've gotten over, but I can be very patient. I'll wait YEARS. I'll bide my time hiding behind the soft underbrush, looking for the perfect moment to strike. Just when you think it's safe to breathe, I'll find a decisive, terrifyingly dramatic way to make you regret what you did.

It's only fair.

Blame yourself. If you hadn't fucked with me, you wouldn't be in this predicament.

I never see myself as a predator. I see myself as prey getting even. The world threw the first punch, and the first hundred after that. Everything I do is just retaliation. Just playing catch-up.

I'm not fighting *against* you; I'm fighting *for* myself.

It isn't the killer instinct, it's a survival instinct.

Has there ever been a victimizer who didn't start out as a victim and decide that he or she liked it better on the other side of the fence?

Watch the little abused child beat the stuffing out of his teddy bear when he thinks no one's looking, and you'll understand everything.

Violence is *très* glamorous when you're winning. It only becomes ugly when you lose.

I've hit a lot of people and I've been hit by a lot, and I can tell you this much:

It feels better to hit them.

I've been on top and on the bottom.

Top's better.

It feels better to punish than to be punished. To control than to be controlled. To hurt than to be hurt.

Your pain never hurts as bad as mine. Your pain relieves mine. My pain is the only pain that matters.

The ebb and flow of violent tension follow an orgasmic pattern. Day after day, month after month, the strain builds as I weather life's ceaseless indignities. The petty insults and major frustrations are like electricity I absorb to be used at a later date. It piles up like shit in my colon. Like piss in my bladder. Like sperm in my nuts.

After a while, I have to release it. If I keep it inside, it'll corrode my liver.

Anger management. Bite it. Swallow it. Shit it out. Toss it away like a pipe bomb, or it'll blow off half your hand. Push and squeeze it away.

So when I'm beating your face in, I'm releasing bad memories through my fists, which are curled tight like scared fetuses. I'm just discharging a bit of this pent-up energy. Just letting off some steam. I'm transferring my frustrations into your body. My cup runneth over, so I'll pour a little into yours.

But it's only a partial catharsis. I couldn't beat you badly enough to get it all out of me. Even killing you wouldn't do it.

A jailhouse joke runs something to the effect of, "I caught AIDS three times, but I'm OK, because I gave it away each time." Same with violence—you can give it away and still not be rid of it.

I have a secret: I'm very sensitive. I take things hard. Harder than most. I didn't want you to know about my pain, but sometimes, well, it just spills onto the table.

If you think it's unpleasant to be around me, imagine how unpleasant it is to BE me. I torture myself, and you don't even give me any credit for it. I've been in constant emotional pain since before JFK was shot, and still you wonder why I'm cranky.

The pain cuts so deeply, I'm driven fairly fucking mad from it. I could scrape out the last fleck of my bone marrow, and it would still be in there. I've never stopped hurting. I may go numb sometimes, but the phantom pain persists.

After a while, you've felt so much blinding, blinding pain, the systems just shut down. It's the emotional analogue to your body going into shock. My apparent numbness doesn't mean I'm unfeeling. It means I feel too much.

Monsters don't have emotions; I have too many. Violent people are supposed to be dead inside—I WISH! I'm a little too much alive. Bad guys—at least as we've been led to understand them—don't feel pain like this.

Maybe violent people are the most sensitive people on earth. Maybe they're attuned to *everyone's* pain, while the "victim" is only in touch with their own. Maybe people who are able to just let things roll off their back don't feel things as strongly as I do.

Did it ever occur to you that if I was happy, I wouldn't be smashing things? Has it dawned on you that maybe I'm in more pain than the people I hit?

Like my parents used to say, this is going to hurt me more than it'll hurt you.

Well, that's not entirely true. When I finally hit my parents back, it probably hurt them more than it hurt me.

I hit them back when I became strong enough to do so.

With mom, I was about twelve…

She's chasing me in the hallway outside a salt-sodden old beach apartment we've rented for the week. Suddenly I decide I don't want to run anymore. I spin around and slap her on the cheek, knocking her goggles askew on her face.

I think,

You don't realize, mommy—I have hands, too, and I can hurt you, too. And the way those glasses are hanging off your face really makes you look stupid.

Mom stops in her tracks, startled. She retreats and goes crying to family members that I'd attacked her. She tells the same story to the neighborhood gossip Guernseys. She omits the part about randomly attacking me during the first twelve years of my life.

Everyone thought I was evil for hitting my mother. No one seemed to care that she'd hit me dozens of times before I finally hit her back.

I never hit her again. I didn't need to. She never hit me again, either. She was afraid to.

I hit my father when I was seventeen.

I'm alone in the house, talking on the phone with a female friend. She's not a girlfriend, but she's my best friend, the first pseudo-adult relationship I've had with someone where I can discuss pseudo-adult problems. She means a lot to me. She has recently moved out of town, and the phone is the only contact I have with her.

Dad comes home, his brain a drunken stew of rotted vegetables.

He rips the phone from my hand while I'm talking and hangs it up. He chases me upstairs and then back down again. We square off in the living room, face to face. He raises his hand to hit me, and I grab it.

I can almost see the alcohol vapors rising from his head. Big oily nose with craterous pores. Tan, leathery skin. Bloodshot, drunken eyeballs.

And then he gives me that smirk, amused that I'm trying to defend myself. His expression says so much. It says,

You're a stain. A slug. A germ. A speck of lint. You're nothing. You don't count. You don't even register on the scale. I erase you. I wipe you away. You're an object. A prop. You're not real. You're dead.

So I show him I'm alive.

I clobber him with a left hook and knock him to the carpet.

My spirit soars to see him crumpled on the floor like an aborted fetus. I think,

Now you know what it feels like, you cocksucker. And if you ever hit me again, I'll collapse your facial cavity. You preyed on my weakness. But now it looks as if I'm stronger than you.

That one punch was so hard that it breaks his dental plate into two shiny pink-and-white pieces. He's so plastered that he ambles down to the basement and tries to glue his false teeth together again.

Dad wails to the rest of the family that I assaulted him. And just as mom did, he neglects to mention the part about trying to hit me first. He says nothing about his history of drawing blood from me. And the family believes him. My brother and brother-in-law threaten to kick my ass.

But dad never hit me again after that. He was afraid to. And I never hit him again, either. I didn't need to.

The day of dad's funeral, after they lower his pickled cadaver into the soil, me and my friend Steve are panhandling outside a subway station so we can buy weed and beer.

A thuggish Italian metalhead who had persecuted Steve in high school passes by us. Steve asks him if he'd sell us a joint.

"No, I don't sell weed to punk-rock faggots," he dismissively says over his shoulder, walking into the station.

I follow him in through the doors and confront him.

WHAT did you say?

"You heard me, fag."

We assume boxing positions, and I land a quick jab to his nose. Blood jumps from his nostrils with a comical spritz. He looks so silly. He touches his hand to his snout and feels the warm stickiness. Realizing that a punk-rock faggot is poised to physically humiliate him, he stops fighting and disappears through the turnstiles.

My father is dead, but I'm not about to let anyone else treat me like he did.

Somewhere around the same time, I'm riding with a goony middle-aged man who'd picked me up hitchhiking. He touches my knee and coquettishly asks if I like to "fool around." I tell him no and demand to be let off at the next corner. He drives a block past the corner before finally letting me out. I grumble something about how he drove too far and slam the door as I leave. I walk back to my corner and resume hitching.

A minute later he's running up behind me, screaming and bearing down as if to attack.

He runs straight into my left fist and falls to the blacktop.

I feel powerful. Justified. How glorious to see his body fall. How sexual it is to be standing over him, dominant. So in a way, we wound up having sex, only not the way he'd intended.

About a year later I'm sulking alone at a New Wave club and decide it's time to leave. Lonely and angry, I walk outside and begin hitchhiking home. People lob smart-assed comments at me from passing cars.

I swear to myself that the next person who says something will regret it.

A stocky drunken Guido leans out the back window of a cab and shouts something flippant at me. The taxi stops about fifty yards down, right in front of the club.

He gets out, a girl on each arm. I run up to him and dare him to repeat what he said. He shoves me instead.

I flatten him with one shot. He falls backward, the back of his skull slamming onto the pavement.

He lies there motionless. A crowd forms around us.

Blood starts flowing out the back of his head. It's more blood than I've ever seen at one time. A syrupy red halo at least two feet in diameter expands around his cranium.

His eyes are rolled up in the back of his head. He looks peaceful. He looks dead. He looks unable to insult me anymore. It isn't pretty, and yet it is.

His tarted-up girlfriends are gasping and gesticulating and probably in some way turned-on by what I did.

I just stand over him and think,

You should have kept your greasy mouth shut. You shouldn't have shoved me. Now you're unconscious on city sidewalk, your head cracked open and blood pouring from it like soda from a spilled can.

The club owners run out and start to revive him. They tell me I'd better leave.

About ten years later I'm married and living in Brooklyn. My Russian landlord calls my wife stupid.

You shouldn't do that.

She's the only person who ever loved me.

She's essential to my survival.

I tell him to apologize. He doesn't. He calls me stupid, too.

I start punching him. I keep punching him. He stands there, taking it. Blood splashes from his face with each shot.

Within fifteen seconds, his head is bloated like a big bloody wad of bubble gum ready to pop. The swelling turns his eyes into thin razor slits.

Who looks stupid now?

Almost a decade later I'm driving in Portland when some skinny slacker geek in a little bubble-bucket car nearly runs me off the road. He flips me off in his rear-view mirror and laughs.

To other drivers, you're just a car, not a human being encased in two tons of steel and glass. The car is another unsafe womb.

I catch up to him at a red light. I jump out of my car and run up to his. He quickly rolls up his window, frightened.

I smash through that window with one punch.

I rain glass into his crib.

Suddenly he's respectful. He apologizes and pulls away at top speed.

I don't want to give you the wrong impression. I don't win every fight. I'm not even sure if I've won half of them.

1979. Hitchhiking again. Blazing on acid. An old Impala containing four drunken teens stops to pick up me and Punk Rock Steve.

I sit up front, in between the driver and a neckless, dark-browed fire hydrant who calls himself Cosmo. Steve sits in between the two hoodlums in back. We do nothing to provoke them. They're just look-ing for prey. They attack while the car's moving. Cosmo's first punch crunches into my face so hard, I can HEAR my nose being broken. His fat working-class knuckles pummel my face over and over. In the back seat, they're beating up Steve.

The driver pulls into an abandoned dumping ground.

They're going to kill us.

Cosmo drags me out of the car. I break free and race home, blood showering from my nose with each desperate stride I take.

By the time I get home, I've bled so much that my jeans are more red than blue. In the mirror, my face doesn't look like my face any-more. My nose is the size of an orange. It looks like a twisted, inflamed scrotum.

Dad reluctantly takes me to the hospital, scolding me the whole way. Bright lights and black stitches and the worst acid crash ever.

Then there's the time someone bashes my face with a steel beer-keg pump. More blood. More stitches.

There's the drunken brawl with my friend Bruce where I tackle him over a cement wall and split my coconut open on black asphalt. More blood and stitches.

There's the black guy in South Philly who socks my jaw just to impress all the black people around him. Yet more blood and stitches.

And every time I get beat up, I think,

STOP! Stop! Cut! Cut! This isn't what the screenplay says should happen. It isn't supposed to work this way. I'm just standing up for my right to exist, and that's a noble thing.

Then there's the domestic violence.

That's why I'm writing this from prison.

It makes a sad sort of sense that when I grew up and tried to recreate family situations, they'd include violence.

The first incident was with my first long-time girlfriend, with whom I shacked up in college.

I say something that pisses her off.

She slaps me. Once.

I slap her back. Once.

And just like my parents, she runs yelping to everyone that I'd hit her, splicing out the part about hitting me first.

Same thing with the girl whose testimony landed me in prison. To this day, she denies punching me first on the morning of my crime.

Throughout my life, I've been punished by being hit.

And now I'm being punished for hitting back.

No one wants to accept guilt besides me, and so I wind up getting blamed for everything.

It's like I'm the only one at the restaurant table who reaches for the check, and so I pay for everyone's meal.

The parents I hated built every cell inside me.

And now I sit inside a cell.

Shadows of cell bars fall on gray paper as I write with a hand that has knocked people senseless. A dim yellow light bulb casts scant rays on the page. Through the meshed wire and frosted glass across the hall, I get the blurry idea that the winter sun is setting.

This building was erected right after the Civil War, and its walls are soaked with desperate generations of male sweat and urine.

I sleep on a two-foot-wide plastic mattress and brush my teeth with baking soda. Three times a day, the cart comes along and dog chow is delivered through a slot in the bars. I'm allowed out of the cell twenty minutes a day to shower and then climb back into the same dirty orange jumpsuit.

I share this six-by-nine-foot cement igloo with a convicted killer about whom there's been a book written and a TV movie made.

He beat his wife to death with a flashlight.

This place is the worst of the worst, a prison within a prison. Its official name is the Disciplinary Segregation Unit, but everyone calls it The Hole.

The most dangerous womb of them all.

An electric fan roars down the block. The drone. The hum. The deceitful peacefulness of the birth sac.

It would be hard to conceive getting any lower than this. Rock-bottom, literally. I've fallen through the cracks and fluttered down to the sewer.

This isn't the best place to nurture my soft side.

I have black bruises inside my lower lip. Scratches on my nose, cheek, ear, back, and stomach. A bump on the back of my head. A slightly chipped tooth. Smears of blood on my shirt cuff from dabbing a facial scab that keeps bleeding.

There's a little red swirl in the white of my right eyeball. A big shiner surrounds that eye and hurts when I squint. I see constant white flashes in the corner of my right eye. I see a jagged ridge of blackness along the bottom of that eye when I first open it. The nurse thinks I might have a detached retina.

My opponent's face was so puffy, other inmates said it looked as if he'd put on weight. Some of them said that his black eye looks worse than mine, and that made me feel good.

A guard saw our black eyes and charged us with assault.

But I hurt myself on the weight pile!

And he got elbowed playing basketball!

Nevertheless, they put both of us in jumpsuits and handcuffs, sending us from our minimum-security kiddie camp to The Hole inside Oregon State Penitentiary.

On the way over here, our transport vehicle passed a motel where my ex-wife and I had stayed five years ago while moving up to Portland.

She had a black eye then.

Come a little bit closer, OK? I don't want to shout.

Since you're the only one listening, I'll tell you: I'm scared. Scared of what has become of me. Scared of what might yet be.

This violence is a part of me. It is not all of me. Yet it threatens to swallow up all of me.

On my eyes' periphery, way on the furthest fields of my vision, I see a badly beaten corpse.

Did I kill it?

Or is it me?

Will I die violently? Will the mortician have to touch up bruises on my face? Will I die before you read these words? Shortly thereafter?

Twice in my life I've beaten someone so badly that if I kept going, I would have killed them. Both times, the sight of their grotesquely swollen faces is what stopped me. I found myself perched on that thin gray sliver between simple assault and murder, yet I was able to throw a leash on my rage and yank myself back.

I'm afraid that one day I won't be able to stop.

In the smudged glass of a prison mirror, I look my enemy straight in the eye.

I'm in prison because of the fists I thought would protect me.

Oedipus didn't realize until it was too late that he was fucking his mother.

I didn't realize until it was too late that I was beating up myself.

Each layer of protection only made me more vulnerable. Becoming a tough guy was supposed to signify that I wasn't affected by what my parents did to me, but all it did was prove how deadly affected I was. Limping along crippled, I thought I could win the race. I keep punching back, but it's never enough. I could give the whole world a black eye and still not get even. The violence protected the wrong parts of me. It killed the higher parts and left the caveman intact.

And that's how the winner of his grade school's spelling bee wound up in prison for assault.

I could have just walked away and let the shit be on my parents.

Instead, I kept fighting and got the shit all over me.

The always loud, always boisterous Negro convicts are shouting from cell to cell about their violent escapades. Dark, nappy men with street handles such as Cherry Bomb, Time Bomb, and Trouble joyfully ululate about slashing other cons with razor blades in the day room, about swinging socks stuffed with combination locks into other inmates' faces, and about how when they punch you, they're trying to break something on the other side of you.

Down the block, a gargantuan Afroman mentions some brutha who beat his pregnant girlfriend so badly, she involuntarily aborted the baby.

In that case, mission successful. And maybe the best thing for the baby.

My parents let me live, which may have been the cruelest of their tricks.

⟩3⟨

A Bad Seed Takes Root

EVERYBODY SAYS I'M a bad kid, so I guess I am. They say I'm a smartass, which means I'm smart and bad at the same time.

I've got a big head and short legs and I'm not good at sports. I get constipated a lot and I pick my nose a lot, which I guess is pretty weird. The parents of other kids keep their kids away from me like I got the measles or something.

When I was really little, I used to wet my bed a lot and wake up screaming and all sweaty from all these nightmares I used to get. Before I'd go to sleep, I'd pray to God that I wouldn't get the bad dreams, but I'd get them anyway.

There was this one time when I was about three that my brother Johnny tells me was really weird. Johnny got back from Vietnam a couple years ago and now he lives in Colorado instead of Philly. But he says that when I was like three and he was like sixteen, mom called him into my bedroom because I was acting all weird, even though I was asleep. He said I was all sweaty and flopping around, and then this sound came out of my mouth like I was gargling Listerine. And then I started talking in a woman's voice, even though I was asleep! Johnny's pretty smart, and he said it wasn't like I was talking like a grownup lady, but it was like a grownup lady was talking with my mouth! Isn't that weird? Then he said the lady stopped talking and I kept sleeping but I looked like I was happy.

Some people thought I had the Devil in me, but mom took me to the psychiatrist, and he said it was because I had a grownup's brain inside a little kid's body, and sleep time was the only time that the grownup could catch up with everything. He told mom not to worry but said don't argue with me because I'll get upset, plus she'll lose the argument.

So a lot of people think I have the Devil inside me, but only because I have a grownup's brain inside a little kid's body.

I don't know, though, because I don't like grownups too much, because they're always yelling at me, especially mom and the nuns here at school. Dad works two jobs so he's never around, so most of these grownups are ladies, and they're always yelling at me and telling me how bad I am.

There was this one time when I was like four years old, which was a really long time ago, because now I'm twelve, and it was New Year's Day, and Johnny and his girlfriend were gonna take me to the Mummer's Parade, which is this thing where these old guys with banjos dress up in rainbow costumes and walk down Broad Street like total gaybirds.

So that morning I woke up kinda cranky like I always do and got a little lippy with mom at the breakfast table. Mom tells me that children should be seen and not heard, and she throws me in my bedroom and locks me in with that little lock dad drilled on the outside of the door.

So I start crying and screaming and I'm all like banging and scratching at the door and mom doesn't answer all morning and afternoon until I fall asleep 'cause I'm too tired from the crying.

I think that what mom did to me is worse than what I did to her, but she says I'm wrong. Mom said that what I did with getting lippy was bad but what she did to me was good, even though I was really crying and really scared. And even when I told mom that it hurt bad, she said that's OK, because it's good for me. She says bad people get punished and good people are the ones who punish them, and that's the way it's always been.

It's like these nuns here at school—they say they're all holy and stuff, but they act like total meanies, and that's what me and a lot of the other kids think. They say they act mean for my good, but it doesn't feel too good to me, and if it's good, I think it should feel good so you can tell the difference. I don't think the nuns are good, I think they like acting mean and bossing us kids around, but they can't say that because then God would never forgive them. Mr. McKee and Mr. Marchese are the only two man teachers in the whole school, and they both act like absolute gaybirds, so they might as well be ladies, anyway. The other teachers who ain't nuns are all ladies, and they call them "lay" teachers, and I think that's because they're allowed to get laid.

The lay teachers are pretty mean, too, I mean, Miss Rooney is always grabbing my hair and pulling me down the aisle and getting this crazy look in her eyes, but the nuns are even meaner. The nuns always used to hit Johnny when he went here to Holy Cross, and when my sister was in first grade, the nuns told her that if she was bad they'd put her in this room they had that was all dark and filled with spiders and snakes.

Sister Brigid Mary has this broom closet filled with all these broken yardsticks that she broke over the hands and asses of the boys here.

She doesn't hit the girls, but that's because girls are expected to be good and so they get away with stuff.

The nuns do other mean stuff, like the time Brian Delahunty and this other kid got into a fight out in the recess yard, they made Brian and this kid kiss each other in front of all the other kids like they were total homos or something.

They say that God loves us and all, but I don't know, sometimes he acts like the biggest meanie of them all. He says "thou shalt not kill" and then goes and kills everybody he creates. He says I got free will but then if I don't go and do everything he tells me, he's going to throw me in hell so I'm screaming and crying forever and ever. It's like he wants to torture me just if I don't want to hang out with him, and that isn't cool. It's like everybody's afraid of God, but they've never even seen him.

They say that priests can make holy water just by waving their hands over regular water like you get from a spicket. They say that the priests can turn those little white wafers and the wine into the real body and blood of Jesus like it's a miracle or something. They say it isn't like it's a symbol, it's like when he prays over the bread and wine during Mass, it really turns into the body and blood of Jesus, even though it still looks like bread and wine, and to tell you the truth it still tastes like bread but they won't let me have any of the wine so I can check, even though Jimmy Boyd and me drank some of it one time when the priest wasn't looking when we were cleaning up after Mass, and it didn't taste like blood because I tasted my own blood once when I cut my finger, and this stuff didn't taste like blood.

There's this big statue of Mary at the end of the corridor here and one day there was this shiny thing under one of her eyes like a drop of glue had dried there by mistake. And the nuns told us that all the kids at Holy Cross had been acting all bad and that Mother Mary was crying because of all our sins.

When I was like eight days old, they poured some water over my head and said I was baptized and that they wiped away all of my original sin. And then they said that I didn't have any sins until I was like seven, because then I was in the "Age of Reason" and then I could tell the difference between good and bad, but sometimes they're telling me that I still can't tell the difference.

They got mortal and venial sins, and the mortal sins are really bad and you go straight to hell, but the venial sins are only a little bad so you can go to purgatory and only scream and cry for a while, then you get to go up to heaven.

They said that Adam and Eve were in heaven, but then they tried to be all like God and God got all pissed off and told them to get out of there and the Devil used to be in heaven, too, but he got kicked out for wanting to be like God and that's why he's in hell now.

Sometimes I go to confession and I tell the priest I had impure thoughts and I talked back to my parents and he tells me to say a few Hail Marys and God will clean the sins off me and let me go to heaven.

After I go to confession we go to Mass and the church is a lot bigger and nicer than all the houses that the people who go to church live in and they give us these little envelopes with our names on them and you're supposed to give money to God and even though my allowance is only a dollar a week I'm supposed to give something.

I don't like going to Mass like I don't like going to the dentist and I don't like eating Brussels sprouts, but it's supposed to be good for me so I go.

It's like I hate going to school, too. We all dress up like I'm a businessman and I hate the way this tie is wrapped around my neck like it's choking me.

And I hate the way they call me "James" and the way everything's so quiet.

I hate having to sit still and shut up and act like I'm scared of them all the time. I like making noise and having fun like any kid, but they want us to act like robots, and I'm getting tired of it.

I hate the kids that the nuns think are good. These are the same kids that act up when the nuns ain't around, but when the nun walks in they're acting like saints and tattletaling on me. I hate that.

They send me to all these psychologists because I don't behave. I think they should send all these other kids to psychologists to see what's wrong with them because they *behave*.

When I don't behave, I get punished. But to me, sometimes it feels even worse when I behave than when they punish me.

They say I break rules, like I'm smashing a vase on their mantelpiece or something. But I didn't make the rules, and I didn't put them on me, and I think they're wrong for putting them on me, but I can't tell them that.

The good people always treat me bad, and I think that's wrong, but they won't let you tell them it's wrong. They always say I should respect them, but they don't act that way to me.

They say I got a bad attitude about stuff. Everyone keeps yelling at me because I won't behave and they say it's hard to discipline me.

I wish one time they'd let me tell them how to behave and let's see how they like it.

I remember when I was real little I had to use the bathroom, but my Grammy Goad was in there taking a long time, and so I yelled through the door that I needed to pee and she should get out of there. She came out and told me I was a real brat. A couple days later she went back to Vermont earlier than she was supposed to, and mom goes that it was all my fault for being such a brat. Grammy died pretty soon after that, and mom goes that I was the one who made her sick.

Mom's got some health problems now, too, and she's telling me I caused them by being a brat. My brother-in-law George, who wears this really plastic-looking toupee, tells me I'm causing mom to be sick, too. George is always giving me mean looks and says he's always gonna beat me up for how bratty I act to mom and dad. One time mom and dad went on vacation and I was staying at George and my sister's house and George was yelling at me and I tried to run out of the house, but he grabbed me and bloodied up my nose pretty bad. Mom and dad say that George is a better son than me, even though he's really only a son-in-law.

My parents are always saying they're going to send me to reform school or military school, or they might even disown me and send me to a foster home. I'm always getting demerits or going to detention and getting suspended and they keep saying they're gonna expel me.

I remember the first time they sent me to the principal's office, back in first grade when I was only five. The nun wrote something on the blackboard, but the grammar was wrong. I'm pretty good at that stuff, and I wouldn't have stood up and told her she was wrong if I wasn't sure she was wrong. She told me to be quiet and sit down, but I told her I wouldn't sit down until she erased what she wrote and made it right. I mean, this is a school, and they're not supposed to be teaching us wrong stuff.

I guess she thought she couldn't be wrong because she's a nun and she's got God behind her or something, but I swear to God she was wrong. Really, God can send me to hell if she wasn't wrong, but she was wrong.

But she didn't correct her mistake, she sent me to the principal's office, and the nun there chewed me out, and they called my mom, who chewed me out, too, and mom goes that dad's going to hit me when he gets home.

Later on that year I got in trouble with the same teacher again, and for the whole lunch and recess period she made me stay in this dark, scary basement part of the nuns' convent, where I fell asleep and wet my pants. And when I got home, mom yelled at me for wetting my pants.

With mom and dad, I get into trouble when I argue with them about stuff, too. I was coloring a picture once and dad said the color was blue, and I go, no, it isn't blue, it's cobalt, and dad started yelling about it. Cobalt is kind of blue, but it's more specific. I mean, even the label on the crayon said it was cobalt, so I don't know why he got upset.

I always get into trouble for arguing about stuff that I'm right about. It blows. Sometimes the dumb kids have it easier, which is wrong the way I see it. They should yell at the dumb kids for being dumb.

I get into trouble all the time, more than all the other kids. In second grade I was getting into so much trouble, my parents went and talked to Monsignor Meyer, and he said I probably acted up because I'm too smart and get bored with what they're teaching.

I told my parents that Monsignor Meyer was wrong and I like to learn stuff but I don't like getting yelled at and being told to stand with my face in the corner and say I'm bad all the time.

They didn't listen to me, and Monsignor Meyer did some kind of deal where I got sent to Waldron Academy, which is where the rich kids go and are supposed to be smarter but aren't really any smarter than the kids here at Holy Cross.

I got into trouble at Waldron just as easy as I do at Holy Cross. I remember one time I got called into the principal's office, and she was some angry little nun with fat ankles that had all these ugly veins running through them. And she was yelling at me and I just kinda stopped listening to her and stared at her while this kinda gray halo thing formed around her body like an outline. She's yelling at me, and I just kinda ignored it and stared at the gray halo.

Over at Waldron I made friends with this colored kid called Tiger, even though his real name was Leland. Me and Tiger used to get in trouble all the time. One time the teacher said that Christmas was Jesus's birthday, and me and Tiger started singing "Happy Birthday" real loud and laughing, and the teacher pulled us by our jackets out into the hallway and yelled at us and said we were going to hell for doing that and God would never forgive us. I started getting all scared, and my cheeks got all hot and red. Tiger's a Negro, so his cheeks didn't get red, but I think he got pretty scared, too.

After three quarters of the third grade at Waldron, the principal told my parents I was so bad that my parents would have to take me out of Waldron or the principal was going to expel me, so mom and dad sent me back here to Holy Cross.

Right after I got back to Holy Cross I was hanging out in the recess yard with a bunch of kids looking at one kid's comic books. You're not supposed to have comic books at school, it's like a sin or something. And the principal looked out her window and saw us looking at the comic books and yelled over the loudspeaker to break it up out there and she goes, you, Goad, come into my office. I got blamed for the comic books, and they weren't even mine. The nun already knew I'm bad, so she started blaming me for everything.

In school they got me in Track A with all the smart kids, but during homeroom class and recess and after school I hang out with all the Track D kids, the ones who get in trouble and the Track A kids are really boring and do what they're told and the Track D kids know how to have fun. I mean, the smart kids are so stupid sometimes.

Steve McGlynn is a Track D kid who sat next to me in fourth-grade homeroom class. He looked like he should have been driving a motorcycle with the Pagans or Warlocks, even in fourth grade. He kinda looked like that Rat Fink cartoon.

When mom was still trying to make me believe in Santa Claus, Steve told me how a man and a woman make a baby. Mom told me my penis was called a "birdie," but Steve said the dirty word for it is "dick." He said that when you put your mouth on it and suck it that it's called "blowing," so after school in fourth grade we'd go to my house or Steve's and go up into the bedroom and get into bed with our dress slacks pulled down and switch around on the bed so his face was on my boner and my face was on his boner and we'd blow each other. We were still only eight years old so it's not like we had semen like they teach in biology class, but we did it a few times and it was kinda fun. There was this three-year-old girl who was visiting my parents one day with her folks, and we got her up to my room and I told her to put her mouth on my boner, so she dipped her mouth down on it like it was a big piece of candy and then popped up with a smile. Me and Steve were laughing when she did it, and when she saw that we were laughing, she started laughing, too.

Mom never caught us doing it, so I didn't feel bad about it.

A year later in fifth grade me and Dennis Hall, who lives across the street, started doing it, too, and we never got caught, either, so I didn't feel bad about it, either. I mean, it doesn't make you a gaybird or nothing, because gaybirds act like girls, and we don't.

Me and Dennis used to go to the swimming pool and hang in the dressing room and watch all the fathers and sons get nude and we'd laugh real hard when we saw their dicks, because it's always funny when you see something you're not supposed to see.

My parents took me and Dennis into Pennsylvania Dutch Country one time, and me and Dennis were sitting in the back seat laughing at all the dirty names they have for cities there, stuff like Blue Ball, Bird in Hand, and Intercourse. We couldn't even believe they'd give the towns dirty names like that.

The nuns all think Dennis is a real good kid, and he acts all good in front of them and says he's gonna become a priest. I don't think he tells the nuns about all the blowing or that he's touched every boy's dick in the neighborhood, even when they didn't want him to.

At Holy Cross they don't make us wear uniforms anymore, but we still have to wear a suit jacket and tie. I mean, my jacket looks pretty "doy-uh," but I'm wearing this thick paisley tie and two-tone purple-and-cream bell-bottom pants over argyle socks and brown-and-butterscotch-color platform shoes, so I still look really cool. The nuns and my parents don't like long hair on boys, and I got the longest hair of any boy in the school. Even though my hair's brown, it's cut like that blond guy in the Rolling Stones who drownded to death in his swimming pool—bangs down to my eyes, flaps over my ears, and so long in back that it totally covers my shirt collar. I look cooler than any other kid in school.

I ran away from home one night because I wouldn't get a haircut like dad told me I had to, and I went over to Keith Heron's house and played strip poker with him and his sister, but we stopped when his sister wouldn't take all her clothes off. Keith had some book where the lady talks about how her and her sister used to eat each other out all the time, and I wondered if my mom and Aunt Marion do that, but probably not, because mom doesn't like when people talk about sex.

We went to see this really cool movie called *Clockwork Orange* where these guys were having sex with this screaming chick, but mom got upset and walked out, and me and dad followed behind her but we were looking back at the screen when we were walking out.

There's this big billboard outside dad's Knights of Columbus hall that says "Stamp Out Smut," which means they're trying to get rid of all the dirty magazines and nudie movies.

Sometimes when my parents aren't around, I sneak into their bedroom and look at their copy of *Everything You Always Wanted to*

Know About Sex, which doesn't have any dirty pictures in it but still talks about a lot of dirty stuff. It was written by this doctor, I think. I was over at Bill Latino's house and he showed me this book that his parents bought called *The Joy of Sex*, which has all these drawings of guys sticking their dicks into ladies' vaginas. There's this other book called *The Happy Hooker* about this lady who has sex with all these guys, and then they give her money for it. Steve Caputi's dad has this book called *The Story of O*, which is about this guy who ties up this nude French chick and then does stuff to her.

I always look at all the ads for the nudie movies in *The Philadelphia Bulletin*. There was this one movie called *Deep Throat* about a year ago which is about this girl who blows a lot of guys. There's another one called *The Devil in Miss Jones,* which I guess is about this girl named Miss Jones who blows the Devil. There's another movie called *Round Robin* where a bunch of people get nude and have sex with each other and another one called *The Organ Trail* where they show a lot of people's private parts. Some of these movies are rated "X," and some of them are rated "XXX," which means it's even dirtier. They even have some that are rated "XYZ," which must be so dirty, I can't even imagine it. They must show people's assholes or something! *The Catholic Standard and Times* rates all those dirty movies "Condemned" instead of "Recommended."

The nuns don't think us kids know about sex, but that's all we ever talk about. There's a kid in our grade who used to be called Tom Dick, but we made so much fun of him, his parents changed the whole family's last name to Dale instead of Dick.

A dick is also called a "cock," which I think is like a regular dick, only bigger and uglier.

There was this one time I wrote "pink dick" on a rubber eraser and passed it to Kathy McNeila during class. She wrote "pink blasser" on the other side and passed it back to me. I asked her what a blasser was, and she said it was a girl's private parts.

The encyclopedia said a girl's penis is called a "vagina," and for a while I was saying it like it rhymed with "Tina," but somebody told me the right way to say it is like it rhymes with "Carolina." Keith Heron said the dirty word for it is "cunt," and somebody scratched "Scat's Cunt" in the wood on one of the desks, talking about Rita Scatareggia. Then Keith said it was called a "pussy," which is the dirtiest word I ever heard, I think.

You aren't supposed to go out of your house from noon 'til three PM on Good Friday, because that's when Jesus was nailed up on the crucifix, but Good Friday two years ago I was over Jeanette Osborne's house, making out with her and listening to an album called *HAIR* that had some song on it that she liked called "Sodomy."

When Potsie Waters told me about some girl who showed her naked body to him and another guy out in the woods, it sounded like heaven to me.

Last Easter Sunday, Potsie, Carol Hall, and me went out to the woods, and Carol lifted her shirt up and pulled down her pants and laid down on this big rock, and me and Potsie took turns putting our boners inside her.

Carol, who's the sister of Dennis who touches guys' dicks and is gonna be a priest, is the baddest girl in school. Some people say she pops pills and ran away one time to downtown Philly where she had a nigger boyfriend for a while.

I'm still kinda confused about these vaginas. I know that girls have this hairy kangaroo pouch thing between their legs, but even when I stuck my boner inside Carol Hall, I didn't sit there and examine the thing like it was a frog in biology class or something. And the time I laid on the couch with Eddie Regan's sister and squished my finger around inside her cunt, I didn't get a good look at it either, but that's probably because Eddie was watching us and laughing plus I was kinda nervous.

Tits I can understand. *Playboy* and the other nudie magazines don't show vaginas, but I've seen enough pictures of tits that I know what they look like. I'm just about tall enough that I'm eye-level with most grown ladies' tits, and in the summertime that's all I look at. Some of these women's libbers burned their bras and don't wear them anymore, which is cool because it makes it easier to see their nipples.

The hippies have love-ins and sex orgies where they run around naked in mud, and I'd love to do it but I'm probably too young for them to let me join. Me and Dennis were talking about running away and joining one of those nudist colonies, and I think we might do it when we find out where one of them is.

This year my science-fair project was all about drugs and how bad they are for you and then you get addicted and they ruin your life. I studied each kind of drug, from marijuana up to pills and cocaine and LSD and morphine. I even studied the nickname for each drug, like marijuana is called "Maryjane" and "boo," and cocaine is called "snow." And I didn't want my science teacher to know this, but even though I said drugs are bad, reading all this stuff about drugs and how they make you feel made me want to TRY drugs! It's like you can take a pill that will send you to heaven, even though you're walking around on earth. I remember even a few years ago I wanted to get tonsilitis just so they'd give me some laughing gas. They had this movie on TV called *Go Ask Alice* about this girl who gets hooked on all these drugs, and they made it look really cool, even though she winds up feeling sorry about it in the end. When I was camping with the Scouts we found some weeds that we pretended was marijuana, and we lit some up and inhaled the smoke and pretended we were high. I'd try some drugs, but I don't know where to get them.

When I was looking at these books on drugs, I tried to find which one was the worst and did the most stuff to your brain and I think it's morphine, so I'll probably stay away from that one at first.

I'm always looking for the most extreme bad stuff like that. I like fast cars, and I look inside parked cars at the speedometer to see how fast it'll go. Most cars go up to 120. The AMC Javelin, which is a cool-lookin' car, goes up to 140, but my brother's Corvette Stingray goes all the way up to 160. Down at the Wildwood shore, there was this car called the Pantera which went up to 200, and I couldn't even believe it!

Last summer we went to my brother's house in Colorado and dad started yelling at me again so I ran away from there for a whole day. When I got back I told dad I did it because he hurt my feelings, but dad told me I don't have a heart so I can't have feelings.

I used to go down my brother's basement there and look at all of his rock and roll albums. I mean, my mom has all these boring records like the Andrews Sisters and these greasy niggers called the Mills Brothers and the Ink Spots. Dad has a record by Johnny Cash which is kinda cool, because he talks a lot about killing people. Plus, there's this one song about cocaine.

The biggest rock and roll band in the world is still The Beatles, even though they broke up a couple years ago. The nuns don't like The Beatles because one Beatle said they were cooler than God. I liked how when The Beatles had those rumors about how Paul is dead and how they put backwards messages on their records and that one song they sing about how it's cool to live in Russia, because the nuns are really afraid of the communists because they say that God died.

My brother has a lot of albums and 8-tracks by The Rolling Stones, and I think they're my favorite rock and roll group. The singer is called Mick Jagger, and he doesn't care if people think he's a nigger or a big homo or anything else people get upset about. He even has this one song where he pretends he's the Devil. There's another song where he says they should just paint everything black, and I think that's pretty cool. They even got a song called "Brown Sugar" that's all about eatin' out black chicks!

There's this other guy who calls himself Alice Cooper, even though he's a man. He has one song about blowing up your school and this other one called "Dead Babies" that's pretty scary. He has black makeup around his eyes and walks around with this big snake on his neck. I heard that he kills puppies and worships the Devil at his rock concerts, so that's pretty cool, too. I was eating dinner one night and told dad that I thought Alice Cooper was cool, and dad got angry and goes, "Alice Cooper? He doesn't even admit he's a *man*!" and I liked the way dad got upset. It made me think Alice Cooper was even cooler.

They got these other guys called Lou Reed and David Bowie, but they dress up like total gaybirds, so I don't really like 'em. I think that Mick Jagger and Alice Cooper dress up like gaybirds just to upset their parents, but I think these other guys are really gaybirds.

My brother had this other album called *Tommy* about this evil deaf and blind kid who gets everybody to follow him like he's Jesus. He had this other album called *Thick as a Brick,* and the album cover was made to look like the newspaper with these articles about a little kid named Gerald who's totally smart and totally evil and upsets all the grownups around him, and it was like they were talking about me!

Last year I was saying that Keith, Eddie, Jimmy, and me should run away somewhere far where there's no nuns or parents to be yelling at us all the time, some place with a lot of woods, so I was looking at this Atlas, and there's this big place up in Canada called the Northwest Territories that has even less people than Alaska. I mean, you look at most maps and there's all these lines and dots that show how many roads and cities there are, but up in these Northwest Territories there's almost no lines and dots. So I said we could run away up there and build a cabin and kill animals to eat with pellet guns that kids are allowed to buy at the local sporting-goods shop here, and we'd have some naked chicks up there, too, although I didn't know how we were gonna get them.

But NO nuns and parents to tell us we're bad, and that way we wouldn't be so bad.

We were all gonna do it, but I guess we forgot about it, so it looks like I'm stuck here for a while.

It's like if God wants me to behave, I think he should have made the good stuff more fun. All these sins are a lot funner than going to

Mass and being in school. They say good is more powerful than evil, but I don't know. I have to TRY to be good. I can't be TEMPTED to be good like I can be tempted to do bad stuff.

In second grade I got called into the principal's office because I drew pictures of Nazi tanks in my notebook. The principal kept yelling at me about these Nazis and how they killed all these people, but I just liked watching *Rat Patrol* on TV, and those Nazi tanks just look cooler than the good guys' tanks.

They got this book called *Maria Monk* that says all the nuns eat each other out in those convents. When I first heard about it I was shocked, but then I kinda wanted it to be true. Same thing with the communists—part of me was afraid of them, but part of me wants them to come over and take over the USA and control my mind with lots of evil stuff.

If there's no God like the communists say, I can stay up late and do whatever I want.

There's this movie called *Rosemary's Baby,* and at the end they actually show the Devil. And just like with the communists and with the nuns eating each other out, part of me was afraid of it, but part of me wants the Devil to win.

I mean, when I received Holy Confirmation they rubbed some oil on my forehead and slapped me on the cheek, and the Holy Spirit was supposed to enter my body, but I didn't feel anything. But they got this movie now called *The Exorcist*, and when the Devil enters the girl's body, you can tell the difference.

Last year in sixth grade I got a "60" in conduct one quarter, which means I flunked it, and I think I'm the only kid in school who ever flunked conduct.

The biggest trouble I got in last year was when I took this little badge they gave me for having the best grade in science that quarter, and you're supposed to wear it on your jacket collar, but I pinned it right on my pants where the zipper is during choir practice IN CHURCH! When the nuns say that they really tried to make me feel ashamed, but the kids at school kept laughing about it for a long time.

Last year I told Mr. Marchese, a music teacher who acts like a complete gaybird, to "beat my meat," and I got sent home for that one, but the kids thought it was funny, too.

I got thrown out of Spanish class this year because I was giving the nun too much trouble. She's about nine hundred years old and even wears this chin strap at the bottom of her habit to hold that old chin of hers up. She's so old that a fly once flew into her mouth during class and she didn't even notice! And she's so mean that I like to make fun of her, so one day I brought this walnut to class and said I was in Spain over the weekend and brought in a rare Spanish walnut that I'd like to discuss with the class, but she could tell I was kidding and so she kicked me out of the class for good.

I like making jokes, because my parents and the nuns don't know how to make jokes. I do an imitation of this nun called Sister Perpetua, who we all call "Peppy," when she walks out of class, and all the kids laugh, and Peppy asks them why they're laughing when she walks back in.

There was this other time when some people came from the Philadelphia Zoo and this guy was standing up there on the stage talking with this big bird sitting on his wrist when all of a sudden the bird pooped out about a hundred little pieces of shit that hit the floor so loud it sounded like a machine gun! The guy with the bird stopped talking and looked embarrassed and the kids were all laughing really loud, and I liked the way the nuns were all running around trying to make the kids stop laughing but the kids wouldn't stop.

So now I'm sitting outside the principal's office because I told Miss Lombardo to shut up during history class, so I'm in a lot of trouble, and my parents are gonna kill me when they find out.

I hate when they yell at me and punish me, because it just makes me want to act more bad to get back at them for making me feel bad.

Sometimes they don't yell at me, and I like that better. There was a time in fourth grade when I ripped some boobie pictures out of my brother's *Playboys* down at Fort Dix and kept them. When mom found out about it, she didn't yell at me that time. She said it was normal, but I was a little young, so I should wait 'til I'm older to look at boobies.

There was another time when I drank some vodka that was in Aunt Marion's refrigerator, and when mom found out about it, she didn't yell then, either. She just told me that it wasn't good for me and that I was too young to do it and I don't want to wind up like dad.

There was another time me and some kids went crawling in one end of this big sewer pipe down near the woods, and when I crawled out the other end there was this big spider on me. And when I told my parents about it at dinner, mom started yelling at me but dad stopped her and goes that it's normal for boys to do stuff like that and I shouldn't feel bad about it.

I wish my parents were that way more often, so that way I wouldn't have to be so bad all the time.

There was this time back even before I went to school when I was so little I had to sit on phone books on top of my chair just to eat at the dinner table, and I said the "F" word at dinner, and mom asked me where I heard that word, and I pointed at my sister even though I was lying, and she got in trouble for it.

There was another time in the first grade when the hall monitor, this girl from eighth grade, saw me acting up in the hall, and when I was walking home from school after that day she ran up to me and said I was a real brat in school, and I told her my twin brother did it, and she believed me, even though I don't have a twin brother.

But now that everyone knows I'm bad, I can't pretend to be anyone else anymore.

All the teachers in school know I'm bad, but there's this one substitute teacher named Mrs. Dorward who only comes in when one of the real teachers is sick, and she never acts like I'm bad. She smiles at me when she calls on me and always acts like what I say is smart and good. And the funny thing is, I never act bad in her class.

I guess they forgot to tell her that I'm bad.

⚡4⚡

Standing Alone at the Edge of a Crowd

ROACHES. If you see one of them, there's fifty thousand more where that came from.

Watch them all scatter as I flick on the light.

Some of them are so big, you can *hear* their disease-carrying little legs scuttling across the linoleum.

Ugly crunchy shiny brown unconquerable unkillable pests, heartless machinelike faces and flailing antennae.

Running and hiding down the sinkhole.

Behind the oven.

In back of the sofa.

Hanging on the walls.

Clinging to the ceiling.

Every little cardboard Roach Motel I've set throughout this place is filled to overflowing with half-inch Orientals and huge lumbering Palmettos, some dead but most still alive, their brown twiggish limbs stuck in yellowish gloppy glue, antennae slashing like bullwhips.

For fun I'll chase one down as it races across the floor, trapping it under a plastic cup then tossing it into a saucepan on the stove, covering it with a steel lid and jacking the flame up HIGH. I'll fry that motherfucker until it explodes, coating the saucepan's inner rim with a sick film of burnt, brownish roach blood.

But you can't catch them all.

They multiply too fast.

Killing one of them is a nice gesture, but it's hopeless. You have to kill them all, and that seems impossible.

I got this apartment so I could be alone, but one is never truly alone, is he? Not with all these roaches.

What can I tell you about myself?

I'm 21.

I got straight 'A's last semester at college.

And I might kill myself or somebody else really soon.

I was born...different. I was stamped "irregular" somewhere along the assembly line.

When I was very young, I thought I was the only real human being on earth and that everyone else was a robot.

But somewhere along the line, a switch was made.

Now everyone else seems real, and I'm the cold, mechanical one.

As far back as I can remember, I felt that I was destined to disrupt things, to leave a big black eye on the world.

One-on-one, I can get along with almost anyone. But facing the crowd *en masse*, I'm always out of the circle.

This aloneness, though, enables me to see things the crowd never can, what with its kicking up dust and obscuring the dustbowl's perimeters. It is too late for me to join the crowd, so I wander on its fringes, checking under rocks and counting the stars.

It's not that loneliness doesn't hurt, because it does. It sucks the life from my bones. But what hurts worse is that I can't see it any other way. Part of me hates being alone, and part of me can't think of another person on earth with whom I'd like to be right now. As depressing as it is to be alone, it's worse to stand in a crowd and realize you don't belong there.

Mr. and Mrs. Goad hatched a strange child, no doubt about that.

My older brother John used to take me along for rides in his Mr. Frostee ice-cream truck, and one afternoon when I was about three, I had fallen asleep beneath the cold-steel ice-cream machines, and when John pulled up to one of his usual stops, a crowd ran up and began banging on the window for their ice cream. I awoke startled and immediately began bawling, scared at all the faces staring at me through the window. When they saw me crying, they started laughing and banging harder. And so I cried harder. And so they laughed harder and banged harder.

When I was around six, some neighborhood kid my age was diddling with my bicycle combination lock when he discovered the secret number—470—and the moment the lock popped open, he started chanting "470" to other kids.

My bicycle lock—my security, the line between me and the predatory prepubescent horde—was now useless. My chain of protection was broken.

The other kids took up the chant—"four-sev-en-tee! Four-sev-en-tee!"—gleeful that my privacy had been demolished.

At least two dozen of them, cruelly, rhythmically shouting:

"Four-sev-en-tee! Four-sev-en-tee!"

How happy they were.

I desperately ran up the alley through the taunting mob, slaloming around all the smiling, chanting, torturing kiddie faces, up into my house and my bedroom's quiet safety.

Alone in my room.

Alone with my thoughts.

Alone with books instead of toys.

I've never had a normal social life. Instead of being connected to a network of friends, I'll take one friendship...or obsession...and plow through it, knock it down and pick it up, caress it and slap it, probe and poke it from every angle, slowly dissect it, and declare it an off-limits disaster area in the end.

And the friends always go back to the crowd and join in the chant against me.

Tommy Fox was my first boyhood friend, a happily dumb, flamingly normal kid who lived next door. From toddlerdom to age seven we played with frogs together, ate Italian water ices together, and pledged to live next door to each other and be friends forever.

We even pricked each other's thumbs with a sewing pin and rubbed the little blood droplets together, swearing we'd be blood brothers forever.

But across the alleyway from our houses lived the Santoro brothers. One summer morning when Tommy and I were between second and third grade, the Santoros turned their garage into a clubhouse and asked Tommy to join their club, with one stipulation—he'd have to ditch me. I was the only neighborhood kid the Santoros didn't want in their club.

Without ever saying goodbye, Tommy walked away from me and joined the club.

For the rest of the summer, I was at war with every other kid in the neighborhood. We even called it a war.

Me v. the rest.

Every morning while I watched, the Santoros would make a grand display of welcoming their friends, then pulling down the garage door and locking me out.

So I'd grab a stick and run up and down the alley, swatting at air conditioners, squashing bugs, and drawing chalk figures on the concrete. I played alone, Robinson Crusoe on a sandless cement beach.

I've been locked outside their garage ever since.

And sometimes I'll lock myself up in my own garage.

Like a clam opening and closing its shell, I'll go through alternating phases of being open and closed to the world. I'm either having too much fun or not nearly enough. And whether I'm playing Satan or Jesus, I'm still a freak, more a mascot than a team player, more an actor than a member of the audience.

Never a part of the world, only reacting to it.

For a long spell through grade school I was a fiendish little hellion, seducing other kids to take off their Catholic uniforms and get naked with me, ambushing them as they walked home from school and smashing their heads into the ground, and disrupting class in whatever way ensured that I was the center of attention.

That all changed the day that Pete Callahan pinned me down and beat my face in.

Pete was tall, goofy, red-haired, and freckle-faced. He had absolutely no style. As such, he was the crowd's perfect ambassador.

Pete had seen me harassing someone else and challenged me to a fight. For two or three weeks, everyone at school knew the fight was going to happen.

Most of the kids wanted Pete to win.

It was over in less than a minute.

Looking down at me as he swung fists, he had a smiling, manic, bug-eyed expression of victory.

The crowd cheered Pete along with every punch and walked home with him.

I walked home alone.

I had been shorn of my plumage in the grade-school pecking order and went from rowdy bully to withdrawn loner.

Alone in my room again.

Obsessing.

Once I focus on something, everything around it gets blurry.

First it was the Marx Brothers—you know…Groucho, Harpo, Chico, and Zeppo. These *schwarzweiss* Jewish funnymen from a dead era became my friends.

I can still recite every one of their movies, first to last, within six seconds (I've timed it on a stopwatch):

TheCocoanutsAnimalCrackersMonkeyBusinessHorseFeathersDuckSoupA NightattheOperaADayattheRacesRoomServiceAttheCircusTheBigStoreA NightinCasablancaLoveHappy.

Two dozen Marx Brothers T-shirts. Three dozen books. Hundreds of clippings. Groucho's autograph. A letter from Harpo's widow.

But I burn out on my obsessions like I burn out on my friendships.

One morning, I threw all my Marx Brothers paraphernalia on a pile and burned it—literally—in a smoky bedroom bonfire because I'd devoted my life to Jesus Christ.

If you read the Gospels, you'll see that Jesus was an extremist.

He said that his believers would be able to drink poison and not die. So I drank a half-bottle of Campho-Phenique antiseptic lotion and crawled into bed, hoping that my faith was strong enough to save me.

It was.

Even the priests and nuns said I was too fanatical.

While other boys were drinking beer and chasing girls, I was all alone in the chapel, saying the rosary.

And then one day after Jesus and I had fucked each other in every possible orifice, I dumped him, too.

But the bottomless melancholy remained. Never been able to dump that.

Depression came in my early teens like a dark winter storm front. It buried me under a ten-foot snowdrift.

And I drifted from the crowd like an old Eskimo on an ice floe, floating out to sea.

I went from being the loudest kid in school to the quietest.

Springtime came, but the flower didn't bloom.

I pulled the cord, but the parachute didn't open.

This rooster crawled back into the egg.

This fly reverted to a maggot.

Depression came and it raped me. It took something I can never get back, and I'm not even sure what. But something's missing now. Something very important is missing. Something came and snatched most of the air out of my lungs. A big block of nothingness came and swallowed me alive.

Adolescence killed something inside me, I know that much.

Cold-steel ice-cream scoopers dug into my chest and carved out huge melon balls of my flesh.

A bomb of emptiness exploded inside me.

A bubble popped inside my head, spreading madness throughout it.

I felt a dread. Oh, what a dread. A foreboding. A premonition of something awful. An urgent, all-consuming, heart-piercing fear that something's coming to destroy me, something that can hide in the sunlight or the darkness. A big vacuum cleaner's coming to suck this pathetic speck of dust off the planet.

Total loss of natural fluid motion. Can't even breathe without a crippling self-consciousness. It's an effort to put one foot in front of the other.

Walking around inside a giant teardrop. I'll step off the curb into the street, afraid that I might fall all the way down to hell.

It's when late spring's light, airy beauty takes hold that I feel my head's going to fly off from depression. I always hit bottom in full-blown summertime, when the heat hatches bloodsucking worms in my brain while all the children play under a screwed-open fire hydrant, running and splashing and squealing, happy children, happy like I never was, strolling lovers, holding hands and kissing and whispering like I've never done. The hot ugly sticky sweaty Philly summer and the sun's melting my brains while air conditioners hum and death's hot breath chases me down the sidewalk.

What to do with this sadness, this sadness, this sadness that knows no end, this sadness like the end of time?

Late teens and mom moved out of the house without leaving a for-warding address and dad's needling me to where I want to kill myself just to spite him, the old cocksucker's all ravaged from late-stage alcoholism and trying to starve me out of the house by refusing to buy groceries until a nun at school finally gives me five bucks so I can get something to eat and each acid trip is more and more like being stuck in a coffin and one night I'm under moonlight wrestling a thorny bush in a cemetery and losing.

Cancer spread from dad's meat-and-potatoes-crammed colon to the rest of his body, and when the surgeons sliced him open they stitched him back up immediately as if the tumors were contagious, because cancer spots were everywhere like freckles on Pete Callahan's face when he was punching me.

Dad would be so doped-up from the cancer medication that he'd fall asleep in his bedroom leaning on the volume button of his remote control until the TV got ear-splittingly loud and would wake him back up again.

White-suited paramedics came and whisked him in a wheelchair to the hospital for the last time and he's all skinny and gray and cough-ing and spasming and that's what he gets for all his hard work and hopes of making it to Alaska one day and never getting there.

Dad's dead and mom moves back home and kicks me out, prying me loose like an aborted baby from the bedroom I'd occupied since infancy, and I move to a basement apartment in Norristown, Pennsylvania, where there's a mental hospital, a methadone clinic, and not much else, and I have to take a forty-minute high-speed screaming train over rickety tracks to connect with the subway into Philly, and at night I could see my reflection in the train window and notice that the hair in my temples was receding slightly and I was fucking only nineteen and already getting old.

That winter in Norristown felt right because it felt dead: dark cold damp basement with only a tiny window peeping up to ground level, privy to only a thin sliver of blackish twilight.

Wheezing Pennsylvania skyline, red smokestacks barfing industrial phlegm, crumbling blood-colored bricks, cracked rubber fan belts on dying leaden machines which leaked oil, my breath a fog, cold alcoholic blackouts, jumping at the slightest noise, lifting weights in preparation for attackers which never came, even my cum was gray and runny like dirty dishwater, nineteen's supposed to be your sexual peak and my hard-on's soft like uncooked dough.

Some skinny black kid with glasses paid me five bucks for the privilege of letting him suck my cock on the concrete stairwell to a fluorescent-lit Norristown subterranean parking lot, and he had his eyes closed all worshipfully slobbering over it and said I could fuck him if I wanted to but I said no, and the way he fawned over my bone was the same way Ardea the fat clothing-industry fag hag knelt down and prayed to it and said it tastes great when she swallowed and she'd be cute if she lost a hundred pounds, and I've never had a steady girlfriend or anyone tell me they love me and thinking about all this makes me want to put a bullet in my head.

Or someone else's.

That winter was when Mark David Chapman, obsessive bookish loner, shot and killed John Lennon and I remember thinking that I could easily do something like that.

Without blinking.

Mom let me back home in the spring because mom likes when I'm depressed and deflated and docile and I kept thinking there's some-thing wrong with my brain, there has to be something wrong with my brain, because lithium didn't work and therapy didn't work and maybe I should try electroshock and deeper I slid down the fatal esophagus scanning my memory banks for traumatic childhood events which would make me feel this way until I finally insisted on a CAT scan to search for organic brain damage, so they shoved my head inside the radioactive white donut, but there was nothing organically wrong with my brain, so the demon remained elusive.

That spring was when John Hinckley shot at President Reagan and when I heard that Hinckley used to sit in the darkness watching TV and glumly eating half-gallons of ice cream I thought, yep, that'll be me one day, and reporters will knock on the neighbors' door and ask if they saw this coming.

A little over a year ago mom kicked me out for good and so I moved into this place here, this shitty, crumbling, Spanish-villa-styled hovel with flaking stucco paint, rusted fixtures, and gas-leaking, ready-to-explode kitchen equipment.

Shortly after I moved here, I accepted a mild acquaintance's offer to attend a keg party at a local Knights of Columbus hall his friends had rented.

He was likeable enough, this stupid, grinning, cut-from-the-mold, party-hearty, pillar-of-dudeosity Philly metalhead.

The moment I stepped into the hall, it was like a nigger walking into a Klan rally. All eyes were on me, and all eyes wanted to hurt me.

A glowering Cro-Magnon looked up from the pool table where he was poised to make a shot and said, "We don't like fucking punk rockers here."

I shrugged it off, and without even bothering to explain the difference between rockabilly and punk rock, I poured myself some beer and sat down.

It was an awful crowd grooving to a retarded cover band sluggishly pumping out covers to AC/DC and Blondie songs, girls with curly perms and yellow teeth, guys with dull eyes and protruding foreheads.

I didn't say a mean word to anyone. The only thing I did to provoke them was being different.

As I crossed the dance floor to the bathroom, the crowd pounced on me from all directions, at least a dozen of them with quick wolfpack instinct, guys swinging fists, chicks scratching my face and pulling on my freaky, gelled-up pompadour, tearing at my shirt, kicking and yelling at me, and I elbowed enough guts and kicked enough shins that I was able to break loose and run outside the dance hall.

As I'm slipping and sliding on the ice outside, using torn shreds of my white shirt to dab blood from my face, a giant thick-necked bruiser walks out of the hall toward me, and every muscle in my body tenses, waiting for him to deliver the death blow.

Instead, he says,

"That was fucked-up what they did. That was wrong."

Individuals have consciences. Crowds don't.

This past spring was when I quit drinking, after I single-handedly guzzled a quart of Colt 45 and an entire bottle of tequila that was so cheap, the screw-off cap was a red plastic sombrero.

The last thing I remember before waking up in jail and being charged with assaulting two police officers was stumbling around in some woods near where I worked and being taunted by a group of schoolchildren who were probably amused at the sight of this silly drunken boy.

Blurry, buried memories of being under siege, of a happy kiddie gang mocking me.

The next thing I knew, I was waking up in a jail cell at midnight with my face all puffy and covered in dried blood. I still don't remember how it happened.

So tell me—where do I run?

Where is the island that holds all the people like me?

Why was I sent to the wrong planet?

Once you see through them, you can't pretend you're a part of them. I will join no movements. No gangs. No political parties. No clubhouses.

Little crowds are just as bad as big ones. Even worse, because they should know better.

The fags and niggers and nerds form their own little lynch mobs and condemn those who are different.

A crowd of nonconformists is just a smaller crowd, bound by the same rules and instincts which guide bigger crowds.

All crowds are bad. Wherever two or more are gathered, there's trouble.

They say I'm crazy, but which is the truer form of madness—the clear perception of their cruelty, or the blind illusion that they're good?

Antisocial acts are only wrong if you accept the premise that society is good, and under the slightest inspection, that premise sinks like a bowling ball through quicksand.

Without flinching, the crowd will do things far more heinous than the most depraved individual on earth could ever come close to doing. Individual crimes can never compete with what an angry school of human piranhas does as a matter of course.

Every serial killer on earth—combined, throughout world history!— can't stack up as many bodies as the crowd does in one eager day on the battlefield.

The crusty old pervert who fondled a kid's genitals likely did so with far less cruelty than the mob which kicks his teeth in and chops his hands off.

The weirdo who gets picked on is never as bad as the gang who taunts and mocks and tortures him.

And yet the crowd must always justify its behavior. It can never bring itself to face the inhumanity inherent in its actions.

The crowd is a big fat ugly frog which blames the fly that it swallows.

The crowd's moralistic outrage is merely a cover for its sadistic bloodlust. The crowd can never admit that it simply enjoys tearing a helpless individual to bloody pieces—it must invent excuses so that this dreaded thing called "guilt" doesn't bounce back to it.

The angry cocks who impale their victim in a gang bang always have to pretend that the filthy whore deserved it, don't they? They can't just get their nut and leave it at that.

The crowd instinctually, effortlessly channels its own guilt onto the individual whom they're disfiguring, the individual who screams out for mercy and gets none.

The crowd needs to see evil as outside of itself. It needs to control and condemn and punish and hurt. It needs to find a scapegoat, that's what it needs to do.

The crowd isn't content just huddling together and being warm. It needs to snatch someone else's blanket and make them cold.

To be different is to invite attack.

Don't join the witch hunt, you become the witch.

Don't join the lynch mob, you'll be hanging from a tree.

It isn't what they do that's so bad; it's how they justify it. They aren't good; they just need to see themselves as good, and they can't tell the difference. They're only "good" because they're bad.

There is absolutely no consistency to their definitions of good and evil except for this: They define right and wrong only by what strengthens or weakens the crowd. If their beloved leader gets killed, they'll flock to the enemy leader who killed him and act as if it was always this way. They'll cluster around whoever has the power, regardless of whether the leader they're now calling "good" was "evil" five minutes ago.

They hate the loner because he reminds them of their cowardice. They hate the thinking individual because he reminds them that they're zombies. They call him a "sociopath," even though they bear their own cruel, pathologically destructive hatred for the lone individual who thinks for himself.

They like to pretend that the loner is the dangerous one, but he's never as much of a threat to the crowd as they are to him. He just wants to be left alone, but they won't allow that.

Join us or die.

The crowd has a mind of its own, a mind which overrides individual thoughts and personalities.

Stare into the shallow pond and watch all the minnows swim in unison, darting back and forth together as if choreographed by an invisible puppeteer.

What they call "society" is only an endless wallpaper pattern of strangers living in apartments next to one another and watching the same TV shows, a vast web of tiny wet brains effortlessly manipulated and rendered compliant.

Creatures of habit and instinct and reflex and thoughtlessness. Not one mannerism or idea to call their own. Never thought or did one thing...one meager, measly fucking thing...which wasn't spoon-fed to them by the crowd.

They aren't individuals, they are imitators. They are programmed. Everything about them was passively received through osmosis. They knelt down, threw their heads back, and accepted everything society told them as if it was a gob of sperm shot down their throats like hot mayonnaise.

What a happy, ginger-spiced twist of circumstance that their tastes and beliefs mirror those of everyone around them. Howzabout that? What are the odds of *that* happening?

And yet each one of these plastic soldiers thinks they're unique, don't they? They're blindly unaware that they're just a little bar of soap that has been whittled into shape by the crowd. They naively believe that they'd be even remotely the same person they are now if they'd been born halfway around the world or a hundred years ago. They're good little Americans here, and they'd be good little Hitler Youth in Germany and good little members of Chairman Mao's Red Brigades in China.

Retarded farting livestock, penned up, shoved down, pushed forward one after the next onto the slaughterhouse conveyor belt.

They're all whipped into line by fear of the crowd's disapproval, by the threat of shame and ostracism.

And loneliness.

Anyone who hides within the crowd is a coward. Anyone. It's the only place where the weak can feel strong. Strength in numbers for weak individuals. Safe within the crowd, a safe place for the faceless. Can't see the forest for the trees. Just a cell in the body. Just a dim little star in the galaxy. A locust amid the swarm. A goose in the gaggle.

Replaceable.

Little minds hide in big crowds. Little specks of toner on a giant Xeroxed sheet. Drowning in their own irrelevance. Striving to be unexceptional. Celebrating their blandness. Lusting after the ordinary. The common. The run-of-the-mill. The middle-of-the-road. The mundane.

Breeding for quantity, the lowest common denominator factored exponentially, mere sequels of their parents, they really think they're so special that they need to reproduce themselves, thinking one of them isn't plenty—or too much already—existing for no other apparent purpose than to squirt out more like them, spraying their intellectually stunted, emotionally arrested genes like pollen, one smelly asshole leading to another, breeding another and another, a big knot of swelling flesh clogging nature's toilet.

I'll bet each little individual fungal spore which clings to my bathtub thinks it's special, too.

I've taken shits which are more intelligent than these people. Ask them why they exist, and they just stare at you confused.

And yet they're happy. They have money and friends and family and love. They're utterly worthless, yet they have an endless network of support. No brains, yet they've been loved all their lives.

Give someone a brain but no love, and this is what happens...

Me.

I'm the Tin Man.

I'm the one everyone says is quiet because they can't hear the explosions inside my head. I seem calm, but that's the only way to contain it all. I'm not quiet—I'm just balled-up with so much tension, I'm paralyzed. One minute I'm polite and silent; the next, I'm smashing everything in the room to pieces. You always have to beware of the quiet ones. Be very afraid of the quiet ones.

I've always felt simultaneously superior and inferior to the rest of humanity. I'm book-smart and socially retarded. I'm a human being amid gorillas—a notch up on the evolutionary staircase, yet weaker and less equipped to deal with nature.

Weirdo gorillas left the herd and mutated into humans.

And I'm a weirdo human.

There's something beyond Homo Sapiens, and I have to strain and stretch to get there. The weirdos experience all the growing pains as they point the normals toward something hidden in our dim evolutionary future.

The freak points to the future. The normals are the present sinking into the past.

If you don't take risks, you become a fossil.

The mainstream isn't a stream at all—it's a backlogged cesspool. Like a dried bloodstain, the crowd congeals at the point where evolution has stopped, at the big fat hump in the bell curve.

Whether it's above or below them, the crowd will destroy whatever is different. In fact, it is far more dangerous to be better than they are than it is to be worse. The crowd will slaughter an inferior individual out of contempt, but it kills the superior person out of envy.

The superior individual reminds them of their obsolescence, and they kill him in a desperate attempt to stave off their own extinction.

I'm harmful to the crowd because I poke holes through the flimsy cellophane they've wrapped around their minds to protect them. But I will ultimately suffer far more from their stupidity than they will from my intelligence.

People my age are getting married and having babies and starting businesses, and I don't want any part of it, this cold new wave of conservative Reagan youth who would have all been hippies ten years ago, rushing lemminglike wherever the crowd leads them.

The others grew into adulthood, and I just went somewhere else.

Here comes the adulthood I never wanted.

Alone I'll sleep tonight, just like every night.

And still, the world is just something I watch.

I booted my roommate Vince out a month ago, only a couple of weeks before Christmas, because that's the kind of bastard I can be. I tired of the cat-piss smell of crank oozing from his sweat glands, tired of the crankhead buddies he'd drag in here all hours of the night who couldn't hold a conversation with tile grout—huge, open acne sores, chipped teeth, misshapen heads hung with drippy black-spaghetti hair, and that open-mouthed vacuum in their expressions—tired of finding used syringes tucked under the silverware tray, so I kicked him out into the wet, slushy snow and wished him a Merry Christmas.

But as much of a lowlife as Vince was, he had friends.

Here I am, a crowd of one.

No family, no lover, no group to call my own. Just me and the roaches. The roaches, bless them, don't seem afflicted with the idea that they're anything more than roaches.

What a mess I've made.

A pile of dirty clothes on the floor big enough to sleep on, big enough to hide a couple of dead bodies under.

Strewn pieces of an old wooden chair I smashed to splinters a couple of weeks ago and never picked up.

I had used a refrigerator box as a trash can until it overflowed and then I gave up and started tossing it all on the floor. Periodically you'll glimpse a small patch of virgin carpet, but mostly it's grease-stained pizza boxes and crumpled garbage with roaches crawling up, down, and around everything. I've started to throw excess trash out of my bedroom window into the alley, and so far no one's complained.

Over Christmas break I went and got the nose job I'd wanted for years. I'd always hated dad's big schnozz, and in my high-school graduation photo I thought my nose looked like a banana, all curved like an apostrophe. And all these fistfights I've had made it look more bulbous than ever.

I figured my nose was the reason I didn't have a girlfriend.

So I was wheeled in on a steel hospital gurney, spiked in the ass with morphine, and I listened stuporously as the female plastic surgeon hacked and sawed at my nasal bones. Feeling her steel hammer's percussive slam vibrating through my skull, I realized that the operation was the first time a woman had touched me in years.

She shoved plastic splints up my nose so the bones would set, stitched me up, and sent me home.

I spent Christmas and New Year's alone here at the trash dump. The only contact with another human being was when I'd swing open the door for the pizza-delivery person, and what a sight it must have been to see me with my face bandaged up, wading amid smelly garbage.

Shortly after I returned to work, this place got burglarized. Someone smashed through my door and purloined my typewriter, TV, and stereo. When a cop surveyed the scene, he gasped, "Jesus Christ! They tore the shit out of this place! Someone must have had a vendetta against you!" The local paper reported, "The apartment had been so thoroughly ransacked, police suspected personal revenge as a motive." Truth was, the burglars had delicately removed my valuables while leaving everything else untouched.

The mess was purely my own.

But revenge had to have been a motive, because the thieves smeared a big "X" in blood on the outside of my front door.

The ancient Hebrews marked their doorways so the Angel of Death would pass over them and leave them unharmed. But I suspect that this bloody "X" was an omen that they'd be back.

I can feel the walls squeezing in on me.

The icy, unforgiving winter sun peers like a telescope into my apartment.

As hard as it is to get up and go outside with my feet nailed to the floor like this, I have to make a move. I can't stay here. They're coming to get me.

I'm a marked man.

The world locked its doors on me a long time ago.

And now even my own locks are broken.

৲5৲

A Womb of Our Own

Photos of us as children, long before we met: I'm about four years old, my oversized space-alien head tilted toward the camera, eyes glaring angrily; you're about ten, sad-eyed and sourpussed, with a tear rolling down your cheek.

YOU PLOPPED INTO this world ass-backwards, a breech baby born with the umbilical cord wrapped around your neck like a noose.

Almost stillborn.

I think if you had the choice, you would've crawled back inside your mother and stayed there.

It's warm in there.

And this world can be awfully cold.

You grew up behind gates. A tiny private community out on Coney Island's far tip, beyond the rusting carnival rides, past the housing projects and broken glass, a cloistered enclave as lonely as the cold breezes lapping Brooklyn's dirty shores.

The cobwebby old house you grew up in was a dusty sarcophagus of moaning, wheezing, kosher sad sacks. A posse of ceaselessly *kvetching* guilt-trippers. Lumpy, whiny, spud-shaped yutzes. You used to say the smell of death was in that house. Was it in their genes? Were they genetically impelled to keep reliving Dachau years after the Allies had shut down the amusement park? Like Old Testament prophets, your folks forecasted doom. Expect the worst. Good times are merely a set-up for disaster. Better not take risks. Better safe than sorry. They protected you to the point where I'm surprised you were able to wipe your own ass without help.

They sheltered you.

Circus trainers sometimes tie baby elephants to wooden posts so that when the elephant grows up, all the trainer needs to do is place a wooden post near the animal—without even tying him to it—and the elephant won't stray.

That's what they did to you.

They immobilized you.

They fossilized your personality.

The car accident made things worse. One morning in the early 80s you drove head-on into a school bus. The crash threw you into a coma's warm womb. When doctors revived you and said you were going to live, you shouted, "FUCK!"

You wanted to stay unconscious.

You were in some sort of half-dead limbo ever since that accident. It must feel like living death to have had part of your brain knocked out, to know that you aren't what you once were. You had a big lightning-bolt scar on your forehead from the crash. You brushed your hair so it would cover the scar. And you dyed your hair blonde because it had turned almost totally gray from all the worrying.

You were still living in your parents' house in your early thirties. By then, it was probably too late. The damage was done. I have no doubt that if I hadn't come along, you'd still be living there. After all, your brother's still there. He's in his fifties and still a virgin. They fucked him up worse than they did you.

A photo of you taken years before we met: You're standing outside your house, frowning and with your hair in pigtails. You'd written, "Please love me forever" on the back of the picture and sent it to me. Underneath your message, I wrote, "I promise I will—forever."

The summer before I met you, I was all alone at a London discotheque as the big black speakers pumped Rod Stewart's sandpaper voice: "Next time I fall in love, it's gonna last forever."

My girlfriend and I had broken up three days into our European vacation. I was all alone in a foreign land. I decided that the next time I fell in love would be the one that lasts forever, because love hurts too much when it ends.

That fall, I moved into a mouse-sized New Jersey apartment right across the river from Manhattan. I was all alone, facing the giant gray city. I worked at night and had no human contact except for the strangers at my job. The strangers on the subway. The strangers on the lonely dark bus ride through the tunnel and back to Jersey.

I used to think I'd lose my mind from the loneliness.

You were lonely, too. Your boyfriend had left you for another girl. You went to a psychic and asked what was wrong. She said that a black aura surrounded you. Thoughts of suicide crossed your mind, an urge to slip beneath the warm black blanket. You compiled a cassette of your favorite gloom-rock songs called "Come Die With Me."

We met in the dead cement-and-ice New York winter the day after

Valentine's Day. Two days after your thirty-second birthday. I was twenty-four. It was a Johnny Thunders concert, and I told my friend Donna I was either going to get laid or get in a fight that night. Donna had known you back in college, back before the car accident, back when you were still somewhat wild and smart.

She introduced us. She said your name was Debbie.

You asked me my name, and I said, "Jim."

"Jimmy?" you asked, and I said, "Yeah, OK." So that's what you called me from then on. You were the only one I let call me Jimmy.

The music was too loud. We couldn't hear each other. We walked out of the auditorium and sat on some marble steps away from the thumping rumble of the show and the crowd.

Away from "them."

You walked splay-footed and slightly hunched-over, as if hauling an invisible boulder of misery. You were pale and bushy-haired, with dark circles under your eyes like a silent-movie siren. There was a sweet chocolatey sadness in your eyes.

But you wouldn't pronounce it "chocolatey." You'd make it sound more like "chawklitty."

Holy fuck, what an accent. It was as if you'd been gargling salt water and vinegar your whole life. So deeply, corrosively Noo Yawk, I almost needed an interpreter.

You wore a button that said I HATE PEOPLE. You said, "They should just drop a bomb and get it over with."

A girl who thinks like me.

You excused yourself to go pee. When you returned, you said, "Oh—you waited for me," as if surprised I hadn't tried to take off and hide in the crowd.

I waited for you. Away from the numbers.

You turned your head quizzically and said, "What's the answer?"

I said it was sex and money.

Soon afterward, I said it was love.

A Polaroid of you taken shortly after we met: You're smiling. On the back, you wrote, "To Jimmy—Good times and passion. Love, Debbie" and sent it to me.

Je t'aime, my goofy, fucked-up Coney Island Jewgirl.

You're an odd duck.

A polka-dotted zebra.

A crippled turtle walking around frightened.

A scowling dodo bird.

The only person on earth with poorer social skills than me.

From the start, I thought you were an airhead. A flake. A space cadet. Clumsy and mopey. Ditzy, daffy, and dopey.

There was something so…*inappropriate* about you.

You constantly misused and mispronounced words.

You cooed over kitty cats but would spit on babies when their parents weren't looking.

You'd make a silly face when you tried acting sexy that looked as if you were sucking a lemon.

You were such a cute little weirdo, it was easy for me to love you. The way you were sweetly childlike and yet disgusted with humanity was irresistible to me. You were crass and uncultured. Free of artifice. Devoid of what you called "chickiness."

You weren't like the other girls.

And I hated the other girls.

For the first few weeks after we met, I wasn't even sure that you liked me. And you didn't know whether I liked you, either. We were two gophers afraid to pop our heads out of the hole.

One night you were dropping me off at my subway stop because it was getting late and you feared your family would start worrying where you were. I asked for a kiss—our first.

I closed my eyes…

Kiss me, and the world will stop.

Your kisses taste sweeter than soda pop.

You're just a cute little girl with a bow in your hair.

Oh, yeah.

…When I opened my eyes, you looked so happy.

I trudged through the snow to the subway station, but nothing felt cold anymore.

We agreed that the next date would be the first time we'd sleep together. You told your family you'd be staying at a girlfriend's house—even at thirty-two, they treated you like a teenager.

We decided to meet at an East Village bar. I bought you a drink. You stared down into the glass as if ready to cry. I asked you what was wrong.

"Oh, that's just my face," you said.

We drove through the tunnel to Jersey. You parked on a big, well-lit boulevard a block from my apartment. But when we were ten feet away from the car, you asked me if it was safe to park there all night. I told you it was. Fifty feet away, you asked me again.

I assured you it would be fine. As we entered my building, you asked yet again. I reassured you, wondering to myself what was wrong with you. At least a dozen times that night, you asked me whether the car would be OK.

When I first saw your naked back, it looked so lonely. Like you hadn't been touched in years. But as I stared at your face after you fell asleep, you were smiling. And I was smiling, too.

And when daylight came, no one had stolen your car.

At the end of our next date, as I stood under creaking subway trestles ready to pass through the turnstiles and hop on a train, you leaned out of your car window and said, "I more than like you."

Soon we were using the most dangerous word of them all:

Love.

Late one night I took a train all way out to Coney Island and spray-painted the station so you'd see it the next morning when you went to work:

JIMMY LOVES DEBBIE

A strip of four black-and-white photos taken in a coin-operated booth underneath a Coney Island Ferris wheel: We're kissing and hugging.

Love is for the needy.

And we were both very needy.

Misery loves company.

And we were both intensely miserable.

Hardly anyone liked us.

But we liked each other.

I felt like I went to the end of the earth to find you and rescue you. I wished that I could have reached inside you and pulled all the misery out. I wanted to solve all your problems because I loved you and didn't want you to be unhappy.

One sunny afternoon we went on a dangerous old carnival ride, and as we spun around upside-down at whiplash speed, you started to get scared. "Hold onto my arms," I told you. "These are the safest arms in the world."

You promised to take care of me, too. You told me that I don't need any other friends, only you.

So it became us...and "them."

Jimmy, Debbie...and the world.

Our motto was "share the bitterness."

We had no support network—only each other. We developed a

bunker mentality and felt as if we were under constant siege from the world. We bonded through unhappiness and a mutual pledge to shield each other from this callous, empty-headed, saturated-fat-filled world. Our love was a sanctuary from a world that made no sense to us. We both hated our families. We both were socially awkward. We both seethed with anger and felt ethically superior to "them."

We promised to never hurt one another like the world had hurt us. I wrote you a letter that said, "Don't worry, little girl—I'll never do anything to hurt you." And I remember the time you slapped yourself in the face because you thought you'd said something that offended me.

We called our love "the granite," because nothing could shake it. I wrote you songs called "Two People, Two Lonely People" and "As Long as We're Together, It's OK."

You lived in Brooklyn and worked during the day. I lived in Jersey and worked the night shift. We grew lovesick for each other during weekdays when we weren't together.

On Friday nights you'd pick me up from work and we'd spend the weekend together in my tiny Hoboken apartment. I remember one Sunday afternoon when we lay together in bed, staring deeply into each other's eyes for what seemed like hours.

I had a dream where we were laying in the same position and you asked me, "Is this love—true love, the kind you only get once in a lifetime?"

And I said yes.

Late Sunday afternoons was when the dread set in, because we knew you'd soon be heading back to Brooklyn and we'd be apart all week again. You called it the "Sunday feelin'," that sick separation anxiety that felt as if a Band-Aid was being ripped from our skin.

"We must not be parted," you'd tell me. We promised that one day we'd be together forever and there'd be no more Sunday feelin' ever again.

You sent me a letter saying, "Let's recluse ourselves together." You'd tell me that "We're doomed to be together."

"Someday we'll get a place," you predicted, "and it'll be just you, me, and the pets, and we'll all sit around being sincere."

We joked that we'd grow old together and ask each other, "Didja shit today?"

I used to say we'd die in a hail of bullets at a Las Vegas hotel, falling into a heart-shaped pool which would fill red with our blood. And I promised that if one of us was ever diagnosed with a terminal illness, we'd hold hands and walk into the ocean together until we drowned.

A picture of us placed onto a tiny color slide and encased in a plastic Vufinder: We're sitting at a dinner table in a Catskills resort hotel, kissing. We look like a hooknosed James Dean and a Jewish Marilyn Monroe.

We felt like a different breed.

No one would want to have sex next to the world's largest trash dump. So that's why we fucked there.

No one smokes crack before going to see Borscht Belt comedy shows. So that's what we did.

Nobody visits Cleveland on vacation. So we took our first vacation there.

Everyone else had something more shallow than we did. The other couples were together just for the sex or to have babies or because it was what their friends were doing. But we *needed* each other to stay alive. *They* all had happy childhoods, good families, lots of friends, and plenty of money, but they didn't have the love that we did.

Everyone said that they could see the love between us. They saw a bittersweet quality in our misanthropic romance. I think we gave hope to a lot of people who saw in us the possibility that two lonely, sociopathic weirdlings could find love. People were amazed that two such hateful crabapples found one another.

For our first Thanksgiving, I whipped up a gluttonous banquet dinner in my broom-closet apartment. I also cut out giant paper alphabet letters, colored them with crayon, and taped them to my wall so it would be the first thing you'd see when you came over. The letters spelled out this:

YOU'RE MY FAMILY

The next summer we moved in together. It was a big Brighton Beach apartment only a mile from your family's house. One room was painted yellow. One was orange. Another was pink. Our bedroom was blue. Jim and Debbie's Playhouse.

A friend had agreed to help us move into the new place. The night before we moved in, he phoned me and said he was still going to help, but he'd be two hours late. I called you and said that we'd start two hours later than planned.

You began crying.

"I knew this was gonna happen! He's not gonna show up! We're not gonna move in! We're not gonna be together! Why? Why? WHY?!? I should just kill myself! WAHHHHH!"

Jesus Christ, what's WRONG with you? Will you shut the fuck up and quit bawling? You're not even going to help us move! I'm doing all of the planning and all of the lifting, and I have to handle your baby-fits, too?

As always, your anxiety was useless. My friend showed up two hours late, just as he'd said. And you stood around sulking while we did all of the work in Popsicle-melting heat.

You owned enough clothes to make Imelda Marcos look like a peasant girl. Enough to stock a supermarket-sized thrift store. And on the night we moved in together, you spent three hours tearing through all your belongings in a frantic search for a white sweater that you thought was missing. Three hours of teeth-grinding neurosis. You made it impossible for me to relax after a day of sweat-soaked lifting. It was a baking-hot summer night, so you didn't need the sweater. I calmly tried explaining this, but you wouldn't listen—you actually cried tears looking for the sweater. I started screaming while you sobbed and tossed clothes around.

You finally found the stupid fucking sweater, but not before nudging my nerves to the precipice. You ignored all logic in your rhinoceros-powered quest to find the sweater. You didn't care that you were driving me crazy over something utterly unimportant.

So we were finally together, but there were already problems.

The problem, as you saw it, was that I got angry and screamed.

The problem, as I saw it, was that you seemed oblivious to why I was angry and screaming.

A photo of us taken by the Reverend Walker Goad outside his Las Vegas trailer home minutes after he married us: We're hugging and smiling.

I never wanted to get married. I had no desire for a stable domestic life. But I loved you so much, I thought I'd give it a shot. Your big fear was of dying alone as a "spinstah." And I didn't want you to be a spinstah.

Our car approached Vegas at night from the dark, desolate mountains above. When we saw the glimmering lights below, it looked like hellfire. Two lonely people staring down at the chintzy world from the vast blackness outside.

I found the Reverend Goad in the Las Vegas Yellow Pages. Nobody we knew attended our quiet little wedding. It was just the Reverend, his wife, me, and you: three Goads and a Goad-to-be. When he pronounced us man and wife, I whispered, "Now do you know I love you?" into your ear. A tear rolled from my eye when I remembered how your sad face stared down into your drink the first night we slept together. I thought that now, maybe you wouldn't be sad anymore.

When we drove away from the Reverend's trailer park, "Happy Together" by The Turtles was playing on the car radio.

Me and you, and you and me...so happy together.

That night we dropped acid and tried navigating through the Vegas streets amid billions of pulsating multicolored lights and the endless sonic swarm of "them." We scurried back to our hotel room and sang our "Two Lonely People" song.

But back home in Brooklyn we shared the bitterness daily, and it began wearing on us. I was angry. You were depressed. You'd complain. I'd scream. I was getting tired of your histrionic false alarms. I said that one day you'd cry wolf, and I wouldn't be there.

But I still felt protective of you. When the landlord called you stupid, I beat him up so badly, an ambulance took him to the hospital.

And yet I was always calling you stupid.

I was tossed in a grimy Brooklyn jail for thrashing the landlord. And when I got out, we decided that maybe it was a good time to move to Los Angeles like we'd been planning.

Actually, like *I'd* been planning. You never did any planning. You did a lot of worrying, but you never took any action. So, like always, I arranged for the move. I put everything in boxes. I rented the truck and filled it with our *tchotchkes*. I drove the truck three thousand miles from Brooklyn to Hollywood.

And you sat in the passenger's seat, complaining all the way.

As the truck chugged through the snowy, ice-laden Smoky Mountains in Tennessee, you started moaning that you had strep throat and would probably die from the infection. I suggested that we stop at a pharmacy to get you some throat lozenges, vitamins, and cough syrup. You didn't want to do it.

All right, then. If you won't do anything to ease your suffering, at least shut up about it and ease my suffering. OK? Is that asking too much?

So you shut up. For about five miles. And then it was back to your strep throat and imminent death.

Debbie, please, I love you, but it's hard enough driving on these icy mountain roads—PLEASE stop whining, or let's get you some medicine.

No, no, you'll be OK, you said. You'll quietly endure the agony. Miraculously, as sore as your throat was, you found the energy to resume howling about the pain within five minutes.

I ran out of patience.

While driving, I grabbed your sweater, violently yanked you toward me, and screamed,

That's it! I can't take it anymore! We're going to a fucking hospital! I don't care if it takes all day! We're gonna see about your stupid fucking throat infection!

So I pulled off the Interstate and headed into the frosty Tennessee outback to find the nearest country hospital. An amiable old hick doctor examined you. No strep throat. No throat infection at all. No sinus or lung congestion. No fever. There was nothing wrong with you.

Physically, at least.

Several photos of us taken by reporters during the *ANSWER Me!* years: We're posing with guns and never smiling.

Picture a wedding cake. Plastic figurines of a man and wife are welded together atop sweet creamy frosted curlicues. Pure white cloudlike innocence. A sugary promise of happiness. So perfectly baroque.

So unreal.

It can't stay that way.

Time slowly wears it down. The frosting hardens. The cake goes stale. Houseflies alight upon it. Ants dismantle the pretty wedding cake one crumb at a time.

Ten years later, the plastic man and wife have collapsed atop a squirming, vermin-laden compost heap.

By the time we reached Hollywood, the slow rot had already taken hold. Year by year, the tender moments grew fewer. The pain became amplified. Our agoraphobic wonderland devolved into a claustrophobic concentration camp.

We were now Jim and Debbie Goad, with a marital umbilical cord wrapped around each other's necks like a noose.

Our love became an open sore. And the sore became infected until it finally required amputation.

As I see things, it was mostly your fault. I know you see it differently. I hit you a few times. I cheated on you more than once. And I was "verbally abusive," whatever that means. But did my actions exist in a vacuum? Or did you play a starring role in our dysfunctional dinner theater?

Here's what was wrong with our blessed union:

You created problems, while I solved them.

You were weak, and I'm strong.

You were stupid, and I'm smart.

You don't think you were stupid?

Is water wet?

Is fire hot?

Is shit brown?

You were as dumb as a lobotomized garden slug. Gullible enough to swallow the simplistic tenets of pop psychology, plastic-applicator feminism, and cable-access religion. Your stubborn imbecility frustrated me to the point of madness. I couldn't treat you as an equal, and I resented treating you like an inferior. After a while, I felt as if I was taking care of a retarded child.

All right, so you weren't retarded.

Your IQ was a blazing 86.

E-I-G-H-T-Y S-I-X.

So your IQ was a hefty eleven points above the standard cut-off line for mental retardation. I'm truly sorry for exaggerating. You weren't retarded—you were just really, really close.

You didn't understand most of what issued from my mouth. You were impervious to intelligence.

Oh, sorry—"impervious" means that it had no effect on you.

I really didn't want anyone to know about your bargain-basement intellect.

Or that your motor skills were so mangled, you couldn't drive a car or operate a simple cassette player.

Or that you lived with your family until you were nearly middle-aged.

Or that well into your forties, you'd get into screaming matches with five-year-old kids—your intellectual equals—because you thought they looked at you funny.

Or that I rewrote all of your ANSWER Me! articles so that they'd be more readable. Remember that? Remember when reviewers would quote passages from your rants as evidence of what a good writer you were? How did it make you feel to realize they were quoting lines I'd ghostwritten for you?

Did it make you feel stupid? It should have. Fuck knows I would have felt stupid if I were in your shoes. But somehow, like all stupid people, you considered yourself smart.

Pssst—you weren't.

You were possibly the dumbest adult with whom I've willingly spent more than five minutes.

And you were definitely the most miserable. Not that I'm Mr. Sunshine. Yes, I have a temper. Yes, I'm moody. Yes, I'm difficult to be around. But I'm a fucking picnic compared to you.

I always said that if you were stranded on a lifeboat with a group of survivors, you'd be the one they'd wind up killing and cannibalizing because you drove them batty with your complaining.

What did you complain about?

Whaddaya got?

Headaches. Backaches. Doing laundry. The way the waitress looked at you. The asshole on TV. The phone never rings. Or it rings too much. You'd whine that we never go anywhere. Then the moment we'd go somewhere, you'd whine that you want to go home.

Moaning about your horrible job in New York.

And Hollywood.

And Portland.

Crying about how nobody liked you in New York.

And Hollywood.

And Portland.

Bitching about how life was unfair in New York.

And Hollywood.

And Portland.

I heard all these complaints in '86.

I was still hearing them in '96.

You were complaining the night I met you, and you never stopped.

Do you remember what happened when you joined a Depressed Women's Support Group? They asked you to leave because you were bumming everyone out. When I tell people about that, they think I'm joking. But it's a true story.

Misery surrounded you like a dust cloud. There was a relentless locomotive thrust to your self-pity. I never saw anyone insist on being unhappy as hard as you did. It was so fun to come home at night to find you sitting in the dark, crying. It was so delightful to watch you hack at your hair and pick at scabs.

My neck muscles knot up just thinking about it. My heart starts racing. Being around you felt like having a nest of mosquitoes humming inside my skull. Like ice water on a toothache. It wore on my nerves like bad road on a bald tire.

How many times should I have been expected to endure hearing that people looked at you funny? Or that your job sucked? Or that you wanted to die? Or that you thought you were having a heart attack? How many times should I have comforted you when you'd burst into tears for no reason?

A hundred? A thousand? A trillion?

What was I supposed to do? Slavishly cater to your every jittery freakout?

I tried that in the beginning. But when I'd solve one of your problems, you'd have two more waiting for me. Your problems multiplied as rapidly as cancer cells.

I guess I wasn't supposed to be bothered by it. I was supposed to untangle every knot, to kiss every boo-boo as if you were a toddler.

Where were all the problems you kept mewling about? Where? WHERE?!?

Actually, you had plenty of problems. You just never worried about them. You worried about strep throat, missing sweaters, and whether your car would get stolen. But you'd ignore impending car crashes that were right in front of your face.

When we first moved to LA, we rented a motel room on traffic-choked Sunset Boulevard. And even though you'd had so many car accidents in New York, I figured I'd be a nice goyish hubby and allow you to drive. But I warned you to watch for traffic. You didn't. You pulled onto Sunset without looking, and a car broadsided you only five feet out of the parking lot. The rent-a-car was totaled.

About a year later, I reckoned it was safe to let you drive again. I mean, fuck, it was an isolated dirt road with no traffic, so what could go wrong? We'd been soaking in some natural hot springs up in the mountains, so I thought I'd let myself relax while the steam rolled off my body. In less than a minute you slammed straight into a tree, shattering the passenger's-side window and salting me with glass chunks. I spent the rest of the day driving to a car-rental agency to replace the smashed auto. And what was worse, you wouldn't shut up about what a loser you were for wrecking the car. The hot springs had actually soothed me, but you found a way to torque my nerves up to the snapping point.

You drove only twice in California, totaling less than a half-mile altogether. And you wrecked the car both times. After that, I never allowed you to drive again.

I didn't want to control you—I just grabbed the steering wheel because the car would have crashed otherwise. I wasn't a control freak—you were a helplessness junkie. A person can only control that which is unable or unwilling to control itself.

You always said that I walked ahead of you. Maybe you were walking behind me.

Your life was a protracted study in human inertia. Emotional entropy. There was a rock-hard immovable mountainous Buddhistic stubbornness to your misery. You were a mule, honey. I dragged you out of your family's house. I dragged you to Hollywood. I dragged you to Portland. I got tired of the dragging. You were like a statue. Wherever I moved you, that's where you stayed.

In the dozen years I knew you, you never read one book.

In the dozen years I knew you, you never developed one skill, whether technical, personal, or social.

In the dozen years I knew you, you didn't learn one thing.

You just got older. More bitter. More stuck in your ways.

You didn't want solutions to your problems. You just wanted problems. You wanted to hold them. To stroke them. To caress them. To sit in a crib and be overwhelmed by problems as if they were a litter of puppies licking your face.

Because if you had problems, you could get sympathy. And sympathy was an intoxicant for you. It was your electric blanket. You were a fetal ball curled within a warm salty sac of suffering.

It's so easy to be a victim. It's the easiest thing in the world. It's easy to blame everyone else for your unhappiness. I never saw you take any responsibility...for anything that was wrong...with any part of your life...at any point in time.

You were a weak person. And I didn't make you weak. You were weak long before I rode into town. Your weakness didn't benefit me. It was a big pain in my ass. I felt overburdened. Solving all the problems. Planning all the moves. Calling all the shots. It wasn't fun.

You were an iceberg.

And I'm a fucking blowtorch.

Remember what it sounded like when I'd yell at you?

A blast of hot liquid mercury from my mouth:

If life is that bad, just kill yourself! Or shut up for five minutes! Please? I can't take it! Please? PLEASE!?!

You'd cower like a scared dog who understood the tone but none of the words. All you saw were enemy aircraft invading your radar field. And the next day you'd remember that I screamed, but never why.

What a downward spiral. You'd complain. I'd scream at you for complaining. Then you'd complain about my screaming. And I'd scream at you for complaining about my screaming....

A photo you took of yourself with a black eye after I'd hit you.

Remember the carnival ride when I told you to hold onto the safest arms in the world?

Those were the arms that hit you.

The first time was about a month after we'd moved to Hollywood. I was trying to buy weed in a graffiti-slathered parking lot behind our apartment building. Police cars suddenly came squealing from all directions, trapping me and everyone else against a wall. A cop slammed me down on his car hood and cuffed me. But since I hadn't yet bought the baggie, he had to cut me loose.

I was still traumatized from my stint in the Brooklyn jail for pummeling our landlord. I rushed back to our apartment, panting and shaking. I told you what happened.

"Oh," you snarled, "so now we have to move to another apartment again?"

I slapped you without even thinking. I was furious that you didn't care whether I was upset, that you could only see my crisis as your problem.

Do you remember what I said after slapping you?

I said,

It's over.

The innocence was gone. I knew I'd tarnished something that could never be made pure again.

I gave you the first black eye on our fifth anniversary. Your birthday had been two days earlier. And for two days, you'd been complaining that I hadn't spent enough money on your birthday presents.

C'mon, Debbie, I spent all the money I had on your presents. And, fuck, you didn't even buy me anything on my last birthday. And I'm sorry if you didn't like what I bought you, but it's pretty rude to keep complaining about it. So stop it, OK?

You didn't. For two days you kept pecking away at my brain.

When you resumed complaining on the morning of our fifth anniversary, I backhanded you hard enough to knock you on your ass.

You sat on the floor, rubbing your eye and looking confused.

It still pierces my guts to think of your startled expression.

You tried covering the black eye with peach-covered makeup. At work there were rumors that you were a battered wife.

But you stopped bitching about your birthday presents, because your anniversary present was so much worse.

The most violent event came during our final days in Hollywood. It was a bright morning and we had a few errands to run. We left our apartment at 10AM to deliver *ANSWER Me!* to two different friends. You also needed to go to the bank, which closed at 5PM. As I motored to the first friend's house, you asked me if we'd make it to the bank on time.

Yes. Fuck, we have seven hours. Don't worry about it.

While we were at the first guy's house, you nudged me and asked me again if we'd make it to the bank on time.

Yes....OK?

It was still well before noon when we drove away from his place, and you asked me again.

Yes. [blood getting hotter]

As we stood at the buzzer outside our second friend's building, you asked it again—are we going to make to the bank on time? We still had five hours before the bank closed.

*Yes, yes, **YES!** Holy fucking Christ, YES!!!!! Have I ever failed to come through? I'm not a fuck-up like you are! Yes, we'll get to the fucking bank!*

"Hit me," you taunted.

I slapped you.

Our friend opened the door only seconds later. We stayed for a few tense minutes and left.

As we got back in our car and started driving to the bank, I howled at you:

Why the fuck did you have to push it to that point? You knew I'd take you to the bank! Why couldn't you shut up?

You looked straight ahead, ignoring me.

I hate being ignored when I'm angry.

I bashed my fist into your nose.

Blood splattered onto your lip and chin.

You made it to the bank with plenty of time to spare. But you went by yourself, wearing sunglasses and a bandage across your nose.

That one punch gave you two black eyes. You looked like a raccoon. The shiners lasted all the way up to Portland.

I cried about that one. It tore me up to see what I'd done to the woman I said I loved. The coily-haired li'l Hebe-girl whom I'd promised never to hurt.

But a few weeks later I shoved you while in the bathroom and you fell against a towel rack, bruising your ribs.

I don't even remember why I did it.

I'd guess there were ten separate violent events in the ten years we were married. Ten ugly candles on our decomposing wedding cake. These weren't beatings in the sense that I never hit you repeatedly during the same incident. It was just one desperate lunge each time. None of it was premeditated. It was always quick and instinctual.

Four slaps.

Two punches.

One shove.

Three kicks.

Ten years.

And I hate myself for doing it.

And I hate what you did that led up to it.

Your actions didn't justify my violence.

But my violence didn't justify your actions, either.

I'm not saying you deserved being hit.

But I didn't deserved being flogged with your neuroses. Being tortured by your indifference to how savagely you were aggravating me.

It wasn't all my fault. You played a role in our sick little tango. You always found a way to pluck my tightly wound strings.

And you didn't care how I felt.

Punching you was the only way I could make a point with you.

When I hit you, I sometimes felt as if I was shaking a baby who wouldn't stop crying. You'd get so possessed by your irrational frenzy, I felt as if I was slapping you back into reality.

I usually gave you warning signals. I'd usually growl before I'd bite. And most of the time you'd just plow ahead with *attacque panic du jour,* ignoring my loudly expressed irritation.

I'll tell you this—if I had pestered someone as relentlessly as you did me, and they warned me to stop, I truly wouldn't blame them for knocking me to the ground. I'd feel as if I deserved in some way what happened to me. And after the first time they did it, I'd make a mental note to not bother them again.

I've been attacked far worse than I ever hit you.

I've had my skull crunched into asphalt.

I've been smacked in the face with a steel keg pump.

I've had my nose broken.

And none of it felt as bad as being assaulted by your full-bore panic attacks.

There are many ways to be aggressive. Hitting is only one of them, and it's hardly the worst.

I've tried to understand why I hit you.

Are you ready for this one?

I hit you because I cared too much.

The problem was that I loved you, and it tormented me that someone I loved was sabotaging my peace of mind. If I didn't love you, I would have left a long time before I did. Maybe other guys wouldn't have hit you. Maybe they just would've said you're a nut and abandoned you at the altar. Would that have been better?

The hitting stopped when I started cheating. So did most of the screaming. I just didn't care enough to get upset anymore. Cheating was my escape valve.

I took all the tension of being with you, channeled it into my cock, and shoved it into one barfly girl after the next. The sex had never been that great between you and me, but at least the first year or two…it existed. Our sex life was abysmal. For years, we'd just jerk each other off, then fall asleep. And every time you were jacking me, I had to think of some other girl. Or even more depressingly, I'd stroke myself in bed right next to you while you snored. For years I'd been telling you the sex was like tepid dishwater, and you ignored me. You didn't seem to care whether you looked good or turned me on anymore. We were married—why try?

I'd be waltzing on sticky wooden karaoke-bar floors with fat, ugly, female speed freaks, yet there was more tenderness in these clumsy slow dances than there had been between us in years. I got an instant hard-on during my first slow dance. It was heavenly to touch another woman for the first time in a decade. She felt so soft and smelled so sweet. Gooey pre-cum left a pancake-sized stain on my shorts.

It felt so good to cheat on you, to cram myself into some anonymous slit. Oh, my God, it felt so good. Did I ever tell you about how good it felt?

Feeling their soft curves in dark motel rooms. Kissing them long and hard. How many years had it been since we'd kissed?

Slowly running my finger down the back of their necks. Having them ride me on top. Always fucking them more than once. How many years had it been since we'd fucked?

These women weren't cold like you were. And though a few of them told me their stories of rape and abuse, they didn't feel nearly as sorry for themselves as you did.

I began to realize what a truly interchangeable appliance the vagina is. In the dark and upside-down, they're pretty much all the same, aren't they? Just a warm, wet place to park yourself for a while.

A photo I took of you on your fortieth birthday, standing alone on the desert floor in Monument Valley, Arizona. You liked the area so much, you said your soul would fly there after you died.

I thought that our love would save my life. And when I knew it was ending, something died within me. It was as if there would never be any innocence again. Everything became sick and defiled.

It was like *The Masque of the Red Death*—they tried their best to seal the castle doors, to quarantine themselves from the disease, and still the disease got in.

It just didn't work. And there was no way to make it work. All the king's horses and all the king's men couldn't put Jim and Debbie together again.

These two misfits were mismatched. These two lonely people couldn't even get along with each other. I loved you as well as I could. I think you did, too. And still it wasn't enough. It didn't save us like we thought it would.

We thought we'd rescue each other from our fucked-up families. And yet we created our own fucked-up family. The miserable world out there became less miserable than our own little world.

Me and you, and you and me...so unhappy together.

"Familiarity breeds contempt," as you'd say. And when you'd mispronounce "familiarity," I didn't find it cute anymore.

It's no longer "us." Now you're just one of "them" to me. And I am to you. We're strangers.

In the end, the granite crumbled.

In the end, I didn't wait for you like I did the night we met.

In the end, you cried wolf, and I wasn't there to save you.

In the end, you were diagnosed with a terminal illness, and I broke my promise to hold your hand and walk into the ocean with you.

I didn't want to share the bitterness anymore.

Love shouldn't make you miserable.

So what was it, if not love?

A sick mutual dependency.

A womb of our own.

You said love should be unconditional. But you had conditions, too.

Don't scream at you.

Don't hit you.

Don't cheat.

Tolerate your misery.

No, I didn't love who you were. I loved what I thought you could be. And you certainly didn't love me for the cantankerous son-of-a-bitch I was. You loved the fact that I was more convenient than your family.

People will love you the way they *want* to love you and hardly ever the way you need it. The ones who need love the most...like you and me...always end up without it.

Hate has always been easy for me. A piece of cake. But love gets stuck in my throat, and I wind up spitting it out.

A photo taken of you by a friend during the summer of '97 while I was out fucking the stripper girl: Your head is bald from chemotherapy. You wear a red clown nose and stare vacantly at the camera.

Back in 1991 you had a routine medical exam which uncovered an ovarian cyst the size of a kiwi fruit. I remember screaming at God for trying to take away the only thing that mattered to me.

But that tumor was benign. When it dissolved, I begged you to have your ovaries removed. Neither of us wanted kids. But you shied away from having the operation.

Your doctor told you that smoking cigarettes heightened your risk of ovarian cancer. Yet you continued smoking. Ovarian cancer had chewed your mother to pieces fifteen years earlier, and it's highly hereditary. But you did nothing to save yourself.

You wanted to die.

Early in '97, you started acting funny. Started talking about Jesus and angels.

One morning you left a shark-bite-sized menstrual stain on the sheets. Something was wrong.

They originally misdiagnosed it as Irritable Bowel Syndrome. But then your stomach became swollen and hard as a basketball.

I remember the look in your eyes when the doctor uttered the word "tumor." But soon you became oddly serene with the diagnosis, as if it was what you wanted all along. You didn't panic. It was almost as if you'd won the Lottery.

When your hair began falling out from the chemo, I agreed to shave your head. I used an electric razor to buzz-cut you from behind. Your back looked so lonely.

Lonelier than it did the first night I slept with you.

One night shortly after I told you about my affair with a girl half your age, I looked over at you while I was driving. Your lips were pursed into something worse than a frown. Your eyes were fixed deadly ahead, little black balls encased in clear jelly, hurt beyond feeling.

You looked sadder than you did staring down into your drink the first night we slept together.

The end of your life is just so unbelievably depressing.

Near the end, you'd say there's no Prince Charming who's going to come and rescue you.

You had a blind date with a fanboy that didn't work out.

And you registered with a dating service, but you were afraid to open the door when the ugly schmuck showed up. He kept knocking on the door and then finally walked away. I wonder what he would have thought if you opened the door and he saw a hairless cancer patient greeting him.

Photos of us that you kept in your house after we divorced, my face ripped out of every one of them.

Our breakup was a slow-motion horror show.

It hurt me to see the hatred you had in your eyes for me, to endure the tragic specter of you, all shiny-skulled and skinny, spitting venom at me.

After our divorce, I didn't say a mean word to you. I took all the blame for what went wrong, even though I never felt it was all my fault. Before you died, I wanted you to know that I had loved you more strongly than most people ever get to be loved. I wanted you to die remembering the good times, not the bad. For a solid year, I tried to get past the ugliness and find some common ground so we didn't feel it was all a waste.

But you didn't want peace.

You were more comfortable playing the victim.

I realized that you never wanted love from me. You wanted pity. And when I withdrew the pity, you sought it elsewhere.

You started making all sorts of false allegations about me to friends and opportunists, yet still I forgave you and wished you well. I figured you'd vent and get past it.

But you never did.

People would have felt bad for you, anyway. I don't know why you had to lie. Or maybe I do—the worse you make it seem, the more pity you'll get. And pity is heroin to you.

I'm glad you turned so vindictive. It'll make your death a lot less painful for me. If you're going to insist I'm evil while I'm trying to be good...well, I might as well be evil.

You want to make it ugly?

Let's make it ugly.

I can do ugly real well.

When I was suffering, you showed no compassion for me like I had for you. You never cared about my happiness like I did yours. Again and again, you relished the idea of me in pain. You kicked me when I was down.

So I started doing something I hadn't ever done: I started wishing you harm. I willed so much pain upon you, they couldn't dope you up quickly enough. I wanted the pain to cut so deep, you felt like peeling your face off.

Die, you miserable, cancer-ridden hag.

Die, you stupid, self-pitying twat.

Just die and stay fucking dead.

Isn't that what you wanted?

Isn't that what you wished for?

Millions and millions of fucking times?

Your foul attitude has finally drained me of every drop of pity I ever had for you. Now there is only contempt. I will no longer allow you to make me miserable. Go cry to someone who cares. Bathe in your own misery.

Suck up the pity, you whimpering child. Soak up all that pain, you sick little masochist with your black-eye photos and betrayal stories and chemo bottles.

Now you have cancer and were abandoned by a husband who used to hit you.

Fuck, you must be on top of the world.

Does it make you cum when people feel sorry for you?

I wasn't the great love of your life.

Your suffering was.

So what was accomplished or proven by your life? Well, I know that you felt bad a lot. That's been established. Was there any purpose beyond that? Anything else you want to add? Any burning insight you'd like to share with the peanut gallery? Any proof that you were better than the rest of the garbanzo beans?

I'm tired of my survivor's guilt. Tired of coddling an imbecile. You had none of the skills you need to make it in this world. Maybe stupid, weak people who constantly whine about how they want do die really don't deserve to live.

Well…no…come to think of it, I don't want you to die. It's too easy. Dying would grant you the ultimate victimhood you craved so strongly. I want you to live for years and years to prove what I've been saying all along—you're incapable of anything beyond self-pity. I want to see you go on welfare and struggle daily. I want you to live a life of middling boredom, of uneventful ordinariness, the same sort of life you would have had without me.

Of course, one risks appearing bitter.

I don't have a right to be angry when the only person I've ever loved turns out to be a near-retarded lump of shit who marinated my soul in misery?

Life is so hard as it is.

I hate you for making it harder.

I hate you for making the situation impossible.

I hate you for failing to do something—anything—to better your life.

I hate you for wasting years of my life on a losing cause.

I hate that your desire to be miserable was stronger than my will to make you happy.

I hate myself for thinking that logic and reason would someday seep into that thick skull of yours.

I hate myself for feeling guilty that I'm better equipped to face this world than you are.

And I hate the fact that I still feel bad for you.

All right, I'd better stop. I'm starting to sound like I used to sound. And I'm sure the doctors and nurses must have heard me.

Look at you.

Gray-skinned and bony, unconscious on a hospital bed.

Your deathbed.

Something tells me you're happy hooked up to all those machines. Tubes stuffed up your nose. A needle jammed in your arm. Maximum masochistic passivity. Everything is done for you with soft, slowly humming efficiency. You don't have to feed yourself. You don't even have to be conscious. The wires and tubes and machines do it all. It must feel like the womb which you so traumatically left.

A womb of your own.

And soon you'll be slipping into the soft cold moist blackness.

A tomb of your own.

Just seeing you again makes me sad. I feel myself being drawn down again.

I'm so stupid.

Here I am again, trying to explain myself to you. I'm not even sure if you can hear me. I just wanted to tell you these things before you died. Maybe I'm saying all these things for my benefit rather than yours. After all, I want to live a little while longer.

I think I figured something out.

You always loved our pets, but toward the end you began idealizing them as if they were supernatural beings. The pets never betrayed you like I did. "Their souls are pure," you'd always say, implying that my soul isn't pure.

That's true. But neither is yours. You lie. You hate. You avoid responsibility. You harm people.

Someone told me that you filled your house with drawings of

angels after I left. You probably felt like an angel, too. But angels aren't rude, bitter, and malicious. You weren't innocent. And you hated me for calling your bluff. More than the screaming, the hitting, and the cheating, you hated me for pointing out that your soul is tainted, too. That you're capable of acting just like me. Just like "them." Just like the rest of the creeps.

You said that in death, you'd be remembered like Princess Diana. Nice analogy, but Lady Di never wrote articles such as "I'm a Piece of Shit," with photos of turds hanging out of her hairy ass.

Yes, the world is fucked-up. But even worse are two lonely people who don't realize they're fucked-up, too.

We agreed that humans are pieces of shit, and that's what brought us together.

The problem: We're both human.

6

You Haven't Killed Me Yet

MOTHERFUCKERS WON'T LET me sleep. Distant echoes of pistols and shotguns prick my ears. Police choppers' machete propellers flutter past my window. Jaw-rattling lowrider woofers and tweeters skim by outside. Glass crashes. Women scream. Dogs bark. And all those sirens.

In the morning, without any sleep, I see the sunshine lower itself in lethal golden slabs through the blinds in this stifling little bedroom. There are poisonous X-rays in this eye-bleaching sunshine. The wicked light illuminates millions of floating particles in this cramped room. Smogbath. I'm coughing again. Evil carbon-monoxide spirits haunt this sick city, this sun-baked crater. It's a medical fact that if you live here long enough, your lungs will sprout lesions.

My apartment building is named *La Leyenda*. The Legend. This eighty-year-old stuccoed edifice hosts the ruins of smashed dreams, the dust of dead ingénues and failed leading men. A half-block away, a grayish, gummy film of spit and blood and exhaust-pipe ash blankets all the stars along Hollywood Boulevard.

The City of Angels. In all the years I've lived here, I haven't seen one fucking angel. But I've seen a man dressed as Jesus Christ, crown of thorns and all, dragging a huge wooden cross down the street. I've seen a man wearing a Darth Vader helmet and black cape swinging a plastic light saber at no one in particular. I've seen an armless Negro dwarf on a dirty blanket begging for spare change. I've seen a junkie shooting up in my parking lot. I've seen a naked woman running frantically down the Boulevard. I've seen a knife-wielding woman get shot by the LAPD, and while she was lying half-alive on her back, the cops exposed her blood-flecked tits for all to see as detectives milled around her, smoking cigs and laughing.

But no angels.

Dry psycho desert metropolis. Countless sand mites infesting an endless dune. You can drive two hours in any direction, and still you're within the Hydra's clutches. Sixty miles away from my apartment, I'm still stuck on some clogged-artery cement cloverleaf. When some snarling old biddy cuts me off in traffic, I pull up alongside her, lean out my window, and start smashing her car door with a steel club. When some rich bitch flips us off in traffic, Debbie reaches over and squirts pepper spray in her face.

There are too many people here. Far too many. You can't escape them. Swirling, teeming bacteria. Homeless bodies splayed everywhere like war casualties.

And the Mexicans. Just billions of them. Tooting *mariachi* music floats from rusted muscle cars. Oceans of little brown people hope to sideswipe your car so they can collect a big insurance payoff and bring *mamacita* plus the other forty-three members of their immediate family up from Oaxaca.

It would be hard to find a better argument against humanity than Los Angeles. Everyone—not only the actors—is acting, as if the sun has sweated all the sincerity out of them. Everyone has fled here from somewhere else so they can pretend they're somebody else. A city built on cocaine and fantasy and ultraviolet light.

Los Angeles, where nothing is real and everything is deadly.

Hollywood, where there are no Hollywood endings.

Debbie and I moved here from New York to mellow out.

What were we thinking?

We stand atop *La Leyenda*'s roof, watching the flames fan out for miles during the Rodney King riots. The flames are so close, we can *feel* the heat. The human pestilence slithers up our street with the camping equipment and cases of frozen hot dogs they've looted from smashed-open stores. It isn't about oppression—it's about wanting to be like the rich people who hire cops to beat the poor people.

A 6.8 earthquake rips us from sleep and angrily hurls everything in our apartment onto the floor. Cracks in the walls. Cracks in the streets. Giant fault lines running underneath downtown. Giant fault lines running along my brain.

The Big One's coming. Everyone knows it is, and yet they still live here. This town begs for disaster. It's a geographical Shit Magnet. And, truthfully, the city would be much prettier if everyone here was dead. No smog. You could see the mountains for once.

Debbie and I have been living in LA for nearly four years, and we still don't have one friend here. We have painted ourselves into a lonely little corner of the world. We hate just about everything in our lives except each other, and even our love is starting to wear thin. We're hurt and mad and ready to lash out.

Debbie has a college degree in Theater Writing, and I have one in

Journalism. And at night, to escape the brain-flaying imprisonment of our day jobs, we write free-lance articles for whatever magazines will accept them. Debbie writes a string of B-movie character-actor profiles for a handful of low-circulation Hollywood trade rags. I write about rap, death metal, and LA gangs for shitty Tinseltown music publications.

We write about other people, not ourselves. About *their* thoughts and feelings, not ours.

And every time I write something, without fail, no turning back, do not pass Go, the editor lops off my favorite passages and lets them crash into the dustbin. It's uncanny. The only sentences of mine that I like are always the ones he *doesn't* like.

It's in poor taste, Mr. Goad.

It's unprofessional.

It's opinion, not fact.

It'll offend the advertisers.

And the readers.

They're steam-cleaning all the life out of my writing.

They're killing the Jim Goad in each article.

Debbie, whose parents never allowed her to show any emotion but fear, has vowed never to reproduce. One day, as a reaction against a nauseating late-1980s wave of mass-media infant-fetishism—*Baby Boom, Three Men and a Baby, Look Who's Talking, et al*—she pens a caustic one-page anti-baby screed. There's a blunt rhythmic economy to this new essay which is wholly different from the pieces she'd intended for publication. And it's the best thing she's ever written. It reads exactly what Debbie sounds like when she complains.

So I decide to start writing exactly what I sound like when I yell.

In school, they taught me to write with the reader in mind.

Fuck the reader. The reader is an enemy. An intruder. The reader is placated with whitewashes and lies. The reader wants to be told that things aren't really as bad as they seem. The reader wants to hear that LA is filled with happy angels and healthy sunshine.

Photo "A" shows the world as I see it.

Photo "B" shows the world as *they* write about it.

I will slowly circle everything that's wrong with Photo "B."

I will sign my literary death warrant. Commit career suicide. And call it like I see it.

Unpardonable sins. Incurable diseases. Unstoppable weapons. Inevitable demises. Everything too horrible to consider.

Hopeless causes? What, like human life? Universal brotherhood?

Love that lasts forever? Peace on earth? How about no rain while we're at it, too?

When I was three or four, my mother told me about some debilitating bone disease wherein your skeleton softens and eventually melts inside you, turning your body into a loose sac of rotting organs.

I was fascinated.

Throughout my childhood, government propaganda machines warned us that we'd be blasted to dot-matrix patterns of blood and bone by H-bomb after H-bomb.

I wanted to know more.

In the early 1980s, doctors announced that a virus transmitted through bodily fluids would render your immune system incapable of fighting disease, causing death in every case.

Now *that's* literature in action.

All the Ugly Things, the things people expend so much energy denying, have more permanence than the sweet sucking-candy lies about equality and justice and everlasting happiness.

Ugliness is God.

And I will pay homage to Him with words. I will spread my hatred like Christ multiplied fishes and loaves.

I decide to do a magazine where I tell the world what I really think about it.

I call it ANSWER Me!

It is the sound of Jim Goad getting upset. A transcribed temper tantrum. My id trampling my slaughtered superego. Gulliver shaking off all the Lilliputians. A thunderous, Wagnerian opus of symphonic loathing. It's an effort to yank myself out of sullen oblivion. Self-administered literary electroshock therapy. A way of screaming to make sure I'm alive.

But writers aren't violent.

And violent people can't write.

Meet the new breed.

Splitting the atom. Tapping into reptile brain. A force which ten thousand years of civilization hasn't been able to kill. Beyond morality. Beyond the need for justifications. Discarding the Rules of Conduct. Peeling away the layers of decorum. Erasing all the boundaries until all that remains is personal power and slain enemies.

The natural human state.

Halfway through my fucking life, and I still haven't spent one day entirely happy. I expected the world to be fair, and it isn't. I expected people to play fair, and they don't. I'm really a decent guy, but there's only so much I can take. I'm very polite for the longest time, and then, well, I just explode. I've allowed myself to be nice to you so I can justify slamming your head against the wall.

The anger runs through me so strongly sometimes, I get the shivers. It consumes me until I feel all cracked and dried and peeled and blistered. I will not quietly accept the deadening of my soul.

So what do I do?

I take out a fly swatter and start crushing all the insects.

I'm not going to wallow in pain and heartache anymore. I'm just going to pick up my pen and start stabbing people with it. I've suffered for being different. Suffered for being superior. Now it's the world's turn to suffer. I'm here to make you all as miserable as you've made me.

Someone has to pay for that unhappy childhood of mine. Those unhappy teen years of mine. This bitterly unhappy adulthood of mine.

Everyone with happy families. Everyone born with money. Everyone who had it easier than I did. Everyone who breezed through life without ever feeling the pain I've felt.

Everyone.

Everyone who's ever told me what's best for me has been wrong. Everyone who's ever had authority over me wasn't even fit to lick my ass.

My parents. My teachers. The bosses who laughed at my quaint little "writing" career. The editors who tried to file down my teeth. Everyone who ever beat me up. Or kept me down. Or insulted me. Or thought they understood me but weren't even close.

Cell by cell, vein by vein, my flesh tells me I'm better than you are. So I will build a cathedral to my hatred. I will throw myself into it with the single-minded dedication of a religious lunatic. It only takes one zealot to fuck up a million compromisers.

Debbie contributes a few short rants for ANSWER Me!, but mostly it's my show. I do most of the writing and all of the production work.

Conceiving. Outlining. Researching. Writing. Editing. Rewriting. Re-editing. Typesetting. Proofreading. Correcting. Proofreading again. Correcting again. Laying out. Proofreading. Proofreading. Proofreading. Blowing it up on 11 x 17 Xeroxes. Proofreading again, this time with a magnifying glass.

Slaving over it. Tweaking and twisting and torquing it. Not one letter can be out of place. Picking every nit until it's perfect. Why don't you understand it has to be perfect?

Because you're sloppy even at things you value, like love. But I strain toward perfection in a world satisfied with bovine flatulence.

I sit at a hacked-up art table, ankle-deep in crumpled proofs and empty Styrofoam coffee cups. Melted wax and an Ex-Acto knife. Ancient typesetting equipment and a blurry old halftoning camera. These are my weapons.

This hatred keeps me working all night under a bare light bulb. Writing until dawn because I can't stop myself. A disciplined automaton. Losing sleep. Losing money. Losing years of my life, but I have to wrestle these primal emotions and pin them down on paper.

So there it is, plastered onto a page—the childhood abuse, the disdain, the arrogance, the screaming fits, the hate, the hate, the hate. All the violence, all the way back to my conception, captured in ink.

ANSWER Me! #1 is released in 1991....#2 comes in '92....#3 in '93....#4 in '94.

And that's all we write.

That's all we needed to write.

ANSWER Me! sucker-punches the world. It strafes the landscape with massive ordnance.

The Great Unwashed were apparently starving for real, raw, animal emotion. At a time when we have no friends where we live, mail pours in from all fifty states and a dozen foreign countries. Many letter-writers give *ANSWER Me!* the best compliment possible: "I've never seen anything like it before." One says that it's "not just a breath of fresh air—[it's] a fucking hurricane!" Reviewers call it "the greatest zine in the history of print" and "the hottest zine in America." A Belgian scribe predicts that "it will change the face of alternative publishing."

The magazine gets banned in England. Customs officials seize it in Canada and Australia. And the harder they try to squash it, the bigger it grows. Bootlegged artwork from *ANSWER Me!* surfaces on T-shirts and punk-rock flyers in Israel, Spain, and Greece.

Zinesters stand in line to interview us. We have saturated zinedom. You can't get away from us. Every zine you open, there we are, hoisting our guns and scowling.

Debbie and I challenged the world to a staring contest, and the world blinked. A pair of Hate Messiahs have arrived. They call us "The Dynamic Duo of Misanthropy" and "The Motorcyclists of the Apocalypse." Seemingly overnight, we become the Exterminating Angels of the Literary Netherworld. People see us as something larger than life. Something mythic.

La Leyenda.

Alone in our apartment, we're an underground sensation.

But I'm not looking for love 'n' cuddles. I seek what's familiar to me:

Conflict. Critics. Enemies.

A few brave soldiers are scoffing that I can't possibly be serious about all the hate and violence.

Excuse me?

I expected people to dislike *ANSWER Me!*—and I'm not bothered if people hate it or think it's shittily done—but it never occurred to me that anyone would think I'm only kidding.

My anger is a survival mechanism. It protects the core of my being. To say it isn't real is to infer I don't exist. To deny my anger is to kill me. When people say it's all a joke, I feel I'm being teased like my parents used to tease me. I feel as if they're laughing in my face while I cry, like my mother used to do.

So you want to test me? You want to provoke me, is that it? Everything is a joke to you, isn't it? Violence is the only thing you'll understand.

One by one, those who question whether I'm for real will get their answer.

You are now on my enemy list. And you will remain on that list until I cross you off.

I draw a stick figure of one critic. In childish handwriting I scrawl, "Little Mikey McP. was a jealous boy—jealous boys get MURDERED." I slice my leg open with a razor blade and wipe my blood—there's a lot of it flowing—all over the page. I send him the letter via Certified Mail. He calls me up, voice quavering, saying he's sorry.

I call up another critic and tell her I'm going to chop her to pieces and piss all over the chunks of her corpse.

I call up another critic and tell him I'll be at his office in ten minutes. When I get there, he's gone.

I call up another one, cock my shotgun, and hang up.

I call up another one, laugh maniacally for two minutes straight, and hang up.

I call up another one, play a re-looped snippet of a rap song that says, "Life is a gamble when you fuck with a psycho," and hang up.

I don't care where you live. No place is safe.

I'll fly to Kentucky and fuck you up.

I'll fly to Brooklyn and fuck you up.

I'll fly to Portland and fuck you up.

I'll fly to San Francisco and fuck you up.

I don't care if you have kids or a girlfriend—I'll fuck them up, too. We WILL meet one day.

Better yet, this is my home address...why don't you stop by and see whether my anger's for real?

Car alarms are wailing outside and my curtains are on fire and machine-gun bullets are piercing holes in my walls, and I really don't feel like being nice right now.

You see, I have a headache. And I don't like loud noises. And your endless chatter is REALLY starting to bother me. And you're too stupid to keep quiet.

Go ahead, asshole. Make me a legend. Turn me into a cult leader. Imbue me with sinister divinity.

You will choke on my words someday. You will be forgotten because you strove to be normal. But I will keep coming. In your dreams, I will keep coming. Just when you think you're finally rid of me, I will keep coming and coming and coming.

Pounding. Pounding. Pounding.

Pounding back.

See the look in my eyes? See how I look straight through you? I can focus my eyes on a speck of dust a hundred yards away and stare at it for hours.

You don't understand—I surround and develop and devour you. I will wear you out. Believe that.

Lone wolf. Solo cowboy. One-man army. Two-legged demolition squad. Wound up like a tin soldier.

From snowballs to avalanches.

From butterflies to Stealth fighters.

From pubic hairs to rain forests.

From a grapefruit to the planet Jupiter.

It's all so small, so very simple, yet you blow it out of proportion every fucking time.

Why?

WHY?!?

ANSWER Me!

ANSWER Me, motherfucker!

ANSWER Me, or I'll shove your nose up into your brain!

Streaks of beautiful flame shoot in ten-thousand-mile arcs across the sun's surface. My anger is the sun. My will is the magnifying glass. And you are the pitiful ant that I burn to a crisp on the sidewalk.

Bring down the hatred. Bring it down. Let it fall like napalm all over the world tonight. Let it burn, burn, burn through the lies until everyone's dead.

All that's left is force. And power. And me rolling over you.

My hammer to your head. My dick in your mouth. My bullet to your brain. My finger up your ass, dirty fingernail scratching into your rectal membrane.

These are my words, the words that will outlast everything. Densely packed matter. Unalloyed. Deadly.

So much power in this psychotic mind of mine. Words and thoughts which burn laserlike through glass, steel, and cement.

My words will find you. They will slip through your fingertips and hit their target.

A brain tumor? A blood clot? A bone splinter pressing in against my aggression center?

Doesn't matter.

I will die for these words. Kill for these words. And you aren't nearly as dedicated about anything.

There's nothing ironic about the way you're sprawled out on the floor. But still I find it funny.

Try to bury me, and I'll dig myself up through the dirt and rocks and roots and worms. I will rise, rise, rise.

Break my nose. Smash my teeth. Crack my ribs, and still I come up swinging.

I will not bend. Or break. Or flinch. I *will* win. You *will* lose. No equivocation. No gradations. No shades or subtleties or nuances.

I am not easily killed. In fact, you may die trying to kill me.

You haven't killed me yet, mother.

You haven't killed me yet, father.

You haven't killed me yet, world.

Not yet.

Obscenity

OFTEN WONDER about my father.

I wonder if he ever fucked my mom in the ass.

If so, did he pull out and spew his shit-smeared load on her back?

Did he ever eat her pussy?

Did he ever tell her to wash the stinking thing?

Did he ever make her cum?

Did he fuck her while she was pregnant with me?

Did his angry blue-collar cock squish up against my baby head?

And what about mom?

I wonder about her, too.

Did she ever suck dad off and slurp his nuts?

Did she swallow?

Did she ever think about his best friend while he was balling her?

Did she ever fantasize about women?

Did she really want a black guy?

Did she ever play with her clit?

Did she even know she had one?

My mother didn't make any sense. She'd go insane whenever I'd say the word "fuck," and yet she fucked my father in order to bear the foul-mouthed child who would say the evil word. To her, the word was more offensive than the act it signified. But make no mistake—she knew, from personal experience, what the word 'fuck' meant. She just couldn't bear to be reminded about it.

Sometimes, I wonder about myself.

I'm not sure how many spermy tadpoles inhabit the average male jizzload—millions? And I was the only li'l fishie strong enough to make it up to mom's egg. How long did I ferment inside dad's sweaty ball-sac before he launched me into mom's equally repulsive gummy womb? How long did it take me to swim up to her speckled ostrich ovum? And did I really crouch up there for nine months?

You've probably pondered some of the same things, then swiftly swept them out of your mind due to the nauseating implications. But trying to suppress something won't make it untrue. Face it—you were once a tenant in your father's scrotal condominium. You once swam inside daddy's hairy, low-slung testes. You once shot out of his cock like a human cannonball.

If that's offensive, then so is the story of your birth. So is universal human reality.

As human beings, there are so many things we have in common: Everyone has an anus, and they all smell.

Everyone has genitals, and most are slimy and deformed-looking.

Everyone has thoughts they might be hesitant to share.

Even you.

I often wonder about you.

And why you think I'm trying to offend you. Sorry, Gumdrop, but you aren't so important in my cosmos that I'd expend any effort trying to bruise your feelings. Hate to break it to you, but you have nothing to do with why I wonder all these things. You could walk out of the room at any time, and I'd keep wondering.

Once and for all: I don't want to offend you. Really. As hard as that might be for you to believe. My life would be a lot easier if you'd just get past being offended.

I understand *what* offends you; I just don't understand *why*.

There is no such thing as right and wrong, only sense and nonsense. And a lot of times, you don't make any sense.

There you are with your Charles Manson T-shirt, gasping at the very idea of date rape.

You contradict yourself. And I consider it my duty to write about such contradictions. I'm very dutiful that way.

The first three issues of *ANSWER Me!* had made me far more popular than I had ever wished or intended. I was tired of being loved for telling people that I hated them. I wanted the alternative underground to finally disown me. I yearned to produce something with an edge sharp enough to prune all the hipsters off the Goad Tree. I desperately sought to winnow down my fan base to the true believers. I desired readers who were able to *feel* the violence and not look away, who didn't merely view it all as some cute postmodern joke to be enjoyed from within their cozy studio apartments.

The kids had gobbled up murder and suicide as if they were peppermint ice cream. Well, what was something they *wouldn't* find cute?

Sexual violence was a good'un.

Ain't nothin' funny 'bout *dat*.

Or is there?

The year was 1994, and the girls weren't playing fair in the gender war. Lorena Bobbitt cuts her husband's *dick* off, and yet *he's* seen as the abusive one. Neo-fem yeastpit Kathleen Hanna kvetches at 120 decibels about violence toward women, and yet she's allegedly hit more women than I have. Wannabe Warhol-slayer Valerie Solanas's *S.C.U.M. Manifesto*—which seriously advocates the male gender's extinction—was considered politically brave, while my own "Let's Hear it for Violence Toward Women!"—which was intended as a *joke*—would eventually lead to an obscenity trial.

In 1994, feminists were inventing several new reasons to feel comfortable about being a misogynist. It was the year that marked the height of the vagino-moronic "riot grrrl" movement, which mixed bad punk rock with worse politics. Riot grrrl implausibly alleged that if a lot of women acted like screeching cunts, it would somehow disprove the notion that a lot of women acted like screeching cunts.

I grew cynical when belching slabs of female swineflesh insisted that *I* was the pig. I got tired of fat, pasty cows shoving chubby fingers in my face and telling me all the things I supposedly wanted to do to them. I'd had enough of being cornered by some whiskery, jowl-laden blob of a woman shrieking about how I wanted to rape her and keep her down. Yeah, Toots, I'm really emotionally involved in your existence. It's not like you could die tomorrow, and I wouldn't blink or anything.

Y'see, there's nothing inherently *wrong* with obese, crewcut-wearing, lumberjackesque women ramming their grimy fists in each other's woolly snatches, but there's nothing innately *righteous* about it, either. It's just one of the kooky things that human animals do.

But radical feminism had become so howlingly sensitive, it was begging to be lampooned. To me, it's a frickin' laff riot whenever anyone gets upset, especially when their pain and outrage has absolutely no effect on whatever upset them in the first place.

It wasn't rape *per se* that I found funny. But the spectacle of crusaders and censors and specialists scrambling around the crime scene wearing blindfolds? *That* was a real hootenanny. The stuff of deepest, darkest tragicomedy.

Of course, if they'd been able to get the joke, I wouldn't have been telling jokes about them in the first place. That's the problem with satire: If it's done well enough, its intended targets will mistake it for the real thing. People got their polka-dotted panties wedged fudgily up their hemorrhoidal anuses as to whether *ANSWER Me! #4*, the so-called "Rape Issue," was intended to be dead serious or pure satire. Their simple jellyfish brains could only conceive of a world split neatly in half as if it were a breakfast grapefruit—it was either supposed to be one big joke or not funny at all. There were no gray areas, and few considered the possibility that it could be simultaneously satirical and serious.

Or that some sections could be satirical while others were serious.

Or that horrifically serious matters could sometimes be terribly funny.

Or that satire could be used to drive home serious points.

And, bless my circumcised wiener, I *was* making some serious points, whether or not you agreed with them.

My primary point was that latter-day radical feminism had become so lost in theory and drowned in self-righteousness that rape became viewed as more of a political idea than a physical act. Feminism had grown unable to distinguish words from actions to such a degree that the two became switched: Women felt literally "assaulted" and "violated" by sexist language and imagery, whereas actual rape was viewed as an ideological tool of the patriarchy, almost more of a statement than an act.

Such muddying of the physical and theoretical led to several propositions that were so irrational, they bordered on the insane:

That all men are rapists.

That all intercourse is rape.

That rape is worse than murder.

That we live in a "rape culture."

That rape has nothing to do with sex.

That cultural attitudes, not biological drives, are what leads to rape.

That pornography causes violence toward women.

That even the word "chick" is an expression of woman-hatred, yet the most bilious fulminations of rad-feminism don't qualify as man-hatred.

[sound of my throat clearing]

You know, when I look down at my hard, throbbing schlong, I see a biological verity rather than a statement about gender politics. And when I look at pornography, I don't feel like beating women, I feel like beating off. In fact, if it weren't for their lovely, objectified naked bodies, I'd beat women a lot more than I do.

When someone tells me I want to rape them…and I don't want to rape them…what am I to make of that? I've never had the slightest desire to rape anyone. I've never had a male friend tell me he wanted to rape anyone, either. Yet several women have told me they've had fantasies of *being* raped. Therefore, I could only interpret the idea that I'm a natural-born rapist as the rank projection of some homely girl's deep-seated fantasies.

To allege that rape is worse than murder, or that it has nothing to do with sex, is evidence of a sheltered mindset incapable of grasping the act's physical components.

Is rape worse than murder?

Sure. And a French kiss is more extreme than a rim job.

Some say it's worse than murder because the victim must live with the trauma, but what about the victim of crippling violence? Why is it worse to have been forcibly penetrated for five or ten minutes than it is to spend the rest of your life in a wheelchair because someone crushed your kneecaps with a baseball bat?

Because the gender-jagoffs have politicized the issue far beyond the realm of logic, to the point where a raped woman's body is somehow more sacred than that of a murdered male. That's why bone-dry feminist authoress Katharine MacKinnon was incensed about Bosnian "rape camps" but made not a peep about all the men and boys being hauled off to mass slaughtering grounds in that war. After all, men started that war. They asked for it.

And, of course, rape has nothing to do with sex.

And that wasn't a penis he shoved inside you, it was a hand puppet.

Saying that rape is fundamentally nonsexual makes about as much sense as claiming that murder is nonviolent. But since the left has traditionally been pro-sex and anti-violence, they had to find some reason, however convoluted, for why sexual assault wasn't sexual.

And their "reason" was loopy in the extreme, although it's gained the half-assed credence of an old wives' tale: Rape isn't about sex, it's about power. The rapist, fueled by hardcore pornography, pervasive cultural messages that rape is groovy, and relentless billboard images of skinny fashion models in frilly undergarments, seeks to psychologically dominate his female victim so she serves him dinner on time and starts shaving her armpits again.

BZZZZT—*wrong!*

Listen very closely:

Animals rape.

Dolphins rape. Orangutans rape. Spider monkeys rape. Scorpionflies rape. Throughout the animal kingdom, living organisms rape one another. I proved it in the "Rape Issue," using scientific documentation.

And when those critters are out a-rapin', it has nothing to do with psychological power. The act is one of sexual desperation—the mating instinct gone awry—facilitated by superior physical prowess.

It isn't about spiritual evil, dummies.

It's about animal force.

Culture and morality are irrelevant to the discussion. Rape doesn't happen because women aren't whiny and self-righteous enough. It isn't caused by the *Sports Illustrated* "swimsuit" issue. The word "chick" doesn't factor into it. Astonishingly, it has nothing to do with anything that the experts think it does.

It isn't even about psychological power.

It's about physical force.

It isn't about morals.

It's about muscles.

Men rape and beat women for the same reason that dogs lick their balls—because they can.

If women were stronger, you can bet your crusty ass they'd be raping and beating men.

Nature, not culture, gave men the ability to do it. So you can blame your precious Goddess for rape and domestic violence.

Goddess. What a hypocritical cunt.

What rad-fems were saying about People With Penises was harsher and more sweepingly negative than any allegedly woman-hatin' comments they could dredge up by men. I have no problems with man-hatred—in fact, I rather enjoy it—but I scoff whenever anyone tries to mask their hatred as something nobly liberating. It wasn't their bile that annoyed me, it was that they weren't playing fair. It feels good to hate, but they weren't allowing men the same pleasure.

I felt that most literary treatments of rape pussyfooted around a sleeping ogre, skipping over the physical act and dealing only with the emotional aftermath.

Trying to understand rape solely from a victim's viewpoint was like trying to understand automobiles strictly from the perspective of the asphalt. I wanted to yank the reader right into it as a participant, experiencing the act from every possible angle, including those of pitcher and catcher. It was method writing, something that would traumatize the reader almost as much as being raped. And yet I didn't see my approach as sensationalistic. To my mind, the sensationalistic ones were those who focused on sensations at the expense of logic, who felt compelled to shellac everything with a sanctimonious glaze. The only difference between me, the tabloids, and the crusaders is that I didn't make a grand display of holding my nose. Otherwise, we were all displaying the same material.

"We're gonna get in trouble for this," Debbie would prophesy while walking past the computer screen as I worked on a layout of a naked man with a giant syringe in place of his penis. The "Rape Issue" was concocted in a sweltering, mold-ridden Hollywood apartment pulsating with the forlorn *angst* of a crumbling marriage. As monster cockroaches slowly scuttled against the hot, dusty, flea-infested carpet, I'd sip oily black coffee and write another five pages about rape. I smeared each page with the most graphic images I could acquire: fucked and bruised children, hacked and dead women, leering and sadistic men. Black eyes, chopped torsos, crushed faces, severed breasts.

At summer's end, I had magically pulled out of my ass what I consider to be the best issue of ANSWER Me!, a malevolent *Meisterwerk*.

But I wasn't merely parading a series of mutilated-snatch photos alongside inept sloganeering. I was presenting some *ideas* with the mutilated-snatch photos and inept sloganeering. And unlike my critics, I allowed the possibility that I could be wrong. It was just that I required proof. But the proof never came. The threats, condemnations, and idiotic allegations regarding my motives came instead.

When the magazine was released late in 1994, it was as if I'd thrown battery acid in my fans' faces. People swiftly reacted as if an acutely unholy event had occurred. They still talk of the Rape Issue as if it was something that never should have happened. For many, it emulated reality too well. It rang too true. People didn't even want to touch it, for fear that some of it might rub off.

And in a sense, it did. The original print job was ink-heavy and smudgy, on cheap grayish paper. Dark and splotchy graphics of nude corpses rendered the whole affair that much uglier.

Prior to the issue's release, I had corresponded with Richard "The Night Stalker" Ramirez a half-dozen or so times. After I sent him the Rape Issue, his letters stopped. One of Ramirez's pen pals later informed me that Ricky had asked him, "Don't you think that issue went a little too *far*?" This from someone who had slaughtered at least thirteen people and skull-fucked an elderly woman after murdering her and plucking out her eyeball.

Words worse than actions.

Distributors were freaked. One Colorado bookstore owner was reportedly so mortified by the Rape Issue, he *burned* all the copies sent to him lest anyone read it and be corrupted. A Toronto bookseller kept his copies in a car outside the store and only sold it to those who specifically requested it. A Texas distributor shrink-wrapped all 1,000 copies I'd sent them before they decided it was even too toxic with shrink wrap and sent back all their copies to me. A Portland bookstore which boasts of being anti-censorship demanded I remove all copies after only four hours on the shelves. A Seattle bookstore owner ruefully told me, "You're gonna lose a lot of your fans."

"I know," I said, satisfied. Suddenly, I had become as uncool as I had always wanted to be.

Early in January '95 I received a letter from a verbally challenged nineteen-year-old girl named Laura. She gave no return address (coward), but the letter was postmarked Bellingham, Washington. Laura wrote that she had encountered the Rape Issue at a local store called the Newstand [sic] International, and she was very displeased with what she saw.

"I am not in favor of censorship," Laura reassured me, "but..."— B-U-T. What a word, that "but."

—"...but this was not free speech, this was violence against women, children, and the developmentally disabled."

So it wasn't a magazine, it was a literal act of sexual assault.

Like many before and since her, Laura compared me to Hitler. "You don't want the blood of another Oskowitz on your hands," she warned me.

I think she meant Auschwitz.

Laura insisted that I retrieve all copies of *ANSWER Me!* #4 and basically apologize to the world in order to stave off the inevitable mountain of ripped vaginas and bloody kiddie anuses that would occur were anyone to actually read my mag. "You alone have the responsibility of preventing a child from being violently raped," she counseled.

She didn't say she *felt* I should remove the magazine from circulation and apologize. She *demanded* it. She dictated the terms of my surrender.

I found the letter mildly amusing and filed it away.

A few days later, I received an answering-machine message from the Bellingham newsstand asking me to call.

The newsstand's female manager told me that a week earlier, Laura had come in the store, insisting that they remove the Rape Issue. When they refused, Laura asked her boyfriend Marcus for advice. Marcus donned his Birkenstocks and marched a copy of the Rape Issue over to the local rape-crisis center.

Hoo-doggie. Rape-crisis workers reading the Rape Issue. That's like a Hadassah knitting circle poring over *Mein Kampf*.

The crisis center's concerned coven of cackling hens waddled over to the District Attorney's office, squealing with outrage.

A detective for the DA's office visited the Newstand and suggested they remove the issue. If not, well, he had a jail cell with their name on it.

I told the store manager that she shouldn't take a bullet on my account—if she wanted to avoid trouble, she should remove the magazine. But she was steadfast. It was the principle of the thing. She didn't appreciate being told what to sell.

She pulled *ANSWER Me!* from sale, wrapped the remaining copies in lock and chain, and made it into a hokey display with some pious quote about free speech. A stalemate developed between the DA and the newsstand. Accompanied by a newfound defense lawyer, the store's owners were called into the DA's office, where the county's chief prosecutor offered to drop charges if they agreed never to sell *ANSWER Me!* or "anything like it" again.

They refused.

The prosecutor's name was David McEachran (pronounced: muh-KECK-rin), and he had been the county DA for something like thirty years. He was a bald, humorless weasel who, like all District Attorneys, pictured himself a gunslinger for righteousness. Mr. McEachran was gonna go out on a limb and take a brave stance against the relentless pro-rape propaganda in this rape culture of ours. He was gonna send a bold message to rapists:

Rape isn't cool.

And sticking table legs up the vaginas of ten-year-old girls is just so immature.

McEachran really couldn't lose. Even if the newsstand owners were found Not Guilty of being smut-peddlers, well, that's what was wrong with ideas such as "rights." He could say he tried his best with limited resources against a high-paid "dream team" of defense lawyers, and the church groups pressuring him from the right and the women's groups nagging him from the left would be happy.

He charged the newsstand owners with Felony Promotion of Pornography, which carried a potential one-year jail sentence. Since I wasn't technically the one who sold the magazine in Bellingham, I wasn't charged.

The day after charges were filed, I awoke in cold drizzly darkness and ate soapy-tasting pancakes at the local Greasy Spoon, opening

The Oregonian to read an AP wire story about the case. The phone calls from reporters began at around 7AM and didn't stop until late into the night, totaling fifty-five messages on my caller-ID device. At one point during the early morning, I peered out my Venetian blinds to witness a TV news team piling out of their truck and walking toward my apartment. A portly reporter knocked on my door, but I didn't answer. I figured that anything I said might possibly incriminate the newsstand owners, so I decided to keep my mouth shut all day. After the reporter left, Debbie and I hopped in the car and drove around Portland, smoking weed and dodging the press. As we puffed on a steel pipe while parked on a freeway overpass, I remember looking down at the rush-hour traffic and thinking, "They're all gonna know about me tonight."

As 5PM approached, we rushed over to a morbidly obese junkie's rat-hole apartment to see what the TV news had to say. As the flabby addict and his friends ran Bic lighters under tinfoil and sucked up their bitter-almond-smelling smoky sky candy, I plugged in a beaten old B&W TV. A fuzzy picture emerged, revealing a graphic of the Rape Issue's cover hovering behind the female news anchor's head.

It was the top story on Portland's evening news.

The anchorwoman said that *ANSWER Me!* had ignited "a firestorm of controversy across the Pacific Northwest." The fat male reporter I'd espied through Venetian blinds was shown knocking on my apartment door and then walking away disgustedly. He interviewed a law expert who said the magazine was possibly obscene. He featured a sound bite from the newsstand owners' primary defense lawyer, a John Denver lookalike who said the Rape Issue bravely tackled "a very difficult subject." A dykey, tight-lipped director of a Portland rape-crisis center leafed through Issue 4 on-camera and yelped, "I'm literally sick to my stomach...Is he giving any of the profits to rape victims?"

Profits?

At report's end, the teletubby broadcaster opined that many people thought *ANSWER Me!* was "not much better than fish wrap."

It made sense that the shit would go down in Washington, home of Riot Grrrl and a state legislature that was about 40% female. Bellingham was a cozy little Nordic-Irish hamlet about ten minutes below the Canadian border, supposedly the continental United States' northernmost city. Bellingham is in the same county as Lynden, Washington, where rumor has it that social dancing was finally legalized in the early 1990s.

Word spread in Bellingham that the magazine was a how-to manual for rapists. Horrified townsfolk were convinced that a literary Golem stalked Bellingham, and it had to be killed at all costs. A town meeting was held, and one concerned father said I should be shot.

Much of the hysteria was fanned by the *Bellingham Herald*, a fifth-rate paper staffed with fourth-rate stringers in a third-rate town. The *Herald* burbled with headlines such as "Rape Magazine Sparks Furor" and "Publisher of Anti-Women Writing Shrugs off Foes." A local judge's wife wrote a letter to the *Herald* saying it was time for responsible citizens to censor themselves before the government was "forced" to do it for them. Another letter said that *ANSWER Me!* couldn't be compared to satire such as Jonathan Swift's "A Modest Proposal" because Swift was a priest—and priests know nothing about rape and molestation. One woman who claimed to have been raped asked a reporter, "What about my rights?"

Uh, what *about* them?

Laura, the girl who started it all, told a *Herald* reporter that she felt "violated" when reading *ANSWER Me!* Then, a few months after initiating the whole spectacle, the typical chickenshit female pulled out, explaining she never wanted the DA to prosecute the newsstand owners.

She wanted them to prosecute ME.

I sat in my apartment staring out the windows at the steely gray rain, wondering when I'd be run out of Portland by a torch mob of lumbering bulldykes.

It became a free-speech case. Again and again the goodniks pondered, "When does free speech go too far?"

Here's the answer: Never. It can't. That's why it's free. It's like asking, "When does a living person become too dead?" You can't abuse something that's absolute. The only ones abusing the First Amendment are those who try to find loopholes around the phrase "Congress shall make NO law abridging freedom of speech, nor of the press," who seek to rope it in with laws about obscenity, treason, and hate speech.

Yes, I realize that those dead white males who crafted the Constitution didn't have "Let's Hear it for Violence Toward Women!" in mind when they drafted the Bill of Rights. But they weren't thinking of *The S.C.U.M. Manifesto,* either. What they *were* thinking about was keeping the government from interfering in the free exchange of ideas. And there were certainly more ideas bandied about in *ANSWER Me!* #4 than in *People* or *Reader's Digest.*

Still, there were those who insisted that I should be grateful that our beneficent, buttery government had granted me the "right" of free speech. Look, it isn't their right to give, only to take. Rights can't be given, only stolen. You're born with all the rights you need. If you're able to form the words and spit them out of your mouth, then obviously nature has given you the right of free speech. Those who steal rights for a living have fostered the illusion that rights are theirs to give.

The "right" of free speech makes about as much sense as a "right" to free air. While being grateful that the government allows you to speak, make sure to also thank them for letting you breathe.

Oh, thank heaven that the government—you know, that giant cherubic force that siphons off about forty percent of our wages whether we want them to or not—is so fucking generous as to allow us to speak. Sometimes. If they approve of what we're saying.

I became politically radicalized when I realized that the same pole-smokers who were forcing me to work nearly half of every year to pay for their massive extortion racket weren't even willing to grant me the meager "rights" which they claimed justified the extortion.

To "prove" that the newsstand owners were guilty of promoting pornography, the DA had to "prove" that ANSWER Me! was legally obscene. To do so, he was burdened with the truck-stop-whorelike task of having to "satisfy" each of three "prongs":

· The magazine must be patently offensive when judged by contemporary community standards;
· It must appeal to a prurient interest in sex;
· Taken as a whole, it must be devoid of redeeming literary, political, religious, or social merit.

I wasn't even going to challenge the first prong.

ANSWER Me! #4 was offensive not only by community standards, but by those of the most jaded hipsters. It wasn't just "patently" offensive, it was painfully offensive. Astronomically offensive.

It was offensive even when judged against the standards of those who'd made careers out of being offensive, the so-called "transgressives." Somehow, Robert Mapplethorpe sticking a bullwhip up his rectum...or Karen Finley's butthole yams...or Andres Serrano's crucifix immersed in urine...were much more complex intellectual statements than anything I was trying to say. And none of those so-called "free speech" cases were even about literal censorship and criminal prosecution, they were about the government's denial of free money to fund so-called "transgressive" art. No one was trying to censor them, they were merely refusing to pay the bill for their psychodrama.

Nobody who had cried about censorship on behalf of such left-wing palefaced shit-slingers was anywhere to be found in the whole *ANSWER Me!* free-speech circus. Transgression had previously been the domain of naughty leftists, yet I took a big, stinky shit in their pool and sent them all fleeing for a lifeguard. I proved that there were limits to their ideas of transgression. I finally silenced all the lisping sissy-Marys who'd been weeping about censorship since the Reagan era's dawn.

Apparently, the "transgressives" were only interested in slaughtering a certain *kind* of sacred cow. In fact, they weren't interested in slaughtering cows at all.

Only bulls. White ones.

Leftists deftly grasp the comic potential in mocking the fears of the pathological racist and the clinical homophobe, yet they're blind to their own easily pushed buttons. And they have an airplane cockpit's worth of buttons.

So when people began blaming "right-wing Republican rednecks" for the Bellingham censorship case, I was always quick to point out that it was a leftist who started the proceedings. A dumb little girl schooled in too much college feminism and too little of everything else.

And *ANSWER Me!* had proven offensive to not only her, but everyone else—left, right, and straight down the middle. So no sense arguing about that.

The second "prong," whether or not *ANSWER Me!* appealed to a prurient interest in sex, was murkier. The Latin root of "prurient" was a word meaning "to itch," presumably one's genitalia. And so a very odd question arose like a thick cock laden with earthworm-sized veins: Was the Rape Issue intended to be a turn-on? Well, I was its creator, and I could honestly state that this wasn't my intent. I know of no one who was aroused by it, either—to the contrary, it was a real weenie-shriveler. I never thought that the issue would give anyone the desire to rape.

And yet the DA did.

So did the radical feminists.

Strange.

What did that say about *their* minds? Why did it have such power for them that they needed to see it banned? Did they feel that if they stared at it long enough, they might fall prey to its seductive allure? The censors didn't want to read anything that would place them in a rapist's mind. But why not, if they didn't feel it could affect them?

Their reaction was almost, "Get it out of my face—it's turning me ON!" It was akin to homophobic panic—"I must destroy the evil that threatens to seduce me!"

Of course, the censor always acts as if she's trying to protect someone else.

Oh, sure.

Yet I couldn't be certain that twelve normal-looking jury members wouldn't secretly get an erotic charge from the Rape Issue, so I was willing to surrender that prong, too.

Which left only the third prong on which to hang the newsstand owners' fate—whether or not ANSWER Me! #4 had any redeeming value. How exactly do you "prove" that something has redeeming value? That's like trying to prove someone's attractive. Why should some sexless prig who takes the Bible literally stand in judgment of my literary gifts? Or twelve overweight mall rats who haven't read a book in years? After all, I don't tell them what sort of sweat suits to buy.

Nevertheless, they were to stand as literary critics, and if I got a bad review, people went to jail.

Never mind that the First Amendment makes no mention of socially redeeming value. What if you object to the very notion of society and don't believe that socially redeeming value is desirable? What if you sincerely believe that concepts such as right and wrong are not only outmoded, but that they seriously cloud an understanding of the world? Shouldn't you be allowed to express such opinions?

Not the way they saw it. Or more accurately, the way they wanted to see it. The way they wished it to be.

To a censor, "good" literature is that which promises life after death, which neatly ties up all the loose ends, which assures the reader that *you're* on the right side and *they're* on the wrong side. It justifies any murders or robberies or lies or rapes—literal and figurative— which your side may have committed. It doesn't ask any difficult questions. Better yet, it depicts such questions—and such inquisitiveness— as inherently evil. In effect, "It has socially redeeming value" is a nicer way of saying "It supports the status quo." They want a literature of denial, of verbal anesthesia, of perfumed reality. And if that's what they want, there's plenty of it out there. I'm not trying to censor it.

And I've never pretended that I'm liberating any individual or redeeming society. Nor am I pretending that the truth is necessarily redemptive. The truth is at least as likely of enslaving you as it is to set you free.

So I didn't act as if ANSWER Me! #4 was good for society, except in a very narrow sense—I felt it was well-written, thoughtfully executed, and discussed serious issues intelligently. Amid a society that was snowboarding headlong into abject illiteracy, I felt that was reason enough to justify its existence. Or at least enough to acquit the newsstand owners on grounds of literary merit.

In the year it took for the case to get to trial, I compiled about thirty different written opinions from published authors, a professional librarian, an English professor, and the occasional layperson as to why the magazine was something more than a depraved smut rag.

A few weeks before trial, as wet snowflakes softly fell in Portland, I sat in my cold basement and gave a telephone deposition to McEachran. While explaining why I published the Rape Issue, it struck me that the prosecutor was entirely unconversant with the feminist authors whose ideas I was challenging and that maybe it was dawning on him that I might be a slightly more complex animal than the bloodthirsty cretin whom he thought was saying rape is cool.

Maybe. Or maybe he was truly as stupid as he seemed.

McEachran was certain that my intent in publishing the Rape Issue was to rally male youth to go out and rape women. He blithely skipped over everything in the issue that could have been construed as anti-rape: the opening disclaimer; Debbie's "He Tried to Fuck Me"; Molly Kiely's cartoon; Donny the Punk's story; and the intro to "RAPEWORLD," where I explicitly stated that not only hadn't I raped anyone, but I never even fantasized about it. As "proof" that I was egging on potential rapists, he focused on the five "RAPEWORLD" articles which addressed the reader as if he was a perpetrator. Naturally, he ignored the thirteen essays which addressed the reader as a victim.

The Rape Issue wasn't intended to be read by rapists, it was targeted at anti-rape activists. Jesus Christ, that seemed so fucking *obvious*.

To me, at least.

Sexual predators don't seek encouragement from literature. People don't beat or rape women based on what they read. Rape is essentially an act for loners—what would be the incentive for proselytizing? What would be the motivation for someone to encourage others to abuse women? What would they gain from it?

No one could answer me.

What could be worse than an opponent of the magazine who didn't understand it?

A supporter who didn't understand it.

"Dude, like, by saying rape is cool, you were just trying to show

how uncool it is."

Shut your mouth and bend over.

The pinnacle of absurdity in the whole debacle was the ironic specter of free-speech wags waxing righteous about one of the most vile publications ever hatched. Imagine the hilarious sight of people getting sanctimonious about what a great thing the Rape Issue was, with "Let's Hear it for Violence Toward Women!" in the vanguard of civil liberties.

Everyone was positive the magazine was something that it wasn't. Like jungle natives encountering television for the first time, both my supporters and detractors were poking around at something they didn't understand. Both sides, apparently, grasped what I was trying to say better than I did. Considering that the Rape Issue was an extended argument against sanctimony, it was galling to watch each side jockey to appear more sanctimonious. It became a war of dueling sanctimony. The prosecution contended that I was saying rape is a very good thing. The defense, without ever consulting me, argued that I was using shock tactics to frighten the reader into believing that rape is a very bad thing. And the defense pissed me off more, because at least I *expected* the prosecution to get it wrong. It was frustrating to have my ideas tossed around by people who didn't comprehend my ideas. The Rape Issue's meaning seemed to have slipped from my hands, and I felt powerless.

You might even say I felt violated.

I arrived for the trial with a fat cold sore on my big mouth.

Bellingham was frosted in ice and snow. Defense lawyers pre-interviewed me and thought I was…insane. The were freaked that I found the whole affair ridiculous—one was never to question the state's wisdom in filing charges. They felt that my lack of reverence for the judicial process, coupled with their discovery that I really hadn't been trying to say what *they* were trying to say I was trying to say, wouldn't play well with a jury. And they were probably right on that account. But since I was still on the docket as a potential witness, I wasn't allowed to see the trial. Instead, I served as the defense's rickshaw boy, taxiing witnesses to and from the courthouse. People stopped me outside the courtroom to tell me what a brave, wonderful statement I'd made with my magazine. I thanked them and tried not to laugh.

The courtroom was stuffed with people pretending they never mas-turbated nor pinched a loaf. Tellingly, no rape victims testified for the prosecution, only for the defense. Molly Kiely, whom defense lawyers said had an "honest face," was encouraged to talk about being anally raped and how ANSWER Me! had supposedly helped her get over it. Annalee Newitz, a Berkeley English professor who had cited ANSWER Me! in one of her classes as an example of "narrative trauma," testified as a literary expert. Reluctantly, she also spoke of having been molested and how the Rape Issue eased her pain. McEachran grilled Donny the Punk—one of the only dignified victims I've ever met—about having edited something called The Encyclopedia of Homosexuality. Apparently, McEachran was trying to infer that Donny had somehow asked for it, or at least enjoyed being raped again and again and again and again and again. McEachran attacked our rape victims because they weren't dealing with their trauma correctly. The prosecutor—who had never been raped—chided actual rape victims because they weren't handling their victimization properly, thus rendering the holy work of the DA's office and the rape-crisis center irrelevant.

The prosecutor seemed to have problems with...reality. He originally was said to have thought Donny the Punk's story was fictional, while apparently believing Peter Sotos's was real. He kept lamenting the "poor ten-year-old girl" in Quality Time, not realizing that fictional characters don't really feel pain. As a star witness, he trotted out a supposed expert on sexual predators, a man whose professional life allegedly consisted of hooking men's genitals to electrodes and then screening porno films for them.

And they had the audacity to contend that I was the pervert.

If Dave McEachran had less personality, he would've been a table lamp. His astonishing lack of courtroom flash, especially in a case that demanded drama, made me wonder how he'd ever reached such an exalted position in the county. Was it possible that every other Bellingham prosecutor was even duller than he was?

During his crashingly boring closing arguments, McEachran used an overhead projector to blast giant lurid layouts from ANSWER Me! #4 onto a huge white courtroom wall. "The author [is]...telling how to sexually abuse everybody," he stated, as if it were a fact. Yawns filled the stuporous air. The judge seemed ready to fall asleep.

The jury returned with a verdict of Not Guilty, but it wasn't an endorsement of ANSWER Me! The defendants were acquitted on a technicality—most jurors seemed to think the mag was obscene, but they weren't sure the newsstand owners knew it was obscene when they sold it.

Two days after the verdict, the newsstand owners held a victory party. The Goads were not invited. Free speech was one thing;

creeps who publish rape mags were another.

About a year later, the newsstand owners sued the county in federal court for Malicious Prosecution. They were awarded $1.3 million, the largest civil-rights judgment in Washington state history.

I didn't see a penny of it.

Of course, the "state" didn't pay a cent for the DA's quixotic boobishness. The taxpayers did. This version of "free" speech carried a price tag of more than a million dollars. It wasn't a victory for the First Amendment. It was yet another bill for ordinary citizens.

The money could have been spent prosecuting actual rapists. It could have paid for another police officer or two. It could have funded women's self-defense classes for a long, long time, It even could have paid the salaries of the idiots at the local rape-crisis center.

How much money did lawyers make in all this?

Lots.

And how many rapes did they prevent?

None.

It's almost obscene.

Still, the Rape Issue was a success in that no one ever disproved—or even attempted to disprove—its basic premises. It also showed that I was right about how hysterical, reactionary, and controlling its targets were. Their reaction to something that was ink on paper—not flesh on flesh—proved that everything I said was true. There was to be no debate. No questioning of their platform. Shut your mouth, or we'll throw you in jail.

As far as I had been able to determine, rape is more an aberration of the sex drive than it is about control.

But let's temporarily appease them and say it's all about a drive for power and control.

They seem quite familiar with such desires.

In demanding total compliance about how the gender debate was to be conducted, what was a permissible opinion and what wasn't, the censors' drive for utter control was not unlike what they were saying about rapists. Rape can be viewed as a very specific metaphor of the power equation endemic to all human and animal relationships. It is simply the ugliest, most immediate symbol of the human will to control others. The censors' ideological M.O.—insisting on total capitulation—was indistinguishable from the rapist's physical M.O. Both the leftoid radical twats and the rightie fundamentalists are sexually repressed control freaks who insist—under penalty of damnation and/or jail time—that everyone else submit to their version of reality. The leftist ideologue, like the Christian bible-thumper, is entirely evangelical—she will not be satisfied until everyone who doesn't think like she does is either converted or jailed under hate-crime legislation.

The censor tries to control the dark patches she fears within herself, the elements of her own personality she's spent a lifetime avoiding. She has a hunger to ban things, an infantile craving to close her eyes and pretend she can make the naughtiness disappear. She wants to slay the demons that haunt her dreams. She tries to create a world without any of the bad stuff. And she isn't above using force to do it. Like the Christian crusader, the leftist censor needs evil enemies who deserve to suffer.

This closeted sadism had its most transparent manifestation in the oft-stated sentiment that if I thought sexual violence was so nifty, maybe *I* should get raped. Hey, I thought rape was wrong! Do two wrongs make a right, or are you finally showing your true pervy colors? And why not rape me yourself? Why sublimate your fantasies and force someone else to do your dirty work?

The government which prosecuted the Newstand International came to power by raping and murdering everything in its path before erecting its noble courts of law. As Union soldiers plowed through the South, they raped the shit out of the slave women they were supposedly freeing. From both eastern and western fronts, the conquerors of evil Nazis raped powerless German women raw. If, as they say, rape goes hand-in-hand with power, then the government is a smidge hypocritical when it fingers the lone-dog rapist as a control freak.

Funny—I probably have less desire to control others than anyone who's ever tried to silence me. Never in my life have I dictated how anyone else should feel or think. I couldn't give an unlubed fuck if someone's opinions differ from mine. I have no interest in controlling the cavernous expanses between someone else's ears. I only have a desire not to be controlled. Silly me, expecting the same in return.

My attitude is that if I can handle it, then it's everyone else's obligation to aspire to my level of sophistication. I'm sick of having to dumb-down everything. Let the slaggards catch up to me for a change.

Being raised Catholic gave me a fascination for the taboo and why it held people in its thrall. I never understood why certain things were unmentionable. If they exist, why not talk about them? The taboo never made any sense then, and it doesn't now. Peel away the layers of inhibition and illogic, and there's nothing left. No solid reason exists for getting offended by anything.

If an idea can destroy your mind, then your mind is weak and deserved being destroyed. You can only be a sinner if you believe in sin. You can only be a transgressive if you believe in the boundaries. You can only get offended if you're offended by something within yourself. Depictions of genitalia should only be offensive if you have problems with your own. Obscenity is such an antiquated concept. The idea of uncrossable boundaries only exists to assuage someone's fears about unpalatable truths.

I've never seen, read, or experienced anything that I felt went too far. People have called for me to be murdered and raped, and it only amuses me. In the way that *they* get offended, in the sense of "that shouldn't be said" or "that's over the line," I can't get offended. I'm offense-proof.

But there are several things which *bother* me. I'm bothered by this culture's celebration of the lowest common denominator. I'm bothered by its rampaging warthog illiteracy and its suspicion of almost all forms of intelligence. I'm bothered by the incessant shrieking of loud-mouthed, self-righteous cunts. I'm bothered by the scary idea that people would pass laws to prevent themselves from getting offended, that they'd weave an insane web of civil lawsuits and demand millions in cash because their piddling feelings were hurt.

I'm bothered by dumb ideas. Like the idea that Jesus rose from the dead. Or the belief that the term "happy ending" isn't oxymoronic. Or the silly ideological construct called "justice," a thing which has never been achieved anywhere on the globe at any point in time. Or the primitive faith in nonexistent phantasms such as good and evil. Or the falsehood known as society, which proposes that people won't actually trample over one another to get off a sinking boat. I'm bothered by all of life's empty promises. Almost without exception, I'm bothered by precisely those things which give others hope. And in a small way, I'm given hope (or at least gladdened) by almost everything which causes others to despair.

A lot of times, the fact that you're alive bothers me. What if you find nearly everything about human existence bothersome? Jesus Christ, waking up in the morning sometimes bothers me. And yet I'm still able to put on my shoes and go for a walk. Imagine that. I'm still able, somehow, to prevent myself from being reduced to tears by it all. How the fuck do I manage it?

There are truckloads of things that bother me, yet I wouldn't censor any of them. I find a lot of anti-rape literature to be fairly tasteless and poorly executed, but I wouldn't ban it. I still don't wish to stop subliterate circus clowns from expressing themselves. As disgusting and stupid and irrational as most people are to me, I still don't seek their elimination.

That's because they exist, so they must be part of the plan. Nothing is unnatural. If it occurs within this universe, it is bound by natural laws and properties. If a fifty-year-old man is able to impregnate a twelve-year-old girl, even against her sacred will, then nature approves of their union, even if the law doesn't.

Rape is natural. Child molestation is natural. Serial killing is natural. Fist-fucking is natural. And so are all the variegated hysterical responses to these things.

Yes, even feminists are natural.

So is arguing with them.

And winning.

But offensiveness only exists as an emotional salve for those too weak to handle reality. Only a dirty mind believes in obscenity. Nothing's obscene. Everything's fair game. As St. Paul said, "To the pure, all things are pure."

Or as the Negroes say, "It's all good."

The White House Shooter

THIS IS A STORY about a little man who tried to kill the Big Monster.

Although no one has ever seen it up close, everyone knows that the Big Monster exists. The Big Monster is so massive, it's impossible to see it all in one eyeful.

The Big Monster is a bloated blob of insatiable power. It fattens itself on the little man's sweat and blood. It sucks up almost half of everything the little man produces, and if the little man behaves himself, it might let him have the rest.

The Big Monster tells the little man what he can and cannot do. It claims to rule through the little man's consent, but that's a lie. If given the choice, most little men wouldn't consent to be ruled at all. The Big Monster rules through a silent, ever-present threat of terror. And yet it's cynical enough to label its opponents "terrorists."

Most little men whose intelligence is above that of a toilet plunger know that the Big Monster lies to them, yet they're afraid to say anything. They know that the Big Monster kills its critics, and they don't want to be next.

The Big Monster is hard to kill. It has millions of eyes and ears, but no face. Where do you aim?

Every so often, a little man gets brave...or foolish...enough to try and slay the Big Monster, but the result is always the same.

The Big Monster always wins.

Little men come and go, but the Big Monster never dies. Every attempt to kill it only makes it stronger. It merely needs to make an example of one or two little men, and the swarm of other little men fall in line and quietly obey. They accept its fearsome power with a submissive shrug. Better to not disturb it. Better to blend in with the other little men.

Our nation was founded by a group of little men who sought to dispose of Big Monsters once and for all. And somehow they gave birth to the biggest Big Monster the world has ever known.

Washington, D.C., is a city of huge white powerful buildings surrounded by little black powerless people.

Outside the Beltway, the former slaves live in roach-bitten squalor, drowning amid the guns and cocaine which the Big Monster will never admit that it supplies. Clouds of crack smoke rise above condemned tenements. Old men with fingerless gloves huddle around barrel fires. Scabby-legged, orange-Afroed hookers wade among broken Thunderbird bottles. Uzi-toting gangstas chuckle while pissing on their unconscious mugging victims.

The Beltway is the puffy white filling inside a rancid, toxic donut. Blinding power is housed within its bleached-white buildings. These buildings are as white as cocaine. As white as the clouds that God hides behind.

At 1600 Pennsylvania Avenue sits the White House, a giant ice-cream cake of stately colonnades, porticos, and Ionic columns. Within it lives the president, a temporal incarnation of the eternal Big Monster.

September 29, 1994, was a gorgeous autumn day at the tail end of the century which saw the rise of the Super State. Polyester-swaddled tourists milled outside the White House gates, marveling at the giant slab of power which ruled their world. Among the crowd of little people was a bearded Hispanic man wearing eyeglasses and a brown trench coat. One moment he seemed like any other tourist. The next, he whipped out an SKS assault rifle from beneath his coat and sprinted sideways along the White House gates, shooting twenty-nine bullets at our president's home. Rat-a-tat-tat. Peeling caps at Uncle Sam. Twenty-nine leaden sperm in orgasmic fury.

A tourist captured the attack on videotape. Panicked civilians are shown fanning out around the camera, running for cover. One hears screams and the popping firecracker sound of automatic gunfire. As the shooter pauses to reload, a pair of porky off-duty agents tackles him to the sidewalk.

The shooter probably felt powerful while he was pulling that trigger. He probably felt freer than most Little Men ever get to feel. For a few seconds, I'll bet he felt like the Big Monster.

His bullets harmed no one. At worst, the White House suffered a few minor nicks. This was a bungled act of domestic terrorism. But federal PR wizards cited his impotent onslaught as evidence for why their new gun-and-terrorism laws were needed.

The conspiratorially inclined said that the assault bore the appearance of having been staged. They noted that the shooter was a disgruntled ex-Army soldier who'd been held in a military prison where there were rumors of top-secret mind-control experiments upon inmates.

At the time, I didn't care. I didn't worry about the government. I figured that if I paid my taxes, they'd leave me alone.

Six months later. March, 1995.

A LOUD knock on my door.

When I answer it, a tall, well-dressed man with neatly cropped peppery hair hands me a subpoena to appear in a District of Columbia court in the case of *United States of America v. Francisco Martin Duran.*

What is this all about?

He says he doesn't know, hands me a business card with a number to call, and is gone.

Within hours, my tenuous link to Duran's shooting hits the AP wire. In a scribbled note found in his van parked near the White House, Duran had allegedly quoted a sentence fragment from *ANSWER Me! #2:*

Can you imagine a higher moral calling than to destroy someone's dreams with one bullet...?

I initially fear that I'm being summoned by prosecution lawyers trying to implicate me as a conspirator in Duran's attack. But a call to the little number on the business card reveals that it's Duran's defense lawyers who need me to testify that this was an actual magazine he was quoting rather than a figment of his imagination. They make flight arrangements for me to zoom into D.C. and attend the trial.

I'm soon being assailed by Portland TV and print-media news leeches for my comments about the Duran case, and I give them all the silent treatment. What do I tell them?

Gee willikers, it was really uncool for him to shoot at the White House like that?

Too bad he didn't kill anybody?

I didn't have anything to do with the shooting—REALLY?

A local TV news report describes *ANSWER Me!* as a "vile" piece of "hate literature" which formed "the Oregon connection" to the White House shooting. It comes close to flat-out calling me an accomplice to the crime. A news jock explains that Duran's lawyers are pushing for an insanity defense, and "as proof" of his dementia, they will demonstrate that he was an *ANSWER Me!* reader.

My gut feeling—and I'll concede that it may be wrong—is that I'm being framed. Something seems artificial about this new spate of trouble. I feel like a stooge. A marionette. A Manchurian Candidate. I feel chosen for a role I don't want to play.

Paranoid?

There are reasons why my sudden "connection" to political terrorism smells fishy to me.

One is that I'd never had any contact with Duran. I scan my mailing list, which was compiled from every piece of mail I'd ever received through ANSWER Me!, and his name isn't on it.

Another reason is that ANSWER Me! had always been aggressively apolitical. My stance was purposely insular, solipsistic, and asocial. I had always written about violence as a personal act, not a political one. I derided antigovernment types as dull, humorless, and sexually sublimated. In the same issue from which Duran had quoted me, I wrote:

I'm not anti-authority; I'm anti-YOU. I don't want you to destroy the government; I want the government to crush YOU.

ANSWER Me! had disdain for *any* socially motivated action. It refused to align itself with mass movements or utopian pipe dreams. It purposely stayed away from the crowd and its silly politics.

But being subpoenaed by two different governmental entities for two different trials within two months of each other changes all that. Against its creator's will, ANSWER Me! becomes a political document. The Bellingham DA and the Federal Public Defender's office dragged it into the political arena. The Duran scandal comes so close on the heels of the Bellingham obscenity trial, my freckled loins chafe. My writing—no criminal activity, only my *writing*—has linked me to major criminal cases on both coasts.

Wowie zowie, what a mountain of shit I've magnetized this time, enough to clog every Port-a-Potty in America. This is the biggest trouble in which I've ever found myself, far more than most people will ever see.

One would suspect that presidential assassination attempts rank rather high on the FBI's list of red-flagged activities. Sure, they fret about drug smugglers and tax evaders and serial killers, but I'd imagine that political terrorists…and the thinkers who inspire them…are at the top of their Shit List. Maybe the thinkers more so than the shooters. When you're quoted by someone who shoots at the White House, the government takes an interest in you.

I feel contaminated by this. Cursed. Bad, bad luck. Bad things will happen. I'm wading into some deep, heavy, deadly shit.

The Big Monster knows I exist.

It no longer sees me as just another little man.

It sees me as a threat.

The Big Monster reaches down and daubs an invisible "X" on my forehead. The black hand of the federal Mafia touches my shoulder. A high-ranking spy sticks pins in a Jim Goad voodoo doll. I receive the Mark of the Beast. A federal *fatwa* is placed on my life.

When someone tells me that the person who videotaped Duran's rampage was found dead of food poisoning in Brazil three weeks after filming the attack, I feel sucked into some sick spy thriller of which I want no part. Area 51. Men in Black. MK-ULTRA. Masonic witchcraft. Interrogation dungeons. Espionage. Intrigue. Deceit. Manipulation. Conspiracy. Humiliation. Torture.

Nanotechnological needle-injected biochips. Sonic mind control. Two drops of FBI chemicals in my shoe, and I'm dead of heart failure six months later. Or they'll take the slow, sadistic route and crush my mind with a high-tech psy-ops program to where I'm drooling, cooing like a baby, and smearing my poo-poo on the walls of the tiny steel crib the nice people have prepared for me.

Men in astronaut suits spray my apartment with carcinogens when I'm not home. They plant tracking devices on my clothes. They tap my phone and place video cameras in my bedroom. They comb through my trash. Take pictures of me as I enter my car. Tail my car. Drive me off the road. I wind up as a smudge of protein on highway asphalt, and the newspapers say it was an accident.

Can't relax for a second. Feverish. Nauseous. Rolling Saharan heat waves of paranoia. I feel like a grizzled old frankfurter impaled on a spinning convenience-store rotisserie, all the juices sweated out of me.

For days I've been running and sweating and freaking. When a TV news team knocks on my front door, I fall belly-down on the carpet and keep quiet as if they're hired killers. If I so much as smile, I fear my eyeballs will pop out.

On the afternoon before I'm scheduled to fly to D.C., I drive with Debbie to Sauvie Island, a paradisiacal squib of wilderness just north of Portland. Blueberry bushes and pumpkin fields and snow-topped mountains which seem as formidable as the federal government. And out there, where my tension has swelled to where I think I might die, the placental sac bursts.

I begin laughing.

I tell Debbie,

If some stupid little magazine I've done is being implicated in a presidential assassination attempt, then life is absurd, nothing makes sense, and there's no point in viewing this situation as anything but a big, colorful cartoon.

And with that epiphany I'm cured, at least for the time being. I decide to make a big joke of it all. With a horror of this magnitude, comedy is the only way to process it emotionally. It's like the temptation one gets to laugh at a funeral.

The government has more guns than me, but not as many jokes. I'm not nearly as powerful as them, but I AM funnier.

I plan on wearing a MEAN PEOPLE SUCK T-shirt on the stand. I'll answer the lawyers' questions in song. Or mime. Or with a game of charades. I'll lift my derby, and a dove will fly off my head. I'll turn it all into an updated version of the Three Stooges' *Disorder in the Court.* If I bomb, it'll be in the comedic sense, not the terroristic one.

How're ya all doin'? I just flew in from Portland, and boy, are my arms tired! So anyway, two Jews, a nigger, and an armed terrorist walk into a bar....

But it's not to be. At the last minute, Duran's lawyers decide I ain't needed as a witness, and I never fly to Washington.

Duran's insanity defense didn't work, even with the story of how he'd stalked the White House for several days, waiting for an "evil mist" to appear above it. In the wrestling match that pitted the United States of America versus Francisco Martin Duran, Big Monster v. little man, Duran received a life sentence and must serve at least forty-five years before he's eligible for parole. He'll likely spend the rest of his life squashed under the thumb of the government he hates. Nearly half a century getting buttfucked by Yankee Doodle.

Almost a year after he was sentenced, I receive a letter from Duran at his Super-Max federal prison in Colorado. The envelope is unsealed, almost as if the feds want me to know they're reading it. In the letter, Duran—or whichever government agent is posing as him—apologizes for getting such "nice people" as Debbie and I into trouble. He requests Church of Satan founder Anton LaVey's address. Beneath his signature he types:

Francisco Martin Duran
"The White House Shooter"

I never write him back, figuring that would be all the "evidence" the government needs to prove that I, too, am a terrorist.

Looks like Big Brother's trying to turn my words into crimes.

Two forms of speech are forbidden in this land of spacious skies and amber waves of grain:

· Obscenity
· Advocating the U.S. government's immediate armed overthrow.

My writing is suddenly associated with both.

Apparently I'm becoming a bit more influential than just a lowly zinester poopstain. I'm fully legit on the danger tip. Not many writers can list obscenity trials and White House shootings on their resume.

Still, jealous zine gerbils continue to carp that I'm an ideological reactionary who in no way threatens the social order.

Gargle my creamy cum, scrawny loser fags.

I don't have body piercings, I have an FBI file.

I don't urge you to question authority, I inspire people to shoot bullets at it.

I foment *literal* rage against the machine, not shopping-mall commie T-shirt slogans.

The oh-so-conventional idea of cultural diversity fails to embrace the violent political terrorist. He is seen as outside the umbrella of acceptable alternative lifestyles.

But to me, Francisco Martin Duran is one swingin' cat, Daddy-O. It took *huevos grandes* to do what he did. And *cerebro estupido*, too. Duran's crime had been unplanned, poorly executed, and ineffective. Twenty-nine bullets aimed at a four-story building.

What a dork.

Couldn't he have at least waited until Clinton came out in his robe and slippers to scoop up the morning paper?

Instead of joining the A-list of successful presidential assassins such as John Wilkes Booth or Lee Harvey Oswald, Duran entered the ignominious ranks of fuckups such as John Hinckley and Squeaky Fromme.

Still, I find something admirable in his quixotic idiocy. Judging by the quote he lifted from me, he felt a "moral calling" to shoot at the White House. Within the confines of his possibly tampered-with brain, he seemed to believe he was doing the right thing.

He was a hopeless romantic, emphasis on the "hopeless." He was a mosquito planting his proboscis into an elephant's hide. A Chihuahua yipping at Godzilla. A gnat flying into King Kong's mouth. A circus midget aiming his pea-shooter at the Cyclops.

And he taught me to hate a government which I'd previously ignored. The fact that they were fucking with me when I had never fucked with them caused me to hate the very idea of being governed.

And maybe that's what they wanted all along.

Don't tread on me, motherfuckers. I'm willing to die over this shit, but I don't think you are. Is anybody with me? Where are the Patrick Henrys who want liberty or death? Where are the intrepid souls who, like James Brown sang, would rather die on their feet than live on their knees?

Duran was one of them. He didn't care about being a doomed kamikaze. It was the principle of the thing. He fired a few pellets at a government which has bombed vast patches of this planet into charcoal. The White House is thought to be inviolable. Immune. Accountable to no one. Duran proposed the heretical idea that it isn't.

After JFK's brains were splattered all over that Dallas limo, Malcolm X said that maybe the chickens had come home to roost. Francisco Martin Duran was one jalapeño-flavored *pollo loco* squawking outside the White House gates.

But one chicken can't do much. The government can deal with one Duran, but not a hundred thousand.

The White House won't stand forever. It can't. One day it will fall, and probably not peacefully. The Big Monster will die, and all the little men will be free.

For a moment.

And then another Big Monster will take control.

9

The Hundred and First Spectacular Suicide

If you want to do something truly radical, kill yourself. We'll have one less reader, but the world will be a better place.

—from *ANSWER Me! #2*

HER DOUR BRITISH voice was as cold as a mentholated cough drop. She left me a distant, tinny-sounding voicemail message saying she needed to verify my address.

Sounding more forlorn, she logged a similar message the next day, adding with a curt finality, "and don't bother calling after tomorrow."

I sit shivering in my dank, mossy, tomblike basement, wondering why I can't call after tomorrow.

I dial her hotel in northern California. The desk clerk connects me to that meek Anglican voice.

The unidentified British girl timidly asks whether my address is the same as listed in *ANSWER Me! #4.*

Yes.

Pause...

Uh, I'm writing a book about white trash and publishing a book by Peter Sotos. You can order them from that address.

Pause...

Trying to fill the silence, I ask,

Is that all?

"Yes."

I don't ask why she wants my address.

Instead, I say,

OK—goodbye.

And she says goodbye, too.

A week later I'm in the same clammy concrete basement pecking away at my computer keyboard when the phone rings. It's a reporter from the local newsweekly, seeking my comments about the three British kids who killed themselves.

What?

"A couple days ago some British kids shot themselves, and Scotland

jim goad

Yard said one of them had made numerous phone calls to your voice-mail number."

I have no idea what this is all about.

He says he'll call back with more information.

The dog starts barking. I run upstairs to find two reporters for *The Oregonian* at my front door. They, too, want to hear what I have to say about the three British kids who committed suicide.

Come on in. Don't mind the dog. I just got a call from Willamette Week about this. What the hell is going on?

"On February 21st," says a tall, graying newsman, "a young British man and woman shot themselves at a gun range in Mesa, Arizona. The next day their friend, a girl who'd been with them in the States for six weeks, drove up a mountain road in northern California and shot herself in the head. Investigators found that she'd called your voicemail number several times and that last week you phoned her at a hotel down near Redding."

British girl...northern California...I called her hotel...oh, FUCK.

A sinking feeling in my stomach like a rapidly falling elevator.

God, yeah, I talked to some girl with a British accent for about a minute last week. She had called asking about my mailing address. I probably still have her messages on tape.

I fetch my microcassette player, and together we listen to the disembodied voice of a girl who's no longer alive.

Over the next few weeks, details of the suicides slowly begin leaking in through police detectives and news reporters.

The fresh young corpses were those of Stephen Bateman, Ruth Fleming, and Jane Greenhow, the girl who called me. Bateman and Fleming were twenty-two; Greenhow was twenty-three.

The trio had lived together in the dentally challenged lily pad called England. They all habitually wore black military-style gear on their pale white skin. They all shared an ideological fondness for the Nazi forces which nearly blitzkrieged their homeland into nothingness. All three were exceedingly brainy.

Jane, who had a pretty canary face and short, carrot-colored hair, played the cello. Ruth, a bit more plumply puggish and with her bangs dyed Aryan blonde, played the violin. Both girls had recently graduated from Leicester University with first-class degrees in physics and astrophysics.

Stephen, who Teutonicized his name into Stefan, was a dropout dreamer who toiled in a potato-chip factory. After his suicide, his mother described him thusly:

Stephen was a very intelligent, kind boy who worried a lot. He was never in trouble growing up, but in his late teens he seemed unable to find an anchor in his life.

His anchor...or millstone...became a Hitlerian nihilism which translated into fascist fashion such as SS uniforms and an affected Kraut accent. He met Jane Greenhow at a nightclub and was soon goosestepping inside her vagina. Stefan, Jane, and Ruth moved into a house in Andover, where their cadaverous demeanor had neighbors calling them "The Addams Family." Stefan's affections gradually shifted from Jane to Ruth, and he started sieg-heiling between her legs instead.

In January, 1996, the three abruptly sold all their belongings and purchased plane tickets to America. Bateman informed a neighbor that he and the girls planned to join a Nazi cabal in Detroit.

The night before leaving, Bateman and Fleming stayed at a Salvation Army hotel in London. They left behind several items which hotel workers turned over to investigators. A notebook entry outlined their last-minute chores:

Check the guns, get rid of the car, clean the house, dye hair.

Bateman had jotted the phrase KILL THEM ALL onto a check stub. A macabre snapshot featured Fleming, garbed entirely in black and with her face caked in white makeup, holding a sign that said

SUICIDE

The word was apparently written in dripping blood.

On January 6th, the three touched down in Detroit. They flew on to Vegas the next day and rented two cars, with Greenhow driving solo. Over the next few weeks, the three wormed their way through the Plains states and the desert Southwest, a trio of pasty Nazi Goths aimlessly stormtrooping through cowboy country.

There were unsubstantiated rumors that they plotted to assassinate wrinkled Republican presidential candidate Bob Dole. It was also thought that they attempted to hook up with aging Arizona white supremacist Jack Maxwell Oliphant, only to find that he had croaked shortly before their arrival.

Jane apparently split off from her friends sometime in mid-February. Bateman and Fleming settled in the dusty, prickly-pear-laden town of Casa Grande, Arizona, taking residence at the Boots and Saddle

Motel and making regular pilgrimages to a local gun range. In their motel room, detectives later found a doctor's prescription form on which Fleming had entered her "name":

OBERGRUPPENFUHER STAATSPOLITZEI
(HEAD SQUAD LEADER—STATE POLICE)

And her "address":

HELL AGONY ETERNAL

On February 21st, Stefan and Ruth entered their beloved gun range, rented a pair of revolvers, squeezed a few shots at the paper targets, stepped back, placed the barrels in their mouths, counted down, and blasted their bright white melons into Valhalla.

Meanwhile, Jane Greenhow ate her meals alone, staring despondently out her motel's dining-room window overlooking California's icily shimmering Lake Shasta. Hotel workers described her as "sad...lonely and real quiet...an odd nut."

On the day of her partners' suicides, she phoned the Las Vegas car-rental agency to tell them she'd be late returning her vehicle. A clerk informed her that Ruth and Stefan had killed themselves. "She freaked out," said a rental agent. "She started crying."

Jane hastily checked out of her hotel. She placed a frantic last-ditch call to her parents in England, but Mum and Dad weren't home.

Greenhow drove a short stretch of Interstate 5 north toward Oregon. She then exited the freeway and headed up a remote mountain road which ended at a spot called Conflict Point.

Once there, she connected a garden hose to her car's tailpipe and sat with the motor running, hoping to die in her own little gas chamber. Then, seemingly growing impatient, she grabbed her black-market Glock pistol, stuck it in her mouth, and sent a 10mm meteor crashing through the brilliant galaxy inside her skull.

What happens in one's head as the bullet's going through your brain? Was there a blip of regret as she pulled the trigger?

Did she hear the gun fire? Did it sound like the roar of a crowd cheering *der Führer?* Did her life flash before her eyes? Did she see Nordic lightning?

Or was her birthday candle instantly blown out?

The human body is such a delicate soap bubble. POP! She's gone.

A forestry official found the body. Blood had gushed from the ears and nose. Black combat clothing and boots. Hair dyed black, cut short, and shaved over the ears. Thick black feline eyeliner. Eyes wide open.

Jane's hand still clutched the gun. A note found near her body was addressed to "My Glock":

I am so sorry I have to leave you now, the only one I am reluctant to leave behind....I am so sorry we never got to consummate our relationship. I know we could have had such fun together. Alas, always too many regrets....[We were] brought together through strength, honesty, purity, always so cold and removed, both designed to be able to act almost instinctively when fully operational. Perhaps my firing pin was under tension for too long. I guess you just functioned more reliably—I jammed.

A phony check for six million British pounds was found at the scene, "one pound per Jew" killed in the Holocaust. There was a photo of Greenhow and Bateman at a German war memorial. Jane's hand-written journal decried all things British, and British men in particular. Greenhow referred to herself as "Ms. Hitler" and likened her demise to that of the Third Reich:

As in WWII, the better side lost. And the better side had a promise, a goal, a clear idea of what it wanted and how to get it. The other side, hopelessly inept....

Jane had also written a letter to Debbie and I, mailing it four days after speaking with me and two days before capping herself. The letter apparently passed through investigators' hands, because although it was dropped in the mail only four hundred miles away from Portland, it doesn't reach my P.O. box—sealed with duct tape, no less—until nearly two weeks after Jane sent it.

Jim and Debbie:
    You can't reply—I'm dead. This is the money I had left. I knew that if you had it, you would use it to contribute to *your* good, and not the "greater good," the "common good." If you don't want it, don't take it. To try and explain all in a letter is futile. I acted. If I thought explaining to anyone else would do any good, I'd be alive, and stupid."
                                                                                        —Jane

Enclosed with the letter are three money orders, each for $700. Two of them were made payable to me, one to Debbie.

The $2,100 seems like blood money, almost as if I'm being paid for Jane's suicide. If I spend a penny of it, I'll appear to be endorsing her death. Jane has thrown a stick of dynamite in my lap, and I need to get rid of it quickly.

I mail the money back to Jane's parents in England.

Because of my one-minute phone conversation with a depressed stranger, most news-media buzzards are certain I'm a *Nationalsozialist* mastermind who orchestrated three deaths. I'm pegged as the sinister puppeteer who'd used the power of literary autosuggestion to nudge these Children of the Queen into snuffing themselves.

The Oregonian headline is "Portland Publisher Goad Tied to Suicide." *Willamette Week* coyly queries, "Did a Portland Publication Goad Three Brits to Pull the Trigger?"

The Limey press, in its incomparably stuffy-yet-tawdry way, seizes upon the story's implications of youthful Britons gone wrong in Wild Redneck America. London's *Daily Mirror* runs a photo of me looking slimy and demented over the caption "WARPED: Publisher Jim Goad and His Evil Magazine." It describes *ANSWER Me!* as a "sick death-and-rape magazine....[that] glorifies mutilation, rape, and suicide and publishes horrendous pictures of death and disfigurement."

As with the White House Shooter, I find myself being blamed for something about which I feel zero culpability. Just as I'd been "connected" to Duran's shooting, I'm "tied" to these suicides, and there seems no way to cut the ropes loose.

I will eventually be hounded by British TV crews, movie producers, and book authors for my comments about the suicides. I refuse every interview. My reaction isn't, "Great—more publicity! More power!" Instead, I sit in my cold basement and cry for the sad-but-brilliant girl who spent her last days alone.

And I find myself angry with Jane that she never told me what was wrong. If I had known she was suicidal, I would have tried to persuade her against it.

Could I have stopped her?

If I said, "Don't do it," and she asked, "Why?," what would I have answered? What reason do I give her for staying alive that doesn't sound silly?

Do I tell her that life is worth living? I'm not sure it is.

That it gets better? It doesn't.

That there's hope? There isn't.

What would I have told her?

Only that I've been there.

I've stared at pill bottles. I've crammed a shotgun shell into the chamber and thought about sticking the barrel in my mouth. I've peered over a bridge's railing down at the dirty river far below. I've contemplated tying plastic bags snugly around my neck. I've pondered rolling up the car window and slinking off to sleep while the engine runs.

I know how sad one can get looking at happy people.

I've gazed around me and wondered what I possibly could have done to deserve being placed here.

I've cried my eyes bloodshot and didn't feel any better for it.

I've felt as if I've been slowly bleeding inside my whole life.

I've felt as if the world was happily engorged on my misery like six billion swollen ticks.

I've felt like shoving my fist all the way down my throat and yanking out the pain.

I've felt like a seagull walloped by an oil slick, flapping about helplessly on frothy black sand.

I know emptiness. And heartache. And wanting to die, die, die.

There is no reason to live. There is no reason to die. Jane, all I would have told you is that maybe I know what you felt like.

You were only an eight-hour drive away from Portland. I would have asked you to come up, have some coffee, and talk with me and Debbie. You can sleep on the couch. Tell us something you like to do, and maybe we'll all go out and do it together...

The three bullets which killed Jane, Ruth, and Stefan would have been so much better spent elsewhere. There are so many brains out there whose rudimentary functioning wouldn't be significantly impaired by a bullet:

Men with auburn halos of feces rimming their gnarled anuses, chicken grease dribbling down their chins while they reach into their grimy boxer shorts and paw at their saggy, misshapen, gray-haired, hang-dog bloodhound balls;

Their squalidly gelatinous twat wives squatting on bean-bag chairs, munching Fritos and picking at bleeding mosquito bites while watching "reality" TV shows.

Those are the non-suicidal. The should-be-suicidal. The never-will-be-suicidal.

I'd imagine that the suicide rate among the mentally retarded is rather low. But the top percentile shouldn't be killing itself.

Why did Jane do it? With most suicides, the motive is clear, especially when a note is found. But Jane's note raised more questions than it answered.

Some speculated that this was merely a soured love triangle, yet that would only explain Jane's suicide, not Ruth and Stefan's.

Others theorized that the trio's possible disillusionment with American Nazi groups fueled their despair. Perhaps a sobering eyeful of Yankeeland's rusted-trailer version of fascism led them to conclude that their war was lost.

There were intimations that the three were adherents of chaos theory and believed that their suicides would set off a chain of important sociopolitical events.

Or maybe they were just tired.

Or maybe their brains grew too big for their heads.

Or maybe they gazed deep enough into the universe to realize there's nothing out there.

Or maybe they wanted to impress me.

If Jim Goad told you to jump off a bridge, would you do it? And if you did, whose fault would it be?

Jane's letter to me contained this crucial sentence:

I acted.

I *wrote* about suicide; she *acted*. So if she was the actress, was I the playwright? Did she turn my words into flesh?

How clearly defined is the line between word and deed? What separates the voyeur from the participant? When do you stop thinking and start doing?

How far can you stray into the shadows before you can't find your way back?

How long does a Christian preacher rail against faggots before he wants to suck one off?

How much can radical feminists write about rape before a few fantasies seep into their minds?

How extensively can you "research" suicide before you want to kill yourself?

Previously, ANSWER Me! had only flirted with death. Now it was married to it. What sort of Pandora's Box had my writing unlocked? Had I willed something into being?

Jane Greenhow had called me to confirm an address listed in ANSWER Me! #4, but it's almost inconceivable that she hadn't seen the third issue, which focused on suicide. Issue #3's centerpiece was a sixty-page compendium titled "Killing ME Softly, Roughly, and Just About Every Other Fucking Way Imaginable: 100 Spectacular Suicides." As a graphic device for that article, I had magnified the word SUICIDE from old newspaper headlines and scattered it throughout the layout.

Ruth Fleming, perhaps imitatively, posed for a photograph holding a card with the word SUICIDE scrawled on it.

Jane Greenhow's note to her Glock was campily fetishistic like my homage in ANSWER Me! #3 to a shotgun I called The Reverend. Fleming and Bateman frequented a public gun range—a form of recreation which doesn't exist in England—just as Debbie and I did for an article in Issue #3.

Drawings of Hitler adorned the front and back covers of the Suicide Issue. Ol' Dolfy was also featured as one of my 100 Spectacular Suicides; like Jane and friends, he allegedly exterminated himself with a bullet to the head. An unhealthy affinity for Hitleria also played a role in the deaths of Dan Burros and Gregg Sanders, two more of our spectacular suicides.

Perhaps the most eerily relevant suicide featured in Issue #3 was that of Ian Curtis, the Joy Division singer who was said to have hung himself wearing a Nazi brownshirt.

Regarding Curtis's fans, I had written:

Regrettably, most of them have failed to pursue their emulation to its logical extreme and hang themselves.

Like Curtis, Jane Greenhow was thought to be the loser in a love triangle. And Joy Division cassettes were found in the vehicle where Jane shot herself.

The British Suicide Kids weren't the only carcasses somewhat murkily linked to ANSWER Me! #3.

Kurt Cobain, the scruffy, moppety, dirty-dishwater-haired helmsman of grunge trio Nirvana, was similar to Ian Curtis in his bellyaching lyrical hopelessness. During Nirvana's final concert in Seattle, artist Jim Blanchard schmoozed his way backstage by giving the concert promoter some free comic books and ANSWER Me! #3, for which he had drawn the cover art. At one point in the evening, Blanchard spotted Cobain sitting on a couch and reading ANSWER Me! #3.

The centerfold to that issue was a photo of a man sitting on a couch with a shotgun between his legs, his head blasted to bloody gristle.

A few months later, Kurt Cobain blew off his clinically depressed head with a shotgun.

Was he influenced by ANSWER Me!? Or did it merely resonate with a wish already buried deep within his smack-addled heart?

Shortly after the British Suicide Kids extinguished themselves, I receive a letter from a woman in California:

Please remove my name from your mailing list. Last summer my son hung himself. Your magazine was found in his bedroom. What you're doing is very sad.

I never answer the woman. I don't know what to say.

In 1993, Debbie placed a prank call to Dr. Jack Kevorkian, famous for helping terminal patients end their lives. She lied and told him she had ovarian cancer, asking for his aid in killing herself. She taped the call and printed the conversation's transcripts in the Suicide Issue.

Four years later, Debbie was diagnosed with ovarian cancer.

Did she wish it on herself? I'll never know.

And I'll never know why Jane Greenhow sent the last of her money to me.

Did she think I'd be pleased by what she did?

Did she choose me as her eulogist, hoping I'd write about her as if she were a morbid sort of pop hero?

Did she think I'd merely play up the sensational elements of her death and turn her into The Hundred and First Spectacular Suicide?

During those pauses in our phone call, was she dying to confide how lonely and sad she was?

Why wouldn't she tell me what was wrong?

I like having answers, but I don't have any answers for this.

So awash in cold sunlight one late-fall afternoon, I sit out on the bleachers staring at the unfeeling sunset and waiting for a hint of Jane's voice.

All I hear is the bitter wind.

≯10≮

My Year With Anne

DEAD. After eleven years with Debbie, we both know it's over. The marriage is dead. I've wrestled with love and lost. Love had been my religion, but I discovered there was no God. For months I've been telling her I'm leaving. I'm just not sure when. I have nowhere to go, but I have to go anyway.

I feel hopeless. Ready to die.

And along comes Anne.

I close my eyes and see an image of Anne in a long white night-gown, floating toward me.

Infecting my life. Sweet Dracula girl. Fifteen years younger than me and a thousand times more fucked-up.

I liked Linda Blair in *The Exorcist.*

I liked Patty McCormack in *The Bad Seed.*

And I like Anne from Oregon City.

Anne has a malevolent, reptilian grin as if she knows secrets about you. She speaks in a Valley Girl accent, her speech littered with "ums," "likes," and "awesomes." She has straight black hair with Cleopatra bangs. A round baby face with thick lips and an upturned, porcine snout. Bugged-out psycho eyes. An emaciated, boyish body with li'l cupcake tits and milky skin. A tattoo of three daisies near her bush. Feature-for-feature she's no great shakes, but she carries herself well. She oozes pheromones like tree sap. She smells like raisins and wine.

Anne says she's "100% sinner." She hands out business cards describing herself as a "Psychotic Neo-Nazi Bitch With a Whip." She claims to be "more of a fucking misanthropist than any of you." She says that she molests children. She says she likes to torture animals. She brags that as a babysitter, she enjoyed dropping infants on their heads, then savoring that stunned, silent moment before they'd start screaming. She's a troublemaker and shit-stirrer with the loudest, foulest mouth I've ever heard on anyone. A stripper. Welfare scammer. Shoplifter. Homewrecker.

So far, so good.

Anne is a diagnosed manic-depressive who'd been hospitalized four times as a teen for suicide attempts. She has tidy little scars on one wrist to prove it. At age fourteen she suffered a breakdown and literally didn't leave her bedroom for three months, pissing and shitting in buckets her mom left near the bed. A male psychiatrist who examined Anne playfully poked at her belly and said she was too young to be so depressed, that she should be out dating boys and having fun. After Anne left the examination room, the shrink turned to Anne's mom and said there was no hope for her. She'd only get worse.

Anne says that the only way she can rebel against her longsuffering hippie parents is by being a homeless, hatemongering, drug-addicted asshole cunt. She tells me that throughout her teens she terrorized the household, threatening to harm or kill her family members. She accused her mom of being a dyke and said she'd burn in hell. She called her younger brother stupid and taunted him about his prominent harelip. She says her family wishes she'd die or at least go away.

She didn't lose her virginity until age eighteen. Then she made up for lost time. Thirty-five guys over the next three years. Of all these liaisons, only two lasted more than a week. Both of them were married men. Both guys got divorced while seeing Anne. The second married man was a milksop who allowed her to dominate him. But all the other boys had kicked her to the curb.

Everyone was always telling her to leave.

I'm Boy #36.

Married Man #3.

In the summer of '96 she sends me her zine *Cryptic Crap*. Its cover collage features cartoon knuckleheads Beavis and Butt-head playing air guitar in front of a swastika and the phrase "Human Suffering Rulez!" The centerfold shows several pictures of a topless, rapturous Anne mincing around captions such as "I wuv myself sooooo much!" She's always smiling in her pictures.

And Debbie never smiles.

I send her a copy of my latest flyer with a note saying I think her zine is funny. I say she can pick a free item from the flyer. She selects the *HATESVILLE!* CD, which spotlights my spoken-word rendition of "Let's Hear it for Violence Toward Women!" Anne later tells me she'd play that track at maximum volume and jerk off to it.

A few months later, she sends me another zine called *ZAP!* It features the obligatory boobie shots, but its tone is much harsher than *Cryptic Crap*. I zero in on an article called "Sex Is...," which shows

Anne naked in the fetal position surrounded by little fortune-cookie sentences. One of them says "[Sex is] something I do to abuse myself." Another calls her a "disposable cunt." Another says something to the effect of, "Please, please, don't think I'm a piece of shit while you're fucking me—or at least pretend you don't." Love to her was pain, torture, psychosis, and humiliation. I wonder what the hell had gone wrong. I feel protective of her. I feel bad that she missed the prom and had never gone on a date that didn't involve porno peep booths and crystal meth. I think to myself that I'd never treat her that way if given the chance.

She had personalized my copy of *ZAP!* with silver magic marker. She wrote, "Hey, Mr. Casting Director—pick me! Pick me! Oh, please, pick me!"

She starts asking people in Portland about me. One of them says I'm very polite when I talk to you, but I grit my teeth as if I can't stand being in your presence. Anne loves it.

In May of '97 comes another zine, *Motherfuckin' Titty-Suckin' Two-Balled Bitch.* Another boob shot. A note with her phone number, asking me to call. I leave a message on her voicemail. Nothing much, just my return number.

A couple of weeks later, I make a live bookstore appearance at Portland's Reading Frenzy to coincide with *The Redneck Manifesto*'s release. A few days afterward I get another letter from Anne, along with a Xerox of her naked ass. She wants to know if I'd publish a book consisting of three articles she'd written:

"100 Shitty Things I've Done to Hurt Other People";
"100 Shitty Things Others Have Done to Hurt Me";
"100 Shitty Things I've Done to Hurt Myself."

She says she'd almost come to my book reading, but she got cold feet a block away from the store and turned around. She ends her letter, "Fuck you, Jim Goad—I'm usually afraid of no one, but you're the only person who scares me." She signs the letter with a drawing of a chicken.

... I've just been obsessing over you the last couple of days. So I suggest that if you don't want me to call you and bother you that you quit calling me, because that's the kind of person I am, very obsessive. And you are my latest obsession.
—*Voicemail message from Anne, 3:53AM, May 26, 1997*

On Memorial Day she leaves a message saying that she might be stripping tonight, but probably not, so I should call her. Maybe we could hook up at her apartment downtown.

When I drive over the St. Johns bridge and head downtown, I know I'm crossing a line. A point of no return.

I phone her from a lonely old phone booth in a dark part of town. She tells me to call back in ten minutes. It seems there's the small matter of kicking her boyfriend out of her apartment and out of her life. When I call back, she gives me the address to a monthly hotel right off Burnside Street's bag bitches and crackheads.

She opens her apartment door and seems taller, skinnier, and prettier than she had in her zines. The place is a matchbox efficiency about the size of a jail cell. She has a hurricane victim's sense of decorative style. Roaches scramble through the debris.

She sits down spread-eagled on a small, sticky plastic mattress. She's wearing shorts and no panties, revealing her black-bushed snapper. She fills a pipe with a nugget of skunk bud and lights it.

"I'm the best fuck in Portland," she boasts, exhaling smoke. She says her boyfriend is a fag. Says I'm a babe. "Wanna see my tits?" she asks, flashing them before I can respond.

Nervous, I suggest we go for a ride. We head for her hometown of Oregon City, slicing through the warm, late-spring mist. As we're driving, she unzips my jeans and begins fellating my schween. She keeps asking when we're gonna go back to her place and fuck.

Despite such overtures, she would eventually wind up feeling used for sex.

She asks me to hit her. I playfully grab her hair and shake her head, accidentally bumping it into the passenger's-side window. I quickly apologize. She laughs as if I'm not a very good abuser.

I ask her,

So, um, exactly how many times did your daddy molest you?

She says he never did.

She tells me she heard that Debbie was bitchy and wears too much makeup. When she calls Debbie "hideous," I tell her to leave Debbie out of it.

We get back to her place and disrobe in the dark. I try going down on her, but she won't let me. I flip over on my back. She straddles me on top. I cum in about three seconds. While forcefully grinding my wilting erection, she asks me a strange question in rhythm with her hip thrusts:

"You're...coming...BACK...aren't...you?"

She doesn't like the idea of me leaving for good.

Moonlight spills in through her window as we lay about naked. "Oh, by the way," she says, "I'm HIV-positive."

I tell her I don't care.

It turns out that she's lying. But I don't care.

When I get home at around four in the morning, Debbie wakes up and asks me where I'd been. I tell her I'd fallen asleep down in the basement.

Two days later I go back to Anne's place with a shaved head and a baggie of crank. She says crank makes her wet. I should've remembered it makes me dry. It siphons the blood straight out of my wee-wee, shriveling it down to thumbnail-size. For twenty hours she tries sucking my prune dick. Twenty hours of her saying "It's not important" and me cursing my luck. I finally hoist my mast—barely—and "experience" her for about a minute and a half.

We go for a walk in the pale silvery morning. Later that day she leaves a voicemail message saying how she was checking out my ass as we strolled the empty streets. She likes my swagger. She digs how I threatened the parking-lot attendant. She calls me "the last masculine man in Portland."

I figure that with her sexual history and general wildness, she isn't going to be into anything heavy. But it gets heavy almost immediately. She starts leaving multiple voicemail messages for me daily, all of them marked "urgent." In one early message she says she's having trouble concentrating at her stripping job and that she's miserable when she isn't around me. So she quits stripping and says she's devoting her life to making me happy.

After a week, we're seeing each other every day. She plasters her apartment walls with blown-up Xeroxes of my photos from *ANSWER Me!* She surrounds herself with Jim Goad. And it's more than a little unsettling to visit her dilapidated micro-pad and be surrounded with Jim Goad, too.

One night I sift through unimaginably heavy Rose Festival Parade traffic to her lice-'n'-scabies soap-dish apartment. And as I sift through rubbish on her floor while she's downstairs in the laundry room, I find a booklet written by her immediate ex, a fey spoken-word wannabe. One line sticks with me, something to the effect of, "Please don't break my little China-doll heart." I think of Debbie, and how my affair with a girl half her age would smash her heart into ceramic pieces.

Anne and I hang out in her sauna-like hovel, watching out the window as brightly festooned parade floats caterpillar their way past sweating onlookers. We can't sleep all night. At daybreak I suggest we drive out to the Columbia River Gorge and rent a motel. In a little town called The Dalles, we find a cool, quiet room with a slowly wheezing air conditioner. She painfully squints while lowering herself atop my wang and mutters, "You've got a pretty big cock...this is the best sex I've ever had." Soon after the best sex she's ever had, she's asleep. She looks almost innocent.

I'm still restless. I sit on a chair next to the bed and watch some Sunday afternoon kids' fantasy show with the sound turned off. A witchlike character appears onscreen. It seem as if something is tormenting her. I think of Debbie and how my philandering will strip her open to the ugly, desperate pain of betrayal.

Anne soon awakes, and we ride out to a gravel turnoff next to an isolated country road. It's near dusk. We face the sunset over the Columbia River Gorge's colossal mouth. The giant sky casts doubt over the greenish-golden fields.

There's doom in that wide-open sky.

I feel my fate setting along with the sun. A tear springs from my eye. I feel like I'm falling in love, and I know how much pain love can bring.

Falling in love. Down, down, down. You *fall* in love. You don't fly upward.

After a police car passes we pull into The Dalles again, fearful we'll be nabbed for a small sprig of weed we've been smoking. I park next to some train tracks in an abandoned section of downtown. We stare out the windows as a cold depression seizes us. I ask her if she knows what it's like to feel so bad you want to die. She sort of derisively laughs and says, "God, yeah," her wide eyes surveying the emotional damage in her life to this point. She seems to be saying, "You don't know the half of it."

The next morning, fog clouds dot the Gorge as we head west to Portland. She's scheduled for an abortion to eject the fetus her previous boyfriend had implanted. As we sit in the clinic's waiting room, she falls to the floor, grabs my ankles, and says, half-laughing, "I'm a lonely and desperate person."

I attend the operation and clutch her hand as they pump her full of anesthetics. "My ass ROCKS!" she shouts to the nurses as they reveal her nether regions. "Don't I have a great ass?...Look at my boyfriend—isn't he a babe?" As they ram a massive steel speculum up her twat, she shrieks, "Give it to me, daddy!" The doctors try to hush her, fearing that her banshee squeals will clear out the waiting room.

After the operation, she gives me some blood-soaked cotton gauze as a souvenir. We drive for a while and park beneath an overpass facing downtown Portland. I tell her I'll need to be getting home. She asks when she'll be able to see me again. With mascara smeared like two black eyes, she adds, "I mean, I'm totally in love with you already."

I tell her that the same dangerous word had occurred to me.

When I get home it's Monday afternoon, and Debbie's at work. She's left a note for me near the computer. It reads:

Here on Sunday thinking about the last eleven years and how we got this house for the both of us and the pets. I held back the tears all day. And then on the World News, they interviewed tornado victims who repeatedly said, "God doesn't give you more than you can handle." I finally sobbed to that.

Igor [our pug], who had been sleeping across the room by the white couch, got up from his nap, and pounced on me and licked my face manically for twenty minutes. It helped, but I'm still not cured.

I gulp and realize I'm falling in love again to punish myself.

God didn't give her more than she can handle.

After all, he didn't tell her about the twenty-one-year-old stripper.

Or that in a week, Debbie would be diagnosed with terminal cancer.

Or that on the night of her surgery, as she lay on a hospital bed with morphine dripping into her arm, the stripper and I would be rolling around on Debbie's bed at home.

And I really wish you could kidnap me right now, or that you could, you would. Because I am so ready to run away from all this. I don't want to deal with any of it.

—11:07AM, Thursday, June 18, 1997

Summertime is gorgeous in Portland, the only time of year the sky isn't smothered in clouds. It rarely gets too hot. The days are long and drenched in syrupy sunshine. The nights are cool and buzzing with possibility.

For a while you can pretend that rain doesn't exist.

Or death.

Debbie's cancer shows me the difference between emotional death and the literal kind. Suddenly, death doesn't seem nearly so romantic. Suddenly, I don't want cancer or AIDS. I don't want to die. I push myself through a rigorous fitness regime: pumping iron, running, gobbling vitamins, and eating health food. I work myself into having a taut, angry body to prove I'm not dead. Or dying. Not like Debbie is.

I run from Debbie as if the cancer will somehow rub off on me. I can't handle the morbid megatonnage of her condition. Watching her hair fall out. Seeing her legs get as skinny as a young pony's.

Every night I tell her I'm going out for a long drive in order to clear my mind. And every night I run straight into Anne's young, healthy arms.

Debbie's cancer dooms us. It casts a long, black ribbon of darkness over our heads.

We tell each other we're going to hell for what we're doing to Debbie. And yet we keep doing it.

We both should be awarded trophies for conducting the most psychotic, contaminated, pseudo-romantic liaison in human history. It's not really love, because love implies sweetness and innocence. It's an intensely eroticized death wish. We both feed off the danger and suffocating closeness. People who know us are sure that we'll kill one another. Two angry psychos headed full-throttle for each other's throats.

Combustible. Borderless. Unhinged. She eats my boogers, and I burn a cigarette on my forearm for her. We wonder what it would feel like if we were to, say, drive to a small rural town and shoot a transient point-blank in the head. Or kidnap a small black boy and pose for pictures with him at rap concerts and the zoo before returning him to the playground.

We indulge in a sort of terroristic fun to scare off the death we feel is chasing us. Driving, driving, driving, as if we don't want to stop for a moment to ponder what we're doing.

Rolling through Portland like the Plague. Running up to strangers on the street and snapping pictures of them as if we're paparazzi. Pulling cigarettes out of people's mouths and telling them it's a filthy, disgusting habit. Walking down hipster-thronged NW 23rd Street, both of us topless.

We call ourselves "Portland's Hottest Young Couple." Everyone's afraid of us. We get kicked out of almost every bookstore, mall, restaurant, and coffee shop in the city, mostly for her ear-splitting public displays. It's almost impossible to overstate how loud she is in public. She'll enter a room screaming and usually not leave until forcibly ejected. She'll be somewhere in the middle of one of her mega-decibel monologues, and people will flash me this stunned look, as if, "Which mental hospital did you find HER in?"

But she makes me laugh. She reminds me of how spontaneous and theatrical I'd been before teenage depression dampened it. Before adult depression killed it. I feel as if she's resurrecting part of me from the dead.

We make a killer comedy-writing team, driving around finishing each other's ideas. I drive while she scribbles notes.

We plan to do several zines:

BLOW Me!, whose premise is that happiness, fitness, family values, and greed are ultimately more offensive than suicide, murder, and rape. The magazine's centerpiece is a cartoon panel about my twenty-hour spate of crank-induced impotence. I suggest a centerfold pop-up where everything pops up but my dick.

Negro Love Child, the heartwarming tale of two ex-Nazis who find love and commitment through the adoption of a small black child from the inner city.

Rashawndasaurus, a coloring book about a strong, young, intelligent black female dinosaur.

Wheelchair City, a zine about handicapped people "by two people who aren't."

We devise comic characters:

Bruno Penilucci, the planet's most homophobic man.

Lord Ashleigh St. John, a sadistic British aristocrat who still owns slaves in Alabama's hill country, and his incestuously attractive niece, Wee Lady Anne.

A rap group called Wiggaz in Jeepz and their hit, "Knockin' Da Boots."

Lonsdale, the flying anti-littering monkey.

The Gay Nazi ("Vee are heer, vee are queer—you VILL get used to it!")

And Stan 'n' Barb Taylor, an annoyingly wholesome, extraordinarily ordinary pair of real-estate agents from Beaverton, Oregon. Stan 'n' Barb are our most fully developed characters, with an extended family of sub-characters and an entire TV fantasy network based on their lives. They are also our normalcy-stricken alter egos, the happy squares we could never be.

Part of us wants to be Stan 'n' Barb. Desperately.

There's a desperation to our comedy.

And our sex.

We really can't spend time together without fucking.

We feel as if we'll somehow break a spell if we don't do it at least once daily.

Up in the hills. Next to the train tracks. On the roadside. Beneath the nuclear power plant. Out in the woods. In the parking lot behind the church.

Fucking even while she's recovering from her abortion and bleeding all over the place.

Fucking so hard, the bed collapses beneath us.

Fucking so hard in my car, she has permanent scars on her back from the friction. Just whomping her with the dick like I'm the LAPD and she's Rodney King.

We play up the age difference. I'm Joey Buttafuoco, and she's Amy Fisher. I'm Travis Bickle, and she's Iris the Teenaged Prostitute. I'm Kentucky coal miner Earl Harlan, and she's his granddaughter Swee'pea.

My cock is her baby bottle. Her ba-ba. She likes falling asleep with it in her mouth. She'll point at its veins and giggle excitedly. She suffers from obvious penis envy, or she wouldn't hover over mine for so long. She dawdles over my prick as if it holds all of life's secrets. She calls it "The Best Cock in the West." Shouts about my "porn-star cock" at a Portland magazine shop. E-mails a friend about how I tear her up with my tool.

Despite all her sexual experience, she didn't even have an orgasm until she met me. She thought cumming was the same thing as getting wet. I take her from that point to where she's epileptically spasming from the second I shove it in her until a half-hour later when I dismount. She cums so hard, I can *feel* her pussy contracting around my cock. I'll push it in her to the hilt and just hold it there without pumping, and she quivers like a jellyfish. Total loss of control. She screams so loud as I stick her doggie-style, I'm afraid someone will call the cops.

Fucking and laughing and fucking and laughing and fucking and laughing with this young girl to prove I'm alive. And after eight or ten hours, she'll ask me to stay a little longer, and I always do. I'm gorging myself on pleasure because there's no pleasure with Debbie. None. There hasn't been for years. Debbie is a straight bummer.

I always get home late.

"Where'd you go tonight?"

Um, up into Washington, near Mt. St. Helens.

I pet the dog, kiss Debbie, and fall asleep, smelling of Anne.

THERE IS NO WAY IN HELL, even, Jim, even if you call me up and tell me you never want to see me again, I AM NEVER GOING TO FUCK ANYBODY ELSE AGAIN. I'm crazy, it may be crazy, that's maybe really obsessive and fucked-up, oh well!...I'm like the woman who stalked David Letterman with you! I'm sorry, that's how I feel. You're IT. So, you know, that may not be what you wanted to hear, but I am that much in love with you, to the point where I am devoted for the rest of my life.

—1:18AM, Monday, July 28, 1997

Anne is a true believer. An apostle of The Gospel According to Jim Goad. She has forsaken everything and taken up my cross. But her devotion comes with a price. Just don't ever, ever, ever, ever leave her.

In June I catch her in a lie. She'd been bragging to a female bookstore owner that she's ruining another marriage, and the bookstore owner tells me about it. I confront Anne, who denies ever saying it. Oh, bullshit. I argue that the bookstore owner would have nothing to gain by telling me this, while Anne has everything to gain by lying. So Anne admits she lied. As we sit on the warm grass in a public park, I say I'm breaking up with her. She pounces on me and wraps her arms tightly around my waist. "Don't leave! Don't leave! Don't leave! I won't let you go!" she sobs. I've never seen anyone cry so hard. And I've never had anyone grab onto me and refuse to let go like this. I tell her I'm leaving—she can either accept a ride back to her place, or she can walk home. I stand up. She's still clutching onto me. I start walking. She still holds on, dragging her feet on the grass. She finally gets in the car. I drive her home. She cries all the way.

She tells me she cried for nine straight hours. She leaves a string of desperate phone messages choking back the tears. And ultimately, my hard ass softens. I feel bad for her again. I say that if she feels that strongly toward me, maybe we have something special. I go back to her.

In August I break up with her again. She screams "FUCK YOU!" at me during an argument, and I say I never tolerate such behavior from anyone, male or female. Fuck you, too, and goodbye. I start walking out of the apartment.

"How can you do this?" she wails.

Like this—watch me.

Barefoot, she follows me out of the building and into the street. As I try opening my car door, she lunges at me and holds on like an octopus. For fifteen minutes she stands there with her tentacles wrapped around me. I say I don't want to get forceful, but she'd better loosen her grip.

"Is it over, Jim?"

Yes. Now let go of me.

She does. And with those bare feet she walks straight into traffic, howling incoherently with tears soaking her puffy red cheeks.

A car slams on its brakes. It misses her by a foot. She runs away screaming. I drive away sighing.

Um, yeah, I know, I can't stop calling....Well, I still can't get over my habit. I haven't kicked
it....I don't know, this is bothering you, probably, I mean I probably should just stop and
leave you alone, but I really can't. Um, I'm really going crazy.
—*3:14PM, Thursday, August 14, 1997*

Nobody exists in my mind except for you. I'm sick....Oh, God, I'm deranged.... I want to hunt
you down, I want you!
—*5:29PM, Thursday, August 14, 1997*

Late in August, Anne's invited to give a live reading at a Portland
bookstore as part of some faggy little zinester fest. Debbie hears
about the event and wants to attend. I try persuading her against it,
but she insists on going. And so we go.

My wife, my mistress, and I...all in the same small room.

Debbie wears her curly blonde chemo wig and a white cotton dress
with little banana and watermelon patterns. Anne wears a sheer
nightgown and no bra. She disrupts everyone else's readings to the
point where people are screaming at her to shut up. She finally gets
up and reads her piece, which lists and describes the first twenty-five
guys she fucked. People are still laughing nervously after the first five
or so guys. By the time she reaches #25, everyone is silent and staring at the floor. People feel bad for her.

Regardless, she resumes interrupting everyone else after her reading and is booted out of the store. And after I drop Debbie off at
home, I go out for one of my "rides" and impale Anne with the dick a
few times.

The next day, Debbie asks me what I thought of Anne.

Oh, well, you know, I guess she was kinda funny.

"She seems like your kind of woman," Debbie says. I change the
subject. I deliberately had avoided eye contact with Anne the previous night. And yet Debbie could somehow smell the connection
between us. She would write in her diary that I fell in love with somebody named Anne that night, and that's what happens whenever a
thirty-six-year-old man sees a cute twenty-one-year-old girl.

The bubble is burst. The fantasy summer is over. No more honey-
moon. Seeing Debbie as someone real, rather than just an abstrac-
tion, ruins our Cartoon Psycho Funworld. It closes down the carnival.
Debbie's contamination becomes ours.

Anne and I drive up to the hills like we always did. But instead of fucking, we cry and cry over Debbie. For hours.

Guilt. Self-hatred. Two psycho assholes who are laughing and fuck-ing while a dying woman stews home alone in the summer heat. Two psycho assholes who are going to hell.

The jig is up. Anne and I become much more comfortable sharing our inner rottenness with each other. We become bottom feeders, eating each other alive.

[N]obody ever killed themselves over me...I always wished, 'cause I was weird, that when I was younger that my mom would kill herself or somebody would kill themselves in my family, 'cause then I wouldn't have to kill my own self.
—1:35AM, Sunday, August 31, 1997

It's called scapegoating. Transference. Guilt-projection. Hypocrisy.

Anne wears many masks, but there's no face behind them. She'll use whatever angle works and say whatever sounds right. It all depends on her audience and who's doling out the sympathy. One moment she's a "flaky liberal chick"; the next, a "psychotic neo-Nazi bitch with a whip." One minute she's the most mentally ill broad who ever lived; the next she's perfectly sane, because her psychiatrist said so. Today she's a raging killer cunt; tomorrow, a tragic victim. She's either the ultimate misanthropist or a paragon of family values.

Which is all fine, on a purely Machiavellian level. But if you want to play at being moral, you should have some moral grounding. Some consistency. And Anne has none.

From what I can discern, Anne is fundamentally amoral and will do whatever is necessary to obtain personal power. But unlike world-class major-league sociopaths, she's extremely uncomfortable with this knowledge about herself. I think she's aware that there's something deeply flawed about her that renders her unlovable, but she wants to be loved. She wants people to see the...ehh...what do you call it...the "good" in her. So she constantly seeks to justify all her actions with some moralistic rationale beyond the blind drive for power.

The girl just isn't happy being Satan. So she tries pawning it off on someone else.

As the arguments escalate, Anne becomes subject to fits of moral outrage and high-holy finger-pointing. My inner reaction is always, "You've gotta be kidding me." She's a turd walking on two legs trying to spray-paint herself with gold. She has the bloated sense of morality that only comes from having a guilty conscience.

Truly ethical people go about quietly being ethical. They feel no need to advertise. But the sinners are always shouting about all the good deeds they've done.

I like Anne's rottenness. A lot. She's very, very good at being bad. A Blue Ribbon winner. It's her hypocritical self-righteousness I can't stand.

She's the proverbial whore who wants to be a virgin again. The master abuser who can only see herself as a victim.

She purposely does something bad and then feels like a good person for feeling bad about it. Better yet, if she can get someone else to feel guilty about it, she'll feel like a saint.

She's on a sacred mission to broadcast everyone else's moral shortcomings. She anoints herself the Joan of Arc of Outing.

Huh. That's funny. Honesty should begin at home. For someone so savagely "honest," she never really comes clean about her wonderful abandonment issues. Or her delightful pussy hangups. Or the role she plays in her alleged victimization.

She lies about everything yet fancies herself a truth-teller.

So when she goes on the attack about my alleged moral failings, what a marvelous coincidence that she's guilty of all of them.

She makes dozens of death threats against me.

Yet she says it's obvious I want her dead.

She mercilessly dumps her boyfriend to be with me.

Yet she calls me despicable for leaving Debbie to be with her.

She says she doesn't understand how I could be with someone as stupid as Debbie for eleven years. More than once, she says she wishes Debbie would die. She even says she's jerking off to the fact that Debbie is shriveling up with cancer.

Yet she accuses me of being insensitive toward Debbie.

She sends insulting letters to my friends, consciously trying to isolate me from them.

Yet she accuses me of trying to isolate her from her friends.

Despite my offers, she's too weirded-out about her snatch to let me go down on her.

Yet when she's angry with me, she'll scream, "You never go down on me!"

She'll skip around in public yelling, "NIGGER! NIGGER!," brag that she's "never had sex with a minority," and claim that "white people are more attractive than other races."

Yet she accuses me of being a racist.

She repeatedly begs me to throw her down and rape her. And I always refuse.

Yet she files a false rape charge against me with police.

She'll say, "I want to be your slave."

Yet she accuses me of trying to control her.

She smashes my car windshield, tears up my books and CDs, and destroyed every window in an ex-boyfriend's 4x4.

Yet she accuses me of vandalism.

She brags about her dozens of sex partners.

Yet she calls me a slut.

She physically attacks me time after time.

Yet she calls me violent.

She says she's pretty enough to get any man she wants.

Yet she calls me vain.

She does all of these things.

Yet she accuses me of hypocrisy.

Er, look who's talking?

Takes one to know one?

Talk about the pot calling the kettle black?

Let she who is without sin cast the first stone?

I'm rubber, you're glue—anything you say bounces back to you?

It's as if she's trying to laser-beam all of her own foul traits into my body. Her guilt and self-loathing are hot potatoes which she tries tossing onto me.

Maybe if she can depict me as total shit, she won't feel so shitty about herself.

Maybe she's the perfect person to scapegoat Mr. Shit Magnet.

Maybe if I kill myself, she won't have to kill herself.

Um, like, y'know?

She thinks violence is wrong.

When she gets the worst of it.

Being "the other woman" is wrong.

Unless she's the other woman.

She's the most aggressively insulting person I've ever met, and yet the most easily insulted. The classic case of someone who can dish it out but can't take it.

She'll make fun of my nose job, and I'll laugh.

I'll make fun of her pig nose, and she'll cry.

She'll make fun of my teenaged homo past, and I'll laugh.

I'll make fun of her prepube lesbo past, and she'll cry.

She'll make fun of the time I couldn't get it up, and I'll laugh.

I'll make fun of her pussy farts, and she'll cry.

She complains that I treat her like shit.

Well, how else are you *supposed* to treat shit?

I used to wish that I had a father that beat the shit out of me so that I could say, "Look, I have the bruises..."

—1:46AM, Tuesday, Sept 2, 1997

Anne wants to be a victim. She wants to have bruises she can show people. To prove that she isn't a bad person. To prove that she doesn't hurt people. To prove that she's the one who gets hurt.

With very little supporting evidence, she's certain she's suffered more than anyone in human history. No one had a worse childhood. No one has more severe mental problems. No one has been hurt worse in love.

It doesn't take me long to start questioning the extent of her victim-hood. None of her victimized situations seemed particularly foisted upon her.

Her traumatic childhood sexual "abuse" at the hands of another girl just seemed like Playing Doctor, with Anne in the submissive role.

And it was so sad that every one of her nearly three dozen male lovers was abusive toward her. Every fucking one of them. God, can you imagine the luck? If she didn't want to feel used by thirty-five guys in three years, maybe she shouldn't have thrown her pussy in their faces. Maybe she shouldn't have been showing naked pictures of herself in Texaco parking lots...or performing fellatio on her boyfriend's dog...or walking around downtown Portland with cum dried on her face from gutterpunk circle jerks...or exchanging blow jobs for heroin.

And if she didn't want her mom to throw her out of the house, harkening a tragic three-month "homeless" phase, maybe she shouldn't have assaulted mommy, called her a dyke, stolen money from her, and published mom's most embarrassing secrets in her zine.

When I mildly suggest that she played a role in her so-called vic-timization, she becomes livid and says she isn't going to fuck anyone who doesn't understand her.

I disagree.

I think she doesn't want to fuck anyone who understands her too well.

...You know, I joke around about it and stuff, but I really am sometimes, like especially now, I mean I swing back and forth, with being anti-feminist, and like, sometimes I get really extreme....I think that feminism needs to be reformed, and I don't think these women are strong enough.... Like the women that I consider to be feminists are like Sharon Stone in *Basic Instinct* or Lorena Bobbitt, ones that used violence, you know, and like beauty and power to seduce men and then, you know, take advantage of them and kill 'em.

Now I know why women have a hole between their legs. That's where they hide all their problems.

Anne hates her pussy. All her self-loathing has become localized in that well-worn Irish twat. She feels that her cunt is a repository for all the world's sewage. She's sure that her labia are too droopy and that her snatch is too stretched-out from all the cocks that have visited it.

A previous boyfriend had traumatized her by asking, "Uhh, can you squeeze your legs to make it a little tighter?"

She actually walks up to strangers on Portland streets, shows them a Polaroid of her bearded oyster, and asks them if there's anything wrong with it. When one guy says, "Yeah, it looks like someone just gave birth," she becomes furious. Not at him—at me, for lying and saying her cunt is fine.

She is particularly humiliated by vaginal flatulence. One time she pussy-farts while fucking me, immediately dismounts, punches me on the back as if it were my fault, and yells, "I TOLD you sexual trauma was for real!"

She isn't *Carrie*. She's *Queefie*.

Yet she knows how to use that farting slop-pit to her advantage.

In her more candid moments, she acknowledges that feminism is just a pastime for women who are between boyfriends. She admits that "sisters" such as herself will scratch each other's eyes out to snag "some asshole good-looking guy."

But she's extremely savvy about latter-day gender politics and knows how much sympathy (and cash) she can garner by playing the victim. She plans on writing a book called *Milking the System*, featuring a whole chapter devoted to how women can use false rape charges and domestic-violence scams to make money.

She's keen on making false rape accusations.

She faced criminal-mischief charges in 1995 after throwing a mortar block through windows in her first married boyfriend's car and house.

He had told her to leave. For good.

During her trial, she received probation instead of jail time after whispering "tell the judge I was raped" into her Public Defender's ear. "The system will believe a woman every time," she brags to me later.

After cheating on her second married boyfriend with a pair of male gutterpunks—simultaneously—she excused it by saying, well, they raped her. When her boyfriend offered to call the cops, she quickly talked him out of it.

During her Fall 1997 semester at Portland Community College, she skips more than half of her classes because she's terrified of letting me out of her sight lest I cheat. As the semester nears its end and teachers are threatening to flunk her, she doefully explains to two different professors that she'd missed so many classes because she'd been victimized by an abusive boyfriend. Her English teacher gives her a 'C.' Her Women's Studies teacher—a woman—gives her an 'A,' wishing her wellness and plenty of safe places. When it comes time to pay her tuition, she's broke, having frittered away her student loan on weed and trinkets. So she marches into the Women's Crisis Center, crying that her monstrously battering boyfriend—who has left the state—has ruined her life and rendered her penniless. The Crisis Center pays her tuition in full. Five minutes later she meets me in the school cafeteria, laughing at how gullible they are.

In the spring of '98, tired of her measly $280-a-month General Assistance allowance, she goes for the big bucks—a Social Security Income check, topping seven hundred smackers monthly. She's going to claim that her disability is mental illness—not a far stretch—but she isn't going to take any chances. She requests that I give her a black eye so she'll look extra-daffy for her screening. So I consent to the punch. As we drive to a desolate patch of North Portland, she guzzles a whole bottle of champagne to blunt the pain. We get out of the car, kiss, and I wallop her in the right temple, leaving a small knot but no black eye. Since she's crying, we decide not to push it further. She appears at her disability interview in piss-stained clothes she's been wearing for days. She gives purposely loopy answers to the psych-test questions. ("Q: What do trees and fruit have in common?" "A: Um, they're both outside?") Remarkably, they don't think she's crazy enough, and her S.S.I. check is denied.

JIM: I was talking to [Sean] Tejaratchi earlier tonight, before I even picked you up, and he asked me why did I think people like Debbie and you were attracted to me, and I couldn't say why. And he says he thinks it's because these are people who feel disgusting and nobody understands them, and I accept them. It's typical Tej.

ANNE: Do you think that's the truth?

JIM: Yeah, I think so.

ANNE: [unintelligible] You should be a motivational speaker or something....You're a little shepherd.

JIM: Oh, Christ.

ANNE: You are! You're a protector. You're a shepherd of the mentally ill.

JIM: Yeah, they come to me.

ANNE: Yeah! It's true, though.

—Taped phone conversation, 9/97

Anne says she admires Glenn Close in *Fatal Attraction*.

She says she wishes our relationship could be like the movie *Misery*, where a star-struck woman holds a writer against his will.

She says she feels O.J. Simpson was guilty—but *justified*—because he loved Nicole so much, he murdered her when he found her with someone else.

She sends out Christmas cards implying we've gotten married.

She wants to bear my child so she can have a "piece" of me.

She tries to get PROPERTY OF JIM GOAD tattooed on her ass, but the guy at the tattoo parlor thinks it's too degrading.

When I tell her that the A.S.P.C.A. implants animals with biochips to track their whereabouts, she says she wants me implanted so she can always know where I am.

I feel very intimidated by you still, and I'm used to being the one in charge, and being in control, and being the smartest one, and you're smarter than me, you're stronger than me, and it's just—I don't like that.

—1:38AM, Tuesday, Sept 2, 1997

Anne is attracted to my reputation and the long, dark shadow it casts. And she has a much more inflated image of me than I ever did of myself.

I always tell her I'm not all that. But she doesn't want to hear it.

She says she has to scrape to find things wrong with me. She tells me she has trouble looking in my eyes. She has an idealized notion of me as some impenetrable fortress. Something superhuman. Something not human at all.

In many ways, I feel like an object.

It begins creeping into my consciousness that her idolatry of me has very little to do with whatever sterling qualities I might possess and everything to do with her own obsessive needs.

Then one day she tells me how, as a girl, she used to carry her baby brother around as if he were a doll.

I feel scared.

To her, I'm an idol. But an idol is a statue. A doll. It isn't real.

And if you carefully sculpt an idol, and that idol comes alive and starts walking away from you, then you have to find a way to smash it to pieces.

She doesn't like that I'm a rock, so she struggles to find a way to grind the rock into dust. She searches for a weakness.

She thinks she found a sore spot in the fact that I'd had a few hair transplants drilled into my dome fifteen years ago.

It doesn't bother me. In BLOW Me!, I'm going to call myself a "skull-stapled hatemonger."

She thinks I'll be embarrassed by a history of domestic violence.

Nope. I'm going to write an article called "To All the Girls I've Hit Before."

She thinks I'll be humiliated by a smattering of teenaged homo experiences.

Nuh-uh. I'm going to write an article called "I'm Not a Nazi, I'm Gay."

She thinks I'll freak if she alleges I'm not really white trash.

I don't. I help her write something called "Reasons He Ain't No Redneck."

Her usual power play of revealing someone's secrets, the one that had so enraged her mom and brothers, doesn't faze me in the least. I'm a jolly good sport about it all.

So since she can't crack my shell that way, she preys upon something much deeper.

My weakened will to live.

She often compares us to Kurt and Courtney, a love story that ended when Kurt creamed his own brains with a shotgun.

Later, she'll liken our "love" to the film Titanic, where the guy dies young and the woman lives to be a wizened old hag.

She wants me, dead or alive.

All summer she's been encouraging me to have sex with Debbie. And when I finally do, she threatens to kill me.

...Oh, but it had nothing to do with revenge—it's just a coincidence that it was right after you hung up the goddamn phone with me, you know? I want to fucking castrate you, I want to stab you a million times all over your fucking body....So, I hate your guts, and I'm going to kill you, and I don't care what happens to you or your fucking wife, and I hope you die.
—1:02PM, Wednesday, Sept. 3, 1997

September is a bad month. The beginning of the rainy season. The start of the long slide into darkness.

All summer Anne had been snorting and smoking crystal meth so she'd be happy and pleasant and bubbly for me. But the speed is scorching her brain. She decides to stop doing crank. And quit smoking cigarettes. And she's going to return to school. And give me the first full taste of exactly what she means when she calls herself psychotic.

What a sick time it is. A hundred yards from the hospital where Debbie is undergoing chemo, Anne's in a cheap motel, exorcising the crank demons from her body. My wife is getting chemicals pumped into her, while my mistress is trying to sweat the chemicals out of her. I drop Debbie off for treatment and drive over to Anne's motel. She opens the door, and the room smells like a thousand dead, bloody fish. A thick cloud of funk. Anne says she's been seeing little green doily patterns on the ceiling. Thick chunks of black gunk are oozing from her pussy. When we drive over to the local mall to try and cash her welfare check, she starts writhing uncontrollably on the parking-lot asphalt. She's certain it's demonic possession. It turns out she's had a tampon lodged way up her snatch for five or six days and is probably suffering the first stages of Toxic Shock Syndrome. Hence the smell.

Thick clots of bad blood ooze between us. I threaten to leave town. She sits in the rain at the bus stop, leaving message after message, begging me not to leave. I toy with her fear of abandonment. And she toys with my fear of death.

I hate your FUCKING guts and I want to RIP YOU APART and DESTROY every fucking living cell in your body. I want to CRUSH YOU and take tweezers and pull out your FUCKING NIPPLES, and cut you up into a million pieces and scratch out your eyes and I want to chop off your FUCKING HEAD.
—8:13PM, Wednesday, September 24, 1997

It's always bad when a loved one is dying.

And when another one wishes you dead.

October crawls in like the flu. Grayer. Damper. Chillier.

I want to die.

Anne wants to die. She wants me dead, too.

And Debbie's dying.

Death, death, death.

Debbie has finished her chemotherapy. The cancer is temporarily at bay. And she's getting more and more suspicious of my nightly "rides." I come home every night, and she'll be working on some silly little clip-art collage. Or watching another video with cute house pets in starring roles. Or telling me about the giant spider in the basement and how I wasn't there to protect her.

All alone. Except for the dog. And cats. And spiders.

jim goad

I handle my guilt in the worst possible way—by being meaner and meaner to her. I become furious when she asks too many questions. And I use my anger as an excuse to go out for another ride.

After nearly five months of high-profile aesthetic terrorism with Anne, it seems as if Debbie's the only Portlander who doesn't know about the affair. One afternoon Debbie and I are watching Portland Cable Access, and who should appear on the screen but Anne, talking about her zines as part of some local documentary.

"That's the girl from the zine night," Debbie says to me.

Uhh, yeah...

The stress of leading a double life is starting to crack my shaven canary skull. I'm getting only three or four hours of sleep daily. Relentless exercise and an anorexic's diet have caused me to drop about forty pounds since I started seeing Anne.

I tell my sister I'm in bad shape, and she offers to fly out from Philly and give whatever support she can muster. The day after she arrives, she lends me some gas money so I can drive her and Debbie out to the lonesome Oregon coast. She snaps pictures of me and Debbie at the beach: Debbie pale and eyebrowless with her wig half hanging off her head, and me the guilty philanderer, making inappropriately goofy faces for the camera.

I bring my sister back to her motel at around 10PM and check my voicemail from her room. Anne has left a message saying I have to call her immediately—it's an emergency. I call her. She refuses to tell me the news over the phone. She has to tell me in person. But she's sure I'm going to kill her when she tells me.

I hang up and tell Sis I have to go. As I leave, she says, "That girl sounds very dangerous and manipulative."

I pull up to Anne's house. She gets in the car. It's obvious she's been crying.

Well, what's the news?

She won't tell me—I'll get too angry. I start to get angry that she won't tell me. Finally, she drops the bombshell: While riding around with her black girlfriend earlier in the day, she pointed at some guy and called him cute.

That's it? That's the emergency? That's why I'm going to kill you?
"Yeah."

Anne felt so guilty after calling the guy cute, she immediately asked her girlfriend to drive her home. She cried salty rivers to all her roommates about her "betrayal." She phoned a mutual friend of ours, and after an hour and a half, he persuaded her to stop sobbing.

Everyone thought she was overreacting.

As do I. Hell, I think plenty of girls are cute. I've even been seeing a couple of them on the sly.

She says she didn't even think the guy was cute—she just said it to impress her girlfriend. And that's when I get angry. Her girlfriend has talked shit about me in the past. She's caused Anne to be late for more than one date with me. She's obviously tugging Anne around on a leash, just like the girl who'd made Anne lick her pussy when they were both five years old. In the past when I'd allege that Anne was being dominated by the bucktoothed Negress, Anne always denied it. I call Anne a guilty little white girl from the 'burbs trying to score points with her soul sister from the 'hood. I tell her to get out of the car.

She doesn't. She pounces on me and wraps her arms around my waist.

Let go of me.

She doesn't.

I grab her keys and toss them out the window, figuring it'll make her leave.

Get out.

"No."

If you don't let go of me, I'm going to hit you.

She doesn't let go.

I hit her.

A punch to the face.

She still doesn't let go.

I slam on the accelerator and start driving around North Portland's industrial shadowlands, screaming and screaming. She's crying. I throw her out of the car along a desolate, rain-slicked highway. Five minutes later I come back and open her door, yelling at her to get in. She's still crying. She had plucked a dandelion from the roadside. She holds it out to me.

I take it.

We make up.

But violence changes everything. Permanently.

I'm extremely upset the next morning. I hadn't hit Debbie in two years. I figured I was past it. But hitting Anne brings back the sickness.

I'm sitting the basement staring at the computer when I hear Debbie scream as if being assaulted. I run upstairs. She's wearing a fuzzy blue nightgown, and her bald chemo head is wrinkled in agony.

"You BASTARD! You're SO mean to me! You can't blame me for everything! It's not all my fault!"

No immediate action of mine has provoked her outburst. It's just all caught up with her. Eleven years of my screaming.

It's the first time she's screamed at me. Ever.

During the months of surgery and chemotherapy, I figured she was too weak to hear about the affair. I thought the news would kill her. But if she's strong enough to scream at me...

Sit down. I have something to tell you. Remember that girl Anne from the zine reading? Well, every night for the past five months when I told you I was going out for a "ride," I was seeing her.

Debbie stares at me intently, as if she doesn't want to believe what she's hearing. Like a sponge trying not to soak up the dirty puddle on the floor.

We're silent for a while. I leave the house and drive over to Anne's.

I walk around back and tap on her bedroom window. She slides open the window and looks out, half-awake. Her eye is puffy from last night's punch.

"What's up?"

I told Debbie about us.

"Oh...so I guess it's over for us, huh?"

No...

I crawl in through her window and into bed with her.

The next morning I take my sister to Portland Saturday Market. I return home in the afternoon to find Debbie in the bedroom, sprawled out with her head at the foot of the bed, zonked on four Klonopin and who knows how much wine. It's as if a giant shoe has descended from the heavens and squashed her, so evident is her pain.

That night she wakes me up at 3AM, screaming, "I want a divorce!"

I start looking for a new apartment.

Anne once told me she liked the relative safety of being a mistress— at least you know your man isn't lying to you. But I'm getting divorced. She's no longer the other woman. She's the *main* woman. Now *she* has to worry about the other woman.

I initially find her jealousy flattering...then protective...then suffo- cating...then frightening.

She thinks every woman I encounter wants to fall to her knees and give me a hummer. Of the women who actually *do* express interest, Anne either threatens or physically attacks every one of them.

When a girl calls me her "secret boyfriend" on the Internet, Anne posts a message threatening to take a bus to San Francisco and "beat you to a bloody pulp with my bare fists."

When another Net gal innocently inquires about an essay I'd written, Anne posts a message saying, "Stay the fuck away from my man unless you want to worship him (but not sexually)."

When a woman phones me asking if I'd like to have a beer with her sometime, Anne marches into the bookstore where the woman works and threatens to beat her up in front of horrified patrons.

In the same bookstore, Anne peruses a zine compilation wherein a girl writes that she's in New Mexico, "Thinking about Jim Goad." Upon seeing this, Anne takes a black Magic Marker and X's out my face on the cover of *The Redneck Manifesto*, running away from me and out of the store.

For the Table of Contents to *BLOW Me!*, she proposes listing the names of girls who'd better stay away from me if they don't want Anne to kick their asses.

Her jealousy isn't confined to women whom I have a reasonable chance of snagging.

I tell her that a year ago, I jerked off to an Internet photo of an allegedly naked Sheryl Crow. Thereafter, Anne becomes enraged at the mere mention of Crow's name. When we drive past a billboard featuring Sheryl's face, Anne becomes livid with me.

She also goes ballistic whenever a Tammy Wynette song comes on the radio, for I'd once let it slip that I thought Tammy was sexy.

I phone the Susan Powter radio show, and Powter makes an innocuous comment about me having a seductive voice. Anne goes from being a fan of Powter's to wishing "the bitch was dead."

She doesn't want me to see the movie *Boogie Nights*, because she can't bear the thought of me looking at another woman's knockers.

Even a tiny cartoon silhouette of a bare-breasted woman I'd included on a CD of mine makes her jealous. A fucking cartoon. She wants to kill a cartoon.

She often bemoans the fact that I don't seem to care whether she cheats, and she's right. To try and make me jealous, she'll say things such as, "I'll fuck a black guy...um, I'll fuck Waylon Jennings," to no avail. I don't care *whom* she fucks. It's getting so hairy between us, I'd be *glad* if some 6'5" mullethead came and swept her away.

Less than two weeks after I tell Debbie about the affair, Anne and I have an argument in her school's parking lot. I say I'm breaking up with her. "It's all because you told Debbie!" she spits, slamming the car door shut and stomping away.

That night, just to rub it in Anne's face that I can live just fine without her, I phone a female weed dealer and tell her I need a place to stay. A few hours later, the girl leaves a voicemail message inviting me to drop by her condo the next morning. She's a red-headed chubster with big taters and a missing front tooth, an ex-stripper from Spokane who's packed on some poundage since her naked heyday. I arrive at her place the next morning. We eat breakfast, buy some peyote, and head for the coast.

That night I rent a motel room in Longview, Washington, and have the worst sex of my life. Mutual hand jobs and then slumber. The toothless redhead seems less interested in carnal pleasures than she is in eating the snack foods I've bought her.

The next day we return to her condo. I call Debbie and tell her I'm OK. Anne grabs the phone out of Debbie's hand—she's over at Debbie's house, looking for me. She asks if it's true that I had slept with another girl. I tell her it is. She vows to do everything in her power to destroy my life, then hangs up the phone. She sounded as if I'd stabbed her in the chest.

She originally asks her landlord for a kitchen knife, but she settles for an axe handle. An old, splintery slab of wood without the axehead attached. Later that night she shows up at the redhead's condo, crying crocodile tears that she's pregnant with my child and is looking for me. The redhead grudgingly lets her in and graciously offers to smoke some weed with Anne. While the redhead's turning her back to fill a bong, Anne whips the axe handle out of her purse and smashes her in the back of the skull with it.

The redhead turns around and deflects another blow from the blunt instrument. Wrestling. Scratching. Kicks. The redhead eventually overpowers Anne and throws her out of the condo.

Anne tells me how excited she was to see red rivulets flowing down the redhead's neck. She proudly poses for pictures with the axe handle. She hangs it up as a trophy on her bedroom wall. She brags to almost everyone in town about what she'd done. She animatedly gloats about her deed to a four-hundred-fifty-pound junkie guitarist, himself no stranger to extremes of human behavior. As she bobs up and down laughing about how much blood she'd drawn and how she wanted to kill the bitch, Fat Boy's jaw hangs open. "I don't want to hear anymore," he says. "This is Manson Family stuff."

He later tells police detectives about Anne's confession, as do several other witnesses to whom she'd boasted. The redhead required stitches in her head from the attack and had notified police. She identified Anne in a photo throwdown. There's plenty of evidence.

But Anne is never charged.

After all, she's a girl.

Anne tells me what she yelled at the redhead while swinging the axe handle at her noggin:

"BITCH! You're fucking with a cancer patient!"

This, supposedly, because the redhead had slept with the cancer patient's husband for one night. This, undeniably, at a time when the axe-wielder had slept with the cancer patient's husband almost every day for half a year.

By swinging that axe handle, Anne was trying to pour all of her guilt into the redhead's body. The club was a magic wand of guilt-projection.

And my infidelity swung an axe handle to Anne's mind. She makes a small mural on her bedroom door with a picture of my head pasted upside-down over the phrase, "Is this the end?" When she learns that Debbie had known all along that I'd been with the redhead but had initially covered for me, she says, "I hope the bitch dies of cancer." And she leaves me a voicemail message saying that ever since I cheated, she's been having flashes of murdering me.

A few nights later in her stuffy dark bedroom, we argue about the redhead again. I say I'm leaving. As I stand up, she lunges at me from behind, wrapping her arms around my chest and refusing to let go.

Get the fuck off me!

"Please, Jim, don't leave!"

If you don't let go, I'll hit you!

Then, whispering seductively in my ear:

"Hit me. Just don't leave."

I hit her. And she jumps on me again. And I hit her again. Then I leave.

She's proud of that black eye. She thinks it proves I care. She shows it off to a horrified girlfriend. Flaunts it in front of a coffee shop clerk. Dances up and down a city street, trilling, "My guyyyy...gave me a blaaaaaack eye!"

Debbie sees Anne's shiner and is amazed she's so nonchalant about it.

November is an odd smear of psychic ectoplasm. I'm getting divorced but still live with Debbie, splitting my time between her house and Anne's. All three of us hang out together, which is surreal.

One bright November morning, we watch a man die. Ambulance-chasers that we all are, our attention is drawn by fire trucks and general hubbub outside a restaurant on Martin Luther King Boulevard. Paramedics are trying to resuscitate a shirtless man lying on his back in a parking lot. After ten minutes of our crouching and gawking, he heaves his last, with blood splurting up into his clear oxygen mask.

Dead.

A week or so later, I move into a new apartment.

A week after that, I get paranoid that Debbie has killed herself.

With divorce piled on top of cancer, she's been threatening to pull the plug if things don't get better quickly. And she has plenty of pills to do it.

At around 9AM one morning I call her to announce that Anne and I will be delivering some items to her. No answer. 11AM—no answer. 1PM—still no answer. I grow worried and decide that we'll drive up to her place to see what the problem is.

We arrive at her house, a weather-beaten mint-green cottage with peeling Astroturf on the front porch. I notice that the screen door has been almost entirely ripped from its hinges. Strange. And when I try inserting my key in the lock, it doesn't fit anymore. Stranger. When I knock repeatedly on the door and am only answered with the sound of the dog barking, my heart begins thumping. I walk around to the side of my house, straining to see if anything is visible through the windows. At this the neighbor, a female Rotunda of indeterminate racial origin, waddles out of the house next door. I ask her if she's seen Debbie, and she says no. Very strange.

I drive to a supermarket two blocks away and call police from a pay phone:

Listen, I don't mean to alarm you, but I think we may have a suicide in North Portland.

A squad car soon arrives containing the police—a dumb female and a dumber male.

Hey, my wife has been threatening suicide and has hundreds of pills, so you have to knock down the door while there's still time to save her.

The male cop says he isn't authorized to break in, but if I've paid rent on the place in the past, I can kick down the door. So I begin kicking—loudly—but although the wood starts cracking a bit, the door doesn't bust open. At all the noise, the fatso neighbor who'd initially denied knowledge of Debbie's whereabouts jiggles over and says that Debbie's downtown, filing a Restraining Order against me. I shout that it would've been nice if she'd told me this fifteen minutes ago, before I called the cops and started kicking down the door. She just turns around and walks away, her ample fat flapping in the icy grayness.

A few hours later I call Debbie, who accuses me of trying to burglarize her house while she was gone. I try asking her why the fuck anyone would call the COPS to come and witness a burglary, but she won't let me talk.

"You LIED!" she fumes. "You LIED! You LIED! You lie about everything!" A male policeman gets on the phone and asks me where I am. He arranges to meet me and serve the Restraining Order.

On the legal papers, Debbie claims I've been beating her daily while she had cancer.

She LIED!

If I'd been hitting her daily—or even weekly—someone would have seen signs of abuse, especially in her weakened, easily bruised condition. But if Debbie had told the truth, which is that I hadn't been violent with her in over two years, she couldn't have gotten a Restraining Order. There has to have been physical abuse within the preceding six months for the judge to grant a Restraining Order. The judge told her this. So when he asked her when there had been physical abuse within the preceding six months, Debbie shrugged and said, "daily."

When Anne and I see the Restraining Order, we laugh at Debbie's hysterical allegations. I wonder why Debbie feels the need for police protection—I've moved out of the house quietly and haven't threatened or menaced her in any way. Fuck, the girl has cancer. There's already enough pain to go around. I think about contesting the Restraining Order, but I don't want to cause Debbie any more stress. With police detectives showing up on her front porch to ask if she knows anything about an axe-handle incident, I realize that my crazy life isn't the healthiest thing for her. If she feels safer with a Restraining Order, I'll give her what she wants.

When I later come to retrieve my belongings from Debbie's house—escorted by a policeman—Debbie has scrawled JIM GOAD IS DEAD! on the basement blackboard.

A few days later, Anne physically attacks me.

We had argued. And just to be a bitch, she called Debbie up and told her that not only had I cheated on Debbie with Anne and two other girls—there were six girls in all.

So just to be a prick, I tell Anne that I'd lied when I said I couldn't get it up with the redhead. I had shot my wad, even if it was in her hand. And the redhead came, too, even if it was by my finger.

Pause. A psychotic glint in her eye as she sits in the passenger's seat. And then she pounces at me like a bobcat, scratching at my eyes. I'm able to wrestle her out of the car and onto the grass. She sits there, sobbing.

"Why are you doing this to me?"

Because I like being an asshole.

More violence less than a week later.

On the last day of November, as we're driving over to her mom's house to do laundry, we argue about money. About the fact that she doesn't have any, and I'm paying for everything.

The argument escalates.

I pull over to the roadside.

GET OUT.

"No. You're taking me to mom's."

GET THE FUCK OUT.

"NO!"

So I get out instead. Pop the trunk. Start piling all her clothes, schoolbooks, and *BLOW Me!* notes on the roadside.

She gets out. Grabs a rock. I assume a defensive position. She drops the rock and lunges at me, screaming full-blast and punching me with both fists. I deflect her shots with my forearms but don't hit back.

Frustrated, she turns and runs down the highway about a hundred and fifty yards and begins scaling a steep, muddy hillside, caterwauling all the while. Fearing she'll do something drastic, I follow her up the hill and into gnarled, bony thickets. She lifts a bowling-ball-sized rock and prepares to fling it at me. I jump toward her. She drops the rock. I punch her in the gut.

Just then I hear the loud BLOOP! of a police car. And then a second bloop. Two squad cars, lights flashing, at the bottom of the hill. I walk down first. Anne follows a minute later.

Someone must have seen her hitting me on the roadside and called the cops.

The female cop takes her story. The male cop takes mine.

Just a little argument, officer. No, there was no violence.

I look over at Anne, whose face is wet with tears. She silently mouths, "I love you."

The cops leave. We walk back to my car. Someone has stolen all of Anne's clothes. All of her schoolbooks. And all of our *BLOW Me!* notes, six months' worth of work. The chronicles of our six months together are gone.

Anne runs away, screaming, "RAPE!"

I get in the car. Go to the bank. Withdraw all my money. Drive to my apartment. Pack everything I own into my car. Fill the gas tank. Head east for Chicago, where a friend has offered me sanctuary.

I sleep that night in Boise. The next morning I make it as far east as

Mountain Home, Idaho, five hundred miles from Portland. I pull into a gravelly, grease-spackled trucker's diner for breakfast, the kind of place with phones right in your booth. I check my voicemail messages in between mouthfuls of undercooked flapjacks. Anne has left a dozen or so frenzied entreaties for me to come back home. Or at least stay wherever I am, and she'll take the next Greyhound to meet me. One message, lasting the entire five-minute time limit, is nothing more than her begging me to turn around:

"Turn around, Jim. Jim, turn around. Please turn around. Just turn around, Jim. We can make it work. So turn around, Jim...."

Five solid minutes of that. She's tortured by the idea that my back is turned. That I'm pulling away from her.

I sit for a minute, maple-slathered pancakes swimming in my stomach acids. The previous night as I was heading east, I passed The Dalles, the town where I "fell" in "love" with Anne earlier in the summer. And then as I was traversing Eastern Oregon's mountains in total blackness, feeling like a flea skirting across God's back, the song "I Never Promised You a Rose Garden" floated out of the staticky radio. That song title was also the title of a book and movie about a mentally ill woman.

I feel bad for Anne again. And also for Debbie. There are two women in Portland who need me. It would be cowardly to abandon them.

I turn around.

I zoom five hundred miles in one straight shot, stopping only for gas and dinner. I valiantly rescue Anne from her apartment near midnight.

We go to my place. Kiss. Fuck. Say we love each other. Fall asleep.

The next morning as we sit on my living-room floor smoking weed, she begins yelling at me for having the audacity to seriously consider leaving her. She grabs my half-ounce weed baggie, bites into it, and spits green buds all over the floor. As I stand up to retrieve the weed nuggets, she bites into my leg like a Rottweiler.

There are kicks. Punches. Scratches. More bites. Both of us are bleeding. Mutual combat.

I'm sure the landlord heard us.

All right, don't panic. Fuck, I've only been here ten days. He's going to evict me. Most of my shit is still packed in the car. Look, Anne, things are too hot in Portland. Come with me. We'll start fresh somewhere else.

We drive to her apartment. I tell her to fetch the few items she still owns. As she's getting out of the car, I say I need to find something in the glove compartment. When she's a safe distance away, I burn rubber.

I drive east again. I begin noticing that my foot hurts whenever I press the accelerator. I make it as far as Troutdale, Oregon, only a few miles out of Portland. As I head into another trucker's lard-hole for breakfast, my right foot is pulsating with pain. I remove my boot. My big toe is swollen and purple from our little violent *tête-à-tête*. I'm limping. I'm not going anywhere.

I turn around again.

I make up with Anne again.

That night we go to the emergency room in the same hospital where Debbie had undergone surgery and chemo. The same place where Anne had been hospitalized for teenaged suicide attempts. They X-ray my big toe. It's broken. I'll have to use crutches for six weeks.

Anne and I agree that we'd better tone down the high drama and bloodletting.

Anne moves in with me.

Into every inch of my space.

Every minute of my time.

Throughout December, I'm not out of her sight for ten minutes. Literally. We bathe together. Sleep together. Shoplift together. Ride around together. Fuck, fuck, fuck together. We don't use protection. I shoot my fishies straight up her gully, trying to impregnate her as part of some warped, desperate life instinct.

She has me just where she wants me. I'm the crippled writer; she's the obsessive fangirl. It's an incarnation of the movie *Misery,* just what she'd been hoping for all along.

The New Year creeps in with Anne and I all alone together.

And Debbie all alone in that house, cursing her ex-husband.

The coldest, rainiest, darkest time of year.

And then one night while I'm lifting weights, all the rottenness crashes down on my head at once. A sappy love song from the early 80s wafts out of my boom box. I picture Debbie in her club days, a year or two before she met me, made up all pretty and blithely unaware of what the future would hold. She's happy in this little vision of mine. And I wish that she could be frozen in time like that. Not sucked-up and ancient-looking from cancer. Not betrayed and abandoned. Not bitter at the man to whom she'd pledged her life, in sickness and in health. Not all alone and stuffing her face with junk food while I'm pumping iron and fucking.

I start crying.

And I really don't stop crying for two weeks. Maybe an hour here and there. Crying so hard, I can *hear* the tears falling on my jeans.

Crying so hard, I seriously think I'll die from it.

I have to make right with Debbie, or I'll kill myself.

Anne calls Debbie and tells her I'm in bad shape. Debbie agrees to talk to me.

I'm sorry. I'm sorry. I'm sorry. Oh, my God, I'm so, so sorry. I'll kill myself if you don't forgive me. You deserve to live, not me.

Debbie says she'll forgive me.

I tell Anne she has to find someplace else to live. What we're doing is too foul. It's hurting Debbie too much. Anne agrees with me. She can be very empathetic and cool sometimes. She calls her mom, who's willing to take her back for a few weeks. As I'm driving over to mom's house, we see a group of revelrous hipsters walking on a downtown sidewalk, toting a JUST MARRIED! sign. Anne looks at me and bursts into tears. She realizes it's never going to happen with us.

By the time we reach her mom's house, both of us are crying. We say goodbye, although it's hard.

I tell Debbie I've broken up with Anne.

And the next night, I start seeing Anne again. She agrees not to tell Debbie we're still together.

Throughout the winter and spring, I'm sweet and gentle to Debbie. Every Saturday I take her for rides, give her weed and money, and buy her dinner. And I lie to her that I haven't seen nor heard from Anne. I think it would hurt her too much to know that every night I'm plunging myself into the girl who helped destroy our marriage.

Anne finds another shoe-closet apartment ten minutes away from my place. A damp, dark, moldy room. She no longer has me to herself. She becomes the other woman again, and I'm not even married any-more. And she knows that in the summer, I'm going on a three-month coast-to-coast road trip as research for a book contract I've signed.

I'll be leaving town. Without her. I'm pulling away. For good.

And the sickness, threats, and violence come back. For good.

Hi, it's me, and I was just saying it might be necessary, ASAP, for you to take out some Restraining Order against me. Seriously, Jim, I'm infected with you....I don't know any other way to describe it. I can't get over this, I can't wash it off me, I'm insane, that's all I can think about, I am so obsessed and possessive of you....I'll go to extreme lengths to capture you, you better restrain me, and we both know what I'm capable of. I mean, you've threat-ened to call the police many times, so let's get this filthy rotten piece of garbage out of your life once and for all.

—10:13AM, February 6, 1998

I don't intend to hurt Anne by pulling away from her. I'm trying to protect myself, to prove there's a part of me she hasn't gobbled up entirely. But she interprets my gradual withdrawal as a total rejection of her, as an aggressive act rather than a defensive one. She's so self-absorbed, she takes it as a personal affront.

Earlier in the year, I had trouble distinguishing emotional death from the literal kind. Now she's the one who can't make the distinction.

To Anne, it's a literal act of murder for me to infer that I have any sort of life apart from her. I'm just another one in a long line of people who want her to leave.

But this time, it'll be over her dead body.

Or mine.

To prove that she's serious, she drinks a half-bottle of cleaning fluid in front of me. She sends me an e-mail titled I HATE MYSELF AND WANT TO DIE. She begins reading the book *Final Exit* in search of suicide tips. All over town she tells people, "I'll kill him or myself if he ever breaks up with me."

I had run into her arms to get away from death.

And now those arms are starting to strangle me.

James, I'm on my way over to your place of residence, and if you're recording this for police, I really don't care, although I would like to talk this over very civilly, if you're willing to do that, LOVER...I'll see you in a bit. Probably twenty minutes? Have the police waiting, please! They'll want to get two squad cars....

—March 4, 1998

The only "control" I wield over Anne is a prolonged effort not to be controlled by her. That's all. I never dictate her actions. Never tell her how to feel or think. Any subservient behavior she displays toward me is purely volunteer work.

She has simultaneous desires to be controlled by me and to control me. To be handcuffed during sex and to implant me with a remote-controlled biochip so she'll always know where I am.

Early on, she told me that she can be a real flamin' bitch, and I said I'd never stand for that.

I think my reply turned her on.

I think part of her yearns for me to tame the shrew inside her.

At one point, she complains to her mom that I'd hit her. Anne tells me that mom's reply was, "Finally you've found someone unafraid to discipline you."

I'm probably the first person ever to give shit back to this snake-bitten little bitch. And for that, she both admires and despises me.

She always acts as if it's erotic that I'm so forceful with her. The sex is always better after violent incidents. We fuck with scratches and bruises all over our bodies.

For Valentine's Day she gives me a card written in her blood.

Love and blood. We can't tell the difference.

Why do you have to be such a stud? I just wish you were ugly and I could tell you to fuck off, that I wasn't in love with you...Jim... [snarling sounds] I put a curse on yoooouuuu! [More evil snarling and squealing] You naughty little boy. Bye.
—11:16AM, February 6, 1998

It's like a one-way street, and, um, of course you're not in love with me like I am you....Of course, when I have nothing left in this whole fucking world except for you, I'm going to want to try to destroy you when you destroy me!
—March 6, 1998

I don't want to destroy her. Don't want to harm her. Don't want to spend the rest of my life with her, either. My feelings toward her don't run that extreme in either direction.

Can't say the same about her feelings regarding me.

When March rolls around we both have jobs, me as a graphic designer and her as a stripper again. And after one of our forty-five billion arguments, I dump her at home and return to my place. She calls and asks if I'm still going to give her a ride to the strip joint.

Fuck no.

She pauses. "Prepare to have your life destroyed," she says, hanging up.

She then leaves a slew of messages saying that she's "out for the blood," that "ya fucked with me, now it's a must that I fuck with you, nigga," that she's going to terrorize me at home and at work—oh, ho, ho, ho, ho, she has big plans for fucking up my life.

A few days later, my boss receives an anonymous letter containing two printouts downloaded from the Internet. The first is an interview with me where I say things such as how groovy the Ebola virus is; a sticky note is attached that says "FYI regarding your new employee." The second printout is a transcription of "Let's Hear it for Violence Toward Women!" with a sticky note saying, "Sample from Goad's magazine." Anne never admits to sending it, but it had to be her—no one else knows where I work.

The next time I see her, she has erected a Jim Goad Hate Shrine in her apartment. She's torn several pictures of me into tiny pieces and taped them around her mirror. On the mirror she's scrawled THUS HE IS AN ENEMY in blood-red lipstick, along with dates she thinks I cheated on her.

All because I refused to give her a ride.

At the bottom of the mirror she's taped a list titled PEOPLE HE'S HURT, a litany of all the shrinkin' violets I've supposedly harmed in my life.

The list includes the redhead whose skull she'd whacked with an axe handle.

Guilt-projection.

[Tight, sneering voice] Hi, lovey-dovey who always wants to be near me and would never cheat on me, you fucking asshole. You better be there in 20 minutes, or a fucking rock is going through your landlord's fucking window. And if you ain't there, I don't care. If your landlord lets me in, I'm throwing away, every hour that you're gone, I'm throwing away all your *ANSWER Me!* magazines, all your letters, destroying your house, and this ain't gonna be a fun night for you, boy, 'cause I'm not in a good mood. And I'm destroying everything you fuckin' own. So you can even have the cops there, because I'm not gonna play quiet when you're not there, in 20 minutes. You're having a rock through your fucking window. And if your fucking landlord doesn't answer the phone, or lets me in, then I'm destroying every single possession you own. So be there in 20 minutes or get FUCKED!

—7:39PM, March 22, 1998

The pattern of violence between us is always the same:

I tell her to leave and she refuses; or

I try to leave and she won't let me.

And she's the first physical aggressor every fucking time.

My parents used to hit me. I don't like being hit. Or bitten. Or having someone try to scratch out my eyes. It makes me angry.

She doesn't just slap me, like you see women doing to men in the movies. She's trying to do damage. And if I throw her off me, she comes charging back.

And she always winds up getting the worst of it. You'd think that after the first or second black eye, she'd search for another mode of conflict resolution. She knows I'll hit her back. So by making a conscious choice to attack me, over and over and over, I can only conclude one thing:

She deserves those black eyes. She asked for them.

As a friend would later say, "I understand why you hit her. I just don't understand why you went out with her."

One morning in March I tell her to leave, and she won't. I threaten to call 911. She dares me. So I dial 911, but she rips the phone cord out of the wall.

She lunges at me. We struggle. I fall backward onto the couch. She jumps on me. We lock arms. I restrain her as she's chomping her teeth, trying to bite me. I threaten to punch her if she doesn't stop.

She doesn't stop.

I punch her.

In the nose.

Blood starts dripping from her nose. She's still trying to bite me.

Stop it...

"No!"

WHAM!

Hard enough to cause a black eye. She finally dismounts.

The cops arrive.

Oh, sorry, I meant to dial 411, not 911. I was calling information, not the police.

One April morning we have another bitch-fest as I'm driving her home. While the car's moving, she lunges at me, scratching my face, pulling my hair, and reaching for the stick shift to try and make us crash.

I slam the brakes in the middle of the road less than a block from her apartment building. It takes a half-hour to get her out of the car.

There's another time in April when I try leaving her apartment and she pounces on me. I push her off. She keeps jumping on me, and I keep pushing her off...all the way out the back entrance...past the garbage cans...down the block...and finally to where my car is parked...me pushing her off...and her jumping back on me.

Did she come by and pick you up? How *sweet!* Listen, Goad, I know for a fact that you're not home. I've just been all around your fucking house, the whole perimeter, I've surveyed it, the inside, and out, and I couldn't get on your roof but I rang the chimes, I know for a fucking fact that you're not there, buddy, the game is up, so get your stuff, have her drop you off, 'cause I ain't leaving the premises.

—8:44PM, April 11, 1998

There's only one thing consistent about Anne: Whenever she says she knows something for a fact, she's wrong.

She knows for a fact that I hate black people.

She knows for a fact that I'm trying to destroy her.

She knows for a fact that those cuts on my face and that blood from my nose is self-inflicted.

And she knows for a fact that I'm not home tonight.

Fact is, I *am* home. Sleeping. I had worked late and got home exhausted, crashing into bed at around 7PM. I wake up three hours later and check my messages. Anne has left a dozen or so of them, saying it was awfully sly of me to park my car outside my apartment as a decoy and have "the bitch" pick me up. Saying she's going to kill me and the bitch when we get back to my place. I've listened to three or four messages when I hear a rock hit the window. Then another.

I put on my robe and go down to the front door. There she is.

"Uh, hi, J.G. I love you. Sorry about those messages. Let me in— *please?*"

I'll be at the 99¢ store buying Brillo pads. Or at the Laundromat. Or visiting Debbie. Or working late. Or sleeping. And she knows for a fact that I'm out fucking some bitch.

On the nights that Anne and I don't sleep together, she almost always takes the MAX train over to my neighborhood and "checks up" on me. She leaves items on my car windshield. One morning she leaves a drawing of herself wiping sweat from her brow with the caption, "Whew, J.G.! Thanks for staying faithful!" Another time she leaves cut-out photos of our faces pasted onto the bodies of happy families in domestic situations. She shows me a sheet of notebook paper with the heading "Times to Check Up on Him." On the left, it lists "11PM. 1AM. 3AM. 5AM." And on the right is a series of disjointed words and phrases such as MURDER, MAYHEM, LIVE APPEARANCES, BUY A GUN, and PRISON. She's drawn a happy face inside the "O" in "PRISON." She explains that she'll do anything necessary—even if it means going to prison—to ensure I'm not cheating on her.

At work they ask me how my weekend went and I say, *Well, I didn't get arrested.*

One Friday afternoon while leaving work, I tell another employee about a crazy girlfriend who's stalking me. I cross the street just as a bus pulls up. As the bus chugs away, I see that Anne is crossing the street over to my workplace. I run to my car, hoping she hasn't seen me. I get stuck at a red light two blocks away. She spots my car and starts running toward it. I screech away when the light turns green. When I arrive home about five minutes later, she's already left a cluster of threatening phone messages, saying she's headed to my house and I'd better fucking be there.

I run down to my car and high-tail it away from my apartment.

When I get back home a few hours later, Anne has left a sobbing phone message saying that she realizes her behavior is driving me away instead of making me love her. She also says that she had seen me leaving my workplace and that I'd looked happy being by myself, happier than she'd seen me in a long time.

It's a rare flash of insight on her part.

And one that won't last.

You will WILL [sic] be killed.

—e-mail message, 4/98

Over the year, Anne has gradually moved from groupie to lover to stalker. She keeps talking about buying a gun or hiring a hit man to kill me. I'll come home from work and check the bushes outside my apartment to make sure she isn't crouching there with a pistol. I take her threats seriously, but I'm not sure how to handle them. I complain to friends that I don't know how to get out of it peacefully.

And I don't want to show her any fear. I say that if she shoots me, she'd better flatten me the first time or suffer the consequences.

One night Anne and I drop by a Portland coffee shop to meet some out-of-town zinester associates, and Anne does her little comedy routine about how fun it had been to thwack the redhead's dome with an axe handle. They sit there stunned, grinning nervously.

The next morning, a friend takes the out-of-towners to breakfast and asks them what they think about Jim Goad's girlfriend. They look at each other, then down at the table, and are silent for a moment.

One of them finally speaks: "She's going to murder him someday."

Darling, where are we at, the Farmhouse? Ah darling, you know what? I ain't gonna wait for that olive branch, 'cause I don't want it. You know what I was hoping for? That it would be you. But it's not, and you have destroyed my dreams....You are going to dispose of me... and you're not going to be able to get rid of me so easy. There's going to be...somebody's going to wind up dead, whether it's me or you. And don't think, [laughs] that I won't find a way. Don't think, for even a second, that you can get away. And I wouldn't be very sloppy about it, believe me. If you hurt me bad enough, you will be fuckin' blown to fuckin' pieces. You will be *assassinated*. And there is no way, unless you never want to make a public appearance again, that that's going to...ah...uh, I'm going to follow you, I'm going to find out where—you are a fuckin' famous personality. I'm going to find out where you are, and I'm going to blow your brains to fuckin' smither-fuckin'-reens!...Your head—it's going to be out of this fucking universe. Your head's going to be blown to fucking shreds. You better pick up the fucking phone.

—8:29PM, April 13, 1998

Anne's biggest flaw is that she doesn't want to be admired for her high-octane freakiness or her skills at psychological manipulation.

She wants to be loved.

She wants to be normal.

She wants to be anybody but who she is.

She's emerged from a hairy jungle of thirty-five guys and wants commitment. I'm coming off eleven years with the same woman and want to mess around. There's bound to be a collision.

Despite all the interplanetary psychosis that had transpired between us, Anne's delusional enough to believe that one day we'll live in a ranch house with rainbows and babies. She thinks we'll eventually metamorphose into Stan 'n' Barb Taylor, our comic alter egos. I tell her we're both way too damaged to have something normal. Which doesn't mean we can't be happy. But we'll never be Stan 'n' Barb.

She won't listen. She wants life in a dollhouse.

I only have one happy memory from our last six months together.

It's a Sunday afternoon in April. We attend an all-you-can-eat spaghetti dinner in the basement of a Catholic church.

We both dress conservatively. Anne even looks sort of sweet, if you can imagine that. We almost fit in with everyone else. All the blue-haired, leisure-suit-wearing Catholic ladies who sit at our table probably think we're just another cute couple from the parish.

For a moment, we're Stan 'n' Barb Taylor, and nobody can tell we're insane.

Nobody can see the bite marks or bruises.

Nobody knows about cancer.

Or the Rape Issue, the White House Shooter, and the British Suicide Kids.

Nobody knows about her death threats.

Or my lonely forays to pick up hillbilly barfly girls.

Or Debbie's death wish.

Or mine.

Or Anne's.

If only she wasn't so suffocating.

If she could just leave when I ask her to, trusting that I'll want to see her again.

If she didn't threaten to destroy me every time she gets angry.

If we hadn't met under such impossible circumstances...

For a minute we're Stan 'n' Barb, and then it's gone.

Forever.

A sweet, sunny Sunday morning early in May. I need to write. I tell her it's time to leave. She refuses. Lunges for my face but winds up scratching my neck. I grab her. She bites my shoulder. I punch her in the mouth. More wrestling. And scratching. And screaming.

The landlord yells from downstairs. "Knock it off right now!"

But Russ, I'm just trying to make her leave.

"One of you has to leave. NOW."

She gives me the finger. "I ain't leaving."

Then I'm calling the cops.

I dash toward the phone. She kicks it off the hook. My seven-week-old Chihuahua puppy, the size of a hot-dog bun, is frantically scampering around, yipping for his life. I pick him up and run downstairs. Anne follows, punching me on the on the back and shoulders.

I knock on the landlord's door.

Russ, please call the cops.

She's still punching me. And screaming incoherently: "His wife has cancer! He's written about rape! He's evil!"

The landlord pries her off me. Takes her upstairs. She begins tearing up my books. Throwing my CDs around. Screaming, screaming. Russ finally persuades her to leave. As she's leaving, she punches me in the back of the head one last time.

Russ, I'm sorry. This is really embarrassing. But at least she's gone.

A LOUD crashing sound.

I look out the window. She's smashed my car windshield with a shovel.

Russ, PLEASE call the cops.

I run outside. Anne sees me. Drops the shovel. Tries to run.

I catch her.

All right, dumbass, now you fucked up. The cops are coming.

She looks up at me, eyes blazing. "Is there something wrong with my pussy, Jim?"

Yeah—it's deformed.

She rips open my T-shirt. Plants her teeth right in my chest as hard as she can bite.

Starts screaming "RAPE! RAPE!" in the middle of the empty Sunday-morning street.

A neighbor runs up, thinking he's witnessing a rape.

She continues biting me, hanging off my chest like a pit bull.

Look, man, I'm not attacking her—she's attacking me. Look at my fucking windshield.

When the cops arrive, she tells them I raped her. Ten minutes later, she recants.

Thank fucking Christ. We had fucked this morning. My sperm is still sloshing around inside her. She could have nailed me on a false rape charge.

They snap Polaroids of us. Blood on her lip. Scratches on her back. Scratches on my forehead and neck. Blood all over my torn shirt. Bite marks on my chest and shoulder. Cops tell a witness that the bite on my chest is the worst human bite mark they'd ever seen. They're calling her "Lady Dracula."

The police report quotes Anne: "I wanted to hit him! It feels good! He deserves it!"

It cites my landlord: "He thought Anne was the aggressor."

It quotes my neighbor: "He said that he did not see Goad as the aggressor."

From the investigative report, quoting my landlord:

He said we went upstairs to make an attempt to get Anne to leave and found her tearing up items in Mr. Goad's apartment and throwing things around randomly. He described Anne as "out of it" and said she "seemed insane." He stated Anne finally came downstairs to his apartment and "started beating the crap out of [Goad]." He said Mr. Goad did not once strike Anne nor become physical in an attempt to defend himself. He described Mr. Goad's reaction as a 'solely defensive position.' He went on to state that Anne, after assaulting Mr. Goad, went outside and took a shovel to the windshield of Mr. Goad's car, doing considerable damage.

Regardless, cops take both of us to jail.

I can't believe it.

Fuck, I was the one who told the landlord to call you guys. Why are you taking me to jail?

Because, as I will soon learn, this is Oregon. And in this P.C. Wonderland, males are never innocent in domestic disputes.

At the police station, I can hear Anne crying through my holding cell's solid steel door. I laugh out loud.

"FUCK you, Jim!" she screams.

And I say,

At least I'm free of you now.

Even in jail, wearing handcuffs, I feel free. As long as there's a wall between us.

I bail out that day. She stays overnight. Tries calling me from jail. Writes "I LOVE JIM GOAD FOREVER" on her bunk.

I call my lawyer friend in Oklahoma City. He says he's tempted to fly out to Portland and kick the shit out of me. "You stick your dick in her again, and you'll deserve everything that happens to you," he warns. "You're an intellectual terrorist; she's just a criminal. But she's lucky; you're not."

The next day, the DA's office drops all charges against both of us. I phone them, incredulous.

She bit me on the shoulder. On the chest. Smashed my windshield. Filed a false rape charge. And you're just gonna let her walk away?

"Yes."

Why?

"Because, as we see it, this was a mutual fight."

How the fuck is smashing someone's windshield evidence of mutual combat? What, did my car attack her?

"The case is closed, Mr. Goad."

Thanks, Mr. Government.

The next morning I take my car to a glass shop to have the windshield replaced. While straining to see the road through shattered glass, with sunlight refracted in a million directions through a spider web of hanging shards, I think,

This must be what it's like to see the world through her mind.

Even after all she'd done, after all the malice, threats, and even a false fucking rape charge, I feel bad for her.

But despite my overwrought, misguided compassion, I don't quite feel like getting murdered. So after dropping my car off, I head downtown to the county courthouse and file a Restraining Order against her. I really don't want to do it. She pushed me really far for me to take such a step. I'm no fan of cops, lawyers, or the prison-industrial complex, especially when they start meddling in something as private as romance. But concern for my safety—and hers—overrides such reservations.

I fill out the paperwork:

DATE AND LOCATION OF ABUSE: 5/3/98...Home
HOW DID RESPONDENT HURT OR THREATEN YOU? Bit at chest and shoulder, clawed at eyes.
DESCRIBE OTHER INCIDENTS...IN THE PAST 180 DAYS? E-mail threats; phone threats; respondent becomes murderously jealous when I tell her I want to see other women.
I AM IN IMMEDIATE AND PRESENT DANGER BECAUSE: She has repeatedly threatened to kill me and/or herself when I broke up with her. I fear what would happen to her if I were forced to act in self-defense.

The courtroom contains three dozen women with shiners...and me. I show the judge some of Anne's threatening e-mails. I show him the Polaroids of my bite marks and scratches. He grants me the Restraining Order without an argument. I feel a little safer, although my lawyer friend says that filing a Restraining Order is usually the first step to getting killed.

Anne sends me an e-mail saying she wants to kill herself. That I destroyed her. That I sunk her battleship. That our love was the Titanic, and we're sinking. That she's the little dog running around scared. That I'd better bring the Chihuahua with me and visit her on our one-year anniversary.

I awake in the middle of the night. Somehow I know she's been by my apartment. I just *know* she left something on my windshield. I throw on my robe and walk outside barefoot. Yep. Three items: a rose, the torn-off cover of a book called *Women Who Love Too Much*, and a Polaroid of her pussy.

She calls me the next night and asks what I'm doing. I say I'm waiting for the cops to serve her my Restraining Order. "Oh," she says, a sad little squeak in her voice. "OK, goodbye."

Again, I feel bad for her. I call her back.

Look, I don't want you to go to jail. I really don't. I don't think you're a criminal, I think you're mentally tortured. But I don't think you're aware of how dangerous this is getting between us.

She seems glad I called her. We talk a bit more. I look down at my crotch, and I'm as hard as an elephant's tusk. A pearly drop of pre-cum oozes from the tip. It's the sound of her voice. The smell of raisins and wine. The thought of love mixed with danger. I'm embarrassingly erect. I tell her about it. She giggles. The connection is still there.

But I tell her I'm not going to rescind the Restraining Order. I need to breathe. Need for things to simmer down. Need to feel safe. Maybe we'll get together again if we're able to flush all the insanity out of our systems. If she could just stay away and obey the Restraining Order, if she could just respect my wishes for a while, maybe there's hope for us.

Silly little boy.

I am such a masochist—I really want to go to jail, so please hand this tape over to the police and tell them I'm calling you, I'm violating the Restraining Order, it's 10:15PM and I really really really need to go to jail. So, have them over here as soon as possible, 'cause I'm ready to go back, 'cause I have nothing to do on the outside. So, if you could do that for me, love of my FUCKING life, I would really appreciate it. I really want to go back there. And that way you could just fuck your brains out and have no problem, you know, with what's going on,

shit magnet

even though I'm working on your goddamned BIRTHDAY present right now. I can't stay away from you, I'm gonna have to be behind bars, so go ahead and do what you will, Jim Goad.

—10:18PM, May 6, 1998

An hour after she's served the Restraining Order, she sends me an e-mail that says, "Your laws don't affect me" and that she isn't going to stay away.

Reluctantly, I call the police. After all we'd been through, it depresses me that she pushed it to this point. I show the police her e-mailing and tell them to arrest her. It's a drizzly Friday afternoon at around 4PM. The cops say they'll bust her sometime this weekend, depending on how busy they are.

Over the next few hours, the Sympathy Angels begin nibbling at my insides. I don't want her to go to jail.

Anne is so certain I wish her harm. If that had been the case—ever—I would have just let her kill herself. And I'd let the cops arrest her tonight.

Instead, I rush over to her place around 8PM. When she opens the door, she looks as if she's been crying all week.

Let's go. I called the police. They're coming to arrest you. I tried dropping my complaint, but the cops who have the paperwork are already on their beat. If you don't come with me, you're going to jail.

She comes with me.

We drive up to Skyline Boulevard, to the hills where we'd fucked and fucked and fucked that previous summer when I was still married to Debbie. When everything seemed almost innocent. I say that I care about her, but I'm confused. I don't want either of us to die.

What I don't tell her is that I feel safer by her side than I do knowing she's out there lurking. They wouldn't have held her in jail very long for a Restraining Order violation, anyway. And if they spring her loose after a few days of lockdown, she'll come headhunting. It's a case where I'm keeping my friends close, but my enemies closer.

I'm not trying to fuck with her head. I just sense an explosion coming, and I want to avoid it.

My darling stalker spends the night with me. We fuck, but of course. And we fall asleep curled up together.

At around 4AM she wakes me up by saying, "I don't love you."

Huh?

"I don't love you."

Oh, really? This is the thanks I get for saving your ass from jail? Well, that's OK. I don't need you, anyway. I'll just call this chick in San Francisco I've been talking to.

"WHAT chick in San Francisco?"

I tell her about the Israeli college girl in the Bay Area.

And Anne's stripper friend who'd called me.
And the girl with pink hair at the coffee shop.
And the wigged-out bitch from Long Island.
And the one who dialed me from a pay phone in Oklahoma.
Bonnie and Linda from the karaoke bar.
And Mieko from the Farmhouse.
Lots of girls.
Lots of reasons I don't need Anne to survive.
She sits on the floor, melting into the carpet like the Wicked Witch of the West.
Suddenly she bolts up and runs into the bathroom. I follow her.
She grabs a pair of scissors and begins hacking at her shoulder-length hair. Chops it all down short and spiky. Fat clumps of black hair all over the bathroom floor. She picks up a cigarette lighter and tries burning the rest of her hair down to the scalp.
Hey, girl, I still have a Restraining Order against you. If you don't calm the fuck down, I'm calling the cops.
She runs past me into the living room.
Picks up a Chihuahua turd.
Puts it in her mouth.
Starts chewing.
Spits pieces of puppy poop in my face.
Says, "*That's* how much you've hurt me."
Wow. I must have hurt her bad.
So she must have been telling a lie when she woke me up. She *has* to love me. You can't chop off all your hair and eat dog shit if you don't love someone.

You don't love me, you don't worship my pussy the way that I worship your cock. You don't worship my features, anything about me....I really gave so much power to you at the beginning, and I really said, "I'm a piece of shit and you're the greatest thing that ever lived, and do what you will with me." And, um, even though we spent so much time together, you were still seeing other women, and you still want to see other women....
—6:01PM, May 19, 1998

It's cold and rainy almost every day in May. And Anne isn't taking her medication. She looks about ten years older than she did when I met her. Her new "haircut" frames her face in Frankensteinian derangement. We're both skinny, pale, and pockmarked from our year of chasing Death around in circles.
And yet we continue seeing each other. I figure that with the Restraining Order in place, maybe it'll work. Maybe she'll be afraid of going to jail. Maybe she'll leave when I ask her to. Maybe she

won't attack me anymore.

Maybe I'm a moron.

One morning in mid-May, I'm dropping her off at her apartment before I go to work. Naturally, we argue. And predictably, she lunges at me. I grab her wrists. I bend one wrist back until she squeals with pain. She agrees to leave. I take her apartment key off her key ring and give it back to her. It's over.

She starts walking away in the rain.

Anne!

She turns around.

I still love you, baby.

She walks to the car and hands me her key back.

Together again.

One night while over at my place she's reading "Women Who Love Too Much" (minus the cover) and flashes me a cartoon she'd scribbled on one of its pages. It's a drawing of her in a bridal gown, tears streaming down her face, with a cartoon balloon saying, "MARRY ME!"

On May 26th we celebrate our one-year anniversary. I buy her irises in honor of Iris the Teenaged Prostitute from *Taxi Driver*. She wears a pretty gold dress her friend had made. She gives me a card signed, "With all my love, sex, bite marks, and bruises—your ex-mistress." We rent a hot tub. I harpoon her with the dick in the steamy, bubbly suds. We stand naked in the dressing-room mirror, preening and laughing.

The next afternoon as I'm driving on my lunch break, a motorist runs a stop sign and totals my Ford Probe. The car in which we'd traipsed around Portland all year is dead. Smashed beyond recognition.

As I crawl out of my mangled auto, I scream, "Like my life isn't fucking complicated enough!"

I call a friend in LA and tell him what happened. He comments about how bad my luck has been in Portland. I say I'm going to stick around just to spite the town.

Debbie says the car crash is karma.

Anne says, "What a bitch!" and comes over to spend the night with me.

jim goad

⊱11⊰

My Last Day With Anne

IT SEEMS LIKE a nice day. The clouds which had constipated the sky for months are finally gone. The virgin sun holds a mild promise of hope.

In the morning I call my Okie lawyer friend to ask him some insurance questions about my crushed 'n' impotent automobile. He asks me if I'm still seeing Anne.

Yeah. In fact, she's sleeping in the other room.

"Well," he sighs, "I'll wear a black suit to your funeral."

I'm taking the day off from work. I have to file an accident report downtown with the Department of Motor Vehicles. I also have to get screened at the health clinic to make sure I didn't suffer a concussion when my forehead bonked against the windshield yesterday.

I put the Chihuahua in his small plastic carrier and bring him along with us.

I don't want him to be all alone.

Same reason I've hung out with Debbie after the divorce. I don't want her to be all alone.

It's one of the reasons I'm still with Anne. I don't want her to be all alone.

And I don't want to be alone, either. That should be obvious.

We have a minor argument at the DMV office. As we wait outside for a bus to the health clinic, she says we should break up if I still want to see other girls.

I smile at her. No skin off my ass. She isn't the only tuna-fish sandwich in the cafeteria.

The clinic is only four blocks from Debbie's house. Anne sits outside with the puppy while a wrinkly male physician flashes a light in my pupils.

No concussion.

We both have more errands to run. We hop on another bus. A big-assed mulatto broad with bushy black hair sits across the aisle from us.

"That's what I picture the Israeli girl from San Francisco looking like," she snaps at me.

I don't respond. She's picking another fight.

"Maybe when we get down to the Rose Quarter, we should split off and do our chores separately," she suggests.

I'm surprised. I thought we had planned to do everything together. But maybe she wants to be alone. So I shrug and say OK.

With that, she stands up and walks to the back of the bus. She grabs the hand railing, looking furious.

Do you want to tell me what the fuck this is all about?

She just stares straight ahead, nostrils flaring.

Five minutes later she sits down next to me again. "I'm not going to be with anyone who treats their dog better than they treat me," she growls.

I stare out the window and say nothing. She continues pissing and moaning and whimpering.

I can't believe she's starting an argument for no reason. It's not bad enough that my car's totaled—now I have to deal with this. Oh, what an annoying little gnat. A fat-faced, soul-sucking slug. I treat the dog better than you because he *is* better than you. Because he doesn't bite me. Or threaten to kill me. Because when he gives me affection, he doesn't demand my life in return. If I could teach him how to suck dick, I wouldn't need you for anything. Isn't it obvious?

Finally, I turn to her and calmly say,

You're not the one.

"WHAT did you say?"

You're not the one for me. You never were. So let's just end it.

Her face starts shaking like water ready to boil.

She begins walloping me with both fists. Maybe a dozen times.

I look her straight in the eye and say,

Hitting me isn't going to make you the one.

She stands up to get better leverage and resumes punching my face. Socking my skull. Grabbing my hair.

I beg for someone to pull her off me.

"I'm not touching her," says one woman. "She seems crazy!"

Seems?

Anne bites into my elbow as hard as she can, trying to rip out a chunk of flesh with her doggie teeth. She digs in deep.

"Girl, you better stop!" someone shouts at her.

"But he's given me ten black eyes!" Anne howls. "He's very abusive!"

"Well, we see who's hitting who *now!*" says a middle-aged woman, clutching onto her bags for safety.

Everyone on the bus is watching. And laughing. It's always funny when a woman hits a man, even when she's giving him scars. Someone suggests that we go on the Jerry Springer show.

When the bus pulls into the Rose Quarter, Anne's one of the first to get off, separated from me by a wall of sweaty bodies. As I exit, an older, Uncle Remus-looking black man shakes my hand.

"You kept your cool," he says, nodding appreciatively. "I admire that."

Gosh, thanks. But I'm not gonna let her get away with it.

Anne's sprinting away from the bus as fast as she can. I give chase, swinging the Chihuahua in his carrier. He squeals every time my boots hit the concrete. Poor baby. But I'm not gonna let the bitch get away.

I catch up with her. She trips and falls against a cement wall, landing on her ass. She stays on the ground, staring into the distance as if smelling something foul. It looks as if all her inner rot has finally sprouted on her face. Invisible fumes of ugliness roll off her body. She's a pink-skinned garbage bag filled with human waste. A crumpled ball of shit-smeared toilet paper sprawled on a city sidewalk.

Standing over her, I say,

Everyone was laughing at you. You're pathetic. I win, you lose. And don't ever forget it.

I begin walking back home with a huge open gash on my right elbow from where she'd bitten me.

I filed the Restraining Order only three weeks ago. And this is already the second time she's attacked me since it was filed.

I don't want the cops showing up at my apartment again, so I walk two blocks away to an ice-cream parlor and call them from a pay phone.

Hey, I have a Restraining Order against this girl. Yeah, she hit me again. Yeah, I want you to arrest her. Yeah, I'm at this ice-cream parlor on NE Weidler Street. Yeah, I'll wait for you.

While waiting, I call Anne's number to see if she's made it home yet. No answer. But a minute later the pay phone rings. She had dialed Star 69 and called me back.

Hello?

"What are you doing, asshole?"

I'm waiting for the cops to come. You violated the Restraining Order by hitting me.

"Fuck you! You're just trying to stall me so they can bust me!"

She hangs up before I can answer. She doesn't pick up when I call back. She probably fled her apartment to avoid the cops.

I stare at the phone. Sending to jail would only make her a tragic martyr in her sick game of love. After all, she begged me to send her to jail more than once. Why give her what she wants?

I call the police again and tell them to forget about it.

I've made a lot of mistakes in my life. That right there was the biggest one.

I walk back to my place and dial Anne's mom. Anne had once griped to her mom that I wasn't suffering in our romance like she was. "If he's been with you for all this time," came mom's response, "I'm sure he's done his share of suffering."

I tell her about the bus attack. I ask her to tell Anne that the cops aren't looking for her and that she can return to her apartment. I also ask her to tell Anne to stay away from me. Her mom says the whole thing isn't healthy for either of us and that we should stay away from one another.

I leave a voicemail message for Anne.

Don't worry, the cops aren't coming. But stay the fuck away. I see through you and your little pious ballerina act. You're the least ethical person I've ever known. The only one who can feel morally outraged when a weed dealer won't front you pot. Or when the asthmatic Okie zinester fanboy whom you've been squeezing for money doesn't send you a second check quickly enough. I'm better-looking than you, I'm smarter than you, more talented than you, and I'll be more famous than you. I don't need to send you to jail. My revenge is in being superior. So stick that in your sloppy pussy. Nyah, nyah, nyah.

Feeling triumphant, I walk a few blocks to a car-rental agency so I'll have some wheels with which to cruise the hillbilly bars for tooth-less snatches. Ominously, the half-retarded ex-gang member who used to be Anne's roommate is now a car-rental clerk there. He's a chunky, slow-lidded white boy who looks like Barney Rubble. We exchange dull, thudding, wary pleasantries. Within minutes I'm cruising P-Town's streets in a new-vinyl-smelling Ford Escort.

When I arrive home, Anne has left a string of snotty voicemail messages. The first lasts five minutes, all the way up to the beep which warns that time is about to expire. After the beep, she tosses in this charming nugget:

"And I wish you had died in that car accident yesterday."

It's the first of five times she'll directly allude to my death today—four times on phone messages, and once on the Internet.

ANNE ATTACKS:

I told your wife not to trust you, and that you're going to talk shit behind her back up until the day she dies and after she dies and before she dies....And just like I said on the bus, I kinda woke up and just punched you in the face about ten times because you deserved it, you fucking prick....Your karma is going to come back to you tenfold, man. You've got so much shit coming to you....Your ego is through the roof, and the day that your wife dies is going to be a cold day in hell for you, buddy. And you know what else, too? I'm going to stick around on this earth just like I decided for my father, because I'm fourteen, *fifteen* fucking years younger than you, and no matter what, I'm going to take care of myself, too, man, I'm going to outlive you, man, and I'm going to dance on your fucking grave.

—*3:59PM*

Better-looking than I am? Oh, my God, have I told you about what I really think about your looks? Let's bring out the truth here, because you're starting to make me sick over the past couple of weeks....You have zits all over your face, you have a hook nose, you look like a lizard, your skin is disgusting, your breath stank today, and you're disgusting.

—*4:02PM*

...More and more you repulse me. But mostly it's your inside, and your attitude, and you remind me of my father in a lot of ways. You're just sick. I can't wait 'til the day you die. I feel nothing for you.

—*4:04PM*

Um, you can do everything you want, by the way, and it still won't shut me up. You ain't going to shut me up, no matter what. And I'm going to do tons of zines about you....You can send me to jail, and I'll get out, and I'll still do my zines, and you are going to be humiliated.... You're UGLY on the inside-out and your karma's gonna come back and you're gonna age, you're gonna wither away, you're gonna die in the ground.

—*4:06PM*

I COUNTERATTACK:
Jesus, Anne, you know, do whatever you want. Your obsession with me is just going to prove you love me....You're skinny as a rail, you just look psychotic, you look like an ugly, drowned rat with your hair cut off...You cut your hair off for me, I never would for you. Write all you fucking want, I got the proof, dumbshit....And when I said you're not the one, that's why you freaked out. Go ahead and write whatever you want—I got everything on my side.

—*4:37PM*

Oh, God, what does it feel like to lose? Just to have everything crushed? All your hopes of marriage and babies, all the hopes that I never had. You say you want to talk about me? That all fucking comes out. And like I said, I got the evidence. You don't have shit on me. I never pledged devotion or worshiped your body or left any message saying those things. Because, let's face it, I fucking don't. You're the one who wanted the eternal life with me, I never wanted it with you. I was never in love with you. Oh, well....Otherwise, hey—you have a pleasant life.

—*4:38PM*

Oh yeah, I kept color Xeroxes of your vagina pictures. And yeah, since we're getting everything out in the open, I always did find it disgusting. The lips really are too big, and they hang too much. And it does have an unpleasant odor....You might want to check into that...Your tits are really kind of small, and your face is pretty ugly. I mean, it really is. I guess you made up for it in attitude, but you do have an ugly face. The things you said about my looks, look, I could give a fuck. I'm not as body-obsessed as you are. I do all right, as you know, and as you know I've got about twelve hours of tapes of you saying how much you love me more than I love you, how big my dick is, how great-looking I am....You might want to comb your archives looking for me saying anything remotely similar about you....Never loved you, fucked around behind—ah, there are *still* women I haven't told you about....The one I'm going out with tonight has a much better body. And I *will* be thinking of you while I'm ramming it into her.

—4:53PM

Ugly little skank girl, trying to prove she's not a dyke, and it's so obvious she is. Because you really are unattractive. What else...hair transplants...big fucking deal, I really don't care about that. But you do care about your cunt, that's why you asked for the pictures back. Good thing I made copies, huh? But again, I really don't care about you that much to do something like that. I *will* say some things in my defense if you come out talking shit....And you know what? You look about forty-five in the morning light. I think it's all catching up with you, Anne.

—4:57PM

You know what else? Your father won. Because you're still pissed at him, and he doesn't care about you. Oh, by the way, last couple months, too, whenever I was fucking you? I had to think of somebody else to get into it. Cheers!

—5:12PM

Yeah, in a year, maybe five, I don't know if I'll be in Portland, but I'll be somewhere, and I'll have some beautiful, much more womanly—'cause let's face it, you look like a fuckin' boy— more buxom, bigger tits, nice firm ass—woman with me. We'll be walking somewhere arm-in-arm, and I'll step over some crabby, crusty, skanky-looking little homeless girl—it'll be you. You'll ask for change [and] realize it's me. And I'll look over to her and go, "It lives!"

—5:27PM

Yeah, I never read *Men Who Love Too Much*. And whatever happens from now on, both you and I know that.

—5:38PM

What a goofy pair o' spaced-out lovebirds we are, eh?

I drop off the keys to my totaled car at the body shop. The mechanic asks me about the gash on my elbow. I tell him I got it from "my asshole girlfriend."

I drive to Debbie's. Take her out for Vietnamese food. We smoke a little weed, go for a little drive. She says she has a hunch that Anne and I will get together again. And I say no, it's over.

But it isn't. Not quite.

Part of me is a romantic sap.

Part of me can close my eyes and pretend I'm not really crashing into a wall.

Part of me wants everyone to be happy.

Part of me should worry about my own happiness.

I never understood why you had to hate someone to break up with them. I can't look at things as all good or all bad. I get fixated on gray areas. And that's why breakups are difficult for me. Why they're confusing. Because, as bad as it gets, I have trouble blocking out the good times.

I don't want another bitter ending. Another breakup. Another failure. Another death.

So, puppy in tow, I knock on Anne's apartment door at around 7:30PM. No answer. She was never gone this long. I start getting nervous. Maybe she killed herself. Or maybe she's out somewhere, plotting to kill me.

I go home and doody myself up for a skag-saloon cunt hunt. I wash my nuts and armpits. Throw on my typical pussy-snatchin' outfit: black denim jeans, black denim button-down shirt, black denim jacket, black engineer boots. And that burning look in my steely gray eyes. Johnny Cash as a serial killer.

First I hit an Internet café for a hot mug of black thunder and a peek at my e-mail. I also check Anne's e-mail. There's a message from earlier in the evening. It confirms her registration with a service enabling her to post public messages on Usenet. I know exactly what that means.

Fucking whore. At the same time I'd dropped by her apartment with the puppy trying to make amends, she was at a computer keyboard, broadening the theater of war from private voicemail to a public electro-forum. She was always escalating things.

I drive to a cum-bucket karaoke bar where I'd had luck with female life forms in the past. But it's a Thursday night. Zero action. All the low-rent honky-tonk honeys must be at home, burning the crabs off their muffs with blowtorches.

I dial Anne from a pay phone situated between the bathrooms and the Chinese kitchen. The smell of greasy egg rolls clashes against that of crank-tainted piss. I yell into the phone receiver over the loudly pumping karaoke music:

Saw your DejaNews posting registration thing....If you want to go on alt.zines or wherever talking shit about me, I would fucking *welcome* it, because I'm a *master* at that type of shit, and I would *destroy* you in a fucking war. I have so much shit on you, it's hilarious. Every phone call, every pathetic, pleading thing is going to be out there for millions to see. Dumb, ugly bitch...

—10:42PM

I drive to a fifties-themed rock 'n' roll bar hoping to bag some mid-dle-aged housewife with raccoon mascara and a husky ashtray voice. But this place is even deader than the last. They're sweeping up the floors at 11PM. I call Anne again. This time she answers.

"Hello?"

Hi.

"WHAT do YOU want?"

I love you.

"FUCK off!" [click]

Restless and frantic, I head downtown and call her from another pay phone. She says her landlord had left a note demanding she see him immediately. She was sure I must have caused a scene or done some damage when I'd dropped by her apartment earlier.

I try telling her I hadn't. She screams "BULLSHIT!" and hangs up the phone again.

I call back, but her line goes to voicemail. I say I had come by with the puppy trying to make up, and that was it. I say I'll call back in five minutes after she listens to the message.

Instead of calling back, I drive over to her building. I knock on her door. When she opens it, she's crying.

"Jim, please, you have to leave! If the landlord sees you here, he'll evict me!"

OK. Can I call you from the phone up the street?

"Yeah, yeah..." Her face is moist and swollen from crying. When I call, she's still crying. She agrees to meet me up the street. And she's still crying when she gets there.

"Jim, I know that part of us loves each other, but if we keep going on this way, one of us is going to kill the other."

Does it have to end like that?

"Remember last summer when we said we were going to hell for what we did to Debbie? Well, I think we're on our way."

I ask her what she posted on the Internet. Two things: One about my hair transplants, the other about my nose job.

Oh, God, why did you do that?

"It's because you're a rock. I was never able to break you. You hurt me so bad romantically, and I couldn't hurt you that way, so I had to find another way to do it. What are you worried about, anyway? Nobody will believe me. I have *zero* credibility."

I feel deflated. What is this thing with love and destruction? My parents said they loved me, yet they wanted me destroyed. They knew I was smarter than them, but they didn't want to see me rise above them. Same with Debbie.

And Anne. Her biggest fear is of being publicly humiliated like *Carrie*. And here she is, pulling a *Carrie* on me. She says that she stopped after typing the second post because she realized she was starting to look bitter and desperate.

Tomorrow night, Anne's going to start a job as a caregiver which requires her to stay at a handicapped person's house from Friday night to Sunday night. She's sure that I'm going to cheat on her. Earlier in the day, news broke that comedian Phil Hartman's wife had killed him and herself because he planned to leave her. Anne calls it justifiable homicide.

Mostly we're silent. At one point while we're sitting, she sidles over to me and holds my hand. And I let her.

We're sick.

I check the clock in the jewelry-store window. It's close to 2AM. I have to wake up at 7AM for work. I'd better get home. We start walking. I'm a few feet behind her. Just as she's about to enter her building, I hold out my hand to her.

Come with me.

She places a hand over her chest and gasps, like, "Be still my beating heart—he still cares."

She asks me why I want her to come with me.

Because we're sick and I love you.

I suggest we head to the east side of town to an all-night diner for breakfast. We drive past the print shop where I work.

"J.G., if you broke up with me," she says, smiling, "I was planning on buying a gun and blowing you away when you walked out of work."

Ahh, you would have found a way to fuck it up. You're the world's dumbest criminal.

And we laugh about it. I'm actually chuckling at a death threat which is utterly serious.

I *told* you we're sick.

I order an omelet. She has garlic bread. She seems happy we've made up.

We get back to my place a little after 3AM, because Howard Stern is just coming on the radio. As we sit on the carpet smoking a joint, she says that we're funnier than Howard. She tells me her dream is for us to live in a Manhattan penthouse and have our own radio show.

Even now, she has hope for a future together with me.

As I shove my cock inside her, this odd infantile voice leaks out of her, not faked at all but coming from some personality buried deep within:

"Love me, love me, please love me! I'm just a little girl, and no one has ever loved me!"

I never heard this voice before. Then she says, in her normal voice,

"Ha, ha, you know me, and that I like to have sex a lot, and that I can't really help it."

As I'm pushing and pushing inside her, she asks if I want to have threesomes with other girls.

Rather than saying yes, I ask,

Is that what you want?

"No, but I want whatever will keep you happy."

What about you? Do you want other dicks in you?

"No, I just want you, and I want to hold onto you."

Right before we pass out, I mention that Debbie has a premonition that she'll suffer a major cancer relapse by Christmas.

"Oh, God," she says quietly.

I close my eyes and fall asleep.

Love and death have always been intertwined in my life, and I could never untie the knots quickly enough.

There was one night shortly after I met Anne when I told her that everything is hopeless. That everyone dies. That there are no happy endings. That love never lasts.

She cried and cried. Was I sure?

Yeah.

I didn't want it to be true, but it was.

She asked me if we could at least pretend it was some other way. And so we tried pretending for a while.

About a year before I met Anne, I decided I was going to separate from Debbie. I filled out an application to rent a trailer about eighty miles east of Portland. I then drove up a remote mountain road covered in snow, even though it was June. A road sign pointed to a natural ice cave buried deep in the forest. A series of creaky wooden stairs led down into the cave's mouth. It was cold and dark down there, with the merest hint of a howling wind. I didn't like being down there. It felt like death, and I wasn't ready to die. But I knew that when I did, it would feel something like this—chilly and lightless and alone. And the "alone" part was what scared me the most. I rushed up the stairs and back into my car. As I was coasting down an idyllic mountain road, past simple wooden homes with plastic flowers planted in the front yard, I spotted a graying old couple holding hands and walking by the roadside.

They were near death, but they weren't alone.

I drove straight back home to Debbie and made up with her.

And I guess this is why I kept coming back to Anne. Even if she killed me, I wouldn't die alone. At least she'd be there, pulling the trigger.

I was asleep for less than two hours. I'm not sure if I dreamed or what floated through my mind, but I wake up feeling very angry with Anne. I have the feeling that I've been sleeping next to a human hand grenade.

You can't build a mansion atop a toxic waste dump.

You can't paint the Mona Lisa with a handful of shit.

Was I crazy thinking this would work?

She makes it impossible to get along with her. If I show any strength, I'm an egotistical asshole. If I display any weakness, she uses it against me.

I throw on my clothes in half a minute.

Get up.

"Huh? What?"

Get the fuck out of bed. I'm taking you home. It's over.

"No, Jim, please don't do this. Let's go back to sleep. I'll leave in the morning."

You can walk home, or I'll drive you home. What'll it be?

She gets up and is soon dressed.

There's been too much damage. There's no trust between us. I'm tired of the mood swings. The attacks. The threats. The jealousy. The insanity. It wasn't what you posted on the Internet. It was your intent. You'll do anything to try and hurt me. Debbie acted as if she forgave me for cheating on her, but she never did. You acted as if you forgave me for sleeping with Darcy, but you never did. I'm the only honest one out of the three of us—I can't forgive you for this. So let's go.

She doesn't say a word the whole way over to her place.

As I drive, I say something like:

Yeah, you and Debbie are real feminists. Real credits to your gender.

She's so full of self-pity, she has to exaggerate her victimization to get the sympathy she needs. And you're the rottenest human being I've ever met. You're violent, you're a liar, an egomaniac, a scam artist, a user of people, someone who rips off her own mother—you're not a feminist.

I also say this:

Between you and me, whatever is said or done in the future, and whatever you try to do to me, just remember that I didn't love the little girl who needed love.

⚡12⚡

Roadkill

SPRINGTIME. **DAWN'S BLUE** light yawns through dead Portland streets. And I'm throwing you out of my life. Finally.

We pull up to your building. I throw the car in park but leave the motor running. And I say...

I'm going to get a girlfriend who isn't so fucking crazy. So just go.

And you say...

"Nooooo!"

You pounce at me, scratching my face. I grab your skinny, trembling wrists. Those bulging goldfish eyes look straight into mine.

With foam flying from your fat lips, you say...

"You'll *never* get rid of me! I'll write tons of shit about you! People'll be laughing at you—it'll be like *Carrie!*"

Because I'm restraining your arms, you try kicking me with your big-ass glam-rock heels. We struggle a few seconds until a black guy...a lone pedestrian...walks up to my window.

You stop trying to hit me.

I release your arms.

"Are you guys OK?"

And I say...

Yeah.

I look over at you, and you're nodding, Yes, Mister—we're OK.

End of fight.

I watch him walk into your building.

But as I turn to face you, your girlie fist clocks me dead on the nose. I grab your arms again.

As we're rocking back and forth, I see myself in the rear-view mirror. I'll remember that freeze-frame for the rest of my life:

My wild eyes. A crescent-shaped scratch on my cheek. And blood dripping from my nose.

My blood. My life essence. You're trying to take my life away.

And then, I swear to God, I hear it—this raw prehistoric roar from deep within.

I rip the rear-view mirror from its mounting and throw it in the back seat.

Bitch.

I was trying to be nice.

I was driving you home.

If I wanted to be a dick, I would've made you walk home.

But you never left without a fight.

There was the time you wouldn't leave my apartment—and I tried calling the cops—and you ripped my phone out of the wall.

Another time when it took my landlord to finally force you out of my pad, and when he did, you smashed my car windshield with a neighbor's shovel. And when the police came, you lied and told them I raped you.

The time I threw you out of my place and you walked right back in.

The time I tried throwing your keys out of my car to make you leave.

The time I tried throwing your wallet out of my car to make you leave.

The time I took your purse and backpack out of my car and dropped them on the sidewalk to make you leave.

The time I took everything you owned out of my car and piled it on the roadside to make you leave.

All the times I had to fucking push you out of my car because you wouldn't leave when I asked you.

All the times you lunged at my face when I was only asking you to leave.

Like this time.

You won't leave, eh?

So let's go for a little ride.

The tires scream like a woman being attacked.

CHORUS:
You say....
"Nooooo!"
And I say...
Yesssss!

(repeat chorus 3x)

Oh, what—now all of a sudden you *want* to leave?
Too late.

You already had your chance.

Get back in here.

Get the fuck back in here.

Come back.

Come on back to me.

C'mere, little girl.

Stay with me, my love.

Where're ya goin'?

Poopsie, I'm catching a draft—close the door.

Look, sweetie, you'll hurt yourself if you jump while the car's moving.

Get back in this car so I can rip your fucking head off your spine.

Gotcha.

BAM! BAM! BAM!

DON'T try that again. And if you honk the horn one more time, I'll bite your fucking hand off.

You know, I'm getting mixed signals from you.

You said you were out for the blood.

You wanted to destroy every living cell in my body.

You threatened to crush me.

To stab me a million times.

To blow my head out of this fucking universe.

You said you'd take it further than I would—all the way into jail.

So what happened?

You said one of us was going to wind up dead.

I ain't the one.

I thought you wanted a Bad Boy—we haven't changed our mind, have we? What was that you said about me being a pathetic wannabe? A big fat poseur? Remember all the times you scoffed and said it didn't hurt when I hit you? Well, how about now? Are we feeling anything yet?

Do you recall telling me that I fuck as hard as I write? Well, I *punch* like I write, too, don't I?

Hard.

You said that all of life, no matter how painful, was only performance art. So tell me—how do you rate *this* performance? Your face is the canvas. My fist is the brush.

I'm taking it where you had only threatened to take it. Somewhere beyond satire and pop culture. Somewhere with zero comfort margin. A place that you can't handle, but I can.

Up to the hills.

Remember we used to fuck there?

Hard.

Now you're going to die there.

Hard.

This is the control that you couldn't wield over me.

This is the fear that you failed to make me feel.

I knew you secretly enjoyed when I'd get suicidal. When I said you'd be doing me a favor if you killed me. Think of all the times you wished me dead.

Earlier today, you said you'd dance on my grave.

That was after you hit me.

And bit me.

After I called the cops, then told them to forget about it.

After I forgave you.

And after I forgave you, you said you'd dance on my grave.

You aren't very nice.

I knew you were serious about killing me. I was so dead inside, I didn't care. I wanted to die. You came into my life at a time when I didn't care if you gave me AIDS or ambushed me with a 9mm slug. I didn't care. I allowed your jagged bitch fangs to gnaw upon my soft suicidal underbelly, and I just didn't care.

Now I care.

Deeply.

I don't want to die anymore.

Seeing my blood—my own life seeping out of me—changed everything. That little red trickle cured my vision. I want to live.

Thank you for punching me.

Now I'm returning the favor.

Each punch is my way of saying I won't let you kill me. Each punch is life-affirming. The experts are wrong—this violence has nothing to do with keeping you down. It's about keeping me alive.

So you say...

"I won't tell anybody that you did this—I'll tell them a black pimp beat me up!"

And I say...

You must think I'm stupid.

BOOM!

Pignosed little slit. Pussy-farting hog. What a high-pitched squeal you emit. Such a desperate, mouselike eek. And I thought that the Hysterical Woman was just a cruel myth. Scream your fat little head off. No one can hear you on this lonely mountain road. All this lush Northwestern greenery cushions the sound. Screaming isn't going to help, but please—don't stop screaming.

Scream, like your cunt ancestors have all the way back to the caves. It's just the two of us, honey, suspended over this lovely twilit city. And here you are, stuck in this speeding car. This torture box.

Did you know that it was a man who invented the automobile?

So you say...

"I'm a bitch, I know, I'm a bitch, I deserve this!"

And I agree with you.

BOOM!

I'm turning a bitch into a lady, into someone who says "please." I'm smearing my manhood all over you. Cock ruling cunt, the way Father Nature intended.

This is why men rule—right here, what's happening between you and me—this is why we rule. It isn't pornography, no patriarchal conspiracy, no bedtime stories such as Evil and Sexism. It's this fist. And if you had this fist, you'd be in charge. But you don't...so you aren't.

And you say...

"Please, God, don't do this!"

So I say...

I AM God.

BOOM!

Are you starting to catch my drift?

I never cried a tear for you.

Never wanted to marry you.

Didn't want the baby.

Didn't want your body.

Or what you call a mind.

Never wanted any of the things you wanted from me.

Yeah, doll, I love you so much, I'm pounding your brains out of your ears.

You said that I hurt you romantically. Yes, I did. This is another way to hurt you.

I broke your heart.

Now I'm breaking your nose.

Wow, you're bleeding a lot. With each lightning jab, the blood sprays from those piggie nostrils onto the windshield. And onto the door. And onto the seats. And onto your clothes. Beautiful red droplets. And that big purple bubble swelling up near your eye? My, that's nasty.

You look like one of those pictures in my magazine.

Better let you go...

You walk away crying.

I drive away laughing.

When you get to the hospital, I want you to take a long look in the mirror—that is, with the one eye which isn't swollen shut.

See that?

I never loved you.

The detectives will snap photos of you flattened out on that hospital bed, your face demolished. You looked like a fly squashed on a windshield. A roach crushed underfoot. Like a fucking train hit you. Roadkill. Smashed and destroyed, leveled by my life force.

Rejected.

Blood was streaming down your cheek. They kept wiping it away, but it kept pouring out of you.

We had quite a messy breakup, didn't we, darling?

I haven't regretted it for a second. Well, I sort of feel bad that I had to use my strong arm to drive.

Something tells me I'll get in a lot of trouble for this ten-minute joyride.

Was it worth it?

Absolutely.

For the fear in your eyes.

The fear in your eyes...

⚡13⚡

I'm a Lonesome Fugitive

I **FEEL SPECTACULARLY** alive. And joyously alone. Breathless. Shaking. Electric. Hot blood catapults through my veins. A thousand violins play out of tune in my head.

What a peak experience that was. I administered a strong dose of the ultraviolence. Left her crying and bleeding in the hills. Didn't even give her bus money to get home.

I don't feel bad for her. I feel nothing for her. She's just a bloody piece of meat. I hope she's in a lot of pain. I'm not worried about her safety. Not at all. Only mine.

I don't feel that what I did was wrong. But I have a strong suspicion that others might not feel that way.

I shoot down those mountain roads and back toward civilization. I take the serpentine curves quickly enough to crash. I carom around those twisting black ribbons like the Olympic luge team.

I drive out of the hills. Over the bridge. And straight to a coin-operated car wash.

Antiseptic wet-naps.

High-powered vacuum shampoo.

Blood really spoils the look and feel of new upholstery. Tell-tale red leopard spots on the dashboard. Windshield. Seats. Steering wheel. Over here. Down there. Under there. Dried rust-colored flecks on my black denim shirt.

Scrubbing, scrubbing.

Wiping away all the memories of our time together. All the traces of our uniquely passionate relationship. Of that bloody wipeout up on Skyline Boulevard.

I drive across town to my apartment. Circle the block to check for cop cars. It's clear.

My landlord stops me as I run up the stairs.

"Did you guys get in another fight?"

Yeah.

"The police were just here. I told them I didn't know anything. I went into your apartment and hid your pot pipe and a pair of handcuffs. They're under the sink."

Thanks.

I grab a change of clothes. Take the pipe and handcuffs. Scoop up the little embryonic Chihuahua sitting confused in the morning light.

At this point in my life, Washington seems like such a nicer place to be than Oregon. I don't know where I'm headed. I just can't sit still.

I cross the state line. Pull up to a shattered old phone booth in an abandoned parking lot. I call my Oklahoma lawyer buddy.

Look, uhh, something fucked-up happened about an hour ago. We got into an argument. She slugged me. I freaked out. Drove her up to the hills and beat the FUCK out of her. If I kept going, I could have killed her. I was that close.

"I don't know what to tell you besides this—don't you ever contact that girl again."

Hey, I may be retarded, but I don't have Down syndrome.

Later—much later—he tells me I sounded scared. That it seemed as if I'd been to a place where few people ever go.

I drive a little farther. Stop at a convenience store for coffee, rolling papers, and phone cards. I call Debbie and ask her if the cops had been by.

"No."

I tell her what happened.

I'm in Washington now, Debbie. I might just keep driving and not look back, but then I'd never get to see you again. And I want to see you, especially if you get sick again. I want to take care of you. I'll call you later.

I'm back in the car, hurtling up Interstate 5, the flat, boring strip from Portland to Seattle, a greenish-gray blur to either side of me, road signs ticking by like beats of my heart. I hit Tacoma by noon. Chewed-up, smoke-belching, chemical-coated Tacoma.

I call the print shop where I work. Police detectives had visited the office, looking for me. I call Debbie. Three cops had come by, guns drawn, searching every corner of her house for me. Anne told the police I was probably hiding at Debbie's. Anne had also called Debbie from the hospital. Said her face was mangled and bloated. Said she didn't understand how Debbie could forgive me. Said the cops would issue a fifty-state warrant for me if I tried to flee. Said I was going to be charged with kidnapping.

If you move someone more than three feet against their will in Oregon, you've kidnapped them. Three feet. Seven-and-a-half years in prison minimum.

I tell Debbie I don't think they'd extradite me if I fled. But I want to see her again. What should I do?

"Come back, Jimmy."

I buy some cotton balls and hydrogen peroxide at a Tacoma supermarket. Dip the cotton in the peroxide. Dab it on my cuts. Watch the white foam fizzle. And then I head back to Portland.

The clouds have returned. Massive blackish anvils in the sky. Hard, hard rain. Windowpanes of clear liquid falling to earth and shattering on the freeway.

Forty miles out of Portland, I pull into a roadside diner and run up to a pay phone. I try Anne's number. It's already disconnected. I call her mom.

Ellen, I'll be brief. I'm sorry about what happened with Anne, but if she's going to press charges, I have no choice but to press charges against her for Restraining Order violations, the axe-handle attack—

—click. She hung up.

Re-entering Oregon feels like crossing into enemy territory. But Debbie's moldy little house is a sanctuary. I show her the scratches on my face, which are already starting to scab over. I show her the gash on my elbow. Blood is still encrusted in my nose. I shove a peroxide-soaked Q-tip in one nostril. It slides in white and comes out red. I ask her to take pictures of my cuts. In one photo, my pale face is shrouded in blackness. There's a haunted deadness in my eyes, like I'd seen something I was never supposed to see.

Debbie gives me the business card of a detective who wants me to call him. I don't want them to trace the call to her house, so I drive to a nearby pay phone.

Yeah, it's Jim Goad. You wanted me to call you?

"Well, are you going to turn yourself in, or do I have to hunt you down like a dog?"

I want to talk to a lawyer.

"All right. Be that way."

I will. You have a nice day.

I fall asleep on Debbie's couch like a houseguest.

The next morning I'm up early, flipping through the Yellow Pages for lawyers. I never realized there were so many attorneys who want to help me. Happy lawyers with nice clothes who really like me and wish to be my friend. They handle all felony cases. Murder. Drugs. Sex crimes. Forget the rest—you need the best. 24-hour hotline. I will fight for your rights. 20 years' experience.

I call one friend who gets me in touch with another friend who puts me in contact with a chipper-sounding female lawyer. She tells me not to talk to the cops. Kidnapping's a serious charge. And if you actually beat the girl up, that's more charges. Come into her office on Monday, and we'll go to the cops together.

Oh, good. I don't feel like spending the weekend in the cee-ment jungle, waiting to see a judge. And once they see all the dirt I have on my accuser, they'll throw the whole thing out. I have a few arrests on my record, but no convictions. I'll get probation at worst.

Temporary relief.

Until I have to step outside again. I need to get more clothes from my apartment and do more laundry.

I peer out the front-door peephole before leaving. No cops.

But I know that they're out there. Looking for me. Coming for me. They want me.

And it's not always good to feel wanted.

On the road, I tense up every time a cop car skims by me. I'm playing a game of Tag with every police car in Portland.

And I'm "it."

Each squad car is a big grinning cat looking for this mouse. Waiting to trap me under its paw.

Queasy feeling like jellied soap floating in my stomach. That old childhood dread when my parents were chasing me and I knew they'd hit me when they caught up.

I'm listening to a radio show. The host says, "If you can't do the time, don't do the crime."

Oh, shut the fuck up.

But the cop cars just whizz by me. Nobody stops me.

And Saturday night I fall asleep on the couch again.

Early Sunday morning I'm bright-eyed, bushy-tailed, and paranoid. I need to fetch more clothes from my car. I warily walk the few blocks to where I've parked. As I'm walking back, a police cruiser rolls past me at about ten miles an hour. The bearded boar who's driving stares dead into my eyes.

I detour a few blocks and head back to Debbie's from another direction. I peek around the corner to check if any squad cars are parked outside her house. Nothing. It must have been a coincidence.

Most of Anne's telephoned death threats are still etched on the phone company's voicemail database, but they aren't yet committed to tape. I figure that if the police were to hear her bloody recriminations, they'd know why I did what I did. It would place my actions in a meaningful context.

I head down to Debbie's basement. I pry open a rusty old cylindrical pretzel tin containing used stereo and phone equipment. I untangle yards and yards of spaghetti wires. Pull out an old answering machine. Rig it to the phone. Dial my voicemail number and try recording Anne's messages. I play back the tape. It's blank.

I unearth another old answering machine. Place the proper plugs in the proper sockets. Try recording the messages again.

No luck.

I rush out to a department store and buy a new answering machine which the saleslady assures me will do the job. I drive back to Debbie's. Plug it in. Try recording again.

I play back the tape.

Blank.

MOTHERFUCKER!

On Friday and Saturday, I felt as if I'd been slingshot through time. But Sunday's becoming one of those nightmares where everything drags along in slow motion.

I run back to the car and head for Radio Shack. Merle Haggard's playing on my tape deck:

Now I'm a hunted fugitive with just two ways/
Outrun the law or spend my life in jail.

At Radio Shack, there are two customers in line ahead of me.

The clerk is a sheepish middle-aged guy far too old to hold such an ignoble position. His first client is an older woman who'd look more at home in Miami Beach than in North Portland—terry-cloth shorts, varicose grapevines, oodles of makeup, teased hair, jewelry, and a goofy smirk. She and the clerk are going through agonizingly slow paces in filling out a credit application. It's like watching heated caramel slowly drip from a wooden ladle.

I'm pacing back and forth on the scuffed linoleum floor. Finally I butt in and ask,

What do you have that can record voicemail messages onto tape?

Eyebrows raised through his horn-rimmed glasses, the clerk points to a pack of gadgets and says, "Uh, over there—I think."

I rifle through the rack's items without a clue as to what I need. The clerk eventually glides over and proves to be as clueless as I am. We finally figure out that I'll need a basic cassette recorder hooked up to some doodad which activates the recorder when you pick up the phone.

Wonderful. Let's ring it all up. Hey, where's the power supply? It doesn't come with a power supply? DC 9-volt?

"Hmm, there's none on the racks. That's strange. Let me look in the back, sir."

Jesus fucking Christ. Hurry, hurry, hurry.

Futzing and fumbling, I rip what I've already purchased out of the boxes and start assembling the parts right on the front counter. The Radio Jackoff finally returns with the power supply.

Look, I don't mean to come off impatient, but if you knew the circum-

stances, you'd understand.

He rings me up. I grab the bag, scoot out the door, and sprint across the sunny street into my car.

Right as I crank the ignition, two police cruisers zoom up the street and block my way. The bearded lawman who'd stared into my eyes earlier in the morning points a pistol at my face. I can see down the barrel.

My transmission is already in reverse, so I reach down and throw it into park. To a cop, it might have looked as if I was reaching for a gun. I'm unaware that Anne has told 911 I'd probably be violent with police if they tried to arrest me. That little move for the shifter could've easily gotten me killed.

I lift my hands and surrender. Beard Boy opens the car door, cuffs me, and throws me in his back seat.

"Good job," says a gray-haired cop to Beard Boy. It's hot outside. Sweat begins beading on my forehead. Tucked into the sun visor above the cop's steering wheel is a printout of my mug shot from when Anne smashed my windshield and we both went to jail. I guess they had a warrant for me. After fifteen minutes of radio dispatching and paperwork, Beard Boy drives me to the Sheriff's station.

I'm tossed into a spacious, airy cell and am informed that a detective will be in to see me within the hour. I sit handcuffed on a cold concrete bench. After forty-five minutes, the detective appears. He looks like the Grinch that Stole Christmas.

"Mr. Goad?

Yes.

"Hi, I'm Detective Little. You have the right to remain silent—"

—I know, and I'm going to exercise that right.

"But that way, I don't get to hear your side of the story."

I'm not talking without my lawyer present.

The Grinch shrugs. "All right—you're being booked on Kidnap I and Assault I....ship him downtown."

⚡14⚡
State of Oregon
v.
James Thaddeus Goad

YOU CAN SEE it in my mug shot.
Smirking. Cocky. Happy with myself.
Coming alive again. Coming alive again.
You never broke me.
You never made me do anything I didn't want to do.
You had to call in the Big Boys.
And they won't break me, either.

They shrink my mug shot down to a half-inch tall, print my name and inmate number alongside it, and trap it within a clear strip of plastic laminate. They wrap it around my wrist. A locking plastic clip ensures I can't remove it. I've been marked and tagged like a piece of wild game.

I'm summoned into a stale little room and sit across a nicked-and-scratched table from a sunburnt toad of a man. He scans my paperwork, grinning.

"Assault I. Kidnap I. And they'll run your sentences back-to-back. That's fifteen years minimum. And you had a Restraining Order. You're *fucked*."

I don't have the heart to tell him the Restraining Order was against her, not me.

"Well, what do you want to tell me?"

Nothing.

I'm shuffled to the filthy cement holding tank they call "Bedrock," glutted with hung-over lushes and snoozing junkies. I tell a scraggly Injun about my charges.

"If I was facing Assault I and Kidnap I," he tells me, "I'd be looking for the nearest rope to hang myself."

Both of my charges fall under a recently enacted get-tough-on-crime bill called Measure 11. The phrase "Measure 11" strikes the same sort of fear in Oregon criminals' hearts that the term "Human Immunodeficiency Virus" does at homo steam baths. If you get

shit magnet

convicted of a Measure 11 offense, you serve every day of your sentence. Even if you have no prior convictions like me. No time off for good behavior. No chance of probation or community service. Mitigating circumstances such as violent psychotic bitch girlfriends don't count. Measure 11 dictates that my crimes start with minimum sentences of ninety months apiece.

A long, dark, vacuum-cleaner bag of time floats over my head.

Back in Philly, this would've resulted in a fifty-dollar fine and anger-management classes.

But Oregon wants to put me away for fifteen revolutions around the sun.

A deep breath.

Then another.

It's OK. It's her word against mine. And her word isn't worth the dog shit she ate.

Six hours of sitting on a cold concrete bench. Then a half-dozen of us—the ones who aren't getting released—are handed blankets and corralled into a caged room with dirty plastic mattresses. Some drunk in a nearby cell won't stop howling, so it's impossible to sleep.

Staring at things, you begin to notice details you'd never ordinarily see: bumps, ridges, and chipped paint on the walls; pubic hairs, toe-nails, and skin flakes on the mattress; veins and freckles on my arm.

Hour after hour.

Around midnight, they take me to a one-man cell. I finally start dozing.

In the middle of the night, they wake me up. I'm going upstairs to a long-term module.

Follow the orange line on the floor. Step into the door on your right.

Take off all your clothes.

Run your fingers through your hair.

Lift your arms. Let me see the front and back of your hands.

Let me see the back of your earlobes. Left. Now right.

Open your mouth.

Wider.

Let me see your teeth.

Stick out your tongue.

Lift your penis.

Now your scrotum.

Turn around.

Bend over.

Spread your cheeks.

Cough twice.

He hands me two pairs of pink boxer shorts. Two pairs of pink socks. Two pink T-shirts. Two pairs of "County Blues," the baggy canvas top-'n'-bottom set. And brown plastic snap-on shoes which look like giant cockroaches. Except for the socks and shoes, the word JAIL is stamped onto everything.

I'm given two towels, two sheets, and two blankets. I follow the other inmates in a straight line for the elevator.

The Multnomah County Justice Center. Dorm 5D. A cavernous glass-and-cement cocoon. Sixteen cells on the bottom tier, sixteen on top. Wall-to-tall blue carpeting outside the cells. Concrete floors inside.

Very dark, very quiet. Time seems to stand still here. An entirely artificial environment. Recirculated air. 72°F, no matter what the season. A self-contained spaceship.

The guard assigns me a cell number. A loud metallic click opens my heavy wooden cell door with its thin vertical window.

I'm supposed to close the door. To lock myself in the cell.

Click.

Two bunks in the cell. For now, I'm the only one in here.

Pale fluorescent light stays on all night above the steel toilet.

White walls with ugly pencil scrawlings:

I LOVE YOU CINDY. I LOVE YOU WITH ALL MY HEART AND SOUL. JUNE 11TH START/OUT AUGUST 14TH.

A huge serpent with bat wings drawn over an iron cross.

PICKLE IS A TRICK. FUCK ALL PUNK BITCHES.

LOOK MA, A MONKEY, with an arrow pointing to a crude rendering of a black male.

MrXDo-Wrong AKA = FRED LINCOLN 1997 AGGRAVATED MURDER.

ANY FAGGOT BITCH WANTS TO PLAY, COME ON 'CAUSE BITCHES AIN'T SHIT.

A drawing of a hairy, cum-squirting cock.

LITTLE SMURF SHOULD OF WORE HIS VEST THAT DAY...AFTER I KILLED LITTLE SMURF, I SHIT AND PISSED IN HIS MOUTH.

I LOVE YOU CINDY FOREVER.

An air conditioner softly roars. Intermittent Sheriff-dispatch static.

Time.

Daylight slowly snakes into my cell window. I'm allowed a glimpse at a small sliver of a downtown Portland street from five stories above. And I hope it doesn't sound too much like bluffing machismo when I say that right now, it feels safer to be on this side of the window. My life out there has been so calamitous, unhappy, and shambles-ridden, it's a relief to be in here.

I fall asleep on my stomach with my face scrunched to the side. I dream that I'm asleep in the same position, lying on the living-room carpet of a house across the street from where I grew up. A TV blares above my head while I snore. A knock on the screen door awakens me. It's Anne. I'm happy to see her peering in, ready for a date with me.

I immediately awake and shake off the dream.

Soon a loud metallic click signals it's time to walk down and fetch my plastic breakfast tray.

A piece of anemic cornbread swimming in brown vomit. Watery white farina. Two stale slices of white bread. A gumball-sized orb of lard. A half-pint of milk. And instead of coffee, they serve me hot chicory, which tastes as if it was brewed in an old woman's colon.

I return the tray and lock myself back in the cell.

Click.

Twenty-two hours a day in the cell. One hour of "walk time" in the morning, one at night.

Your walk time is the only chance to shower, make phone calls, and mingle.

What a party atmosphere this is. Every blob of bipedal shit in the city passes through this human septic tank.

Shuffling, scratching, sneezing, farting, coughing death. One dumb, inbred face after the next.

Ravaged white crank-shooters who are literally toothless, their chins sucked up almost into their noses, making those involuntary chewing motions that old people make.

Lice-covered homeless losers who commit petty crimes just so they get a bed and three meals a day.

Braided black gangbangers with names such as "Nubian" and "Silk" who are one wrong look away from exploding.

Skeletal junkies, pus-oozing scabs covering saggy, bony arms.

A black guy in a wheelchair who smells like rancid chicken soup and keeps spilling his urine bottle all over his cell floor.

Clusters of tiny, butterscotch-colored Hispanics with parrot-sized Incan noses.

A fat white biker with only one arm. I wonder how they hand-cuffed him.

The smell of men. Their foul armpits. Their unwiped asses. Their rotten-toothed breath.

A sea of human shit. And I'm treading water.

I can't speak freely to anyone. Every cellmate is a potential informant. Every phone call and visit might be taped and used against me.

The best thing about being in jail is that I know I can't die in a car crash.

The worst thing is waking up in the morning and realizing where I am. They throw on the lights around 7:30AM, and even with my eyes closed, I can tell the lights are on—my eyelids go from black to gray.

I'm getting arraigned this morning. I finally meet my lawyer through glass on a hand-held telephone. She has blonde hair, blue eyes, and thick, fluttery eyelashes. She looks concerned for me. Says she's hoping I'll bail out by my birthday, which is in eleven days.

Are you kidding? That long?

These things take time. And cost money.

She'll need $20,000 for her services. Six thousand up front. Another 5Gs for an investigator. And this isn't counting bail.

At my arraignment, they've already dropped the Assault I charge down to two misdemeanor assaults. But the kidnapping charge is still hanging there. I'm still looking at a minimum of seven-and-a-half years.

My bail is $260,000. They require ten percent to cut me loose. Twenty-six thousand dollars just for bail.

I don't even have the six grand for the lawyer.

Two days later, my lawyer's secretary hangs up on me when I try calling collect. My lawyer tells Debbie that since I'm unable to come up with the retainer fee, she can't represent me.

Now it's just me against the State of Oregon, and Oregon's in a bad mood.

I call Sean Tejaratchi, the gentle Iranian graphic-arts genius and erstwhile Zine Shaman. He saw Anne and I together more than anyone else did. He tolerated her self-impressed loudness better than anyone. Anne once told me there were only two people in the world that she respected: Sean and her mom. He says Anne had called him. She told him I bashed in her face pretty bad. Pressing charges is her revenge for what I did to her face. She told him she just wants me to dangle in jail for a little while, and maybe I'll get probation. She doesn't want me to go to prison. She said it again and again: She doesn't want me to go to prison.

The next night, Sean visits me from behind the glass on the two-way phones. "The problem," he tells me, "is that she was unable to control you."

I know. But what a way to control me. At least in jail, she knows I'm not fucking any girls behind her back. She has me in a box.

Sean leaves a message for Anne saying she should think hard before testifying for the Grand Jury. Once you take that step, there's no turning back, he tells her.

A few days later, Sean's sitting in the courtroom as I'm arraigned on four NEW assault charges. Anne told the Grand Jury that I hit her last October. And November. And December. And sometime this February or March, she wasn't sure.

In the courtroom I'm represented by a mousy female Public Defender. The inmates call them Public Pretenders. They also call them Dumptrucks, because they pick you up in jail and dump you off in prison.

An hour after my arraignment, Minnie Mouse phones me in my dorm and says she can't represent me due to a conflict of interest. It seems that her office represented Anne when she smashed out her first married boyfriend's windows in '95.

But I need a lawyer!

She's sure they'll assign me one. She wishes me luck.

Thanks. And don't you fall off a cliff or anything.

Every night I dream I'm out of jail. But in every dream I'm wearing my County Blues. And I know they're coming after me with a big butterfly net.

I dream that I'm milling around in some Portland coffeehouse. Suddenly, a Sheriff's deputy taps me on the back. He handcuffs me and throws me in his squad car. But while he's standing outside, a transmission gear slips and the car flings into drive without a driver. It rolls through a public park, headed straight for a tree. I tense up and prepare for a wallop, but the car just plows through the tree, digging it from its roots. The car careens into a residential street, smashing into parked cars until it finally runs out of gas. I exit the car and look down the block, where police are pointing assault rifles at me. I surrender and promptly awake, my heart thumping.

In another dream, I'm the subject of a board game. The game features a drawing of me, handcuffed and wearing County Blues. Anonymous hands reach into the frame from all directions, pointing at me.

Ever been stuck in an elevator? Or locked in a room? Extrapolate that feeling for days and weeks and months.

In the whale's belly. In a coffin, buried alive. Trapped inside a box. Layers and layers of locked doors between me and freedom.

Loud, maddening, insipid, all-night monologues from some snaggle-toothed jerkoff in another cell.

"And so I tell the bitch, 'Bitch, you better quit making me sandwiches with that mustard—you *know* I hate mustard!" And so the bitch goes, 'Well, maybe you better start makin' your *own* sandwiches.' So I'm like, 'Maybe I *will*, bitch!' So she goes, 'Maybe you *should!*' So I'm like, 'Bitch, where's the bread?'..."

I stare at the towels hanging on a wall five feet across from my bunk. I have a momentary urge to wrap one around my neck and let myself hang.

I feel that big green sickly wave washing over me. Ninety months. Ninety months. Ninety months. And I haven't even been down a month. I spend all of my walk time on the phone, hanging onto the receiver as if it were a life preserver, calling everyone I know for advice.

Still no lawyer.

A fat, slit-eyed hedgehog of a Sheriff's deputy has been interviewing my friends and relatives. He's trying to suss out whether I'm a safe risk to have my bail lowered to $5,000 and be released before trial.

Everyone—*everyone*—tells him they aren't afraid of me, they're afraid of Anne.

My boss says he'll pay the five grand to bail me out. Oh, thank God. I can't take much more.

I spend my birthday alone in a cell. But at least I'll be out in a few days.

The day before my bail-reduction hearing, I finally meet my new court-appointed lawyer, a short, frizzy-haired woman with a high-pitched goo-goo voice. On the loudly buzzing phone through the smudgy glass, she tells me they're having a problem obtaining my release.

Don't tell me this.

All of my references checked out OK, but the hedgehog Sheriff is concerned about two things:

ANSWER Me! #4, particularly "Let's Hear it for Violence Toward Women!"; and Debbie's Restraining Order against me, where she lied and said I was beating her daily.

FUCK! I haven't touched her in two years! I'll take a lie-detector test!

I squirm. I can't believe what I'm hearing. They're going to hold me in a cage because of an article I wrote as a joke and a Restraining Order based on lies? I'll remain in jail because of two things which aren't even real?

The lawyer scrunches her bunny-rabbit nose and tries to look compassionate.

I awake the next morning at around 6AM, drooling on my pillow. An inmate slips me the new edition of the local alternative newsweekly. There's an article on my case titled "Goad Rage." Cute. Anne called them up whining about how I'd "pounded" on her, and they smelled a hot story. There's a picture of my mug shot. Another of the Rape Issue's cover. My prosecutor says he intends to enter my writings into evidence as proof of criminal intent.

I fixate on this paragraph:

In June, 1997, Debbie Goad learned that she had ovarian cancer. After that, her husband of 10 years began beating her almost daily until October, according to a Restraining Order filed in Multnomah County Circuit Court. Debbie Goad accused Jim Goad of kicking her, spitting on her, hitting her, and threatening to kill her, among other things.

I feel like peeling off my skin and screaming until I shatter every window in the facility. Everyone in town thinks I was beating down a weakened, chemo-sapped cancer patient. That'll look real good in court. And when I deny it, I'll look like a liar, even though I'm telling the truth.

As I trudge through this vale of tears, part of my unique karmic curse is having my actual guilt—which is often considerable—severely compounded by allegations of crimes for which I'm entirely innocent.

Hate me for what I am. I generously supply you with plenty of reasons to hate me. I don't understand why you need to make things up.

I've never pretended to be a nice guy. I don't try to whitewash my misdeeds. I don't suffer from a desire that you see me as something better than I am. In that regard, I'm unlike most people.

I smacked Debbie about ten times over eleven years, and I don't make excuses for it. At the time, I felt like doing it. I know why I did it, and I couldn't care less whether it taints your opinion of me.

But this is ridiculous. If she's going to accuse me of hitting her every day, she should have at least afforded me the pleasure of actually DOING it.

Thankfully, Debbie has agreed to attend my bail-reduction hearing and admit she lied on the Restraining Order. I'm not asking her to lie and say I never hit her. I just want her to sift the truth from the fibs, because the fibs are fucking me over. I'm being fib-fucked.

"GOAD!" The Sheriff's booming voice ricochets down the cellblock. Yes?

"You have court—let's go."

The module door unclangs and my plastic shoes click-clack down the cold corridor.

"Name?" asks a grizzly bear with a badge.

Goad.

"Hey, you're the guy who was in the newspaper today."

Yup.

I'm handcuffed. Two deputies marshal me into an elevator and down to another floor. Outside the courtroom, I skim past civilians sitting on wooden benches and eyeing me as if I'm a captive gorilla.

Still cuffed, I'm escorted into a small, quiet courtroom. I walk past my boss, my landlord, Debbie...and Anne...up to a broad table where I'm ritually unshackled. I sit down and pour myself a cup of water.

At a table across from mine sits a tall, gaunt, blond man with long, veiny fingers. He mulls over a stack of papers and—*[insert ominous symphony music]*—a copy of ANSWER Me! #4. He also has a picture of Anne flat on a hospital bed with blood pouring down her cheek.

My attorney rushes in, looking shorter and frizzier than she did yesterday. She sits down next to me and whispers in my ear, "This is going to be a big media case....I saw the newspaper today. That really sucks."

The Honorable Judge Old Guy enters the room. We rise, then sit, and he mumbles some preliminary statements.

My boss is called to the stand. He has nothing but sweet things to say about me.

Next comes my landlord, a kind, wizardlike gay man with a greasy goatee. He says he wishes all his tenants were as quiet as me. He fears nothing if I were released...except Anne's presence. "I've never seen someone so psychotic and violent," he says, recalling the time she pounded on me and smashed my windshield.

Debbie takes the stand. The prosecutor asks her about her Restraining Order. "It's not true," she says. "I was mad at him for cheating on me."

At this the judge waves his liver-spotted hand and says, "I think she may need counsel." Either Debbie lied on the Restraining Order or she's lying now, which means she committed perjury at least once. The judge won't allow her to admit she lied without first getting a lawyer's advice.

I'm allowed to read from a statement I scribbled in my cell. I list some of the evidence I have against Anne. I say it's unfair that my writings are being used to deny me a bail reduction. My tone is meek and respectful. After I finish, my lawyer tells me I was eloquent. At the mention of Debbie's cancer, my voice even cracked with emotion. But a reporter for *The Oregonian* would write that I was "combative" and "lashed out" at Lady Anne.

The prosecutor summons the hedgehog deputy to the stand. Deputy Dean Martin. I'm not kidding. Apparently, Corporal Frank Sinatra and Officer Joey Bishop were unable to testify. Dino says that until yesterday, he was willing to grant my release. But yesterday he saw Debbie's Restraining Order and a copy of *ANSWER Me! #4*. He admits that he only read one article, but that it "told about beating women, raping women, and murdering them. Uh, it told you how to do it, so I've reneged my decision." After Dean leaves the stand, the judge says that I'm a significant danger to the community and should remain behind bars until trial.

I get rehandcuffed. As I spin around to leave, I catch Anne's eye. She stares back. What an odd expression. It's as if she's trying hard to look angry, but only because I hurt her. And not physically—romantically.

Baby still loves me. But if baby can't have me, nobody can.

I just smile and keep walking.

My landlord packs all my belongings into boxes and says I'll have to find somebody to come and pick them up. My boss finds a permanent replacement for me.

Jail is now my home.

Beautiful, beautiful summer, orangey sunshine evening, the light illuminates green trees from behind silhouetted hills. The clouds are all lifted, and a clear sky smiles down on warm streets. It's the only season that gives hope, the only time of year I feel half-alive instead of fully dead...

...I can see it all behind the dirty Plexiglas window in this suffocating little cell.

Anne is trying her best to ensure that this here caged butterfly is kept in a jar for years and years. She lets detectives take DNA samples from her so they can try and prove that the blood found in the car was hers. She rushes them copies of *ANSWER Me!* She gives them the CD containing my spoken-word version of "Let's Hear it for Violence Toward Women!"—the same track she told me she used as jackoff fodder. She leads cops to her ex-roommates, who say they remember seeing her with black eyes and that she told them I did it. She puts police in contact with the English teacher to whom she *lied* about abuse in order to get a passing grade. He tells police he remembers her saying that I hit her, too.

She also gives them wacky photos of us cavorting around Portland together. A picture of me smoking a bowl of weed. A shot of us smiling and holding the Chihuahua. She even gives them an article I'd written about our shoplifting spree, which is weird considering that it implicates *her* as a criminal much more severely than me.

The hospital reports and police photos show that I fucked her up righteously. Two hairline skull fractures. Two black eyes. The white part of her left eye was bloodshot solid red. A gash under that eye required twenty-six stitches to close. A bite mark on her left thumb penetrated to the bone.

Four days after I smashed her face in, she sat down with detectives for a taped interview. My lawyer sends me the transcripts. I finally get to see Anne's version of how it started:

...I turned to him, I looked him in his eyes and I'm like, I'm not afraid of you, Jim, I can say whatever I want about you and I will, and I'll tell people about your domestic violence, you know, and I, and that's when he lost it....He, his eyes just glazed over and he just went insane.

In her own scorpionlike way, the girl is a genius. She knows exactly what they want to hear. She threatens to "out" me about domestic violence, and I jackhammer her skull with my fist.

What a great story.

Too bad it's entirely false.

She leaves out the part about lunging at my face and scratching my cheek. About me holding her arms while she tried to kick me. She mentions the black guy who saw us, but she skips the part about punching me in the nose after he entered her building.

And in place of all that, she inserts a threat to tell the world about my domestic violence. A threat which she never made. A threat which makes no sense, because Debbie already *told* the world. But a threat which sounds good to the nitwits who call themselves experts about domestic violence.

She plays beautifully to the eager detectives' prejudices and sympathies. She's so surgically precise in the way she omits her culpability and foists it onto me, I have to admire it.

When she called 911, she told them I'd threatened to kill her many times before.

No, she was the one who did that.

She told the operator I'd smash through windows.

No, that was her, too. Wind*shields*, to be exact.

She told 911 I'd gone to jail the previous weekend for beating her up.

No, we'd *both* gone to jail almost a *month* earlier when I told my landlord to call the cops after she attacked me, bit me on the chest and shoulder, and shattered my windshield. And let's not forget the false rape accusation when cops arrived.

Anne told 911 that my ex-wife had a Restraining Order against me. She didn't tell them that I had one against Wee Lady Anne.

She tells detectives about all the mean phone messages I'd left her the day before this happened. She even gives them her voicemail password so they can tape them and use them against me.

She makes not a peep about all the messages she left me that same day. Nor about the fact that her messages alluded to my death five times, while my messages were just petty insults.

She says that the first time I hit her, I just "flew off the handle" after she called some guy cute.

She leaves out the half-hour or so which elapsed between her calling the guy cute and me hitting her. She doesn't tell them that we argued about her girlfriend. That I requested she leave the car. That she grabbed onto me and refused to let go. That I threw her keys out of the car hoping she'd leave. That I finally told her I'd hit her if she didn't let go.

She definitely doesn't tell them that *she*, not I, was the one who'd get violent over jealousy.

For the second of my "assaults," she admits to jumping on my back and begging me not to leave. But she edits out the part about me warning that I'll hit her if she doesn't release me. She doesn't tell them how she whispered "hit me" in my ear.

Regarding the scuffle which led to my broken toe, she splices out the fact that she started it all by biting my leg.

When she tells a magazine reporter about the roadside incident where I wound up punching her in the tummy, she didn't tell him about socking me with both fists and twice attempting to hurl rocks at me.

When telling the same reporter about smashing my windshield, she snips out the segment about how she kicked my phone off the hook, bit my shoulder and chest, and falsely accused me of rape.

So it's natural that in recounting the incident for which I'm facing felony charges, she omits the part about scratching me and punching me in the nose.

And placing a cherry atop the parfait, she says the whole thing started when she threatened to tell the world that I wasn't being honest about how violent I am.

No, that's her, too. *She's* the one who can't cop to being violent.

I beg my lawyer to find the black guy who saw us struggling in the car. He'll support my version of events. He'll prove she's lying. He'll be able to create reasonable doubt in a jury's mind. He'll save seven-and-a-half years of my life.

I can't take seven-and-a-half years of this. I'll die. I know I will.

My lawyer says that one of Anne's ex-boyfriends saw the "Goad Rage" article and sent a letter to the paper. The letter contains some of the first good news I've heard since I was busted:

A little over three years ago I had an affair with Anne. Soon after separating from my wife, I got an apartment, and when Anne found out I wouldn't let her move in with me, she refused to leave my car for over six hours. I finally talked her into getting out and the next morning, she came by my house and threw a concrete block through every window of my Toyota station wagon. By the time police arrived to arrest her, she had also taken out a 6' X 8' picture window in my house.

Debbie Goad says Anne wants to be the next Courtney Love; shortly before Anne's arrest she told me how she thought of herself as Courtney Love and me as Kurt Cobain....It's Anne's dream to become famous by destroying her man, as many people believe Courtney has.

I believe Anne is totally capable of inflicting wounds on herself (or having an accomplice do it) in order to generate publicity for her sick 'career.' After I had her arrested for destroying my property, she proudly published the police reports in her own zine. The woman is seriously ill, and was known by me to be under psychiatric care; she also has so little conscience that I believe she would destroy even someone she loves if she could get enough publicity for doing so... Anne knows where I live and I believe is capable of inflicting violence on me and my property if she becomes aware of this correspondence.

So I wasn't the first.

Get this man as a witness.

My lawyer says the DA called her from his cell phone today. He has a new witness, too.

No. No. No. NO....

It's Friday afternoon. My stomach will bubble and boil all weekend wondering about this new witness.

I call Debbie. She reminds me that we're divorced. She feels ready to snap from all the stress I've reintroduced into her life. She says that Big Brother is watching me. And evil forces are controlling my life. And I wasn't a model husband. And sometimes you have to be cruel to be kind. And maybe I'd better get someone else to handle my business on the outside.

*But I came back to Oregon so I could take care of you if you got
sick again. If I hadn't come back, I'd be a free man.*

"Well, maybe you shouldn't have come back."

*Thanks for telling me now, honeycakes. And thanks for telling me to
come back when I first told you about this shit.*

I call Sean Tejaratchi and tell him what Debbie said. Sean asks me
if I want him to handle my business.

A year ago when he knew I was broke, Sean sent me a $200
money order without me asking him. I sent it back and said I may
need a favor someday.

Like today.

Sean has nothing to gain by allying himself with an accused
woman-beater. Yet he knows both Anne and me. Like most people
who saw us together, he instinctually feared more for my safety than
for hers. He never said he approved of me hitting her. But he feels
that for her to press charges after all the chances I had to send her
to jail—without doing it—is savagely fucked-up.

So day after day he starts to accept multiple panicked, high-stress
calls from me. He retrieves all my belongings from my apartment and
stores them in his already cramped studio. He meticulously transcribes
all of Anne's taped messages to me. He makes long-distance calls to
people who may be willing to contribute to my defense fund.

And he never complains about it.

Never loses his cool.

Never demands anything in return.

I'm in a thoroughly infantilizing situation. And even though he's
almost ten years younger than me, Sean makes sure that my diapers
are changed and I get enough baby food.

The weekend passes. On Monday morning, I call my lawyer's assistant and ask him about the new prosecution witness.

There wasn't one witness. There were two. Both of them called 911
at around the same time Anne says the shit went down. One of them
lives in Anne's building and said he heard a woman screaming. The
other was a female jogger who said she saw a car speeding by. She
saw the passenger's door hanging open. She heard a woman crying
"NO! NO! NO!" and saw the male driver lean over and pull the
woman back in the car.

My life is over. I'm dead. I'm never getting out. This is it. This is the
final act. My death wish has finally been granted.

I close my eyes and see an endless expanse of dead, gray desert.
No colors here. But rather than blissful blackness, just dull gradations

of gray. Lifeless lunar landscape. No love, no other humans, no end or beginning, just parched, cracked tundra leading out to an eternal horizon. No violence, no tears, no hope—just pure, insulting, shameful, soul-destroying existence. Can't taste, smell, hear, or feel anything. But my sight remains to show just how trapped I am. I'm stuck in the middle of nowhere with my legs cut off. My stumps softly bleed into the powdery gray ground.

I'm through.

I dream that Anne is standing over me, triumphantly biting into an apple.

I awake face-down with my heart beating hard enough to leave a dent in the plastic mattress. Get me out of here, get me out, get me out, this isn't happening, it's just a dream, I can't imagine ninety months of being nailed to a wooden board.

If only I had kept going east when I was in Idaho last winter. If only I hadn't dropped the Restraining Order complaints against her. If only I'd gotten laid in the bars on the night this happened. But now I'm stuck in the Roach Motel.

Sean tells me he was bent down fixing his bicycle at a local supermarket when he heard Anne's voice.

"Hi, Sean."

He just looked away.

"I guess you're mad about the whole Jim thing."

He said there's nothing to talk about and pedaled away.

The guards wrap chains around me and transfer me out to Inverness Jail, situated in toxic swamplands near the airport. Instead of a cell, I'm in a giant open dormitory with fifty-six steel cots fanning out in a horseshoe around the guard's desk.

On the plus side, I'm free to walk around from 9AM until 11PM. There isn't the choking claustrophobia that comes with being locked down for twenty-two hours in the Justice Center's tiny aquariums.

On the down side, there's absolutely no view of the outside world. Just white walls. White floors. White ceiling. And fluorescent white lights. The kind that depressed me as a child during dead winter days locked up in school. Surgery lights, the kind the make your veins look bluer. Cold and plastic, industrial rather than human. Everything has the color and flavor of aspirin.

And there's no privacy. No place to hide. From every spot in this 100' x 100' white room, you can see everyone else at all times. And they can see you. The only semi-private cubicles are the shower stalls and toilets.

The shower nozzles emit a constant atonal metallic squall, like drag-ging your teeth along a sheet of aluminum. Not the best sound for someone who's trying to maintain his sanity as if it were an egg yolk sliding around in his hands.

It's just too loud in here. Too loud to think. Too loud to relax. Too much trash in the trash cans. Too much encrusted piss around the toilet seats. Too much toenail fungus and cum on the shower-stall floors. Too much hyperactivity crossbred with low intelligence. Too many rats in this cage for comfort.

I'm assigned Bunk #7. A few feet away, in Bunk #3, sits a chubby white guy with huge tattoos strangling his canned-ham biceps. Stringy bangs hang down in his beady wolverine eyes. People are calling him Branch.

Oh, no. How many guys are named Branch? It's one of Anne's ex-boyfriends. Anne always said that of her thirty-five Abusive Male Lovers, Branch was the King Abuser. She said he stole her Camaro and left her tweaking on crank in a motel room. Forced her to watch him get a blow job from another girl. He was awful, awful, awful.

I ask Branch if he remembers her.

Yeah.

He says he pulled into a Texaco station one night a few years ago and spotted her showing naked pictures of herself to a circle of boys. He told her he had some speed. She asked him if he wanted to fuck. He said yeah. They drove to a cemetery, snorted some fat rails on her dashboard, and fucked all night. Did crank and hung together for a week. A friend took pictures of her blowing him in a porno-store peep booth. After a week, she started acting psychotically posses-sive. Her lips began swelling up from all the meth. When some of Branch's stripper friends visited his place, Anne started screaming at them to stay away from her boyfriend. Branch told her he wasn't her boyfriend. When some criminal partners of his dropped by later, she was still acting psychotic. He told her that if she didn't cool down, one of his friends was likely to kill her. There's a lot of money and a lot of dope and a lot of guns here, and they don't take kindly to crazy broads. Hysterical, she threatened to call the police on his friends. When Branch told her she had to leave, she ran out to one of his friends' cars and began looking for the TEC-9 with which to blow everyone away. He caught up with her. Branch finally calmed her down by giving her his beeper and promising to page her.

Immediately after she left, he had the beeper disconnected. He never saw her again, although his friends say she showed up a few times at his place, wanting to hang out with him.

Golly, it looks as if Anne omitted a few details in her saga of wretched abuse and wanton victimization at the hands of Mr. Branch.

Quelle surprise.

One early July morning I join the chain gang headed for the downtown courthouse. The prosecutor, my lawyer, and I are slated to appear before the judge to schedule a trial date.

My prosecutor is pale and lanky, not unlike Lurch from the original *Addams Family* TV show. He wears a crispy navy-blue suit and sports a blond combover hairdo.

His first name is Rod. Let's just call him Big Rod based on the phallic implications and the fact that he's trying to fuck me.

Big Rod is the chief prosecutor for the DA's domestic-violence unit. And Jim Goad is a mighty big fish on his hook. My investigator says this is the biggest media case of Big Rod's career.

There's an obvious political motivation in his prosecution of me. There is *whenever* a DA gets publicity for a case. Part of a prosecutor's job is to use symbolic gestures to sate the public's appetite for blood vengeance. And what could be higher drama than for the head of the domestic-violence unit to nail the author of "Let's Hear it for Violence Toward Women!"? I'm a perfect sacrifice.

I notice that Big Rod never looks in my eyes. Possibly it would complicate matters for him to see a human rather than the monster his textbooks tell him I am. And he has an annoying way of saying my last name: "Your Honor, in the matter of the State v. James Thaddeus GOAD...." He lets my last name drop as if it were a turd falling from 'tween his buttocks. My lawyer tells me that Big Rod thinks I'm "vile" and "not human."

One Portland defense lawyer describes Big Rod as "a Boy Scout who waves a white flag with one hand and protects his female clients with the other."

Another lawyer calls him a true believer in his cause, an ideologue who's only capable of viewing domestic-violence situations in black and white, with females always wearing white.

Yet another lawyer tells me that Big Rod has boxes and boxes stuffed with pictures of crushed, smashed, bloody women's faces. I'm told that his office's waiting room is always packed with bruised, swollen, fractured women. Only Big Rod, in his darkest, sweatiest moments alone in his bedroom at 3AM, knows whether his interests go beyond mere justice.

There's a possibility, however remote, that this whole obsession of his with savin' the wimmin has something to do with getting enemas from Amazon gals. Or maybe he enjoys being powdered and diapered at Lesbian Avenger keg parties.

Anything's possible. But I don't claim to know what's in Big Rod's mind. Not like he claims to know what's in mine.

Domestic violence is the bugaboo of the new millennium, what Satanic ritual abuse was to the 1980s. And Big Rod is Portland's chief DV witch hunter. Supposedly, he's one of P-Town's chief experts on domestic violence.

And yet I wonder if he's ever hit a woman. Or been hit by one. Probably not.

Then how the fuck can he claim to be an expert?

It's like these New York Jewish lawyers who say they're experts about farm-owning Christian militiamen in Montana. They couldn't be further removed from their subject matter.

If the experts actually cured domestic violence—just as if psychiatrists cured mental illness—they'd be unemployed. So there's a built-in financial incentive to misunderstand the problem and thereby perpetuate it.

The experts believe that there's some magical, conspiratorial confluence of "denial" which causes all batterers to lay some blame on their...uhh...batterees. Is it possible that *all* abusers are afflicted with this same departure from reality? Or is there more complexity to the dance than the experts realize?

As I define experts, I'm a domestic-violence expert in the fullest sense of the term—I have experience in the trenches. Note the similarity between the words "expert" and "experience." And I'm not in denial about being violent. I freely admit to every altercation, and I don't underplay my role.

The one who's in denial about domestic violence is Anne, the girl who hit me first almost every time there was violence between us. The girl who systematically denied her guilt when recounting these incidents to police.

And the experts suffer from even worse denial, because, unlike Anne, they don't even seem to grasp that women are even *capable* of domestic violence.

I've heard the same story too many times while behind bars:

The acid dealer whose girlfriend threw a ceramic tiger at him...and he shoved her...and *he* wound up in jail.

The young Blood who woke up to the sight of his white girlfriend clutching his dick in one hand and a knife in the other. When he jumped out of bed, she slashed his hand. And when he called the cops, she said, "I'll just tell them you RAPED me." And when the cops got there, he told them to forget about it, even though his hand was bleeding.

The guard—not an inmate, but a *guard*—whose brother went to prison for domestic violence. His crime? His psycho wife doused herself and her *kids* with gasoline, lit herself on fire, and he pulled her dress off to save her from getting burned. The guard witnessed the incident and testified at trial, but his brother still got two years in prison.

And yet in her book *Fire With Fire*, quasi-pretty neo-fem Naomi Wolf has the audacity to spew sentences such as these:

> Men harm women disproportionately because they are able to. Women do not harm men as much because they can't get away with it.

Do we live on the same planet, Sweet Tits?

In June, 1994, *USA Today* featured an article citing twelve sociological studies, all of them conducted independently of one another. In each of these studies, researchers interviewed married couples about who hit whom. And *every one* of the studies concluded that women hit men more often than men hit women.

A November/December '99 issue of *Psychology Today* cited three different studies—two of them concluded that women hit men more frequently than the inverse, and one said that the rates were about the same.

A recent issue of *Mother Jones* cited a study, conducted by a *female* psychology professor, in which 860 men and women were interviewed about domestic violence in their lives. This was the study's conclusion:

> A surprising fact has turned up in the grisly world of domestic violence: Women report using violence in their relationships more often than men.

In her book *When She Was Bad*, Patricia Pearson cites a 1985 study conducted by "highly respected family violence scholars" Murray Straus and Richard Gelles in which "several thousand households" were surveyed; the results, according to Pearson, were that

> ...women initiated the aggression as often as men. About a quarter of the relationships had an exclusively violent male, another quarter had an exclusively violent female, and the rest were mutually aggressive.

But how often do you see women going to jail for domestic violence?

America isn't in denial about male violence toward women—Jesus Christ, every other TV movie features some stubbly ogre walloping his bitch for not folding the towels properly. But female violence toward men is pervasive, although largely denied. Or if it isn't denied, it's excused. As a friend of mine put it, "When a man insults or hits a woman, it's 'abuse'; but when a woman insults or hits a man, it's 'assertiveness.'"

The popular mood dictates that you should never hit a woman, even if she's clawing at your eyes and biting you. Women bristle at being called the weaker sex unless they can work it to their legal advantage.

Sorry, Naomi—women harm men precisely *because* they can get away with it. In this limp-dick "patriarchy" of ours, a woman's pain always carries more weight. Justice claims to be blind, but it *is* a woman holding those unbalanced scales.

O.J. Simpson fucked it up for a lot of guys. But O.J. didn't have a Restraining Order against Nicole. O.J. was never punched and bitten in public by Nicole. She never falsely accused him of rape. She never smashed his windshield with a shovel or cracked Paula Barbieri's skull with an axe handle. She never left death threats on his voicemail. She never stalked him.

Or maybe she did, and we just haven't heard the full story.

A frozen snapshot of Anne with a black eye doesn't begin to tell the whole story of what was a yearlong slasher movie between us.

Our situation was so unlike what people have come to think of as domestic violence.

But Big Rod is apparently working from a model of how these situations operate. And despite all the evidence that our situation didn't work that way, he struggles to make it all fit. He strains to shove a dodecahedral peg into a round hole.

Big Rod tells my lawyer that Anne is a "lost little girl" who "got in over her head" in a seedy world of violence and depravity when she met me.

Yessirree, a lost little girl is likely to describe herself as a "psychotic neo-Nazi bitch with a whip." She runs welfare scams and makes false rape accusations. She wrecks three marriages by age twenty-one.

Sure, she's a lost little girl.

She's lost her mind.

And she has the emotional maturity of a three-year-old.

Big Rod says that my Restraining Order against Anne was just another tool in my gallery of control and domination over her.

Right. By attempting to peacefully get her out of my life, I was trying to extend my sphere of influence over her.

Big Rod says that Anne's death threats were part of the "cycle of abuse" and are only evidence of a woman finally standing up for herself against a wicked batterer.

Never mind that her recorded death threats began almost two months before she says I started hitting her.

Big Rod believes Anne's story that on the night in question, she calmly turns to me and says she's not afraid of me, and I can't handle that.

This was after all the times she'd warned me to summon police cars to protect myself.

After all the death threats.

All the lunges at my face.

All the scratches and bite marks.

After I got a Restraining Order against her.

After the ominous promises that she'd hire a hit man to kill me or buy a gun to do the job herself.

Finally, after all that, she was standing up for the first time and telling me she wasn't afraid of me.

By not lifting a finger to me.

Mm-hmm.

It makes sense that Anne's Shirley-Temple-with-bruises tap dance fools the domestic-violence experts and almost no one else.

Not even her mom.

"This isn't the poor little battered woman," her mom tells my investigator. "Anne was giving as good as she was getting."

The PC Portland hipsters who knew Anne are also cynical about her victim shtick.

One guy tells me he's opposed to domestic violence but would make an exception in her case.

A woman who works with rape victims but has known Anne for years says Anne isn't the victim in this case—I am.

A girl who works in a coffee shop both Anne and I used to frequent says Anne deserved it and hopes that I beat some sense into her.

A stripper who used to work in the same club as Anne also thinks she asked for it. She says she hates these chicks who throw the first shots and then cry like babies when they get their asses whupped.

Why are Big Rod and his domestic-violence elves the only ones who don't see the complexity of our situation? Is Anne blowing Big Rod? I'm not the only one to wonder.

While I'm wondering, Big Rod agrees to a trial date of October 29th, and I'm led out of the courtroom in handcuffs.

During one of my endless calls to Sean, he tells me that Anne's on the other line. Is there anything I want him to tell her?

No. But of course I'll call back to hear what she had to say.

Maybe she's dropping charges?

Not a chance.

She calls him up five or six times, angrily hanging up on him each time. She's furious that he's supporting me. She calls him a scenester geek, tells him to suck a fat dick in hell, and says she knows he's talking shit about her to people.

And I thought *I* was the one who couldn't stomach the idea of people talking shit about me.

A week later, Sean is paying a bill at some dump on Burnside where Anne keeps a PO Box, and who walks in, hugs and kisses him, then spins around and dashes outside? Who could it be, with her face buried in makeup and her hair recently dyed blonde? Why, it's the same girl whom Sean follows out of the store, knowing this is a precious chance. He walks with her and nods appreciatively as she tells him her side of the story. After they part ways, she shouts back at him. Sean turns around. "I still like you," she tells him in her dizzy, bouncy way. Sean says that she should call him sometime.

One of the only good things about Oregon law is that you're allowed to tape someone over the phone without their knowledge and use it against them in court.

I tell Sean to buy recording equipment, because we know she'll call. She does. The next day. And Sean gets it all on tape.

She asks him how I'm doing. Sean says I'm not taking to jail very well, that I look awful and had spoken of killing myself. He says that I'm stunned and confused and still can't believe I'm in jail. Regarding our failed "romance," he tells her I said I just couldn't give her what she needed.

And with that, she begins crying.

"I haven't had sex since he was arrested," she tells him. "I still love him, Sean. Do you think he loves me? It's *so* important. I *have* to know if he loves me."

A long pause. Sean, flabbergasted, says nothing. Anne breaks the silence:

"Do you think we'll be together again someday?"

My fate rests in the hands of an emotional retardate.

A few days after my arrest, Anne told a Portland bookstore owner that she still loved me.

Her mom told our investigator that Anne recently said she still loves me, will never love anyone else, and is very remorseful over losing me.

And now, in early August, she's telling Sean that she loves me.

She sure has a zany way of showing it.

From the moment I beat her face in, I never thought of the word "love." I never lamented our breakup. I never hoped to reconcile with her. I don't even wish I'd treated her better while we were together. In fact, I was way too nice. Even if it will save me from prison, I don't want to get back with the little genital louse. If this is what it takes to get her out of my life…well, it's a heavy price, but I'm willing to pay it. That's how miserable she made me.

The next day she calls Sean again and says, "I know what you guys are trying to do—you want me to drop charges, and when Jim gets out, you'll both treat me like shit again!"

Keep dreaming, sister. With or without me, someone will eventually treat you like shit.

Sean steers her toward talking about the violence between us. She mentions attacking me on the bus:

I just started hitting him as hard as I could….Because, like, in public, you know, that was the only time I could do it, 'cause then he wouldn't hit me back.

BACK. Wouldn't hit her *back*. She's implying that in private, I'd hit her back—after she hit me *first*.

She adds a "You GO, girl!" feminist slant to what she supposedly said to me outside her building on the morning of May 29th:

I finally look at him, I go, "Okay, Jim, you know what? You're right, this is it. But you know what? It's not going to be like it was, I'm not going to be all subservient to you, I'm not going to shut up….And that's when he's like, "No, you're not, bitch." And that's when he fuckin' locks the car door, turns into a maniac, gets out of my building with me in the car, and me trying to open up the car door, and trying to honk the horn, with him screaming like a maniac, laughing and punching me as hard as he can in the face about twenty times.

She admits that when it comes to domestic violence, she certainly didn't fail for a lack of trying:

SEAN: …I'm saying that when it comes down to you guys fighting, you gave as good as you got, you know?
ANNE: Sure! We both did…And I never did get to beat him up as bad as he beat me up. That's not fair! I wanted to, fuck yeah! I wanted to cause him as much pain as he caused me.

SEAN: Well, and you certainly tried!
ANNE: Well, yeah!

So basically she wants me punished for being better at a sport in which we were both willing athletes.

This emotional roller coaster is starting to give me mental whiplash. One by one, the planks of hope are being removed beneath me.

Trapped. And suffocating. How can anyone claim this makes you a better person? It just deranges you, leaving pits and nicks and scars on your mind, ulcers forming like purple leeches up and down your intestines, pulsar headaches, fear, paranoia, irritability, mistrust, despair. I don't feel rehabilitated, I feel dismantled.

What can I do? Pull at my hair? Bite off my lip? Rip a testicle straight from the sac?

I'd love to scream.

But you can't scream in here.

So in lieu of screaming, I awake in the middle of the night flexing so hard, I think I might have caused a brain aneurysm. Just stressing every muscle to maximum tension, thick veins popping in my forehead as if I'm bound with rope and trying to break free. I do it five or six times with such intensity that I seriously fear I caused brain damage. So I force myself to recite the alphabet backwards to make sure my cerebrum isn't hemorrhaging.

Tighten up. Tighten the screws. Tighten them so hard you snap off half the screwdriver. But make sure those screws are so deep in the wall, no one will ever be able to loosen them. Work hard at embedding those screws. They'll have to tear down the entire wall before they can pry the screws loose. The little screws will destroy the big wall.

Pounding. Pounding. Pounding. Pounding.

Pounding back.

Ooh, this is a new level of stress. My mind is entering some cracked, shattered terrain it's never inhabited before. I'm almost catatonic with tension. Exactly how gruesome will it get? Will further bad news be the thing that finally sends me to The Hole, naked on a steel floor under a light bulb, howling at passing guards and slithering around in my own excrement?

Deep, deep depression.

Microscopic water roaches swim through my bloodstream, laughing at me.

Lately my mind has felt like an exploded eggplant, a crushed chicken wing, and a half-opened can of spaghetti which has dried to a crust because it fell behind the refrigerator undetected.

Have you ever seen a hair dryer overheat, where the inner coils glow red-hot, and it finally just stops whirring and shuts down? My brain feels close to overheating. I can almost feel the wires short-circuiting in my head.

What do fried nerves smell like? Probably something like burning hair. Or like boiled radiator water swirling with rust. Or like a paintbrush which has dried rock-hard after all the turpentine has evaporated. Bad chemicals surround my neurons. My nerves recoil and stiffen like a rat who's been fed a lethal dose of poison. Neurological rigor mortis. I try to laugh, but my lips crack and fall in pieces to the floor. I sweep it all up with a broom and dustpan, walking away ashamed.

My adrenals are like dried prunes. I have so very little energy, like a toy whose batteries are dying. Or a car running on only a damp smear of gasoline.

Lines form on my face like ice on a windowpane. My gums bleed. I'm as pale as toilet tissue. I'm Auschwitz-thin, with collarbones jutting out as if they were bicycle handles. I look worn, with the bones under my eye sockets nearly poking through the flesh. My joints are all stiff—achy, unlubricated. Bile and boogers and blood and an unwiped ass.

I'm not feeling well.

How do you purge the toxins when you're living in a toilet?

There's crust in my tear ducts, which dried up long ago. When will I cry? If I don't cry soon, I'll turn to stone. Or a pillar of salt. Or a statue of shit.

Do I fantasize about kissing pretty girls and walking under bridges and driving past wheat fields and swimming in ponds and sleeping in cozy little motels while the rain pounds outside?

No, because that would only make me sadder.

My brother says my mom is close to death. The cancer has spread from her breasts to her ribs to her brain. She doesn't know where she is half of the time. She has trouble identifying him and his wife. She's constantly shitting herself and coughing up blood.

Slowly free-falling through time...time...endless time...I wish I'd bump into something. Some crag on the side of this bottomless pit where I can rest for a while and try to climb up again.

Tell me one good thing.

Just one piece of good news.

A log I can grab onto while drowning in this foamy whirlpool.

I call my lawyer's assistant.

Bad news. REAL bad news.

Big Rod is reindicting me on much more severe charges. My Kidnap I beef is being split into TWO kidnapping charges: one with the intent to cause injury, the other with the intent to terrorize. There's a new Assault II charge for biting her. A new Attempted Assault II for repeatedly striking her. Plus misdemeanor Assault and Menacing. Six fucking charges based on a single ten-minute car ride.

My possible maximum sentence balloons from seven-and-a-half years to just over twenty-five years. That's longer than Anne has been alive. My bail swells from $260,000 to $780,000.

I am reindicted through the miracle of interactive television and a fax machine. I sit in front of a TV set which beams images of a downtown courtroom to me. Atop the TV is perched a camera and a smaller screen which captures my pale, pimply likeness. A microphone attached to the wall juts into my face like a Dick of Justice demanding a blow job. I see a stand-in lawyer from my Public Defender's office on the lower screen. He asks me how I'm doing.

Swell.

The new indictment rolls out of the fax machine. A fat, Polynesian-looking deputy hands it to me.

Sigh.

I recall all the times I had the shit kicked out of me and didn't even think of calling the cops. And none of my attackers, including my parents, ever did a day in prison.

My Assault II charge is for biting her. When she bit me on the chest, police said it was the worst human bite mark they'd ever seen. When she bit me on the elbow, it left a permanent scar. And in both cases, there were witnesses to her biting me, while in my case it's her word against mine. But she wasn't charged.

Justice.

I fetch my legal papers and return to the dorm.

Eighteen years' worth of new charges.

And I looked really old on the video screen.

And mom's dying.

And Debbie's on her way.

Why are you all looking at me?

Dead time. Dead dust flecks floating in the afternoon sunlight. Dead skin peeling away on my toes. Dead soap bars pasted to the shower-stall floors. Dead brain cells. Dead emotions.

My life is over.

I'm dead.

And into the dorm floats Anne in her silky nightgown, whispering seductively in my ear:

"Kill yourself."

I know where they keep the plastic bags and rubber gloves.

Late at night. Two or three plastic bags slipped over my head. A pair of rubber gloves tied together and wrapped around my neck. Tightly. Make sure it's tight. Then a blanket over my head so they think I'm only sleeping.

Dead before morning.

"GOAD!"

I sit up.

Yeah?

"Let's go. Got a visit."

I rub my eyes and wait near the door for my escort.

When I see Debbie and my literary agent sitting on the other side of the glass, something within me snaps. For almost the entire half-hour conversation, I look down rather than in their eyes, my thumbnail chipping away at a patch of flaked paint, uncovering a layer of red beneath the newer coat of blue.

I tell them how helpless I feel.

Nothing that they say helps.

Two angry tears reluctantly squeeze out of my right eye and fall to the counter. My agent says I'm scaring her. Debbie looks scared, too.

When the Sheriff says it's time to go, I stand up and leave without saying goodbye. I return to the dorm in a red-eyed daze.

As I'm squirting disinfectant on lunch tables right before noon, three rubber-glove-wearing deputies rapidly enter the dorm and head for the Sheriff's desk. I'm summoned to the desk and ordered to surrender my squirt bottle. I look over at my bunk and notice that two deputies are rummaging through my belongings.

What's going on with my property?

"We'll take care of that. Let's go."

On the ride downtown, I see things I haven't seen in nearly two months: cars, trees, streets, houses, and an ocean of natural light.

I'm escorted into the cold cement basement of the Justice Center, the same place where I was first booked, and tossed into an itsy-bitsy concrete room.

Can I ask what this is all about?

"Yeah," says the macho deputy eyeing me as if I'm emitting radioactivity and he doesn't want to get too close. "You're being placed on Suicide Watch."

I guess my agent and Debbie told them about the visit.

The guard leads me to the Suicide Cell, an 8' x 8' white room with a hard-as-rock wooden slab and a steel toilet. Nothing jagged, nothing protruding, nothing upon which the would-be suicidal can harm themselves. The room is meat-locker cold.

Take off your clothes.

Run your fingers through your hair.

Turn around.

Bend over.

Spread your cheeks.

Cough.

I'm handed a one-piece suit made of white paper. No socks or shoes. I look like a malnourished Pillsbury Doughboy.

I try lying down on the wooden slab. On my back, my elbows grind painfully against the hard wood. On my stomach, it's my kneecaps that hurt. Curled into a fetal side position, it's my hip bones and ankles.

I rest my head on a roll of toilet paper.

The blinding lights never go off, day or night. Every fifteen minutes a deputy looks in, smirks contemptuously at the monkey he holds caged, and jots something on a clipboard attached to my door.

Every meal is a baloney-and-cheese sandwich with a cookie, a half-pint of milk, and either an apple or orange. The apples are so cold, they hurt my teeth. It's so chilly in here, I slip lunch bags onto my feet to keep them warm. I stuff toilet paper in my ears to deaden the sound of newly booked winos yelling and slamming against cell doors.

Lice crawl on the wood. Flaky crumby food particles give the cement floor a grainy texture. A puke-stained water fountain dribbles steely-tasting H_2O.

Lying in a paper suit on a wooden bed under scorching white lights, with dark circles under my eyes, stubbly, zit-ravaged cheeks, my hair a woolly mess, lunch bags on my feet, and toilet paper crammed into my ears, it's a pity that no one is here to snap fashion photos of me.

The environment is—how shall I say this?—nontherapeutic. If you seized anyone off the street and placed them here, it would *make* them suicidal.

I mention this to the bearded, bespectacled, clipboard-toting gent in a white frock who visits my cell in the evening. He tells me the main reason for Suicide Watch is to avoid lawsuits from surviving family members of people who've killed themselves while in custody.

Nice. So you just don't want to lose your investment in me.

After he leaves, I think about biting a deep gash in each of my wrists.

During one of the brief patches when I'm able to fall asleep, I dream that I'm walking in my hometown of Philadelphia. I head down a hilly street which affords me a panoramic view of the monstrous, brick-colored city. I approach something which looks like a cathedral, only massively larger—about three hundred feet high. As I get nearer, I can see that the cathedral is condemned, with fencing all around the perimeter and the building's lower half crumbled into orangey brick piles. And up around a hundred and fifty feet high, people are walk-ing amid the bricks. *Why are they up there?* I wonder. *Don't they know they could cause an avalanche?* And as soon as I wonder this, an avalanche begins. I turn away from the church, but small brick chunks are flying sideways through the air, as if propelled by a hurricane-force wind. Women and children are running around screaming in the brickstorm. I calmly walk, cradling a tiny living creature in my arms— a baby or a puppy, I'm not sure. But I'm protecting something small and alive and vulnerable.

And then I awake.

Looking out this cell's thin vertical window, I can see the orange-suited trustees sweeping the floor and preparing the lunch cart to feed new arrivals. At the Justice Center, the orange-suited inmates are usually serving the last few months of their sentences. One orange trustee duti-fully takes orders from an arrogant deputy. The trustee is obedient. Deferential. He knows who is master and who is slave.

He's had his will broken.

He's ready to be reintegrated back into society.

I'd rather die.

After two-and-a-half days of Suicide Watch, I'm deemed a safe risk to return to the Justice Center's general population, with its airless cells and twenty-two-hour-a-day lockdown.

Almost immediately after I arrive in my new dorm, Recreation Yard is called. With a dozen other inmates, I take an elevator up to the tenth floor. I walk out onto a cement basketball court shielded from downtown skyscrapers by a steel fence. Although it's nighttime, I'm blasted with turkey-oven heat. It feels like 100°F, and fireworks are exploding in the early September sky.

Insanity.

Back in my cell, I'm unbrushed, unshaven, and funkily reeking from three days of showerless Suicide Watch afterburn, flailing like a pesticide-sprayed roach about how my belongings and legal notes are missing, and my cellmate, a nineteen-year-old black kid from DC facing bank-robbery charges, calmly offers me an orange.

Thank you.

The next morning is the first chance I've had to use a phone in seventy-two hours. After I dial Sean and manically unspool my Suicide Watch experience, he takes a long pause and tells me that Debbie received the results of her latest cancer test.

Any score over 35 is considered evidence of cancer.

Two months ago, it was 19.

This time it's 130.

I feel as if someone has pricked me with a pin and let out all the air. My eyes become red and swollen. I choke on each word as if it were a chicken bone.

I call Debbie and tell her I wish it was me instead of her. I say that I might kill myself on the day that she dies. "I look at the pets," she says frantically, "and—and—I love them so much! I'm scared! I'm so scared! Why, why, why? I'm too young! Why is this happening? I'm all alone! You should be out!"

A few days pass.

My mother dies.

Over the past two weeks I've been dealt eighteen years in new charges. I made it through Suicide Watch. Debbie suffered a relapse. And mommy croaked.

Let's see how strong I am.

My cell is seven floors above the street. As I try falling asleep after breakfast, I look out the window. I picture a rack of body bags being wheeled out from this building toward a van parked on the sunny street. One of the bags contains my dead body. I imagine medical scavengers picking at my spleen and kidneys like hungry inmates grabbing at bread and eggs from an extra breakfast tray.

Why live?

To see what comes next.

To see how much I can take.

Because I've yet to figure out why I should live.

Because my death would satisfy all the wrong people.

Because the world doesn't want me to live.

Because I'd rather be an asshole than a martyr.

Because the kids need a role model.

Because nonexistence would get boring awfully quick.

Because this TV channel, even with the twenty-four-hour horror movie, is better than the one with around-the-clock gray static noise.

Because it would show that they haven't killed me.

Because I don't want to die in jail or prison.

Because I still need to make a gift to the world of all that's bottled up inside me.

Because over the years, the guilt will gnaw away at my accuser rather than at me. Of that I'm sure.

Because not for a moment have I felt like a less worthy person than the lunatic whore who wishes me dead.

Nor, despite all my agony, have I felt like I deserved any of this suffering.

The forces arrayed against me are considerable. And yet I think they've underestimated me.

With the help of some good friends, I finally scrape together enough cash to pay for a real lawyer. We appear in court alongside Big Rod and bump the trial date from October 29th to January 18th.

Time to prepare. Time to fight. If I gotta go, I'll go down swinging.

I'm not going to kill myself. You'll have to do it. Here—take the gun.

Debbie tells me she left a voicemail message for Anne to the effect of, "I'm dying, Jim's in jail, and I hope you're fucking happy."

Anne calls back, hisses, "You're just a masochist for wanting him out of jail!," and hangs up on her.

She calls again and apologizes. She asks if she can visit Debbie, and Debbie says yes.

Anne brings her milk and chocolate. She tells Debbie she hasn't so much as kissed anyone since my arrest. She says she still loves me.

Good thing she doesn't hate me.

She tells Debbie that after she dies of cancer, *ANSWER Me!*'s legend will expand and Debbie will be immortal in a sense. She compares the three of us to the British Suicide Kids. She says she believes in karma and realizes that she's doomed just like the Goads are.

How thoroughly romantic.

She says that she's "always suicidal" and will probably kill herself or be murdered by an *ANSWER Me!* fan.

Any idea *when* this will happen? Before trial, *peut-être, ma cherie*?

She says (hopes?) that I probably hate her for what she's doing. When Debbie implies that it might be difficult to feel the warm fuzzies toward someone who wants you locked down for twenty-five years, Anne says I'll "only" do ten to fifteen and that I need to "learn a lesson."

She tells Debbie that she never wanted to press charges in the first place, that it was all Big Rod's idea.

That must be why she pressed charges in the first place.

And appeared before two Grand Juries.

And gave a lengthy taped testimonial to investigators.

And gave them *ANSWER Me!*

And led them to witnesses she thought would bolster her case.

And called every print-media outlet she could think of.

Must be.

She admits that she did some crazy things while with me, but says I forced her into it all.

I guess my evil, Svengali-like influence over her was also retroactive, because she did a lot of crazy things before she met me.

I sent telepathic messages through a time tunnel and forced her to attempt suicide four times in her teens.

And I forced her to threaten and assault her family members before she met me.

And to sleep with thirty-five guys in three years before she met me.

And to walk around Portland with gutterpunks' cum plastered on her chin.

And to blow one of the gutterpunks' pet dogs.

And to throw a concrete block through her first married boyfriend's windows.

And the article she wrote about the hundred shitty things she'd done to hurt other people before she met me?

I forced the bitch to do all hunnert of 'em.

And, naturally, by sleeping with the chubby redhead, I forced Anne to bop the girl's noodle with an axe handle.

And by telling her I wanted to see other women, I forced her to chop off all her hair and eat dog poop.

And by telling her to go home, I forced her to do things such as drink cleaning fluid and smash my windshield.

And by telling her she's not the one, I forced her to punch me in the face and bite my elbow.

And by pulling away from her, I forced her to stalk me and threaten to kill me.

I'm a very powerful man. Not only am I wholly responsible for all of my own actions, I'm totally to blame for all of hers, too.

In mid-October a reporter for SPIN magazine gives Anne the Publicity Slut her first taste of national attention. He interviews her for hours via telephone. He later tells me she's obviously "not a stable person." He says he made the mistake of informing Anne that he'd also interviewed other Portlanders about the case. He says he feels like calling everyone back and warning them that she'd be on the warpath.

At 5:50AM on the morning after her interview, Anne calls Sean, apparently incensed that he had the gall to talk about her to the press. She's doing exactly what she falsely accused me of doing the morning of my crime—freaking out because people were going public with negative opinions of her. Over the next three days, she'll call Sean over twenty times. And Sean, bless his Middle Eastern gemstone of a heart, captures it all on tape.

These excerpts boldly take you within the mind of our tragic victim:

From October 12, 1998:

CALL 1 from Anne to Sean, about 5:50AM
SEAN: Hello.
ANNE: I hate you so fucking much. [hangs up]

CALL 2 from Sean to Anne, about 5:50AM
Sean calls back. **Anne** picks up and says, "Your boy is going away for 15 years. 15 years, 15 years, 15 years," then hangs up.

CALL 5 from Sean to Anne, about 6:00AM
SEAN: Last time I talked to you it was a matter of you biting him so that you could do damage. Every time you attacked him you tried to do damage, but you weren't able to.
ANNE: Same with him on me! Same with him on me! Why wouldn't he go to court on the 29th? Because he knows he doesn't have a case! The DA is so confident about this, it's not even funny. He's GOING to prison. It's going to be so funny, and I will spit on your face and laugh at you on the day he does.
SEAN: That's exactly it...
[Anne hangs up]

CALL 6 from Anne to Sean, about 6:05AM
ANNE: [singing] You ain't getting out on the 29th! You can say I did everything [unintelligible]
SEAN: I remember when you ate dog shit.
ANNE: I assaulted Darcy, I ate dog shit, I did all that, [still singing, gloating, disgustingly gleeful] and I ain't going to prison for it! And Jim's going to prison for the 20 months, baby! Lick my twat! Lick my twat!

SEAN: You don't care what you did?

ANNE: I care, I care, and I ain't—I'm getting off! I don't got charges against me, Sean! Jim does! Jim has charges! He's going to prison!

SEAN: No matter what you do? No matter all the things you've done?

ANNE: He's going to prison! Where's the charges at, baby?! Where's the Darcy charges?! They haven't been brought up!

SEAN: You can hit someone and—you're just gloating. See?

ANNE: There's no case! No case! Yes, I can! I can do whatever I want! And he's going to prison, baby! Bye-bye! [hangs up]

CALL 7 from Sean to Anne, 6:20AM

ANNE: [picks up] He's in that little jail cell now, in that blue uniform—

SEAN: Nothing that you do matters?

ANNE: He hasn't had it on for four months! He hasn't had a woman in four months! I love it! I love it! I love it! Love it! Love it! Love it! [hangs up]

CALL 10 from Anne to Sean, about 7:20AM

ANNE: [N]ow I'm having my revenge and I'm destroying all of you, it's just pretty beautiful to me. It's complete victory!

SEAN: You're not destroying me.

ANNE: Your little boy that you've been taking care of...he's going to go to prison.

SEAN: He's a friend of mine. I know you and I know him, and I think I can figure out what went on.

ANNE: He's going to prison, Jim—er, Sean. He's going to prison. He is going to prison! [kissing noises, then whispers] He's going to prison! [hangs up]

CALL 11 from Anne to Sean, about 7:25AM

ANNE: And um, pull out a single fucking picture out of your ass, besides those ones of him that he scratched up his face right after he assaulted me, and fucking bloodied up his nose—find ONE...where it's EQUAL to where he kicked my ass. Find one! Find one!

SEAN: Yeah, you clocked Darcy in the back of the head and you didn't take pictures of it—

ANNE: Baby—

SEAN: —it doesn't even matter to you?

ANNE: Baby—where's the case? Where's the case? Where's the case? Where's the case? Hey, it'll matter to me if there's a case in my face, but there ain't no case! Because it was a catfight. It was not the same as what Jim did—

SEAN: —a catfight is where one person clocks another in the back of the head when she turns around? That's a catfight to you?

ANNE: Where's the case? This is about May 29th.

SEAN: This is me telling you exactly what you're all about.

ANNE: Jim Goad v. the State of Oregon, May 29th. May 29th. He talk about it? Tell me what happened May 29th? Tell me what happened that morning.

SEAN: Tell me what happened with Darcy.

ANNE: It's not about that. I'll tell you about it when I'm on the stand.

SEAN: That's what my point is all about.

ANNE: I'll tell you about it when I'm on the stand, motherfucker....You fucker. You mother-fucker—

SEAN: Who pulled the weapon out of the bag and clocked her?

ANNE: You motherfucker. Suck my fucking dick, you motherfucker. You're going down.

[hangs up]

CALL 16 from Anne to Sean, about 7:50AM

ANNE: How's our cancer patient?

SEAN: Like you care.

ANNE: I love it, I hope she dies today. [hangs up]

CALL 17 from Anne to Sean, about 7:52AM

ANNE: I'm soooo happy right now. Just tell that to Jim and Debbie both. I am so fucking happy.

SEAN: She's feeling like shit lately, she's going through chemo again.

ANNE: That's awesome! [hangs up]

CALL 18 from Anne to Sean, about 7:55AM

ANNE: Ha ha ha ha! We'll see him in prison. It's so fucking wonderful. It's so beautiful, I couldn't be happier. And Debbie'll be dead, soon, too. My life is wonderful. I'm going to jerk off to it, I love it. [hangs up]

From October 13, 1998:

CALL 2 from Anne to Sean, 11:25AM

ANNE: I just have one last thing to say to you...I just—I have no guilty conscience whatsoever, and you can tell Jim I take great pleasure in the fact that he's suffering, and I know exactly what he's going through, because I've spent time in jail, of course not as much time as him, and I think he fully deserves everything he's getting, and I hope he goes away for a long, long time. And that's it.

CALL 3 from Anne to Sean, early afternoon

ANNE: I think it's funny that you think he's going to get off just totally scot-free and going to walk. It think that's pretty funny.

SEAN: I think it's pretty funny that you're so damned confident. I think it's even funnier that the DA is so damned confident. That damn near makes me piss my pants.

ANNE: Why?

SEAN: Because being around you, and he's still confident, that makes him an idiot.

ANNE: Well, he's not an idiot, he's won like 95% of his cases.

SEAN: I guess that makes the legal system incredibly stupid. But it still makes him an idiot.

ANNE: Well, you probably think most defense attorneys are idiots, most cops are idiots.

SEAN: Unlike you, who's got nothing but the most solid respect for the law.

ANNE: I do now.

SEAN: Uh-huh. Well, are you going to go turn yourself in for the Darcy thing, then?

ANNE: No! Because there's no charges.

SEAN: It would be the right thing to do, Anne.

ANNE: There's no charges, Sean...It's not a crime.

SEAN: It's not a crime to clock people in the back of the head with axe handles? Well, you should come over here!

ANNE: It's not a crime unless there's a charge....

SEAN: If you commit a crime, and you tell people, they will make a case for it.

ANNE: It's a fairy tale. It doesn't even exist.

SEAN: It's a fairy tale that you've admitted to all these different people.

ANNE: Where am I being charged? Who's knocking on my door to charge me? Where are the charges?

SEAN: Why don't we start some charges?

ANNE: Try. Try, boy. [hangs up]

CALL 9 from Anne to Sean, 11:30PM Tuesday night, after Sean leaves a message back to her

SEAN: Hello?

ANNE: Debbie dead yet? Do you think she's going to make it 'til January?

SEAN: I don't know, do you think she is?

ANNE: I don't think so.

SEAN: Hmmm. I bet you're going to just masturbate furiously over that.

ANNE: Probably....

From October 14, 1998:

[one of several calls from Anne on this day]

ANNE: Ha ha ha, she's gonna die, he's gonna go to jail, see you, motherfucker—I hate your fucking guts. [hangs up]

[start of call]

ANNE: ...The entire drive I was screaming at the top of my lungs, and pleading for my life...I tried to open up the door. And I couldn't fucking get out.

SEAN: Why couldn't you open the door?

ANNE: I couldn't open the door because he's punching me as hard as I could [sic] in the fucking face! And my eye was fucking bleeding—YOU DON'T FUCKIN' KNOW THE FACTS, MOTHERFUCKER! [hangs up]

[start of call]
ANNE: [E]ven if I wanted to be beaten on past occasions, it does not mean that I wanted to be beaten to a bloody pulp *that day*. Okay?...I was honking the horn, and I tried to open up the door, and he bit me on the right wrist, and on the left thumb. And I couldn't get out. And he locked the door. And that's when he started punching my face as hard as I [sic] could....WHAT THE FUCK DO YOU THINK? WHAT THE FUCK DO YOU THINK? Why would I want to stay in that car and be repeatedly beaten?! What the fuck do you think?!
SEAN: I think you were probably involved in a fight with him. [Anne starts fake laughing, hangs up]

Don't you feel sorry for poor widdle baby? Don'cha just wanna cuddle her and say it'll be awright?

I knew that if I gave her enough time, she'd do something to fuck up her case. The girl has loose lips on both ends of her body, and she can't keep either set shut for very long.

In her manic quest to rebuild the fragile female ego which I'd apparently crushed, she's concocted a revised parallel universe of how things had been between us.

In this New World, I was the one who was out of control.

I was the one who said I couldn't live without her.

I treated her like a whore, demanded daily blow jobs, and would wake her up to say "let's fuck." Even though she initiated sex every time. EVERY time.

And on the night in question, she was just trying to end it between us, and I got violent.

Yeah, and those Jews sure gassed a lotta Germans in WWII.

Oh, how time changes things:

"...everything that you said was true, about me being more obsessed with you and loving you more..."
—Anne's phone message to me, 5/4/98

"...he was just as obsessed with me as I was with him."
—Anne's taped phone conversation with Sean Tejaratchi, 10/13/98

******

"...I'm violating the Restraining Order... I can't stay away from you..."

—Anne's phone message to me, 5/6/98

"After the Restraining Order...I would have gladly stayed away..."

—Anne's taped phone conversation with Sean Tejaratchi, 10/13/98

* * * * * *

"According to [Anne], Goad woke up [on 5/29/98] and said, 'Get the fuck out of bed. I'm taking you home. It's over. I'm never seeing you again."

—Anne quoting me in SPIN *magazine*

"...on May 29th, in the morning, I turned to him and said, 'Jim, it's over. For good.' He kidnapped me..."

—Anne's taped phone conversation with Sean Tejaratchi, 10/13/98

Poor li'l victim.

Dumb little bitch.

We're going to make you look like a chimpanzee on the stand.

Try explaining your death threats to a jury. Your false rape charge. My Restraining Order. Your nutty phone calls to Sean. We're laying so many land mines for you, your head will pop off. And then the jury will see you for what you are...

A willing combatant rather than a victim.

The prosecution is coming at me with a big black wall of evidence, seeking to snuff the life out of me. Each hole in that wall allows a little sunshine into my cell. Each hole is another reason to live.

As the days shorten, my cell grows grayer. Darker. More dismal. And my resolve strengthens. A sickening monomania consumes me. I have twenty-two hours every day in this cell to probe every hole in their case. Tiny golf pencils. Looseleaf paper. I sit in the lotus position on my upper bunk, diligently working on my defense. Fighting for my life.

I'm in a strange position—I committed the crimes according to the legal definition, but not the way she said it happened. And I can *prove* it didn't happen the way she said it did. My task is to disprove her version of events so thoroughly that it creates reasonable doubt.

HER IMPLAUSIBLE THREAT TO "OUT" ME

When the 911 operator originally asked her the reason why I beat her up, Anne said, "He's insane, I don't know….I don't know if this is his temper, I don't know."

But four days later with detectives, she said I "lost it" when she threatened to "out" me about domestic violence. The problem with her story: My domestic violence was no secret. In both public and private forums, Debbie had already blabbed to anyone who'd listen that I'd been violent with her.

Anne also knew that for our collaborative zine *BLOW Me!*, I was going to write an article called "To All the Girls I've Hit Before." So we could prove that on the morning in question, Anne was already aware that my horrific domestic violence was common knowledge.

The truth was that after she'd gone on the Net squealing about my plastic surgery, she had no secrets on me. And I was so "upset" by her posts, I took her out to breakfast and then fucked her.

THE DISAPPEARING BLACK GUY

For months I've been pleading with investigators to find the black male who saw us struggling after the first time she lunged at my face. It shouldn't have been too hard, because he had a key to her building. Plus, there are only about a dozen black guys in Portland, and most of them play for the Trail Blazers.

Anne mentioned the black guy in her first interview with detectives. But in all subsequent versions of her story, she omits him, because she knew he'd be troublesome for her case.

She told detectives the black guy saw me punch her so hard that she collapsed in her seat. Then Brother Darky asks ME if everything is OK and leaves after I assure him we're all right. In Anne's version she's totally silent, allowing the chocolate-coated Good Samaritan to quietly walk away.

And if such a world-class loudmouth as Anne had been slugged so hard by me that she goes down in her seat, and someone came offering assistance, she would've yelped for help and exited the parked car. And if the black guy—or anyone—had seen a man bru-tally punching a woman, he wouldn't merely have taken the man's assurance that everything was dandy.

What actually happened is that Mr. Superfly saw us wrestling, asked us *both* if everything is OK, and walked away after we *both* told him we could handle it.

THE POWERLESS POWER LOCKS

Twelve different times—to policemen, detectives, reporters, Debbie, and Sean—Anne claimed she was trapped in the car because I pressed the power-lock button.

He locked the doors so I couldn't get out of the car. When I was tryin' to, um, open the door, the locks were automatic. I tried that and I tried that.

—*To detectives, 6/2/98*

Impossible. The car was a 1998 Ford, and Ford hasn't made a car since the late 1960s in which you can be locked from the inside. Even with power locks, all you need to do is pull the handle, and the door opens.

THE MYSTERY BITE MARK

Two weeks before trial, my lawyer shows me a picture of a bite mark on Anne's right wrist. The photo was taken in the DA's office, but the date wasn't noted.

What's that?

"That's what you're facing the Assault II charge for."

But I thought it was for the bite mark on her left thumb.

"No, it's for a more severe bite mark on her right wrist."

But I only bit her thumb!

The hospital reports make ten different mentions of a bite mark on her left thumb.

The police reports mention the thumb bite three times.

Three days after the shit went down, Anne called a detective and told him I bit her left thumb.

In a taped conversation with detectives four days after the incident, she says I bit her left thumb.

But in none of these reports—*none* of them—is there mention of a more serious bite mark to her right wrist. You would think that if I had caused it, there would be at least one mention of it in these early reports.

Maybe she's insisting I inflicted my own wounds because honey-chile did a little inflicting of her own.

BLOOD FOR CHRISTMAS

My mug shot showed cuts on my face. So did several pictures that Debbie took. A big scratch on my cheek. A smaller one on my nose. An even smaller one on my forehead. That was it. Nothing major. If I was going to inflict wounds on myself, I would have done a much more drastic job of it than Anne wound up doing to me, especially knowing the damage I'd done to her.

But Anne has consistently denied hitting me on the morning in question. When Debbie tells Anne she witnessed blood caked up inside my nose, Anne theorizes that I must have inserted a razor in my nostril and slit it myself. Ya, *that's* reasonable.

Big Rod, seeking to discount any claims of self-defense, orders that a DNA sample be taken from me to prove my blood wasn't found in the car.

And so comes Grinch the Detective, along with some forensics geek, to stick cotton swabs in my mouth and scrape for DNA.

The results come back right before Christmas—my blood is found in six samples—five in the car, and one on her clothes. Even more significantly, my blood is found *mixed* with hers in some of the samples, meaning we bled at the same time and the blood dried at the same time.

There was no way I could have deliberately mixed my blood with hers after the incident, especially on her clothes.

When I was booked, police noted no scratches or cuts on either of my hands during a routine check for signs of assaultive behavior.

The blood came from my face. Even after I tried cleaning the blood out of the car, my blood was found all over the place.

The blood evidence proves my version of events is true.

PROSECUTION WITNESSES

I found several minor flaws in the testimonies of the two prosecution witnesses who'd dialed 911.

But I kept fixating on the female jogger who said she saw a car speeding by, heard a woman screaming, and saw a male driver leaning over as if pulling "something or someone" back in.

She's the one who worries me.

A lot.

She was around the right place at around the right time, and if jurors are able to forgive the defects in her story and believe the kernel of it—that she saw me pulling Anne back in the car against her will—I'd be convicted of kidnapping and forced to serve at least seven-and-a-half years.

I dream that I try crossing a bridge back home to my apartment, but the bridge keeps falling in the water.

I dream that I'm in a cheap, scummy restaurant in Southeast Portland eating a hamburger. One of the patrons says, "Jim Goad's trial is coming up." I look outside, and the sky is glutted with dark, menacing clouds. The stratospheric blanket is only pierced by a small, sunny hole in the far-off distance.

I wake up in the middle of the night to the sounds of screaming, only to realize it's all in my head.

In the morning I look out my cell window across a snowy public park to the county courthouse, the place where I'm almost certain they'll hang me.

During my walk time, I catch peripheral glimpses of television. I see ordinary things—people wearing jeans, couples dancing, freeway traffic at rush hour—and I fear I'll never be part of that world again. If I'm convicted, the outside world will remain outside. It'll be as impossible to enter that world as it would be to walk up to the TV and step inside it.

On New Year's Eve, Debbie tells me the doctors say she has only two months to live. I fall asleep crying at around 8:30PM. At midnight I'm yanked from slumber by the sound of inmates pounding on their wooden doors to ring in the New Year. I stay awake and cry throughout the night. And for most of New Year's Day. All of my tears are for Debbie, not for me.

In a fit of cockeyed romanticism, I'm willing to go to trial on the outside chance that I get acquitted and am set free in time to take care of Debbie during her final days.

But then I realize she hasn't shown me nearly the same degree of compassion.

My survival instinct swells up inside me. Just like it did when Anne punched me on the morning of May 29th.

Protect yourself. Remember that small living creature you were guarding during that dream where bricks were flying everywhere? Protect it.

One of the biggest reasons I'm in this predicament is that I worried too much about Debbie and Anne's well-being and not enough about my own. I had numerous chances to disengage from both of them but hadn't done it because I didn't want them to die.

And look where I've landed.

I picture myself as a juror. Despite all the fluffy meringue about "innocent until proven guilty," most jurors start with a presumption of guilt. They *want* the guy to be guilty and usually have to be convinced otherwise. If all the evidence was presented to me as a juror, I probably would've figured out what happened—Anne was lying about how it started, but the most serious charge of Kidnapping had been committed according to the letter of the law. I had moved her more than three feet against her will.

Early in January, I ask my lawyer to ferret out the possibility of a plea bargain. She brings Big Rod some of our evidence. He starts to realize that his lost little girl is lying about key elements of what happened that morning. He reportedly "blanched" when he saw the transcripts where Anne's gloating about getting away with violent crimes and how she's jerking off to the prospect of Debbie's death.

Big Rod offers me a deal. If I plead guilty to Attempted Kidnapping in the First Degree, Attempted Assault in the Second Degree, and Misdemeanor Assault, he'll drop the other charges. My sentence will be three years. Counting good-behavior credits and the seven-and-a-half months I've already served in jail, I'll have another twenty-one months to go.

That's a lot better than fifteen years.

I'm also forced to pay $500 in court costs and $1,820 for Anne's psychiatric bills.

As if I caused her mental problems.

As part of some Victims' Rights law, Big Rod is required to ask Anne whether she approves of the deal.

At first she says no. She wants me buried for much longer.

And then Big Rod apparently scolds her for fucking up his case by lying and making all those insane phone calls to Sean. He tells her there's a chance I could walk free.

Reluctantly, she agrees to the deal.

In court, my lawyer tells the judge that Anne and I had the unhealthiest relationship she'd seen in her ten years as an attorney and that what happened was almost inevitable. I tell the judge that I contest the accuser's version of events but that in essence, the crimes had been committed.

I sign the papers and walk out of the courtroom. Even in handcuffs, I feel a hundred pounds lighter.

I'll be free in less than two years.

My life isn't over.

She hasn't destroyed me.

She wanted me, dead or alive.

She didn't get me.

⸮15⸮

Angels With Black Eyes

IT SOUNDS LIKE steam escaping...

PFFSSSSSSSSSS

...the hydraulic hissing sound which opens my cell door in the morning...

PFFSSSSSSSSSS

...sounds like my nerves decompressing from the emotional G-force of my time in jail...

PFFSSSSSSSSSS

...get up. Stretch out. Exit the steel door and walk up and down the hundred-foot cement corridor which runs along the cells. Up and down, up and down this artificially lit concrete pod. This piss-stained, steamy-hot, echoey wind tunnel. This gray catacomb.

I saw the fences and razor wire coming into this place. They made me strip naked, peeked at my anus, and gave me a new set of blue canvas pajamas.

They took a new mug shot and encased it in a new plastic wristband. I look drastically worse than I did on the mug shot from back when I was first arrested.

I look like I have no soul.

I could be here a week, could be here a month. They won't tell me. They call this place the Oregon Correctional Intake Center, located in Oregon City, OR.

Anne's hometown.

Everyone headed to prison in Oregon has to pass through this processing station. We're all in the mouth of the beast, headed down into the belly.

The amphetamine desperation of county jail is gone, replaced by a churchlike solemnity. Inmates slowly walk up and down the pod like monks in a monastery.

No books. No television. No visitors. We are here to be observed. Each cell has a two-way mirror so the guards can snoop on us at all hours. They can watch us shitting on steel toilets or jacking off on steel bunks. At mealtime, we stand in line to be handed steel trays through a slot in the wall. We're all bacteria on a giant petri dish.

They poke me with a needle to draw blood. They jab me with another spike to test for TB. They stick a steel dental pick in my mouth to probe for cavities. They administer rudimentary math and English tests. A five-hundred-sixty-seven-question personality test.

And at 10PM, I'm back in the cell to be locked down for the night.

My cellmate is an effeminately Chaplinesque gent who calls himself Jericho. His skin is saggy and yellowy from the Hepatitis-C he shot into himself with a dirty needle years ago. The disease has progressed into the first stages of liver cancer.

Jericho has been dealt a fifteen-year sentence for armed robbery. Plenty of time for his cancer to slither into its final stages. He'll die in prison.

We talk most of the night. Jericho says when he was a boy, his father used to suck his dick, then beat the shit out of him, call him a faggot, and lock him in Jericho's toy box. Dad once tied him to a post in the basement, flooded the room with three feet of dirty water, and left for the weekend. Water rats nibbled at Jericho's flesh until dad got back, untied him, sucked his dick, and beat the shit out of him again.

Dad never spent a day in prison.

At age eighteen, Jericho was arrested in Utah for being in the getaway car with some friends who'd pulled a robbery. He spent almost five years locked in a toy box called The Point, which he says has been rated one of the country's worst prisons. His eyes grow cold and haunted as he recalls knife fights and murders and the sight of a bloody eyeball impaled on an inmate's long, unclipped fingernail.

After being released from The Point, Jericho became a heavy-metal singer whose band once opened for Dokken. He starred in a porno film called *12 Inches and Counting*. He says a friend in southern Oregon once showed him a room in his house whose walls are covered with Polaroids he snapped of his victims' faces while torturing them.

Although he says he's a Christian, Jericho keeps begging to suck my dick. And I almost let him, but it'd be too much of a head trip right now.

In the morning comes the loud sound of steam escaping again...

PFFSSSSSSSSSS

...news of my plea bargain has hit the press. The AP wire story's headline is "Satirist Sentenced in Beating." *The Oregonian* opts for the yellow-journalistic "Promoter of Violence Guilty in Attack." The local alternative freebie *Willamette Week*'s account is surprisingly balanced, the only article which raises questions about Anne's innocence. It quotes Big Rod saying he wished I received a longer sentence, but that Anne's history of violence and wackiness impelled him to offer a deal. Big Rod expresses compassion for Anne, who he says placed herself "in harm's way" by choosing to be my girlfriend.

And I suppose I was entering a safety zone by dating *her*.

The piece ends with me shrugging off guilt: "I'm not sorry at all....I have absolutely no remorse."

And why should I?

I've had my ass kicked several times in my life, a few times as bad or worse than Anne got it that morning, so I know what it feels like. For the most part, the suffering is over when the swelling goes down. If the punishment should fit the crime, I'd gladly volunteer to have someone pummel my face for ten minutes in a moving car—it wouldn't be the first time. The Bible dictates an eye for an eye, and that would be fine.

But a week—only a *week*—in jail is worse than a week spent nursing a shiner. I'll wind up doing two-and-a-half YEARS. So on top of the punishment being far, far worse than the crime, I'm supposed to emotionally flog myself about it, too?

I'm supposed to feel bad while Anne gloats about getting away with so many violent crimes? When I dropped so many police complaints against her? When she did her best to bury me after I'd done my best to keep her out of trouble? If I was as malicious as she is, *she'd* be the one headed to prison now rather than me.

Sorry? Don't think so.

If a *man* had shown the consistent pattern of menacing and violence that Anne did, and a woman finally smashed his skull with a frying pan—or even *murdered* him—she'd be considered a hero rather than a pariah. So I'm required to hate myself merely because my penis casts me on the heavy side of the gender-war seesaw?

No. I won't do it.

I did the right thing that morning up in the hills. I saved my life. I spared hers, too.

The authorities want me to make a Pavlovian link between my suffering in jail with the suffering I inflicted on Anne. They want me to think that her suffering was totally undeserved, while mine is wholly justified. But what if you think it's *all* wrong...or all right? Why is human suffering wrong in one context and right in another?

So I'm not sorry.

Sorry.

If I'm going to pay for the crime so heavily, I might as well savor sweet memories of it. I might as well fondly recall the sound of Anne squealing for her life and the sight of her blood spraying through the air like slow-motion photography of a sneeze.

Especially since she's out on the streets, saying she gets "great pleasure" from my suffering.

What's good for the goose is good for the gander.

Isn't that what equality's all about?

Anne, the Psycho Succubus of the Neo-Matriarchy, leaves a voice-mail message for Sean Tejaratchi saying she's bought a gun and I'd better stay away from her when I parole. She tells him that "you men" will never understand the horrors of being victimized by violence and that us guys don't even deserve to express opinions about it. She says she's going to milk the situation for all the publicity she can get.

A few days later, she phones Sean again in the middle of the night. She gleefully tells him that Debbie and her are now best buddies and will do everything in their power "to piss Jim off."

I call Debbie to ask if this is true.

In the year since our divorce, I've apologized over and over and over and over for the pain I'd caused her. While I was rotting in county jail and she said I deserved being there, I bit my lip and said I loved her. When she told me she wouldn't cry if I died, I bit my lip harder and said I hoped she lived another forty years to hate me, if that's what kept her alive. I have made every sort of conciliatory, shit-eating gesture short of killing myself.

I remind her that Anne had recently claimed she was masturbating to the idea of Debbie's death.

"But she apologized," Debbie says.

Hmm. Now why didn't *I* think of that?

I say that if she wants to ally herself with someone who's been campaigning for my extinction, that's cool—she'll just never hear from me again.

"You deserve to go to prison," she spits.

And does Anne deserve to go to prison for all of her violent crimes?

"You should never hit a woman," she non-answers.

So is it OK to hit a man?

"You should never hit a woman," she replies, zombielike. Then, planting the incisors deeper: "Your life is destroyed. You lost your house, you lost your car, you lost your dog, you deserve everything that happened to you and worse."

And guess what? I'll be ALIVE in a year-and-a-half, and I'll walk out of prison stronger than ever.

Soon afterward, she hangs up.

She tells people I said,

You're gonna die! You're gonna die!

I didn't. I said,

I'll be ALIVE...

It makes all the difference.

She equates my survival with her destruction. And my destruction with her survival.

I return to my cell, crawl under my sweaty, cum-stained blanket, and ponder the improbable union of my ex-paramours.

Debbie's motivations are transparent. She's dying, desperate, and aching with loneliness. Before she steps into the grave, she needs someone to pat her on the head and say that nothing was her fault. She thirsts for the unquestioning sympathy I refused to give her.

So into her life flutters Pixie Anne, doing her little Florence Nightingale routine for the cancer patient.

On some level, perhaps deeper than the thin, flaky crust I suspect it is, Anne seems motivated by compassion for Debbie in the way one feels protective of a wounded animal. And that's admirable.

But part of it is an obvious ploy to expunge her own guilt for stealing Debbie's man.

A big part of it is vindictiveness toward me.

Part of it is an addiction to the nuclear-fallout energy which continues to unspool from this shattered love triangle.

And part of it seems to be a *Whatever Happened to Baby Jane?*-styled sadistic urge to see just how thoroughly she can swindle the dying invalid. Anne has a quasi-sexual attraction for any morbid, pathetic, intense situation. A Psychic Vampiress of the highest order, she enjoys siphoning the life energies from those who are dying.

She likes being in control. She told me she resented that I was smarter and stronger than her.

Debbie's easy pickin's. She's dumber and weaker. Anne will hold Debbie in her thrall by manipulating her bitterness and self-pity. She will take Debbie's brain, already softened by chemo, and work it like Play-Doh.

There are obstacles to their union, chief among them a heapin' helpin' of hypocrisy. If the tables were reversed and Debbie had shanghaied Anne's husband, Anne would have *murdered* Debbie instead of befriending her.

I'm sure she won't tell Debbie about all the nasty things she said about her. She probably won't recite any of those cancer jokes. Or mention the time she told me, "I don't see how you could have been with someone so stupid for eleven years." Or the time she watched a videotaped interview with Debbie and told me, "God, she comes off dumb." Chances are good she won't remind her of the Internet posting where she said she never pretended to be Debbie's friend, and that anyone who did was a hypocrite. Or the time she responded to Debbie's announcement that we'd divorced with a post saying, "Give it up, grrrl. Nobody cares...[signed] The 21-year-old Stripper." I don't think she'll tell Debbie about how she'd laughed at the pain and anger in voicemail messages Debbie had left me after our divorce. Or the time she said, "I hope the retard dies of cancer" after learning that Debbie had lied to her about my whereabouts on the night I slept with the redhead.

Debbie, for her part, has to forgive the woman who sucked her husband's cock on the night of Debbie's cancer surgery. I'm sure Debbie won't inform Anne about the time she said, "Between you and me, Anne's just a joke." Or the time she said, "Anne's so loud and annoying—how can you stand it?"

I'm positive she won't tell her what she said the time I showed her the Polaroid of Anne's cunt.

But these girls share some character traits which should help them overcome such formidable hurdles:

Self-loathing.

A history of self-mutilating behavior.

They both view themselves as tragic figures.

And the biggie:

We both share a hatred of Jim Goad.

—*Debbie, quoted by a reporter*

In other words, they both still have feelings for Jim Goad. And if they can't have a relationship *with* Jim Goad, they'll have one *about* Jim Goad.

Both of them announce they'll write "tell-alls" supposedly designed to destroy my "legend."

Both publicly express a desire that I get the shit stomped out of me in prison.

Both flaunt precisely the same sort of cruelty of which they accuse me.

There's a strong iconoclastic element to their vengeance. They act like rabid Italians kicking Mussolini's corpse through the streets. Or like Judases with vaginas, offering up their ex-savior to appease a bloodthirsty mob.

These days, the mob turns victims into saints.

"Abuse Victims" has a haunting melody, ladies, and you've obviously memorized all the words, but do you know any other songs? How about "Jilted Lovers"? Wanna hum a few bars of that?

Let's eavesdrop on one of their hate-Jim hysteria-fests:

DEB: Jim Goad is such a prick!
ANNE: He's TOTALLY a prick!
DEB: He hit me!
ANNE: He hit me, too!
DEB: He yelled at me!
ANNE: He yelled at me, too!
DEB: He rejected my pussy!
ANNE: He rejected my puss—um, like, let's change the subject, 'kay?

In their numerous public vituperations against me, they're strangely silent on the manner of my cheating. It's odd, because both of them repeatedly told me that the infidelity bothered them far more than the fisticuffs.

Debbie always said I could do anything to her—just don't cheat. She said the cheating made her feel as if she was being split in half with an axe.

Anne always told me that the violence was a sign I was passionate toward her. Her death threats didn't start until I told her I'd slept with Debbie one night during our affair. Her assaults upon me had nothing to do with *my* violence—it was all sparked by *her* jealousy and fear of abandonment.

But my ex-lovemuffins don't advertise about the cheating, because it would call their own desirability into question. It would also lay bare the roots of their vengefulness.

Hell hath no fury like two mentally ill women scorned.

The female ego. Such a fragile little ovum. Women seem hard-wired to believe they own the Earth's only desirable cootchie. It's incomprehensible to a gal that once you've basked in the soppy glories of her hole, you'd ever want another. When you reject that pungent little honeycomb of theirs, no degree of vengeance seems too severe to them.

There's a biological underpinning to this behavior. The male is pro-grammed to spray his seed like a tomcat soiling every curtain in the house. The female plays the role of selector/rejecter. So when a man circumvents this natural tradition and rejects a woman, her mind goes haywire.

About a week before I crushed Anne's little baby face...and little baby dreams...with my fist, she had e-mailed Debbie a message stating how they both knew I was a "good catch."

Now, all of a sudden, I'm a bad guy.

It's called sour grapes. If they couldn't have me, then obviously I wasn't worth having.

I lived with the prick for quite a few years....Prison is the correct place for the scum to be.... Jim Goad is a thief, a liar, a fraud, a wife-beater, and a psychotically sick individual who should be kept in jail or institutionalized the rest of his life.

—Debbie, posting on Usenet newsgroup alt.zines

Asshole Jail Scum...I'd tell you to go to hell, but you're already there. Have a happy '99 behind bars. Prick...BAN his book! This man is awful, evil, beyond cruel, and DESERVES TO DIE!

—Anne, posting on alt.zines

Can you feel the love in the air?

Laying it on a bit thick, are we, ladies?

I'm "scum," eh?

I wasn't the one who ate shit.

Or the one who called myself a piece of shit.

I just attract shit. Opposites attract.

Some will say I'm merely in denial. I'd be happy if that were the case. Being a monster would be easy.

Being a tortured human being who tried his best is pure hell.

But Debbie and Anne know that unless I'm constantly depicted as Dr. Evil, their own purity is called into question. If I'm not Satan Incarnate and they're not cottony-soft angels, the possibility is raised that what they're doing to Mr. Monster—with far more malice and deliberation than I ever acted toward them—is itself monstrous. They know that if I'm not a monster, there's no way to justify what's hap-pening to me. Human beings don't belong in cages, monsters do. But to relent even the teeniest bit on my monstrousness would render the story too complex, too muddy, something more than a nursery-school parable of Good (them) v. Evil (me).

If their intent is to hurt me emotionally, it's working. Just when I felt as if I'd hit rock-bottom, they shove me down a little deeper. I feel as if my entrails have been ripped from my abdomen and strung around my cell like Christmas garland.

If their intent is to make me regret the way I treated them, it's working, too.

I regret ever treating them well.

I'm sure they wanted me to think,

Holy Moly, these Brave Daughters of Venus are finally standing up against my iron-fisted tyranny.

Instead, I'm thinking,

What was I ever doing with these termites? Why did I ever care for either of them? Why did I stay in Portland hoping to stave off both of their deaths, while they're repaying me by wishing me dead?

Their juvenile shenanigans only confirm my instincts for rejecting them in the first place.

When I pounded in Anne's skull, I did it with class. But these girls just have no class about anything.

Neither of them is acting with the thinnest sliver of dignity about the whole situation, preferring to turn something supremely tragic for all parties involved into a tabloid-TV free-for-all, broadcasting our pain to the delight of people who never cared for any of us. Neither girl displays the merest shred of gracefulness in the wake of this emotional Hiroshima that waylaid all three of us.

But to them, there still hasn't been enough suffering. At least on my part. Long after whatever suffering I'd inflicted on them had ceased, they wish for me to continue suffering. For life. Or until it kills me.

These sweetie-pies want more blood from me than I'm willing to give. Definitely more blood than I drew from them. They are prime examples of the nymphomaniacal insatiability of female vindictive-ness. Guys can break each other's noses, shake hands, and then go out for beer. But women remind me of the allegedly "forgiving" Christian God who casts sinners into eternal torments to pay for a few years of masturbation and pot-smoking. No wonder they say the ancient matriarchal cultures were bloodthirsty.

The funny thing is, both Debbie and Anne were so loving and sweet and made me so, so happy. Life with them was nothing but rainbows and unicorns. They were just all-around swell dames. T'weren't a thing wrong with 'em.

It was all my fault. And they have the black-eye pictures to prove it.

Debbie went on the Internet and posted a picture of herself with a black eye.

Anne sent photos of herself with a black eye to every magazine that interviewed her.

Obviously, the black-eye pictures are supposed to make me look guilty. But there's an even grander purpose. They're supposed to make Debbie and Anne look innocent.

Poor babies. Will the swelling EVER go down? Not when you have photos. Those shiners last forever. They remain innocent victims forever.

I've endured a dozen or so black eyes in my life, but I never had the masochistically exhibitionistic impulse to take pictures of them. And even if I did, no one would feel sorry for me.

Because I'm not a woman, so I deserve it.

The sympathy gap has nothing to do with Strength v. Weakness... and everything to do with Man v. Woman.

If I had assaulted, say, an eight-foot-tall Negro gentleman as many times as Anne attacked me, and the Negro gent finally hauls off and pulverizes me, everyone would think I deserved it, even though the eight-foot Negro is stronger relative to me than I am compared to Anne.

If I had broken the nose of a man smaller and weaker than Anne, would anyone think I deserved life in prison?

Did I miss the *New England Journal of Medicine* article which concluded that a woman's black eye is a million times more painful than a man's?

So why is a woman's black eye considered a million times worse?

Because of what it symbolizes.

You should never hit a woman.

You should never hit a woman.

You should never hit a woman.

Why?

Because you should never hit a woman.

What if she drew first blood, like Anne did on the morning of my crime?

You should never hit a woman.

But she attacked me three times the last day we were together!

You should never hit a woman.

But she was stalking me!

You should never hit a woman.

She was threatening to kill me!

You should never hit a woman.

But if I'd stalked her, threatened to kill her, and attacked her three times in the same day, people would think I deserved to be beaten up— or even murdered!

You should never hit a woman.

Why?

Because women are innocent.

What?

Women are innocent.

What makes them innocent?

The fact that they're women.

Women are innocent because they're women?

That's right.

There's a pervasive cultural belief that females, merely by virtue of their boobs 'n' bushes, are sacred.

But they aren't. They are no more sacred than men.

There are currently—what?—three billion human vaginas on the planet. Methinks they're replaceable.

What makes women sacred? The ability to squeeze out offspring? Female hamsters can do that. So can female guppies. It ain't special at all.

But hamsters and guppies can't conquer nature and build nations and devise philosophies and develop technologies, which is what men were doing while the ladies sat at home knocked-up like barnyard sows.

So again—what makes women so bloody special?

Only the *idea* that they're special.

Having a hole doesn't make you holy.

There is no proof of female innocence. In fact, all the proof runs in the opposite direction. Yet our culture clings to the idea of female innocence with a cognitive-dissonance level of tenacity. Anyone who darest challengeth it is branded a heretic who deserves eternal damnation.

The idea is universal. The political left and right both believe in the myth of vaginal sanctity; they just disagree on what should be done about it.

Perhaps our very civilization teeters atop this delicate concept of female innocence. Maybe some reproductive stasis is achieved by balancing male docility alongside the notion of female irreproachability.

Women are hardly innocent, yet they're always rushing to splash some perfume on their stink. They instinctually know that if they don't maintain the mirage of having a moral edge on men, they don't have any edge at all. If women were to concede that they can act with every bit the ill will that men do, they'd invite man-styled retribution. It'd be back to the days of getting clubbed and dragged by their hair. Women know that their safety and power reside behind this Veil of Vaginal Innocence. Once that veil is pierced like a bloody hymen, their moral virginity is forever lost. I believe that on some level, females know they aren't angels, and they laugh at men who think they are. But they also aggressively demonize males who call them on their shit, because those males threaten their whole game.

So people want me dead not because my life is just payment for a dozen or so punches—it's because my fist shattered a sacred social myth. People seek much harsher vengeance if you break their illusions than if you break their nose. In society's eyes, I committed more than a crime. I committed a sin. I broke a taboo. I fiddled with a sacred idea.

The vagina, despite the way it looks and smells, holds a quasi-religious significance in our culture that the male organ could never approximate.

If society was the least bit serious about equality, then women who hit like boys should expect to get hit back like boys.

But women know that they can take a few shots, then run and hide behind their snatches. It's like the old movies where a guy punches someone, then quickly throws on a pair of spectacles and says, "You can't hit me—I'm wearing glasses!"

Male physical strength actually becomes a weakness, because men are forbidden to hit back. Men become slaves to their strength. While men stand there with their hands tied behind their backs, women are free to dance around wagging their fingers and sticking out their tongues. They're also free to hit men—even to draw blood and leave scars—because hardly anyone considers it wrong. And if they go too far and kill the guy, they can beat the rap by claiming to have been battered or raped.

As it stands, "domestic violence" implies "male violence." When the ladies get violent, it's seen as comically empowering. TV is filled with images of women hitting men, backed by roaring laugh tracks. You go, girl!

When Lorena Bobbitt sliced off her husband's bratwurst, comedians joked about it for a year.

Imagine the laughter if he'd mutilated her vagina.

I talk to a prison guard who tells me that when he tried splitting up with his girlfriend, she broke his nose and left twenty stitches in his lip—roughly the same amount of damage I caused to Anne. But he didn't even press charges, knowing how the system...and society... wouldn't feel sorry for him. He's a guy. He must have deserved it.

Some will claim that this sort of double standard has been a long time coming.

Sufferin' Sappho, they say, women have been oppressed for so long, turnabout is fair play.

Well, Leapin' Lesbos, when exactly was the Gilded Age of Male Privilege?

When was it that females were the ones who died in war?

When was it that women were the ones who went to prison?

When did the ladies clear the forests and remove the boulders?

Yeah, they were beaten and raped. But they weren't slaughtered on battlefields or chained down and forced to row galley ships, so it really doesn't sound like a bad tradeoff to me, darlin'.

A thousand years ago, most men weren't kings, they were serfs. And most men today aren't corporate executives, they're sperm donors and worker drones. And more often than not, their "oppressed" wives hold the power in the equation. On average, wifey also lives nearly a decade longer than her demon hubby.

Clearly, the rule in our culture is women and children first. Men take most of the blame and do most of the grunt work.

And pussy-whipped males quietly accept this arrangement, with all the concessions of will and dignity it demands.

It would seem that a bit of Boy Power is long overdue.

The gender war's current lopsided standards will only encourage a new wave of unharnessed bitchiness that will lead to a male backlash like you wouldn't believe.

Is that what you want, girls?

Then keep acting like you've been acting.

We boyfolk got tired of it thousands of years ago, when we over-threw the goddess cults and blamed Eve...and Pandora...and Kali...for everything.

Anne the *Ubercunt* is the least innocent person, male or female, I've ever known. She's a skilled practitioner at the game of female inno-cence, but she's not perfect. She leaves too many clues. The mask keeps falling off.

Debbie isn't Little Bo Peep, either.

But team 'em together, and let those self-exculpatory feminine instincts work their synergistic magic, and suddenly they're the Sisters of Mercy.

Debbie bragged that long before she met me, she stabbed her uncle with a kitchen knife because he broke her bong.

Anne bragged that long before she met me, she attacked her mom with a pair of scissors.

Debbie once gloated to a reporter about how, a long time ago, she fantasized about killing her father and poisoning her mother.

Anne once gloated to me about how, a long time ago, she enjoyed scaring the bejeezus out of her family.

On the night I met her, Debbie wore an I HATE PEOPLE button and talked about dropping bombs.

On the night I met her, Anne wore no panties and talked about dropping babies on their heads.

And yet nowadays, they're both claiming that Mr. Jim Goad was the Rasputinlike scoundrel who introduced them to darkness and violence.

Debbie, who wrote, "On one end of the earth stands society...on the other end stands me," is now calling me "a menace to society."

Anne, the self-described "100% sinner," is now calling herself a "born-again virgin."

Good luck.

As the jailhouse saying goes, if she had as many dicks sticking out of her as she's had stuck in her, she'd look like a porcupine.

Anne, who bragged, "I'm more of a fucking misanthropist than any of you," now tells a reporter, "I crave normality."

Bon chance.

She's missing the main ingredient:

You have to be normal.

Nowadays, Debbie says she can't even look at *ANSWER Me!* anymore, that she was never really into that whole death trip, that I forced her into it.

And Anne says she only ate dog shit because I'd shown her a coprophilic video and implanted the wicked idea in her head.

I've witnessed both girls threaten to kill people, and never at my suggestion. But now that became my idea, too.

Both girls willfully dabbled in darkness, then went screaming for the light after a few shiners. They both expressed loud-throated loathing for all that society represents, then scurried and hid within the flock when the going got a little rough out on the fringes. Both of them eagerly played a game of Misanthropic Musical Chairs with me; now they're acting as if they never played the game when I wound up the only one without a chair.

Pussies. Hypocrites. It's so typically female.

Ever been arrested alongside a woman? The moment the cops slap cuffs on her, she's crying and snitching and pleading for mercy. And she'll throw all the blame on you to save her own candy ass.

Chicks can't hang. Never engage them as partners in crime or evil. There is no such thing as a hardcore girl. A few of them may *play* at being hard, but when the shit really goes down, they're just...women. Deep down, they're only...girls. This doesn't mean they can't be destructive, it only means they can't own up to it. Fuck, even fags have more guts. I've taken the biggest, brashest "bad girls" and sent them running to the police.

And to Jesus.

You heard me.

In my absence, Jesus has become Debbie and Anne's new boyfriend.

I wish I was kidding about this, but the information comes from several reliable sources.

Debbie has been telling people, "If you don't accept Jesus as your personal Lord and savior, you're goin' to hell, and that's not a good place to be, let me tell ya."

Jesus can have 'em. But I can't help feeling that after a few weeks, Jesus would be backhanding 'em, too.

Anyone whom these Brides of Christ perceive as their adversaries...in other words, anyone who calls me a friend...is labeled "evil" and "satanic."

They have inoculated themselves with a very convenient strain of the Christian virus. This brand of Christianity doesn't require them to do good to those who've harmed them. They don't have to forgive their enemies.

They definitely don't have to turn the other cheek.

And they aren't forbidden from contacting dead spirits through a Ouija board, a practice which most Christians consider satanic.

Debbie has become a cancer-stricken, formerly abused female Criswell, making several startling discoveries through her newfound ability to contact dead souls on the weegee:

• The world will end in the year 2006.
• In a past life, she was an Egyptian princess, and her pug dog Igor was her baby camel.
• In another past life, I was an evil Civil War general who abused three daughters who, as luck would have it, were named Debbie, Anne, and Giddle.
• Satanic organ-grinder Anton LaVey, feces-slinging shock rocker GG Allin, and beer-bellied misogynist El Duce are all in heaven, and they're all Debbie's guardian angels.
• Deceased film critic Gene Siskel is alive in the spirit world and imparted this coy message: "[Film critic] Roger [Ebert] is satanic—just kidding."
• I will mention Debbie's frigidity eighteen times in this book. (I guess I just did.)

The Ouija board also makes Anne's car headlights go on and off.

Debbie seems to believe it all out of deathbed desperation. But I doubt that Anne swallows any of it, or that she's sincere about the Christianity.

Or did I really bash her brains that badly?

She's obviously guiding Debbie's hands along that Ouija board. Part of it seems rooted in a genuinely compassionate urge to give a dying woman some hope, however false. But part of it seems a darkly sadistic exploitation of Debbie's pathetic gullibility. Inwardly, I'll bet Anne's laughing like a witch.

However phony Anne's recent "conversion" may be, she does suffer from a need to think of herself as something nobler than what she fears she is:

A piece of useless skin surrounding a vagina.

Anne craves a spiritual douching. All religious impulses arise from a desire to be made clean, to exorcise the Shit Within. Such an exorcism is usually accomplished by an act of scapegoating.

You can blame the Devil.

Or you can blame Jim Goad.

It's all very tidy.

Jesus is merely a handy symbol. These girls have concocted a Wiccan folk religion based on the idea of my guilt and their innocence. Of me as Satan and them as angels. What they're doing has very little to do with me as a person and everything to do with me as an idea. A religious idea.

Despite all their aspirations to moral purity, they've chosen a telling name for their tag-team vaginal lynch mob. Their jilted-lover version of *Revenge of the Nerds.* Their sequel to *Of Mice and Men,* with an all-lesbian cast.

They call themselves the "She-Devils."

It's quintessential femalia. Good and evil, thoroughly compartmentalized. They are simultaneously born-again Christians and she-devils. Wilting victims and vindictive cunts.

Debbie has been telling people that violence is wrong. In the next breath, she says she wants to slit my throat.

By acting as Debbie's caregiver, Anne convinces herself that she's a good person. By flailing out against me with demonic fury, she satisfies her need to be a bad person.

It isn't evil when you aim your evil at someone who's evil. It isn't murder when you try to kill the Devil.

The She-Devils will even make a pilgrimage down to my prison in Salem, Oregon. Down to Salem, looking for witches. They'll sit in the parking lot trying to catch a glimpse of the man they're certain intends to kill them upon his release.

Both Debbie and Anne are wailing that they'll need police protection when I parole, that I'm such a vengeful maniac they'll never get a good night's sleep again.

If I tried to kill them, that would prove I'm evil and they aren't.

And so they taunt me while I'm locked in a cage, trying to get a rise out of me.

They've told everyone how their hatred for me is undying. As they say, there's a thin line between love and hate.

But both emotions are miles away from indifference.

Sorry, I just can't get that worked-up about this whole "revenge" thing. I think they have it bad enough being who they are. They're facing much harsher sentences than I am—they are forced to remain Debbie and Anne for life, without the possibility of parole.

You don't need to get revenge against two pieces of shit. You just scrape them off your boot and keep walking.

During the Internet guerrilla wars regarding my case, some guy suggests that Anne is hypocritical in screaming for my blood. He says that with her documented history of violence, justice would be served if she did some prison time as well.

Her response is creepy:

Oh, no, it's just me. Just me. Just me. I'm the only guilty one. The only crazy one. The only one who deserves to be shut up, locked up, hung up to die.

NO one—not even me—is saying she's the only guilty one. Truth is, both Anne and Debbie are saying that about ME.

Projection, projection.

Who are they trying to shut up?

Me.

Who was locked up?

Me.

Who was hung up to die?

Jesus.

Who was Jesus, if not the ultimate emblem of the world's guilt-projection? The poor skinny bastard took all of the world's sins upon himself.

Dumb galoot that I am, I tried playing the hero for both of these girls.

I pictured myself as Debbie's savior when I rescued her from her demented family.

I pictured myself as Anne's savior when I tried rescuing her from her whorish past...and from the cops.

Anne had called me "a protector...a shepherd of the mentally ill." I was the only man who accepted Debbie and Anne's flaws.

I thought I could save us all, myself included. It wasn't until too late that I realized their salvation necessitated my destruction.

Ever since Anne was a child, she had wished for a family member to kill themselves so she wouldn't have to commit suicide.

When I was in county jail, Debbie seemed intrigued when I said I'd hang myself with a bed sheet if I received a long prison sentence. She also acted flattered when I told her it should be *me* dying instead of her.

This is a twisted Passion Play, no doubt. I'm aware of how ridiculous the Jesus metaphor sounds. True, he never broke Mary Magdalene's nose.

But he *did* create the illusion that she wasn't a whore anymore.

By going to prison and being publicly vilified, I took all the heat off Anne and Debbie. I paid not only for my sins, but for theirs. I allowed these two girls, who felt like steaming turd-piles before they met me, to transfer all their guilt onto me and finally feel good about themselves. Before I gave them their precious sacramental black eyes, I was the only person who viewed them as sympathetic characters. After I did it, they got plenty of the sympathy for which their souls lusted.

Maybe Debbie can die with a little peace if she thinks it was all my fault.

Maybe Anne *has* changed, as much as it defies all laws of logic, psychology, and astrophysics. Maybe miracles *can* happen.

Maybe.

Or maybe one day she'll look in the mirror and realize all the guilt's still there.

One thing is for sure—Jim is NOT a masochist.

—Anne, posting on alt.zines

Wrong.

By staying in Portland, I subconsciously set myself up for slaughter.

When I let Anne out of the car instead of killing her, I knew I'd get into trouble. So I was offering myself as a sacrifice.

A few hours later, when I told Debbie I was driving back to Portland so I could take care of her when she got sick again, I knew I might go to prison. So I was offering myself as a sacrifice for her, too.

In a warped way, what I did was chivalrous. I became the fall guy. The patsy. The scapegoat. The Shit Magnet.

But I was half-assed about it. I cared enough that I didn't want them to die, but not enough that I wanted to die myself. I wanted to leave, but I didn't want to leave them hanging.

And so I wound up hanging on a half-assed cross. I became a half-assed savior who experienced a half-assed fall in a half-assed tragedy.

I performed an act of Jesus Interruptus. I allowed the Roman soldiers to drive the nails into my hands and feet. Then I screamed, "Hey, that HURTS!," demanded that they remove the nails, and hobbled away with a few bloody wounds.

Only hours before I used Anne's face as a punching bag, she said we were both going to hell. Up on those mountain roads, I told her I was God. I gave her a taste of hell, and she fled from it screaming. I had a gutful of hell in county jail, and I decided I didn't want to go there, either.

By taking a plea bargain, I'm going to purgatory instead of hell. The She-Devils are angry that I avoided a trial and a public crucifixion. It seems unbearable for them to conceive that one day I'll emerge from the crypt. They're furious that my fall hasn't been complete.

Too bad.

Jim Goad died for their sins.

Almost.

This entire situation is the penultimate example of my Shit Magnetism, my desire to redeem my loved ones by becoming pure evil.

But Debbie and Anne have redeemed me, too. Their fuming cuntliness has absolved me of any guilt I had for abandoning them. They've freed me from the obligation to ever rescue a damaged woman again. They've taught me not to feel bad about feeling superior.

I will never again cast my pearls before shit.

The biblical legend says that after Jesus was entombed, he spent three days in hell, then rolled away the boulder and was resurrected.

In less than two years, Jim Goad, The World's Unlikeliest Christ Figure, will walk out of the prison gates.

And inside my head, I'll hear the sound of steam escaping.

ϡ16ϟ

Hell, Inc.

THIS CELL of mine is bigger than a coffin, but not much. Without straining, I can spread my arms and touch both side walls simultaneously. I can touch the cell bars with my toes and reach back at the same time to touch the rear wall with my fingers. I lay corpselike on a plastic mattress that is so narrow, my pinkies fall off both ends when I rest my hands by my sides.

This cell's much smaller than a chimpanzee gets at the zoo, but animals live free of ideas such as guilt and punishment.

This cell's so cramped and claustrophobia-inducing that everything clamps down and collapses and presses in all the way to my skin's surface until all I have is an internal life.

I *wear* the cell more than I inhabit it.

I can stand up in here, but I can't stretch—I'll bump into something. Not enough room here to pace. Not enough room to do push-ups. Barely enough oxygen to fill my lungs.

My bunk is made of steel. My clothing drawer is made of steel. A tiny writing table and seat are both made of steel. A small steel shelf drilled into the wall juts out at face level over the toilet, so I have to arch my head backward while pissing to avoid breaking my nose or knocking out my teeth.

Even the walls are made of steel, but a steel so thin that they bend when inmates in the cells to either side of mine get in their bunks, making a sound like a giant soda can being crushed.

About three feet outside the cell bars, another steel screen of bars and fencing runs along the tier, preventing me from pushing someone to their death or jumping to mine. A good twenty feet beyond that are the cellblock windows, outside of which is welded yet another web of steel bars. And beyond that are the penitentiary walls, thirty feet high and lined at the top with electroshock wiring.

Those tall, tall, rain-stained cement walls. The demarcation line between me and real society. Real citizens call this place Oregon State Penitentiary, but convicts call it "The Walls."

A few very tall trees peer in over the walls like judgmental patriarchs, but that's about all I see of the outside world. I can look up and catch glimpses of a purplish-orange sunrise, then lower my eyes and see the walls.

Boxed up inside a cell…which is enclosed within more bars and fencing…which is further encased within more steel bars outside the windows…all of it penned in by giant cement walls…I'm unpleasantly reminded of those gag gifts which are delivered in a huge box…but once you open that box, there's a smaller one…and a smaller one…until the "gift" is encased within a matchbox.

I forgot to mention there are two of us inside this matchbox, two angry bumblebees stuffed in a tiny steel cell of this mammoth honeycomb.

From the small landing area at one end of the cellblock where the guard enters his monkey cage and pulls the steel lever which pops my cell door open, you can get a sweeping view of this Felon's Valhalla.

Forty cells along each tier.

Five tiers high.

Cells on one side, windows on the other.

A shiny gray floor runs straight down the middle to the opposite wall. My first glance of this massive, airy chamber immediately reminded me of a cathedral, with the gray floor a church aisle leading to the bare altar at the other end.

Sheets of dusty sunlight, gusts of cool wind, and even a spray of rain filter in through the open windows, reminding me that natural elements exist beyond this basilica of glass, steel, and cement.

Little sparrows sometimes squeeze through cracks in the cellblock windows and fly around this enormous room. And then they get out—I think, because I don't see them anymore. They come and go, and who knows what happens to them?

My wings have been clipped. If I had wings, I'd be able to fly over those walls. I'd be able to fly away and get clean.

I can never get clean in here. They won't let me.

You're only allowed to shower twice a week, on Tuesdays and Fridays, so I get used to having a three-or-four-day crust of dried sweaty dirt clogging my pores. The shower bell rings louder than a firehouse bell, my cell door clicks open, and I join the beeline down into the muggy basement to get my twice-weekly change of clothes, this "new" set of clothes that has been worn by a hundred guys before me.

The shower bears all the naked humiliation of a communal delousing. I undress myself elbow-to-elbow with other inmates along a hundred-foot wooden bench and then turn to face the showers—fifty or so nozzles packed within the same hundred feet. I squeeze somewhere amid this subterranean waterworld beneath a meek warmish aerosol spray, sudsing and shampooing myself along with forty-nine other criminals, elbow-to-elbow again, all of us spraying one another with foamy airborne filth, and the guy next to me could have an open cut and be spraying infected blood on me, and I'd have no idea until the test results came back positive.

The water washes down our bodies into a tile-lined drainage ditch teeming with cloudy, soapy water, my liquid sludge mixing with everyone else's.

And even though I wear plastic flip-flops to avoid contracting jungle rot from the shower floors, my feet still come away covered with inexplicable, ineradicable strawberry fields of red dots.

I towel off…elbow-to-elbow…and get dressed…elbow-to-elbow…and as I leave, I pass another hundred guys in a beeline waiting to wash off all their dirt.

And then I come back to my dirty cell.

Back to this protozoan hodgepodge.

This jambalaya of filth.

I get new bed sheets only once a week. I sleep under itchy wool blankets that only get washed four times a year. I've been in this particular cell five months now, and the piss-coated scuffed-cement floor hasn't been mopped once. In county jail they'd come by with mops twice weekly, but not here.

There's a battered old straw broom in the cell, and I try to sweep the floor daily. I scoop up a full cup's worth of dust every time I sweep. And every morning there's another swarm of dust bunnies populating the floor. It's as if they breed. I don't know where the dust comes from, only that it keeps coming back. The air vent's always clogged with a mossy gray dust blanket, so I know I'm breathing lungfuls of the shit, and who knows what sort of carcinogenic crystals inhabit my lungs like microscopic death pollen?

Death is never too far from my mind here.

A few months ago I was gathering up my bed sheets for the weekly sheet exchange and as I stood up, I slammed my eyebrow into the HARD steel corner of the bunk above mine, ripping open my flesh and spurting blood all over the cell. I immediately dropped the sheets and grabbed the small cylinder of powdered bleach cleanser on the floor near the toilet, mixed some powder with hot water on a washcloth, and began soaking my open gash with liquefied bleach.

This place will infect you.

I'm terrified of letting *anything* here come in contact with my blood-stream. A third of the inmates in Oregon Department of Corrections are infected with the deadly Hepatitis-C, so odds are good that if I don't have it, my cellmate does. And Hep-C isn't like HIV—it can live for weeks after being exposed to the air. It can live on sinks and tabletops...and the steel corners of bunks. My cellie usually bleeds when he shaves, so his blood could be all over the cell.

About a tenth of the nearly two thousand inmates here are said to be HIV-positive. That averages out to one future immolated AIDS matchstick every fifth cell. At the joint I occupied prior to this one, there was a sloe-eyed, HIV-positive inmate who bragged to everyone about how he'd jack off and squirt his goo all over the walls and floors of the communal showers. The warden, aware of sloe-eye's medical condition, threatened to charge him with attempted murder if he got into a fistfight with anyone, but still this guy picked fights with people daily.

Soon after I was transferred here I ran into Jericho, my cellie from back at the Intake Center. He had lost about a hundred pounds and looked like a puff of thinning hair atop a chicken bone—"all sucked-up," as convicts say of the emaciated.

Jericho told me he recently contracted a "super-virus" strain of HIV from sharing a needle in a phone booth out in the yard here, but I don't think AIDS develops that quickly, and now I'm glad I didn't let him suck my dick back at the Intake Center.

A few months ago I was sitting between Jericho and another inmate on the faded wooden bleachers out in the card room. I commented on the palpable tension between Jericho and the other inmate and, jok-ing, I asked Jericho whether he thought the tension might be sexual.

Just like a bitch, Jericho reached over and dug his long fingernails into my neck, scratching me. I politely excused myself and then scur-ried around to other inmates, asking if Jericho had broken the skin on my neck. Most said they could see pink scratch marks, but it didn't look as if the skin had broken. Well, maybe...it was hard to tell...but probably not.

Back in my cell I emptied a half-bottle of after-shave lotion on my neck, desperately trying to kill whatever microbes Jericho had implanted there. I had run out of powdered Ajax a few days earlier, and I was frantic.

In county jail they had supplied each dorm with one electric razor for all sixty-four inmates. And even though you were allowed to soak the detachable razor heads in a blue-green antiseptic solution, dusty stubble nubs were still pasted on the body of the razor onto which you reattached the heads, and you weren't allowed to clean that part—the Sheriff was watching you the whole time. And every time I used that dirty razor I'd rush back to my cell and check in the blurry steel mirror for cuts on my face and neck, panicking every time a blood droplet emerged on my newly shorn facial terrain.

If fatal microbes entered my bloodstream during my journey behind bars, how could I ever forgive society? They KILL me merely because I thrashed a bitch who was seriously endangering my life? I don't care what your law books say about justice—I don't think that's a very good deal, and if it's the case, I think society owes me some blood. If I get infected with a fatal little germ, you can be sure I'll get my pay-back. I'll become a killing machine. And I'll waste a lot of bodies before I get caught.

It's a great time to be alive and incarcerated.

I make myself a mug of coffee with water from the sink that barely rises above lukewarm, and some of the freeze-dried granules invari-ably float at the top, half-dissolved into a mucky brownish paste.

The rumor among inmates is that the guards are instructed to bring bottled water in from the streets and to never drink the water here. Up until the late 1980s, the water was pumped from a contaminated well. When inmates started sprouting tumors, officials apparently con-cluded it was more financially feasible to pump water directly from the City of Salem's reservoir than to face all the inevitable class-action lawsuits from dying inmates.

I had a cellie a while back who did a twelve-year stretch here ending in the early '90s; he's now back in for a parole violation. But near the end of that twelve-year set, he developed cancer in one tes-ticle that made it swell up to baseball-size. He was so weakened from chemotherapy that he fainted and lapsed into a coma after walking up the stairs to the prison infirmary. He eventually awoke to find himself handcuffed to a hospital bed. His cancer went into remis-sion, but lately a brain tumor has sprouted which is severe enough to give him periodic black eyes. They won't treat it, claiming it isn't life-threatening *yet*. He thinks he contracted cancer from working as an inmate plumber during all the years here. He says that although they changed the water supply, they never changed the pipes, so all the carcinogens still leach into the water with which I fix my tepid morn-ing coffee.

I take slow sips of Cancer Java and stare at the Sleeping Beauty who's crammed into this broom closet with me, the one snoring in the bunk above mine...my darling cellie.

I am forced to cohabitate in suffocatingly close quarters with a living neural web of accumulated pain and ignorance.

I must endure the sour nasal burn of his foot stench and the rancid-peanut-butter smell of his farts and his greenish toenail clippings and the way he keeps slapping his fat belly because he likes the sound it makes and how he bangs the heels of his ugly bare feet on the cement floor and the way he sucks food particles from between his teeth and his off-key whistling and his middle-of-the-night groans and his sad stupid face.

I hear about how his old lady's sister has to get an operation on her finger and so she's going to quit her job as a McDonald's manager and move in with his old lady and all the kids, and he runs through his well-rehearsed litany of excuses for why he never amounted to anything and why his brother's fucked-up because he won't accept his collect calls anymore, and I'd love to break his nose but that would only buy more time being forced to listen to stories like his.

And there are so *many*...just...like...him.

Children with pubic hair. Oversized baby boys never properly weaned, so now they're violent, drug-addicted toddlers with hair on their backs and wrinkled faces.

And all of them have kids, with an 's.' Hear the cons wax righteously wrathful about child molesters, yet they're oddly silent about men who spawn kids and then neglect them.

There's a paucity of what might be considered radical thinkers or revolutionary outlaws here. Most guys are normal, only three notches lower. They want a normal life, but they're too stupid to achieve it.

I'm starting to get the feeling that a lot of these guys aren't too bright. Judging from their facial expressions, it looks as if they've been eating Retard Sandwiches their whole lives. On rainy days, they'll have a bowl of Mongoloid Soup along with the Retard Sandwich.

When the Nobel Prize Committee passes through Salem, I think they're going to skip over this place entirely. The Mensa Society, too, won't find many recruits here.

Shockingly illiterate. One slow-lidded, drooling troglodyte after the next. Men whose mental energy couldn't power a wristwatch. Ugly, stupid, belching, conscienceless, unfeeling, driven-by-instinct, worthless turd dumplings whose only purpose in life is to remind us that forced sterilization maybe wasn't such a bad idea. Even the word "worthless" is too kind, since it conjures the very idea of worth. They insult the air by breathing it.

I can't ever escape the sounds and smells and presence of the pinheads. There is eternal, soul-flattening agony in never being alone. I've been down for more than two years now, and I haven't been alone for one minute. Never, ever, ever, ever, ever alone.

Always someone in that bunk above mine.

Always three hundred or more men on this side of the block.

Always two thousand or so at this institution.

When the AIDS crisis broke, common wisdom was that if you had sex with someone, you were also fucking everyone they'd fucked for the past ten years. The same applies to doing prison time with others—I'm also doing *their* time, rubbing up against all *their* misery, all their coiled tensions and simmering resentments and bad breaks in life. And not only am I smelling *their* shit, I'm smelling the shit of everyone who's crammed shit down their throats since infancy. I'm doing time with these husks of men and all the ghosts inside them.

The noise is a constant ice pick to my brain.

The punishing metallic sound of cell bars clicking open and smashing closed. Rude white-noise blasts of a guard's radio static. Some snoring fat fuck's eleven-dollar alarm clock beeping for hours. A crew of welders on the tier above mine, hammering steel and showering sparks and making it impossible for me to sleep.

Ignorant voices from above, below, and side to side. The booming sonic ricochet of belly-laughing clodhoppers tickled silly by dirty jokes. Juvenile middle-agers making fake fart sounds and calling each other homos. An angry elderly Negro screaming out his cell number because the guard forgot to pop it open for pill line.

My tier is perched directly over the protective-custody row, which houses the rats and cowards and weaklings too fearful to mix with the general population. Since their tier is caged-off and no one can get to them, they're the loudest ones, shouting all day from cell to cell, holding deafening conversations about *nothing* for hours and taunting us about our inability to administer instant justice to them.

The noise never stops unless it's the middle of the night, and even then you'll hear crocodilian snores and distant flushing toilets.

I am officially in state "custody," just like a child in thralldom to its parents.

My parents have grounded me and sent me to my room...for *years*. And even though I'm old enough to have grandchildren, I'm treated with sub-nursery-school condescension.

It's worse than being an infant, because an infant can usually cry and get what he wants.

Many of the cons here pretend to be outlaws, but they are addicted to the system, to the structure and security, to the only family they've ever known, to the "three hots and a cot." Tattooed skin sacs of sick need, baby piglets sucking on the Big Sow's carcinogenic teats.

They're happy having no control, no responsibilities, no decisions to make, being fed and bedded down and wearing Big Brother's state-issued diapers. They say they hate Big Brother, and yet they keep choosing him as their dance partner.

But for me, licking boots gets tiresome.

Control over my identity, environment, and destiny is a primary need of mine, and they've stripped it away from me. Almost my entire fate is now in the hands of those who've proven hostile toward me. While they move around in the shadows, I'm squashed under glass and trapped under a microscope.

My name and Social Security number are now etched in government databases as those of a felon, an enemy of the state's laws.

They have copies of my fingerprints.

My DNA code.

And with periodic urinalyses, even my bodily fluids are in state custody.

Humans need hope almost as much as they need water, and the Department of Corrections exists to siphon all hope from the convict's wishing well. They remove all hope, and the rest falls in place.

The fates have unspooled a finite strand of time for me to be alive on this Earth. The justice system wields a cold, gleaming pair of scissors and snips out a few years right in the middle of that strand.

The semantics are cockeyed. They didn't "give" me three years. They *took* them from me. And I count every fucking day they've taken. I take a cold blue pen and mark off every fucking day on a little calendar up on the wall. I blot out every day they've stolen from my life.

Every day I endure a hundred indignities, any one of which would have been intolerable on the streets. The thudding regimentation of wake-up bells and sitting up on my bunk to be counted and strip searches and pat-downs and flashlights in my face at midnight when I'm trying to sleep and the omnipresent imbecilic inmates and the smirking condescension of subliterate guards who aren't qualified to lick my sphincter, much less have an attitude with me.

And to my terror, I realize I've grown *used* to the hundred daily indignities. If I didn't get used to them, it would kill me. But the getting-used-to-it is a form of death, too.

The pride I swallow—where does it go?

I know this—it doesn't disappear.

Grinding my teeth into chalk dust having to pretend these guards aren't beneath me. The torment of being charged with assault by someone who spells it "assualt." Being barked at and ordered around by someone who can't even pronounce my name—he calls me "Go-add." Go add. Go add two and two together, and when you get the right answer, you're allowed to bark at me.

Having to defer to two-legged nothings who aren't fit to catch my turd in their mouths as it plops from my ass. Motherfucker, you don't even deserve to inhabit the same planet as me. I'm so elevated above you, it isn't fair to say we're from the same species.

Key-jangling doofuses peering through the cell bars asking me unnecessary questions as I'm sitting on the toilet taking a dump. Ransacking my cell when I'm not there, looking for contraband and leaving everything turned upside-down. Popping my cell door open, and when I peek out to see what he wants, he'll shout, "Shut your door!" as if I was the one who popped it open.

They're never required to cop to their mistakes.

Not like we are.

The jelly-bellied closet homo with little frog hands who incessantly drops sickening sexual innuendos at inmates he thinks are cute.

The guard at county jail whose wife left him for a bad-boy felon and so he has a nasty habit of spitting into inmates' Kool-Aid and forcing the trustees to serve the saliva-tainted bug juice.

The Sherman-tank-shaped carpet-munching dyke guards who took this job to flaunt a palpable hatred of People with Penises.

Imagine being *proud* that your job is to stand in Receiving & Discharge all day, scrutinizing felonious anuses to make sure that contraband doesn't pop out of them like a mischievous little gopher. When these guards kiss their partners at night, do they think of puckered anuses?

Some guards radiate an arrogance which is near-suicidal, since many of the guys here are lifers who'd have little to lose by cracking a broomstick in half and stabbing the air out of their lungs.

But I have a lot to lose, and these walkie-talkie-toting pricks have the power to falsely accuse me of something and be believed. To beat me unconscious and claim it was self-defense. To act like a criminal and look like the good guy.

God, how these cocksuckers milk their puny positions of micropower. Fat-necked, pink-faced, buzzcut, slack-jawed nobodies a notch above security guards but too stupid to graduate from Police Academy, regular spuds whose brief moment of glory was as a nose tackle on the high-school pigskin squad, and it's been all downhill from there, wearing one uniform after another as a hired guard dog of power.

Take off that uniform, and you have a portrait of human failure. Dress them in convict blues, and watch all the power drain out of their faces.

"Power" seems little more than an excuse to abuse in the name of "good." So when one of these ex-jocks-with-a-GED flashes a vicious glare at me as if I committed my crime against them, I strain every tendon resisting an impulse to righteously erase that expression from their face.

I'll step out of a guard's way as we're walking past one another, and then I'll catch myself, realizing how reflexive it's become. Then I'll bite my lip and send a little more rage down into the arsenal where it's all being stored. I'll blink twice and think, *that's all right, cowboy, you'll be stuck working this cattle ranch until you retire; this is just a temporary hitching post for me, but this is as good as it gets for you, so enjoy it.*

If I were to get feisty enough to, say, punch a guard's teeth out through the back of his skull, I'd be shackled and shoved into a lower stratum of hell called the Intensive Management Unit (I.M.U.).

Inmates call it "Thunderdome."

The artificial lights never go out there. The psychopaths never stop shouting. Instead of cell bars in your solitary chamber, your "door" is a plate of steel that has been punched through with a continuous pattern of dime-sized holes. The holes are often plugged up with dried, encrusted human feces. I.M.U. inmates like to "shit-bomb" one another by stirring up their own shit and piss in a shampoo bottle, shaking it until it's a frothy yellow-brown elixir, and squirting the foul excremental nectar from cell to cell.

Once a day, guards will come to handcuff you behind your back and lead you on a leash to the shower, where you're locked in for thirty minutes. After showering, you get a half-hour to walk in the "recreation yard," a six-by-ten-foot room.

The guards in I.M.U. wield complete control over these self-contained pods. More than one inmate has told me that if guards don't like you there, they'll mix in some human shit with your food. If you get defiant, a half-dozen black-booted emissaries of the state will rush your cell and smash you down with Plexiglas "shock shields" which deliver an electric jolt that stuns you into slobbering submission no matter how tough you are or how strong your will is.

A typical stint in I.M.U. lasts six months to a year. All the cons say that once you spend some time there, you'll never be the same. Some guys languish in there for years and get so wacked by it that they never leave, night after night standing naked in their cells chewing their own shit and howling at the mirror.

Not that being in the general population here is a boon for your mental health.

Any psychologist not hired by the prison industry would tell you that smashing a steel door shut on someone and cooping them up in a tiny room for years, severed from every tentacle to the outside world which gave their life meaning, would produce drastically negative personality effects. It might even make them dangerous.

Judging from some of the dreams I've had lately, incarceration has jarred my psychic equilibrium a smidge. My mind is a pinball machine that reads TILT.

In one dream, I'm driving a figure-eight pattern in a gravel-strewn church parking lot, each time getting closer to a light-bulb-sized glowing red-eyed skull on a stick.

In another, a female accomplice and I murder a waitress at an all-night diner. In the dream's final sequence, I can see through the diner's windows...past the empty countertop and fallen waitress...out the other side...where I see myself walking with my accomplice. I'm dressed in drag in the fallen waitress's uniform, stumbling on her high heels and muttering, "I can't believe how low my life has sunk."

I had a dream a few months ago where I'm calmly staring at pictures in an oversized children's book. The pictures are high-magnification black-and-white photos of cockroach faces.

And last night I dreamed I was a voyeuristic spectator at a clumsy orgy of elderly men and a retarded girl in a dark, moldy house. We all suddenly rushed to the bathroom, but I wound up last in line. So I shat in my hand, held it up for all to see, and everyone ran screaming.

What do you think this all means, Doc?

There's even an air of surreal dreamy unreality when I receive a letter and the address says I'm at the state pen. I can't really be in prison, can I?

Before they sent me to this place, I spent nearly a year at Santiam

Correctional Institution, a tidy little minimum-security joint on the other side of Salem.

When they first "dressed me in" over there, I put my blue T-shirt on backwards, with the large orange Department of Corrections shield and INMATE decal on my chest, and the inmate worker said, "No, you've got it on wrong—the bull's-eye goes on your back."

The bull's-eye. That's what I am to them. A target.

Santiam had four dormitories housing four hundred men total. Instead of cells, each brightly lit white-linoleum dorm contained neat rows of bi-level Army-barracks-styled bunks with a small wooden locker painted orange at the foot of your bunk. You could see out the back windows to the yard and watch denim-clad cons in ski caps shooting hoops in the rain. You could stare out the front windows at huge flocks of geese huddled together in the fields beyond the prison fence.

After nearly eight months in county jail and the Intake Center breathing nosebleed-inducing stale recirculated air, I hit Santiam's yard the first chance I got, walking determined laps amid the icy winter mist, sucking in lungfuls of real-world air under the unforgiving nighttime sky and slowly feeling the blood come back into my cheeks. And even though I still had almost two years standing between me and freedom, I somehow felt there was hope whistling through those bare trees outside, and at night I curled up in my bunk, closed my eyes, and felt the clean, cold wind come through holes in the windows and roll all over my body.

But ironically, the time over at the minimum-security joint was more stressful for me than being in a cell at this maximum-level penitentiary, because a cell at least affords a *little* privacy, and the ceaseless day-and-night cacophonous evil dragonfly hum of that big dorm with a hundred-plus men was starting to frazzle my brain.

Because I was shaving my head over there and having a friend send me news clippings about Jane Greenhow and her neo-Nazi *ANSWER Me!*-reading British suicide friends, I was placed under investigation for being a suspected white supremacist. When Santiam's "gang expert"—a fat, oily, middle-aged man resembling Wimpy from the *Popeye* cartoons, a bloke who would have cut quite a figure going undercover in gold chains and a sweat suit and trying to buy crack—called me into his office and asked if I was a white "supremist," I told him about *The Redneck Manifesto* and my line,

I'm no fan of white supremacy—everyone knows the Jews and chinks are superior.

But he didn't think it was funny, and with an eyebrow arched, he said, "Oh—so they're *chinks,* are they?"

And I felt the cold existential shudder of realizing I was under the ironclad dominion of people who thought they had my number but were utterly clueless about my thought processes and belief systems. And what's worse, I could have laid it out for them with blueprint precision, and they would have been none the wiser.

So after my...alleged...fistfight with another inmate that...purportedly...took place in the laundry room there, I was shackled and dumped in The Hole over here. After three days in The Hole, "assualt" charges were dropped because the guard at Santiam forgot to attach the Confidential Informant statement with his paperwork.

I was sprung loose from The Hole into the general population here at The Walls, but after only a few weeks they rolled me up early one morning and shipped me to Columbia River Correctional Institution in Portland.

Columbia River felt less like a prison than a Community College which you couldn't leave: shiny-clean, ultra-quiet little dorms, food that tasted as if it might have originated in the real world rather than some penitentiary dungeon, and—good God!—

Female inmates.

The dorms were sexually segregated, but the chow hall and yard were coed, and as much as I've seethed toward womenfolk during my Hegira behind bars, their presence had an immediately soothing effect upon me. Granted, these weren't exactly primo specimens of femininity; as the joke went,

Q: What has a hundred legs and two teeth?
A: Women's chow line at Columbia River.

But seeing the other half of the human race up-close after nearly *two years* of separation from them somehow grounded me and made me feel halfway steered back to reality.

But after only five days at Columbia River, I was rolled up again and sent back here to Oregon State Penitentiary, where I've remained. No one told me why I was shipped back, and it took a few weeks of pestering my case manager until she called up my file on her computer screen and asked me,

"Uh—do you have a problem with women? You write about beating women or something?"

Yup, that's me, the woman-beating author. I guess they feared I'd start battering bitches in the chow hall or something.

So my confidential prison file—which I'm never allowed to see, therefore never able to challenge—has me wearing two "jackets," that of a racist mastermind and that of a compulsively violent misogynist. They put the jackets on me, and there's nothing I can do to remove them. And even though my offender-risk score has me classified well within minimum-custody status, my mere *reputation* as a transgressor of politically sensitive belief systems will keep me here at a maximum-security joint.

Five days a week at 5:15AM or so I'll hear the loud steel shotgun-pump sound of my cell door popping open, and I'll head down into the chow hall to serve hash browns to serial killers and dope fiends.

The chow hall looks like a giant old Woolworth's cafeteria that has started to rot like an abscessed tooth. Sickly artificial lighting. Cracked yellow wall tiles. Scuffed, sky-blue tabletops.

Along one wall run three huge framed paintings done years ago by the same inmate:

A brook with a sunny meadow in the background;

A rocky Oregon coastline;

Ducks flying over a lake.

Upon first inspection, these bucolic settings seem intended to soothe. But staring at them, one apprehends the heavy shadowing, the menacing clouds, and the ocean's unnaturally dark-blue water. You realize the sunny meadow is shoved far in the background, dominated by the turbulent brook; the coast is empty and forbidding, its waters possibly shark-infested; and the ducks look as if they're trying to escape, but their wings are frozen in mid-air.

These are the scariest paintings I've ever seen.

Back in the hot sweaty smoky broiling lard-misted ashy-carbon kitchen, I'm drowned in the sounds of smashing pots and pans, the roaring spray of water hoses blasting crust off dirty utensils, creaking carts and boiling vats and workers running around screaming about the missing trays of greasy kielbasa.

There are rumors that some food crates came in through the loading dock marked UNFIT FOR HUMAN CONSUMPTION. I've been told we've been served ground frozen hamburger left over from Operation Desert Storm, and I'm sure it was fresh when that war ended almost ten years ago. I've seen them wheel in boxes marked "Fresh Pack 1998 Tomato Sauce," and while '98 may have been a good year for wine, tomato sauce doesn't age nearly as gracefully.

And I've served fruit cups on which the expiration date passed four months ago, but the prison newsletter assures us this only means it was "best" before that date.

The stereotype is that in prison they starve you on bread and water and maybe the occasional bowl of cold cabbage soup swimming with dead cockroaches. In Oregon prisons, the food may be lousy, but you're allowed to pile it on your tray and ram it down your gullet until you explode. One is initially amazed at the specter of so many FAT convicts, roly-poly oompa-loompas who've let their bodies melt into shit, stuffing their yaps with big ploppy lumps of starchy comestibles that turn to papier-mâché sculptures in their colons, sweat coursing down their pink hog jowls as they desperately chew, chew, chew, weighing their bodies down until they're unable or unwilling to escape.

Most of prison life seems to consist of standing in one line or another. For food. For showers. For canteen. For phones. Waiting, waiting. Dependent. Compliant.

There are two entrances to the chow hall and two chow lines, each hugging the side walls along old steel guard rails. It takes an hour and a half of nonstop serving to get through breakfast; lunch takes two hours. The lines seem never-ending, as if they're manufacturing new cons every second.

The chow lines are filled with the sort of faces you'd only see in prison, wrinkled and ashen like elephant's hide, lines etched in their cheeks as if they've cried acid teardrops, faces with the hardened detachment of ceramic Buddhas heat-treated in a brick oven, faces ravaged by gin blossoms and knife scars, faces of skeletons and scarecrows, the faces of walking, rotted dead men.

You can tell a new fish just by looking at his face: It carries the dewy freshness of the free world. Three months later, his face doesn't look that way anymore; now it carries bitterness like invisible whip marks.

I can say "hi" to a face in here for months without ever knowing his name. I'll see familiar faces from other legs of the journey like county jail or Santiam and notice how his hair's changed or he's put on weight, and, yeah, it seemed really hopeless then but he's getting out soon.

Sometimes a week or two will pass before I realize a certain face isn't in the chow line anymore, that it must have gone to The Hole, or to another prison, or even released to the free world.

But that face isn't important, because another face will soon replace it. Faces aren't important to the Department of Corrections— bodies are.

The inmates grab their plastic food trays from tall stacks and scrutinize them for flecks of hardened food which the hot bleachy dish-washing machine failed to blast loose.

A con will reject four or five trays before he finds a clean one.

Hard, callused hands with scraped knuckles and missing fingers shove their trays at me.

Feed me. Feed me.

And I wonder—*what exactly am I feeding? To whom am I providing nourishment? Am I helping a body grow or feeding a tumor?*

The cons will look down at a dented steel bin containing a huge plop of puddinglike substance the color of Turtle Wax Car Polish over which I stand with an ice-cream scooper. They'll ask me,

"What IS that?"

I'll point to the handmade paper sign that I've fashioned with a pen and placed in front of the bin that reads CUSTARD and say,

Custard.

"Custard?"

Yes. Custard.

"Is it any good?"

I haven't tried it.

They'll pause and then hold their tray toward me suspiciously as if they're doing me a favor by taking a dollop of the stupid fucking custard.

Or I'll be stuck serving bacon on a Sunday morning wearing flimsy clear-plastic gloves, digging my paws into an Auschwitz pit of dead grizzled hogflesh, the Negro guard barking in one ear that I'm giving too much bacon and non-Muslim pork-gobbling Negro inmates barking in my other ear that I'm not giving enough.

Or I'll be scooping out macaroni salad and they'll say,

"I like black olives—pick out some of those black olives for me."

Or it'll be tossed salad and they'll say,

"I don't like cucumbers, man—take the cucumbers out."

Or it'll be Oriental mixed vegetables and they'll say,

"I don't want any pearl onions, but give me lots of those baby corns."

A thousand felons standing behind them, and they think they're at fucking Spago. Look, motherfucker, on the streets you shoot speed with toilet water, and all of a sudden you're a gourmet?

But unless they're baldly prickish about it, I'll try to give them what they want, because living squeezed in a vise like this, the only freedom and control they have is to ask for extra olives in their macaroni salad. A lot of them will die in here, so I'll kick down a few extra olives and consider it my good deed for the day.

Some days I'll slap a glob of butter onto the tray of Jerry "The Lust Killer" Brudos, who made fetish items of his female murder victims' severed feet. He's been down now for over thirty years and is hopelessly obese, mostly bald with a tightly sheared laurel wreath of strawberry-and-gray hair around a large pinkish head, beady eyes magnified by a pair of thick-lensed, black-rimmed glasses.

Or I'll ladle out corn chowder for The Happy Face Killer, who drew happy faces on his raped female prey's corpses. He's an enormous man with tortured eyes and thick, wolfmanlike beard and hair. I'll see him out on the yard sometimes walking the track wearing headphones attached to a radio.

Or I'll slide a pair of hot biscuits onto the tray of Randy "The I-5 Killer" Woodfield, who raped and murdered women up and down the west coast and who, according to what another inmate tells me, to this day insists all his victims deserved it. I'll notice that Randy has received yet another coiffing and dye job out at the Vo-Tech hair salon.

And I'll remember my cellie back in county jail who thrill-killed two people on Larch Mountain above Portland and told his friends it was "better than sex." Just blew 'em clean away with a rifle for the fun of it. I spent two months in a cell with the guy, and he was clean, amiable, polite, and agonizingly nerdy. He was a member of his high-school History Club and excitedly told me of how the club had once made a field trip to DC. He liked classic rock such as Pink Floyd and Steve Miller and was an obsessive collector of *Star Wars* memorabilia. His mom and dad loved their son and visited him every week in jail.

I also recall a taped phone conversation an acquaintance of mine had with Richard "The Night Stalker" Ramirez where Ramirez gripes that the artwork on the new line of serial-killer trading cards made him look like child-loving ex-Negro pop star Michael Jackson.

And I think...

The Lust Killer still wears glasses because he likes to read.

The Happy Face Killer enjoys circling the track while listening to his radio.

My thrill-killing ex-cellie knows everything about Star Wars.

And The Night Stalker doesn't want people to think he looks like Michael Jackson.

To me, these trifling idiosyncrasies of theirs are far more disturbing than their crimes.

It's much easier to view them as pure monsters, but one can never fully become a monster, can they? You can commit isolated acts of pure monstrosity, yet you retain your humanity. There is no act you can commit that can make you cease being human.

You can never become a monster, you can only flirt with guilt and wind up tortured by it. You never become a monster, only a severely damaged human being incapable of functioning in "their" world, and although that's not the same as a monster, it'll do for them. It isn't about whether you *are* a monster; it's about their need to *see* you as one. You serve a mythological purpose for them.

From my vantage point in the kitchen, the chow line to the left is entirely Caucasian—you might see a black guy in that line once a week, and he's probably a newbie unaware of the chow hall's unwritten, self-imposed laws of racial segregation. The guards don't dictate these laws—the inmates have segregated themselves, following tribal laws written in their DNA.

The dining room is split in half by a wide aisle straight down the middle, and the seats on the left side are occupied by a solid sea of Caucasianity, with the hardest peckerwoods seated closest to the kitchen, filtering into gradations of weaker white boys back toward the entrance. I've never seen a Negro sit on the left side.

The right side starts off 100% dark chocolate near the kitchen, turns Mexican, then a smattering of Injuns and a handful of white freaks back near the doors. It's presumed that if you're white and sit on the right side near the rear, you're a rapist, child molester, or some unclassifiable weirdo unwelcome in the "woodpile" to the left.

I'd reckon that the population here is 60% white, 20% black, 10% Mexican, 5% Indian, and the occasional lapsed Asian or Jew. Oregon is an incredibly white state, and its prisons boast a racial quotient so lopsidedly in favor of the peckerwoods that an odd sort of racial stasis is achieved. The Negroes don't get too rowdy, or they'd be swarmed in an ocean of white sunshine.

Racism is an accepted fact of prison life. Nonracist whites don't seem to get much respect from anyone, black or white. One white inmate after the next has told me he wasn't racist until he came to prison and was forced to live in close proximity to blacks. And black convicts have consistently told me that Nazis are the only whites they respect, since blacks assume all whites are racist and that Nazis are at least honest. Truly, it's the white boys with WHITE POWER tattooed on the back of their neck...or SS lightning bolts on their throat...or TRUE PECKERWOOD emblazoned across their stomach...who seem to mingle most easily with black cons.

And since I'm just about the only white guy here with no kids, no tattoos, no history of intravenous drug use, and all my teeth, I'm a race unto myself and don't mingle well with anyone.

After lunch, I'll wait until the bell rings for Yard Line and hustle out to that giant evil drag strip of death and dissolution, that amphitheater of atrocities, that cement-rimmed wildlife preserve teeming with human beasties.

Guards stand in towers that rim the walls, somberly clutching rifles and ready to blow your head off if things get too crazy down here in the pit.

There's a perpetual pall about the yard, a light coating of dust and soot, a feeling of death so close that you might be able to stick out your tongue and catch a piece of death as if it was a gray snowflake. When I first saw a red-and-white chimney belching smoke in the distance, my immediate instinct was that they're incinerating bodies. This place has the feeling of a death camp. This is where you come to die.

Cons walk around and around the eternal track. A small red-haired man circles the loop obsessively every day with a grimace welded onto his face, walking rapidly as if he's late for a business appointment, around and around until his shirt is entirely sweat-soaked. Even in winter, his shirt is sopping-wet as he slogs endlessly around and around in his quest to get right back where he started.

Cons sit at picnic tables working with meditative diligence at prison artwork, images of clowns in striped prison uniforms tethered to a ball and chain, peace signs rendered in barbed wire, and a thorny rose clutched by a hand with blood squeezing through its fingers.

Cons stroll shirtless, their skin inked with inmate hieroglyphics: spider webs on elbows; barbed wire around wrists; LOVE on one set of knuckles, HATE on the other; guard towers on backs; State Prisoner ID numbers on necks; and a permanent teardrop under one eye.

An inmate they call French Fry has scars from third-degree burns all over his face and body, his skin melted into a yellow-and-pink tapestry of chewed-bubble-gum-textured flesh. A con they call Bug-Eyed Bob has peepers which fairly pop out of his skull, and whenever he makes eye contact it's as if death is looking straight through you. A con with a small pink stump for one arm clutches his coffee mug to his side with that stump. Another con's torso is scarred with dozens of self-inflicted razor slashes. An AIDS-ravaged black inmate with a plastic tube sticking out of his Adam's apple sits on a bench, staring out over the field.

A gay Mexican with breast implants and plucked eyebrows circles the track coquettishly. A Negro homo in short-shorts minces around trilling that his pussy smells good today. A slender white male with high cheekbones and shaved legs playfully grabs the crotch of the male "jocker" who protects him.

Among convicts, Oregon's most legendary inmate is Angel, a former Golden Gloves boxer turned den mother of the queer contingent. The fags affectionately call him "Mother Love." Angel is a white male with long, shiny, chestnut-colored hair and a face which is starting to age rapidly. Angel's swishy mannerisms and high-pitched voice are indelibly female, yet he's a convicted murderer known to exact lightning justice upon anyone who preys on homosexuals. The story I heard back in county jail is that if Angel likes you but you don't swing that way, he'll knock you out and suck your dick while you're unconscious. I heard another story about how Angel was jogging around the track one day and twice passed a convict who called him a punk. The third time around, when the convict again called him a punk, Angel knocked him to the ground with a quick combination. Standing over his fallen antagonist, Angel wagged a finger and said, "I am a *homosexual—you*, sir, are a punk."

I'll slide on my old fingerless leather gloves and hit the weight pile to crunch some rusty steel, losing my mind temporarily, throwing my awareness somewhere else like a psychic ventriloquist, focusing on a spot in the far distance and placing all my consciousness there to avert the tear-duct-wringing pain of shredding my muscle tissues into shocked, bruised, inwardly bleeding flesh. Filling the cracks in my wall with cement. *You want to break me down, motherfuckers? I'll just rebuild myself using stronger bricks.*

As Yard Line is called in, a thousand or so inmates converge through a small exit in the gates back toward the housing blocks, and it's this little bottleneck area where you're most likely to be shanked in the lungs by an enemy who can quickly get lost in the crowd.

Some days there are fights in the yard, and as I walk back in, I'll see a series of orange Day-Glo highway cones marking off where blood was spilled.

Little bright-red splashes on the concrete.

And the biohazard team will come in and scrub the concrete clean.

We had ourselves a little race riot in the yard a few days ago. Nothing major. And nothing that anyone thinks is settled.

jim goad

It's a violent little story which shows how the idea of guilt and indebtedness can get out of hand.

Down in the catacombs where we shower, white boy and black boy are soaping themselves. Black boy owes white boy money for tobacco debt. White boy tells him to pay up. Black boy says fuck you, you're burnt. White boy dries off and walks away.

Later out in the yard, white boy dislodges brick from building and walks into card room, where he clobbers black boy in head with brick. White boy disappears. Black boy and black friends lead guards to the weight pile and point at white boy.

Black boys commit grievous infraction against the Convict Code by involving the guards.

At evening yard, group of white boys confront group of black boys about being rats. A small brawl ensues. Guards snuff it.

Angry little racial pockets form in the yard, groups of tense white boys alongside clusters of edgy black boys. Glares and taunts are exchanged. The tension finally erupts in a racist mosh pit of a hundred convicts punching and clawing, trying to rip flesh chunks out of the other color.

Tower guards fire warning shots until everyone hits the ground. Out in the field, lone guards walk warily amid a sea of prostrate bodies, guards aware for possibly the first time how much of their power is merely in their heads.

Two inmates are taken to the infirmary to be treated for injuries. The warden declares an institutional lockdown. We don't leave our cells for two-and-a-half days, trapped in these steely sweatboxes amid summer heat so intense, you can hear invisible flies buzzing in your head.

On the third day after the riot, they finally pop my cell door open to let me go work in the kitchen. When I get there, everyone's eyes seem wider, alive with a supercharged feeling of evil. Everyone's ready like soldiers. Everyone wants something more to go down.

A friend of a friend of a friend of a friend—you have to cover your tracks in here about who knows what and when they were told it—tells me that one of the riot's main instigators is a white kid, twenty-one, who's been down for two years on a murder beef. Like the song "Mama Tried," he turned twenty-one in prison doin' life without parole. He was recently discharged from the Intensive Management Unit and told someone that he wants to kill as many people as he can in here. That's his goal—to stack bodies up to the sun.

A big invisible serpent sits coiled out in the yard. Everyone knows something's going to go down, they just don't know when. For the first time since I was arrested, I have a feeling I might be killed.

I was tear-gassed for the first time in my life today.

Prison officials say it was an accident, but some inmates say it's impossible to accidentally set off a tear-gas canister—there are too many deliberate steps to the process.

After a torrid lunch shift in the kitchen serving up piping-hot biscuits, I returned to my cell and began dozing off amid high-90s temperatures, covered in beads of today's sweat floating atop a film of yesterday's sweat. I was yanked from groggy reverie by the sound of clanging cell bars and desperate yells of, "They're gassing us! MOTHERFUCKERS! They're gassing us!"

I bolted upright and looked out the window the see a half-dozen or so guards wearing gas masks with oxygen tanks on their backs, walking amid a ground-level cloud of white vapors.

It's one of those rare moments in life when your brain doesn't want to accept what your eyes are showing it.

Within moments, a foul smoky chemical smell permeated the cell, a mix of burnt tires and bitter lemon. My eyes, nose, and throat were burning.

I looked in the mirror at my red, watery eyes—stared straight at myself and said,

This is wrong.

What they're doing is wrong.

It doesn't matter what I did to her, what they're doing to me is wrong….

If incarceration is supposed to make me feel sorry for crime victims—or for the beleaguered taxpayers who supply me with room and board—it's having quite the opposite effect. It makes me resent their whining. I swear on all that's holy, I don't want to hear a peep out of *any* of you about how bad you have it out there. You just don't know. Whatever it is, it just doesn't compare.

I'll read some magazine interview with some pampered Hollywood creampuff fag whimpering about how the last five years were very painful for him because, well, his grandmother died, but somehow he's managed to reach down inside his puny little soul and find the faith to press onward, but fucking Christ, *everyone's* grandmother dies, and I wish Hollywood Boy could spend some cell time with me, and I bet he'd be crying out for grandma pretty quick.

Or I'll read some mealwormy prose by some ivory-vagina college feminist about how she feels "raped" when men whistle at her on the street, and it's like, yeah, Betty Boop, you've had a rough, rough life, I simply can't fathom how traumatic it must feel to be whistled at, better lock yourself in a six-by-eight-foot cage like I am so's you can sidestep all that abject martyrdom out there in the cold...cruel... free...world.

In this era of acutely hemorrhaging sympathy toward the plight of Negroes, women, homosexuals, the disabled—and crippled Negro lesbians especially—society's bleeding hearts have apparently bled so profusely that there isn't a drop of pity left for the average convict. While everyone kowtows to a wheelchair-bound nigdyke, her brother who's in jail for selling crack is utterly forgotten.

This exasperating phenomenon of confused compassion alongside callousness reaches perhaps its purest state of polarization in the person of ex-Grecian-Formula-using TV game-show host Bob Barker. The gray-haired emcee is a fanatical animal-lover who once sued artist Joe Coleman for biting the head off a mouse during a live performance. Barker went to bat on behalf of the dead rodent in court. But Barker also rakes in bookoo bucks supplying the corrections industry with items such as soap, shampoo, and plastic snap-on shoes. He throws a hissy-fit over decapitated vermin yet feels no twinge of conscience against making a profit on caged human beings. Well, as they say, if the price is right....

The Human Suffering Gold Rush engendered by the recent prison boom has also given birth to an insufferably righteous, shirt-rending, parasitical entity known as the victim's-rights advocate. It's funny how these advocates were never around when *I* was being victimized. They rarely seem to know the sort of lifelong adversity so familiar to the average convict from childhood onward. Victim's-rights advocates are only attuned to a certain *kind* of human suffering, usually that of fragile little embryos whose lives have been so trauma-free that they're utterly waylaid by their first brush with crime. These self-anointed Protectors of the Overprotected endlessly yammer about breaking the "cycle of abuse," oblivious to the concept that imprisoning someone is a particularly vicious *perpetuation* of that cycle. Imprisonment doesn't settle the score, it ups the ante.

Of course, it isn't a power trip for the victims or their advocates. Not at all. Nuh-uh. No-sirrree, Bob. *Nein. Nyet.* No traces of sadism in *their* demeanor. No willful infliction of human suffering going on with *them.* As they see it, you can't inflict suffering on someone who isn't human, and criminals aren't human to them.

The "justice" system should be grateful that scientists have yet to devise a machine which measures human suffering, for it would incontrovertibly prove how many thousands of times convicts suffer more than their victims, assuming their crime wasn't victimless.

But the average law-and-order armpit-sniffer out there will deny even a molecule of malice on his or her part. No, they seek "justice," that's all.

With the veins in their heads ready to burst open and spew forth hot red waterfalls of righteously angry innocent-lamb's blood, outraged citizens tell us they want perpetrators to know what victims feel like.

Is that so?

By the way you're acting, the rabid manner in which you're seizing control and inflicting harm, I could've sworn that y'all want to know what a *perpetrator* feels like.

The righteous rabble's thirst for blood is unquenchable. They exhibit a sadism more sustained and dishonest than anything a criminal is capable of doing. Or *interested* in doing, even.

They're being "hard on crime," which subliminally raises a phallic hard-on. They're wielding a stiff cock against crime. Both Republicans and Democrats campaign with hard-on-crime platforms. You can't get elected these days without promising to smash criminals' testicles under a pile-driver.

You faggot cowards.

Subconsciously, every one of you who wails about how we aren't being punished severely enough knows you couldn't last twelve hours in here without sobbing and clawing at the walls and crying about how unjust the system is. You'd melt down into a little yellow chicken strip before the sun set. If you're so sure that we're coddled and pampered, commit a fucking felony and come join the country club!

Fear of crime is fear of the masked burglar which prowls in everyone's subconscious. It is fear of one's own dark potential, externalized. The War on Crime becomes a black comedy, an endless hall of mirrors where everyone reflects everyone else's worst fears.

Underlying the outraged citizen's cheap histrionics is an abiding envy of the criminal's boldness. The puffed-up law-abider's craven demands for criminal blood serve to mask his own shame and self-hatred for being cowered into submission without ever having to be punished. Those who've been scared into playing by the rules reserve a special animosity for those who haven't. Buried within every oversocialized buffoon's psyche is a profound humiliation at having been whipped into line by the law. No one hates a criminal more than someone with the nagging awareness of having been frightened into compliance.

Shoved deep within his long-abandoned savage heart, every tough-on-crime goody-two-shoes knows there are several crimes he would have *loved* to have committed but was too chickenshit to make a move:

"Goddamnit, I'm so afraid of the rich and powerful that I've buckled down and followed their rules, even though it's given me ulcers and driven me into debt, so, Officer, please, string up his balls for daring to act out his baser impulses."

If you are suffering, people will find a way to rationalize why you deserve it. This refers, of course, only to *your* suffering. *Theirs* is always cause for outrage.

No, criminals don't suffer—it's a "debt" they owe. They committed crimes, so they deserve it.

Deserve WHAT?

How much punishment is enough?

And how much is so severe that it turns the petty criminal into a murderer?

This whole idea of someone objectively "deserving" punishment for their actions is an antiquated, pseudo-biblical concept and almost entirely foreign to me. "Crime" is "sin" which doesn't trust God to do the punishing.

But the justice system, which peddles such myths for profit, must scramble to depict the victim's suffering as never-ending and the convict's suffering as nonexistent. It becomes a situation where the criminal "deserves" everything that happens to him—and worse—while the "victim" never does. Where I "deserve" punishment for beating her up, but she didn't "deserve" being beaten up for threatening me and attacking me and draining my forgiveness until there was none left. The line of responsibility is never that clear, yet the system has to pretend that it is.

"But if you didn't beat her up, you wouldn't be here."

But if she didn't bloody my nose after nine months of threatening to kill me, I wouldn't have beaten her up.

More to the point—if the prosecutor didn't decide to press charges against me, then hand me over to people who would strip me naked, dress me in a jumpsuit, place shackles on my ankles, run a chain through a small steel black box which locked over my handcuffs, put me on a bus, and then *drive* me here, I wouldn't be here.

Let's make it clear about everyone who made a decision in this process, all right? No one's hands were tied, except mine—*literally*—at the end of the process. But my actions alone didn't land me here.

She made a decision to hit me.

I made a decision to hit her back.

And the justice system made a *series* of decisions which sealed me in a bug jar.

Guilt. No one wants to claim it, and with good reason. If they did, it would create two immediate problems:

They couldn't speak well of themselves;

They couldn't talk shit about others.

The stereotype is that everyone *in here* cries that they're innocent, when in truth, everyone *out there* is acting innocent. Prisoners don't claim innocence nearly as much as they insist they aren't the only guilty ones.

A recent book about the prison industry stated that more than 70% of all adult Americans have committed at least one felony offense in their lives, yet fewer than one percent of Americans are incarcerated. So if you're one of the invisible unconvicted felons who still roams free, I'd suggest you speak softly, step lightly, and consider yourself lucky.

Me, well, luck's never been my bag.

It's not like I have a vagina and can get away with being violent.

It's not like I'm a Kennedy and can get away with rape and murder.

It's not like I'm one of the Bush boys, who can do millions in fraudulent banking deals and not do a day in jail for it.

It's not like I'm the son of Portland's police chief, who gets caught with a fat sack of cocaine and doesn't do a day in jail for it.

It's not like I'm the Portland judge who received eighteen citations for Driving Under the Influence and didn't do a day in jail for them.

It's not like I'm the seven-foot-tall pear-shaped guard in here who was rumored to have slipped his schlong between his niece's legs and didn't do a day in jail for it.

It's not like I'm the guard down in the laundry room who was rumored to have hid in the penitentiary for three days while police were looking to serve a warrant on him for wife-beating and who never did a day in jail for it.

It's not like I'm the chubby, red-nosed bulldyke guard rumored to have battered her lezzie lover in the penitentiary parking lot and who didn't do a day in jail for it.

It's not like I'm one of the estimated fifty percent or more of police nationwide who've assaulted others, particularly their spouses, without ever doing a day in jail for it.

It's not like cop-killers get treated far more severely than cops who kill.

It's not like I'm one of the wealthy, who can afford good lawyers to exonerate them from all sorts of crimes so they never have to do a day in jail for it.

No, it's not like I'm one of the wealthy, whose smooth, easy lives will be seen by a wealthy judge as working in their *favor*, rather than against them, when the truth is that they have far less reason or need to commit crimes than a poor person.

What was that you were saying about justice? Speak up—it's *really* hard to hear you.

I might buy into your definitions of good and bad, of crime and punishment, if they weren't so selectively applied.

But the word "good," at least as it issues from your mouth like a halitosis cloud, only seems like a nicer word for "powerful."

So don't talk to me about justice and accountability. I'm in NO FUCKING MOOD to hear it. Your softly spoken homilies are starting to make my ears burn.

You know, my brother was brutally murdered, and yet I don't blame every criminal on earth for it. I don't even blame every murderer—only the person who did it, who was never caught.

Crime may be a human sickness, but so is an inability to forgive. So is a sadistic lust to punish which cowers behind bullshit notions such as "justice."

I've been on the receiving end of crimes throughout my life. Note that I don't say that I've been "victimized" by crime—I've had them happen to me.

Ouch, I've been burglarized.

Ooh, I've been sexually molested.

Yowie, I've been robbed at gunpoint.

Yikes, I've been stalked and threatened.

Criminy, I've been assaulted—repeatedly, so I have a keen sense of how much suffering my brave "victim" endured.

I know what the immediate effects of being on the receiving end of crime are, and I know what the long-term effects are.

But unlike the professional victims, I *also* know what it's like to be incarcerated. And unless you know it from both ends like I do, you aren't qualified to comment on it like I am. Really. You're just another hundred-percent expert with zero-percent experience, so sit down and quit yappin' before I give you several good reasons to keep feeling like a victim.

I speak from hard experience when I tell you this—being burglarized, molested, robbed, stalked, threatened, assaulted, and incarcerated all made me suffer...

...with one big difference—incarceration is *much* worse than any of the others.

Of all the bad things that have ever happened to me, being thrown in a box and stripped of all freedom, dignity, and respect—for months and now *years*—is more painful, dehumanizing...and *criminal*...than everything else combined.

Just because the system has so much power that it is afforded the semantic privilege of defining its predations as "justice" rather than "crimes" doesn't mean the state isn't inflicting human suffering on a scale much more massive than all "criminals" combined.

No matter how hard they try to focus all the attention on what I've done, my "criminal act" doesn't justify their "act of justice."

Two wrongs don't make a right. As Gandhi said, an eye for an eye just makes the whole world go blind.

And then someone killed him.

And putting someone in a cage is a passive-aggressive way of killing them from the inside-out.

Part of the new sharp-fanged torture-the-criminals ethos is a jettisoning of even the pretense of reform or rehabilitation. They don't even use those words anymore, rubbing our noses in the idea that we are here to be PUNISHED. Lock 'em up...throw away the key...and maybe rape or murder 'em in there, if they know what's good for 'em.

Corrections officials argued that since the recidivism rate was so high, programs designed to rehabilitate the felon didn't work.

They never seemed to question whether it might have been the putting-people-in-cages part that didn't work.

Still, to appease concerned citizens who might murmur about the adverse effects of pure punishment, the D.O.C. makes a limp-dick gesture at wallpapering our minds with happy faces through a series of "cognitive restructuring" classes which most inmates have to attend in order to earn good-time credits.

These classes boast snappy titles such as "Pathfinders," "Breaking Barriers," and "Cage Your Rage." They teach us to correct our "thinking errors" so we won't want to shoot meth, steal cars, or beat bitches anymore. They peddle the self-help movement's idiot-level happy-speak, dumbed-down even further to make it digestible for convicts.

By harping on our "thinking errors," the teachers of these classes seem never to have considered that maybe *they're* the ones whose thinking is screwy.

As it stands, these are the golden lessons the system is teaching me:

Throwing me in a toilet will help me get clean.

Depriving me of respect will raise my self-esteem.

Denying me love will make me more loving.

Treating me as if I'm subhuman will bring out the best in me.

Constantly acting as if I'm not to be trusted will make me willing to act more trustworthy.

Removing me from society will facilitate my social adjustment.

I owe a debt to a society which owes nothing to me.

Placing me in a cage will make me less violent.

What I did to my victim was bad, but what the system is doing to me is good.

Hurting me far worse than I hurt my victim will make me feel bad about her suffering instead of mine.

I am accountable to the government for the suffering I inflicted on my victim, but the government is not accountable for the suffering it inflicts on me.

It was a bad thing that I held my girlfriend in a car against her will for ten minutes, but it's a good thing for the government to hold me in a cage against my will for two-and-a-half years.

It's a bad thing to steal $10 from someone in a dark alley, but it's a good thing for the government to steal nearly half my wages in full daylight for as long as I live.

It's a bad thing to kill one person, but it's a good thing when the government kills millions all over the world.

It's a bad thing to sell marijuana to someone who wants it, but it's a good thing for the government to shove pharmaceuticals down the throats of inmates who don't want them.

It's a bad thing to force someone to strip naked, but it's a good thing when the government does it to me and tells me to spread my cheeks and cough.

I freely chose to commit my crime, but the government had no choice but to lock me up for it.

The government and its corporate friends aren't the ones forcing the taxpayers to pay for this—I am.

I, not the government, am the one who fails to see the victims of my actions as human.

I should never take the law into my own hands.

I should never presume that the right to hurt others is mine.

The leader of a class insultingly titled "Thinking for a Change," a protected-looking dyed-blonde woman who let it slip that she lives in a community so wealthy that ex-felons are forbidden from home ownership there, kept telling us, "The public is fed up with you guys."

Yes, the public is fed up with all that crime they see on their TVs, and, gosh-diggity-durnit, they feel something has to be done about it.

Their TVs tell them very little about how the American standard of living is free-falling and how kids' test scores and workers' wages are plopping into the toilet and how our fine country is violently cleaving into a moat-rimmed wealthy few surrounded by vast flatlands of peasants, but their TVs tell them a lot about a crime wave that's right around their corner.

Hot, delusive cathode rays inflame you by overhyping sensational cases, wispy little white girls ass-fucked and decapitated, bloody cum stains on Sunday-school dresses, wispy little white girls who went to school where persecuted nerdlings spray classmates with locust swarms of bullets, persecuted nerdlings whose hotheaded disgruntled-worker fathers heave hand grenades at McDonald's Playland, splattering innocent skulls open like squashed tomatoes, TV-industrial prison pimps hyping freakish crimes to where you're hiding behind your couch, afraid of all those psychopathic crack-puffing black-brick nigga thugz smashing through your TV screen and snatching your family heirlooms, afraid of all those lizard-skinned chomos lurking in the bushes ready to slice a yellow fingernail through your six-year-old daughter's hymen.

It can happen anywhere, they tell you. No one is safe.

The public is hypnotized and snake-charmed and brain-damaged by television to where they're mentally crippled, utterly incapable of analysis or discernment. It's all image, myth, and emotion now. They're easy to play.

They've played you.

There's no crime wave. It's a hoax.

Fear of violent crime is through the roof. It's like mercury shooting straight up a thermometer and bursting through the glass.

Actual violent crime is lower than it was in the 1970s, when no one was quite so afraid of it.

TV has created a mass crime panic in order to justify the mass prison buildup.

Two-thirds of American inmates weren't convicted of doing *anything* violent, not even simple assault, much less serial murder or child rape.

The government doesn't give a fuck about your safety, you idiots.

They WANT you to get robbed, raped, and murdered, suckers. Then they'll cage the perps and make money on *everyone's* suffering. You think they'd care about your precious victimization if they weren't getting paid for it?

It's a business, honey.

The sickest business there is.

Sometime in the mid-1990s, total spending on corrections in America eclipsed total spending on education. More money is now spent on jails than on schools. The nation grows dumber and more enslaved.

They aren't building prisons to keep pace with rising crime, because crime is falling. They're expanding the definition of crime to fill all the beds they've built. It's like the hotel business—they have to keep the beds filled.

There are now more than TWO MILLION Americans filling those steel beds.

Thirty years ago, it was less than two hundred thousand.

A thousand-percent rise...and rising, rising. The largest, most rapid prison expansion in world history. The Land of the Free imprisons more people than anywhere else on earth. More than Russia. More than notoriously repressive China, which has four times as many people as America yet fewer total prisoners. Less than five percent of the world's population lives within the USA's borders. A full *quarter* of the world's inmates live within the USA's jails and prisons. Other industrialized nations function fine with similar crime rates and drastically lower incarceration rates.

I'm one of the ten thousand or so unfortunates currently penned up in Oregon's human zoos. Over the next eight years, Oregon's justice officials plan to cram another five thousand people within cages.

That's not in response to a rise in crime, which is declining—yet Oregon's officials plan to increase the state's number of prisoners by fifty percent.

The predictions have been steady enough that their author joked Wednesday that she simply places a ruler at a slant and draws the same line every time.
—*The Oregonian*, "State Predicts Prison Population Will Continue Steady Rise,"
3/30/2000

She *joked* about it.

So what's the Oregon Department of Corrections' main objective? Public safety? Victims' restitution? Inmate rehabilitation? Inmate *punishment*?

No:

Maintaining growth is still the main issue for the Department of Corrections.
—Corrections Director David Cook, quoted in the same *Oregonian* article

Jokes and slanted rulers and maintaining growth. They've become so arrogant and stricken with feelings of omnipotence that they don't even hide what it's all about anymore:

Money.

Crime doesn't pay? For the prison-builders, it does. For judges and lawyers, it does. For every parasitic industry which provides goods and services to the prison-industrial complex, it does. Crime is their bottom line.

They've made a huge business out of defining sin and punishing sinners. They've made Hell into a highly profitable amusement park. Hell, Incorporated.

The only ones who seem to realize it's a business are the prisoners and the entrepreneurs. Everyone else—the poor saps stuck in the middle paying the tab—think it has something to do with right and wrong.

I am money in the bank to them. Job security. Their children's future. I'm a tiny ink spot on a bar graph pointing upward erectionlike toward maximum profits. I don't owe a debt to them; they're making money off me.

The prison boom. A bull market for crime and punishment. America's fastest-growing industry. And the same Wall Street hairy-backed swine who made billions in the defense industry by lying to Americans that the Russians had more weapons than us are now making billions by fanning the public's fear of a nonexistent crime epidemic.

And those millionaires and billionaires will push for harsher laws and longer sentences to ensure their death camps operate at peak capacity. And like always, they'll get their way.

First-time offenders are now going down for years. Repeat offenders are getting buried for decades. No more probation, no more good-time credits, no more diversion programs or community service. Those are all nice, but not nearly as profitable

The tumor grows. Crime. Guilt. Punishment. Money. Money. Money.

One day when it's far too late, all the tough-on-crime TV-nation dupes will fear going to prison more than they fear being victimized by crime, but by then the system will be so engorged on human blood, they won't be able to stop it. They'll put a big wall around the country, and you'll either be a prisoner or a guard. And you think I'm speaking metaphorically, don't you?

There are only two constant principles in all moral systems:

It's good if it enhances my survival; and

If it harms you in order to enhance my survival, it's even better.

So it's natural that I'd see things differently than the prison-builders.

You're using my life as a bingo chip just so you can feel snugger all nestled in your den with the crackling fireplace and shag carpet and seven-foot TV screen and bowl of hot popcorn? I'm to roast in hell just so your pampered, protected mind can project a fragile hologram of security? You'll justify any atrocity against me just so you can feel safe? No. I don't think so.

You can't slice a turd into perfect squares. And you can't isolate guilt and wrongdoing like the Department of Corrections tries to do.

Incarceration will always fail in its stated purpose because it tries to pull off a psychologically impossible magic trick:

It attempts to quarantine all potential for evil outside of itself.

Despite the best efforts of those whose foolish law books seek to crystallize good and evil, to etch right and wrong onto stone tablets, these pixie-dust-sprinkled cosmic forces remain much more ethereal than that. You can't trap the laws of cause and effect within a yellowing, gilt-edged law book.

All moral systems seem destined to boomerang upon themselves.

The justice system, by weight of its *own* guilt, will one day fall to the ground like a sick, old, dying elephant.

It will fall prey to *poetic* justice, which is always more powerful than official justice.

Things change. One era's good guys become the next era's villains.

Society used to view slaves as barbarians, but now the slaveowners find that role foisted on them.

And so—one day—it will be with humans in cages and those who put them there.

One day, the guardians of public accountability will be held accountable for *their* actions, and it won't be pretty.

One day, the finger-pointers will have millions of fingers pointing at them.

Like the key-holders keep reminding me, you can't harm someone, pretend it's a good thing, and not suffer the consequences. They'd do well to learn the same lessons they keep force-feeding me.

Maybe one day, using the same specious two-wrongs-make-a-right logic the justice system is using to step on my back and make money, I'll be able to put them in cages and show them it's wrong to put people in cages. Maybe like them, I'll be able to inflict pain and in an emotionless voice tell them how very much they deserve it.

Ahhh, justice....

I'm not suggesting that the world would be a rosier meadow if we just let everyone run around raping, robbing, and stabbing, although it would be fun to watch how truly "tough" all the tough-on-crime fanatics are when left to their own devices.

But some questions, class—why does crime happen? And what's a logical response to it?

Whoops—sorry for getting so pragmatic. I should've realized that the anti-crime industry doesn't exist to understand crime and prevent its occurrence. No, it operates more like voodoo than a social science. It uses crime as an excuse to set up a grand psychodramatic spectacle, a High Mass based on the Big Tribe's ceremonial needs of guilt and expiation.

I currently reside at a "penitentiary," which uses the same root word as "penance." But penance leads to absolution, and I don't think that's what they have in mind here, at least not for me. *Society*'s being redeemed through my suffering, but I ain't.

Purgatory is where you suffer for your sins and are cleansed. Hell is where you suffer for them forever.

This isn't purgatory, this is hell.

This is the Sin Factory—I'm not here to be washed of sin, but to be stained with it. I'm not being held for years in order to be purged of guilt; I'm trapped here to ensure that I'm removed for as long as possible from everything that might help me get clean.

I'm being used as a pawn on a giant playing board called *Sin: The Game*. They don't want to redeem *everyone* in this little sporting event—the victim's redemption, and by extension society's ability to view itself as good, comes at my expense. Like a seesaw, they are elevated only to the degree that I fall.

For me to get better would ruin everything for them.

Most guys never get better.

Perhaps the main reason criminals keep coming back through the "revolving door" revolves around this mystical psychological carcinogen known as guilt.

Shortly after I came to prison, I thought of getting the word FELON tattooed on my chest. My version of a pink triangle, a scarlet letter, or a dunce cap. An emblem of the fact that I'm forever branded, stained, and stigmatized in society's eyes.

Once a felon, always a felon. It's never over. You are never absolved. Nothing ever gets stamped that says, "Debt paid...sins forgiven." Society seems to hate you at least as much for the fact that you've been to prison as for the fact that you've committed crimes. Probably more.

The idea of forgiveness has been eliminated. If the state's attitude was, "Look, we feel you've done wrong, but if you accept the punishment, we'll forgive you and make you a part of us again," the recidivism rate would plummet. But by refusing to forgive the criminal, they imbue him with an attitude of defiance, of desperation, of what's the use, of nothing will make them happy.

There is a sense that once you go to prison, your life is irreparably damaged. Things spiral downward from that point on.

It's like that TV show *The Prisoner* from the 1960s—every time he tried escaping the island, a big white balloon came and swallowed him up, spitting him back where he belonged.

Imprisonment becomes an incurable psychological syndrome. Convicts refer to it as being "institutionalized." It means, as one forty-three-year-old convict who's spent twenty-five years behind bars told me, feeling more at ease in here than out there. It means they've not only captured your body—they have your mind, too. And even if your body gets released into the real world for a little while, you'll be back, because your mind never leaves.

With a recidivism rate somewhere around 90%, the Department of Corrections is free to explain exactly what it's correcting. They'll just shrug, say they don't know why criminals aren't responding to their treatment, and keep building more prisons.

The truth—which the D.O.C. will naturally deny—is that they don't want criminals to get better. That's the *last* thing they want. The system is designed to keep feeding on itself. It thrives on repeat customers.

The system exists to cement your failure.

If you weren't a criminal when you went in, you will be when you get out. And it has little to do with learning new criminal techniques and everything to do with trauma and ostracism and having your emotional landscape firebombed and your hopes crushed. It isn't a "crime school" in the popularly understood sense, meaning that cons give workshops on lockpicking and meth-cooking, but it's a devastating psychological modification program which renders you almost totally incapable of reintegrating into society. It isn't a crime school so much as it's a University of Hatred.

When I ask cons what they're learning from all this, the answer is always the same:

I'm learning to hate.

I'm learning to hate.

I'm learning to hate.

Oh, God, you can't imagine the hatred.

The hatred one might feel if he'd been subjected to forced brain surgery under bright lights with no anesthesia which altered him so extensively that there was nothing he could do to get back to his prior state, but not so thoroughly that he wasn't constantly, painfully, humiliatingly aware that he'd been changed.

A dangerous, dangerous hatred.

A hatred that makes me want to peel my skin off, twist it into a noose, and lynch you with it.

A hatred that makes me want to eat these cell bars and spit steel shanks through your rib cage.

A hatred that cakes into my soul like burnt crust inside a casserole dish that's been baking in the oven too long. Can't scrub it off now; it's permanent.

A hatred so intense, I feel I can faint from it. A hatred so dizzying, I'll hold the guard rail as I walk down the old steel stairwell to keep from falling. A hatred so exhausting, opening my eyes in the morning feels like Band-Aids being ripped from raw skin.

An emotional biohazard. High-torqued. Ratcheted up to maximum tension.

My diastolic blood pressure shot up ten points.

There's a stabbing pain in my chest.

There's a lot more gray in my hair.

And when people—even friendly ones—are within arm's reach of me, an urge erupts to start swinging wildly at their heads. I never felt that way before.

Look what they've done to my brain.

There's a big blood clot in there that I struggle to lance and spill onto paper.

There's a big white balloon in my head that's being squeezed on all sides. They're making it squeak. Stop them, they're making it squeak.

Low-level chronic claustrophobia slowly driving me mad.

I can't leave.

They won't let me leave.

Motherfuckers won't let me leave.

They won't forgive me for what I did—and I didn't even do it to *them*—but I'm supposed to forgive them for what they've done to me? Won't happen. Couldn't happen even if I wanted it to. The human mind doesn't work that way. The human *body* doesn't work that way. When you've been made to suffer at another's hands, you want revenge. They understand that principle in the crime victim, but never in the criminal. My thirst for vengeance isn't evidence that I'm a monster; it's proof that I'm a human being. Only an android could go through this and not want revenge. Only a totally broken individual wouldn't want to reclaim the power they've taken away.

Prison aims to break you.

Instead of fixing what's wrong with you, they destroy everything that wasn't already broken.

They seek to crush your will and render you as toothlessly, droolingly compliant as the law-abiders, to beat all the fight out of you. To break you and laugh that you're broken. To keep you alive for the pleasure of watching you die.

They place roadblock after roadblock in front of you, hoping your engine finally stalls and coughs up a last smoky puff of surrender.

They shove you down so far and make it such an effort to climb back up, it's a relief to stay down. You're trapped inside a thousand-foot-high steel drum whose cylindrical walls are greased, and every time you get ten feet up, you slide back to the bottom again.

It's their institution, and they exist to institutionalize you. They'd love for you to succumb to their state-sponsored lobotomy.

They smash you so thoroughly that when you get out, you'll either commit no crimes...or really big ones.

Charles Manson was a car thief until he spent some time in prison.

Jeffrey Dahmer was a two-bit child molester until he spent some time in prison.

I won't beat anyone up anymore. I might not touch them...or I might kill them...but I won't beat them up anymore.

And my rage, naturally, will be entirely my fault. They inject me with a virus, strap me to a steel bed and refuse medication, then blame me for getting sick.

It's like a parent who beats his kid until he's crippled, then beats him again until he can't walk anymore.

Society's starting to realize that spanking kids doesn't improve their behavior, yet they're still tragically blind about the long-term effects of putting adults in cages.

When a sacrifice is needed, understanding only gets in the way.

And yet the ugly, ugly truth is that criminals, over the long trajectory of life, have typically suffered far more than any of their victims.

This may be why crime victims come unglued over their victimization to a degree far beyond any immediate suffering—because the criminal pops the little bubble in which the victim had heretofore encased themselves. The criminal gives them a taste of the pain, ugliness, and severe emotional spoilage which *defines* the criminal's life rather than interrupts it. The criminal plucks a shiny pear from the tree and shows that it, too, can be bruised.

I look at all the buff, tattooed, evil dudes in here, and I wonder how many little boys were crying a generation ago. How many families totaled by rage and despair. How many dads missing. How many cold, cold mothers. Look at all the dead faces. Too much crustacean shell to ever peel away—only newer, harder, deader layers piled on top. Too late now.

The black kid who told me of blurry memories just before he was sent to a foster home of sitting at the dinner table in front of a plate of human shit his parents were forcing him to eat.

The wacky skinhead whose parents were such druggies that he was delivered in the hospital room frying on acid and has heard voices in his head all his life.

The morose middle-aged Injun who says that ever since his older brothers coerced him into shooting the neighbors' dog when he was five, he's had an invisible magnet around his head which attracts trouble.

The ones who call themselves "state-raised," who've leapfrogged through their lives from group homes to juvenile detention centers to adult prisons. They were born needy and never had those needs met and those needs festered and grew uglier until now they're fossilized and unreachable.

Seeking to defuse little firecrackers, society turned them into time bombs.

An old peckerwood with the stolidity of a felonious Otto von Bismarck told me of how he wants to become a sniper when he's released, specializing in justice officials. His fantasies were chillingly elaborate, right down to the sort of rifle he'd use and what the best sort of escape routes would be.

A robber who's spending twenty years told me he wants to murder his parole officer and every family member of the crime partner who ratted him out—but he doesn't want to kill his partner. Just all of his family members, and let the cheese-eating little rodent live with that.

Similarly, an impossibly muscular meth cook with veins in his neck the size of tree roots wants to slaughter every child of the DA who prosecuted him.

An Indian with over two hundred felony convictions has a plan for the next time they raid his trailer to bust him on some minor parole violation—he'll press a dynamite plunger and blow up everything within an acre of ground zero. He'll get killed, but so will all the cops.

A pensive punk-rock kid who grew up watching his mom shoot dope tells me he wants to blow up things when he gets out. It doesn't matter what—he just wants to blow up things.

Explosions. That fantasy comes up a lot. Everything they've internalized for years finally comes out in a scorching, all-destroying flameball.

I've been down for over two years now, and being on the "outs" is just a dim, long-buried memory, the stuff of dreams.

I've lost sight of the world beyond these walls. Can I ever truly be a part of that world again?

All the hard-boiled convict types who looked so extreme to me when I first fell now look utterly normal. And when a new guy fresh off the streets moves into my cell, he looks like a new fish and I feel like the convict.

And I find myself using prison slang without a hint of artifice.

And I wish I could get one of those high-paying prison jobs, the ones that pay $48 a month.

And, well, this prison's better than the last one.

And that chicken stir-fry we had for lunch was really screamin'.

And, oh, how luxurious that tiny plastic mattress feels when I crawl atop it at night.

And here I am with all my friends.

Oh God, please God, please please please please God, don't tell me I'm getting used to this.

This here caged gorilla will spend another three months in captivity before the gates open like a dilated anus and excrete me.

I'll leave prison more superhuman and subhuman than when I entered—but not more human. More shell-shocked than I've ever been before, and yet forced to walk a tightrope.

A friend of mine who knows Charles Manson once asked him what he'd like to do if he were ever released. Charlie said he wanted to go and sit under a tree.

I'm with Charlie. I'd like to take a bath and play with my Chihuahua. Then maybe open a door, walk outside—I haven't been able to do that for more than two years—and go buy a cup of fresh-brewed coffee.

Police lights spinning in my rear-view mirror will have an entirely new meaning now...the real possibility of being resealed in a living coffin.

The crowning jewel of my Paranoia Pyramid is the knowledge that I'll be released into the same state inhabited by that foul-tempered, huge-nostriled, gaping-cunted voodoo doll I beat up.

Having to breathe the same air as her...knowing that since they believed her baby-faced victimology rumba the first time around, all it would take from her would be one phone call to lock me up again.

"Um...he raped me, officer...oh, *sure* it was horrible...sure, I'll testify."

Anne is telling people that she's bought a gun and that she'll never be able to rest as long as I'm alive and I'd better stay away from her, and let's just forget that *she's* the one on record saying she can't stay away from *me,* and on record threatening to follow me wherever I go and kill *me,* and the one who kept saying she was going to buy a gun and kill *me* before any of this happened, and let's not think about the fact that she used to say she *wished* I'd stalk her like she stalked me, and that *she* was the one who'd show up uninvited on my doorstep like a stray cat begging for more milk, and that *she's* the one who stalked ex-boyfriends with names such as Rod and Branch and some dude who works in a Portland restaurant and would prefer I didn't mention his name. Let's forget that in the year we were together, people named Brandon, Jane, and Darcy called the police on Anne for stalking, threatening, and attacking them, respectively.

Let's just put all that out of our minds and pretend that *I'm* the one who fits the stalker mold.

OK?

Anne, the most ambitious practitioner of psychological projection on earth, has gone so far as to say she fears I'll want to get back with her and be her boyfriend again.

Yeah, snookums, and those Negroes sure used to lynch a lotta Klansmen down South, didn't they?

Ms. Pignose is giving me a swamp thicket's worth of reasons to suspect foul play from her camp when I bust loose from the gates.

And then, on the day I'm spending my third consecutive birthday behind bars, the clouds part and Jehovah God winks down on me:

Wee Lady Anne is in jail for assault!

The frail li'l orchid plowed over a bicyclist with her car after screaming "I hate bicyclists!" and then fled the scene! Ay yi yi, if it's heinous for a man to hit a woman because of the strength differential, how much *worse* is it for a motorist to assault a bicyclist with her car?

Upon hearing the news, a cannonball of white-light energy shoots up my spine. A giddy, volcanic surge of righteous revenge splats out of every pore.

She who kept mentioning karma!

Little Lady Macbeth couldn't wash the stain from her hands!

Now she can't pretend her violence was only a response to mine anymore. She's out plowing bicyclists while I'm safely chained down.

A-ha-ha-ha-ha-ha-ha!

Her dedicated campaign to scapegoat the honorable, almighty, somewhat-cuddly Jim Goad has finally backfired. Now all the guilt she tried foisting onto me falls back onto her fishbowl-shaped head.

The twat's so out of control, even twat-friendly Oregon had to do something about it. And even though she was convicted of Assault II, she only got five months for it, while I was convicted of *Attempted* Assault II and got twenty-four months…and even though we all know I would have been charged with Attempted MURDER if I did what she did…and even though her victim wasn't threatening to kill her like MY li'l victim was…it would be untrue to say I'm unhappy about the news.

It's a hollow victory, though.

She'll be worse when she gets out.

But so will I.

Every prison sentence is a death sentence.

One sweet spring morning a few months ago before the big yard riot, before prison officials cut down all the trees because cons were hiding shanks in them, I sat on a bench as some grinning peckerwoods tiptoed up to a tree and violently shook its branches. A scrawny, barely feathered baby bird flapped away from the tree and flew straight into the bench to my left, where it fell. And even though this bird was so young that its eyes were still closed, there was a look on its face as if it was fighting for its life. The peckerwoods ran up to the fallen bird, grabbed it, and walked around with their prey, passing it among each other like a pet. Then when Yard Line was called in, they walked back to the tree and returned the bird to its nest.

But even though the bird is no longer in their dirty hands, its mother will peck it to death. She'll sense it isn't the same bird who left the nest.

Not at all.

It spent some time with convicts and was forever changed.

⸮17⸮

The Nicest Guy on Earth

GENTLEMEN AND, UM, ladies of the jury:
I have been summoned before this tribunal today to offer some statements in defense of my life, to dissuade you from handing me the death penalty as punishment for my words, deeds, and relentlessly spunky attitude.

Rumor has it that I'm not a very nice guy. I cite two recent Internet postings in which I'm described as "a remarkably worthless man" and "the lowest of the low."

Awww! Bad people say mean things 'bout Jim-Jim, and me get boo-boo in my tum-tum. Shucks, it appears as if the Mr. Congeniality Award will elude me yet again this year.

What to make of their righteous piffle? Is it something I said? Is it what I wrote? Can mere words inspire obscenity trials and White House shootings and triple neo-Nazi suicides?

What happens when two worlds—Jim Goad and Planet Earth—collide?

Why do bombs go off with every step I take?

Why does the shit always fly to me—and stick?

Why am I so hated? I actually find myself quite lovable. On some days, I even manage to be cuddly.

I don't mind that you hate me; I'd just prefer that it be the real me you hate.

And to understand the real Jim Goad as the real Jim Goad understands himself, to savor me in the fullness of my musky, sunshiny, honey-waxy, chewy goodness, youse jurors hafta understand how I define terms such as "truth," "guilt," and "evil."

So let's start off with truth:
Everything you believe in is false.
Everything. Top to bottom.
Everything you hold sacred reeks of putrefaction, especially your life.
You want easy answers, don't you? Meaning—you want me to lie to you.
You want to hear lilting arias which convince you that you're some-

thing other than a shitting, farting, life-gobbling pillar of selfish motives, and I'm not going to do it.

I might punch you in the face, but I won't lie to you. I can't. It's like a compulsion. I'm a pathological truth-teller. I'll commit the most grievous acts and hold the most contemptible opinions, but if I'm not honest, I feel as if I've sinned against the gods.

Here's the difference between you and me:

I hate it when you lie to me.

You hate it when I tell you the truth.

If at daybreak everyone decided to tell the truth, everyone would be dead by nightfall.

In this world, you are never punished for blurry vision. It's only when you see things too clearly...that's when they put your name on the Shit List. That's when the shit flies toward you from a thousand fecal catapults.

I'm smart enough to figure out the world and too stupid to keep quiet about it.

I was born standing on my feet in a world turned upside-down. A world where governments commit far more crimes than criminals. Where blacks commit more hate crimes than whites. Where women hit men more than men hit women. Where millions more Germans died than Jews in WWII. Where human chattel slavery still exists in Africa but not in America. Where pacifists are more hostile than murderers. Where the "good guys" are always the ones causing the most suffering.

A world where people "fight fire with fire" and then condemn their enemies for using fire.

A world where telling the truth is the quickest way to get called a liar.

How many lies have you told yourself? You know which ones they are, don't you? Think of the lies you've recited so many times that you actually believe them. You were the one who constricted and hemmed-in your mind's vast inferno until it was the size of a cigarette lighter, the cheap plastic kind you buy at convenience stores that wear out after three or four lights.

This endless black universe is devoid of meaning. Everyone's projecting. But although truth is utterly subjective, most people spend their lives running away even from what their own minds tell them. There are two kinds of truth: the kind which validates you, and the kind which scares you. The latter type generally tends to be truer.

OK, now, guilt...

It's just another word for shit. The toxic waste we're always seeking to purge.

Guilt is a uniquely human idea. Animals aren't afflicted with it, even when eating each other alive. The gods, judging by their actions, don't seem to be burdened with it, either.

But to humans, guilt—how it is defined and where it is localized—seems to be the moving force behind the tragedy that is homo sapiens.

Even the Eden myth says as much—the trouble started not with the act of sin, but with the *idea* of sin. Adam and Eve were happy as clams until they ate from the tree of the *knowledge* of good and evil, and that's when Eve became stricken with PMS and Adam had to work a forty-hour week.

This isn't the Garden of Eden here, it's a big meat-grinder.

There are no good guys and bad guys, just a lot of bad guys shifting the blame.

In the end, we're all manure. Ashes to ashes. Dust to dust. Shit to shit. To be alive is to feel dirty. We are all, at base, shit machines. Shitmakers. Predators. Cannibals. Devourers. Our bodies are just big donuts with shit filling. You say you aren't full of shit? I bet if we sliced up your guts, it would tell a different story. Just as there are always untold pounds of excrement slowly snaking through our digestive pathways, there's always more than a little sin on all our souls.

All life feeds on other life. Think of all the death which must occur to give you life. All the dead plants and animals. All the vanquished civilizations atop which your prosperity floats.

It's hard to swallow the blazingly murderous implications of what it means to be fully alive. Most of you would have roughly the same chances at directly confronting your guilt as a housefly would have against an electric bug-zapper. To face one's destructive potential is terrifying, and that's why there's so much guilt-projection going on.

Guilt and willpower cannot coexist. Guilt is the idea that we are finite, that we are mortal, that we decay, and such notions dampen one's life instinct.

Guilt is an obstruction of the psychic colon. It is a virus which disables one's will. It operates like a disease, especially if left untreated.

Humans typically try to cure themselves of guilt by infecting someone else. Guilt becomes something you wish on your enemies. When you can make someone feel guilty, it's easier to control them, to stymie them, to step ahead of them in the grocery line. Guilt is a tranquilizer dart intended to immobilize the enemy.

When a society feels guilty, it starts to decline. When it can isolate its guilt outside of its borders and punish the scapegoat, it prospers. Human history seems little more than a saga in which the winners— meaning the superior predators—impregnate the losers with guilt and slay them for it. The winners write history, and it's astonishing how they never seem to seize the losers' land and resources because they *wanted* them—no, they *had* to do it, because the losers were evil. When you look at heroes and villains throughout literature, the only real differences seem to be that the heroes wear brighter costumes and are better at killing.

The biggest killers always declare themselves saints. Throughout history, the Jew-gassers, the Negro-lynchers, the firstborn-son-slaughterers, the Spanish Inquisitors, the Salem witch-hunters, the Christian Muslim-killers, and the Muslim Christian-killers all viewed their acts as purification rituals. They sincerely felt as if they were acting in the name of the highest good. I challenge the jury to recall any remotely comparable atrocities which were committed in the name of evil.

[Goad pauses for effect. Jury members cough and shift uncomfortably.]

Call me a wisenheimer, but I'm very suspicious of any group which hides behind the idea of its innate innocence, whether it be women-folk, the Negroes, the Catholic church, the US government, or the Ku Klux Klan.

Take those crazy, mixed-up, matzoh-gobblin' Jews, for example.

Will the Holocaust excuse anything Jews might do, now or in the future? Did the Holocaust make them innocent?

Did slavery somehow make American Negroes blameless?

Did the patriarchy's historical crimes wash all sins away from the ladies' souls?

Does suffering make you innocent? No, it only makes you unhappy. But the idea of having been wronged is universally used as an excuse to do some sinning of your own. The idea of someone else's guilt is used as justification for preying upon them. The notion of righteous revenge against a guilty enemy serves as a shield to cover the raw animal urge to dominate, destroy, consume, and flourish.

I call it the Scum Principle.

Lots of *Volk* think Nazis are scum. Why? Because Nazis thought Jews were scum. Or people will call Klansmen scum because Klansmen call Negroes scum. Or they'll call misogynists scum because misogynists call chicks scum. Or they'll call homophobes scum because the 'phobes call homos scum. Or they'll call right-wingers scum because the right-ies call leftists scum. Or they'll call the rich scum because the rich call the poor scum. Or they'll call the cops scum because "those filthy pigs" call *them* scum.

It's like a huge game of Tag, and no one wants to be "it."

It's as if guilt were a Christmas fruitcake no one wants, so they rewrap it and give it away again.

And no one seems to see any hypocrisy or contradictions in all this. Truth is, most alleged "humanists" have no qualms about dehumaniz-ing those who stand outside of the in-crowd, it's just that they insist you pick the *right* groups to call scum.

All individuals and social groups tend to ascribe filth and scummi-ness to their enemies. What is scum, if not a lower life form? Degrading the enemy and depicting him as something less than human justifies any suffering which may befall him, especially at your hands. The pretense of one's own purity is always a precursor for perpetrating atrocities upon the "scum."

I say that we're *all* scum, but especially the ones who consider themselves pure. I think I'm generally a decent fella 'cos I have tran-scended the need to sequester all potential for guilt and scumminess outside of myself. I can be scum, but I can also be quite sublime. And yet I find myself nearly incapable of the sort of detached cruelty all too common among the do-gooders.

Here's where I deconstruct good and evil.

Very dangerous, this thing called "good." To be good has a much more sinister aim than is commonly acknowledged. Any gesture at portraying oneself as good is essentially dishonest, since it masks an attempt to wrestle to the top of the food chain. To be good is to wish that the sun will shine on you and not your enemy. That's why light and darkness so often figure as metaphors of good and evil. The radiant glow emanating from being "good" is merely the life-stuff that comes from winning the battle and destroying your enemy. "Good," therefore, is the ultimate form of evil; it is evil^2.

One seeks to be moral only to the degree that one senses they're shit. A need to convince yourself that you're good can only arise from a suspicion that you aren't. Goodness is evil trying to escape itself. God is the Devil in denial.

The Good People can barely conceal the rage they aren't permit-ted to express. Society has repressed so much of what's vital in them, their animal aggression comes out in dissociatively sadistic perversions.

By necessity, their cruelty becomes more extreme due to its indirectness. Because they're too timid to strangle someone with their own hands, they need to watch a thousand murders every year on TV. Or they cheer when the Army slaughters a hundred thousand foreigners every decade. Or if they're *really* good, they fantasize about ten billion souls eternally broiling in hell.

It's difficult to bring any intelligent scrutiny to bear on the subject of good and evil, because under the most trifling analysis, these things melt like an Italian water ice on a hot summer day. Intellectual curiosity dies on the vast steppes where taboos come alive. People who are intelligent about everything else become kindergarteners when they talk about right and wrong. They understand spatial and temporal relativity, but morality seems etched in stone for them.

And yet morality, like truth, is entirely subjective. What's good and bad depends on whether you're throwing the rock or getting hit by it. One's own life—surprise!—is often very high on the list of good things, right up there at the tippy-top.

Basically, you are here to reproduce. And you are programmed to demonize others so you can increase the survival odds for you and your squalling progeny.

All in all, evil is much less offensive to me than good. Nothing that humans do to one another makes me cringe, because I expect it of humans. The way people try to *clean up* their actions is what sickens me. Nothing disgusts me about humans more than their attempts not to be disgusting. The true foulness always lies in the great pains people take not to appear foul.

What I see through the window doesn't bother me, only the window-dressing.

Metaphorically speaking, I don't find shit nearly as repellent as I do toilet paper.

"Goodness" is merely cheap deodorant on the armpits of existence. Being "civilized" only means hiding the inner animal behind some well-trimmed bushes.

I've been harmed by "goodness" far more than evil ever damaged me. All my life, whether it was my parents at home, or nuns at school, or my darling ex-lovers, or a corrupt judicial system, I've been punished by people who were frequently as guilty as I was, if not more. And I always cop to my shit, but the finger-pointers never do.

Good people have made my life hell.

By contrast, the Evil Ones have been pussycats.

I used to wonder why the assorted philanthropists and worlduplifters were always bitter, petty assholes, while the misanthropes were warm, honest, and genuine. Sweethearts, even. I've observed a pattern, too consistent to be coincidental, wherein "evil" personages, whether they be racists, sexists, or murderers, are polite and rational and a pleasure to deal with, whereas the professional condemners and full-time tattletales are irascible, humorless schlubs who'd plunge a steak knife in your back the minute it was turned.

And I've concluded that "good" people are so unpleasant because they're constipated with evil. Just as your innards slowly putrefy without regular bowel movements, one's personality grows toxic without an honest outlet for evil.

To be redeemed, one must first go down into the bowels.

To be truly ethical as I define it, one must embrace the scum within and rise above it. Or harness it. Or take it for a walk from time to time. But you can't run away from it. Only when you've fully digested your capability for wrongdoing, your own murderous selfishness, pettiness, and vanity, are you capable of wrestling with the divine.

I'm nose-to-nose with my capacity for evil. But that also allows me to French-kiss my potential for heroism.

[Goad pauses to fill himself a glass of cold water. A group of day laborers enters the courtroom, hauling a huge item covered in canvas tarpaulin.]

Pay no mind to those sweaty men in work boots and overalls—they're helping to move my ego into the courtroom.

Only an ego this massive could absorb all your guilt like a big fluffy towel soaking up a tiny piss puddle. My ego's big enough to think I'm seeing something here that most of you are missing. I've been through the wilderness, brothers and sisters of the jury, and I've brought back something from the fringes that I think is worthwhile.

It's all about being the right kind of asshole. I mean the type who tells the ugly truth even when it causes pain and lays waste to cities. The righteous asshole is always a sociopath, because society only exists to tell comforting lies about itself. To the righteous asshole, truth is more important than approval. Truth can slay entire civilizations. But truth doesn't exist to make the righteous asshole look better—looking better is the sole concern of petty assholes. The righteous asshole realizes that the truth is often unkind to him. But he'd rather shake hands with the truth than fight it, or else he'd fall into the pit of petty assholes.

The petty assholes have tiny sphincters which scatter their rabbit pellets atop things they'll never be able to comprehend. They act out of socialized fear, often with no sense of self beyond a patchwork quilt of ideas which others have fed them. The petty assholes invariably tag the righteous asshole as the problem, not realizing it is he who cleans the bottom of their cages and provides them with fresh water. The petty assholes are incapable of grasping their subordinate role in the fecal food chain.

By telling the truth about himself, the righteous asshole sets himself free. By telling the truth about the petty assholes, he enslaves them.

I used to be a petty asshole. But more and more, as the shadows stretch longer on the sundial, I grow righteous. I look better and better because I no longer desire to look better.

The worse they speak of Mr. Shit Magnet, the more evidence there is of my magnetism. There is a magical transfer of energy flowing in one direction—from them to me.

You haven't beaten me, only a Jim Goad piñata in your head. You threw all your ammo, and still I'm standing. That's what happens when you try to blow up the Empire State Building with firecrackers.

You tried to kill me, but you killed all the wrong parts: the weakness, the compassion, the self-doubt, the suicidal blips. This dark night of the soul, more like an arctic winter because it began years ago, only strengthened my resolve. The flames of hell only managed to burn out everything that was half-assed about my personality.

Every time I commit career suicide, I rise from the grave stronger. I go double-or-nothing each time, and if I get wiped out, I just start again. I'm unflinchingly Berserker and tirelessly willful enough to stack the odds against myself and still try to win the game.

I never saw the power that my detractors saw in me, but maybe this is a new beginning, a new start where I gloriously fuse with my public image.

I will rise to greet the new dawn like the Promethean being I'm charted to become. Stronger. Wiser. More powerful. Nearly legendary, if in a dark sense. And fairly reeking with humility.

Some would say my life is out of control, and yet I feel oddly serene. Above it. The master. Not the shit, but the magnet. At the center of the controversy. Eye of the hurricane. Lord of my domain, king of my castle.

A real *mensch*.

Delusions of grandeur? Messiah complex? Yeah, OK, so what?

Quite frankly, Sir and Madame, I feel I am better than you. I'm not perfect, but I'm a lot closer to it than *you* are. I don't want to be anybody besides me. Can you say the same thing?

If there's such a thing as karma, most people have very dull karma. If it's true that everyone has demons, what boring little demons they are. I know high drama and low comedy, while all you know is TV commercials. I run to extremes. I push it to the edge and then shove it off to see whether it flies.

I work hard for you, sweet spirits of the jury, harder than you know. One day you'll realize just how much I've sacrificed on your behalf. The world needs probes and lookouts and kamikazes. You need at least one person who won't lie to you. I can't be bought. I can't be scared into silence. In a world where everything's so tied down and circumscribed, where they try to smack the soul out of you as soon as you're born, you need someone willing to make some bold moves.

I choose the path of most resistance. I'll stand up for what I think is the truth even if there isn't a crowd behind me...or even if there's a crowd facing me with torches and nooses. It's a matter of conscience, and fuck the risks. I've sacrificed money and security, and almost my life, just to express my opinions without sugarcoating them.

All the shaming devices which usually keep people in line don't have an effect on me. I am free of the need for social approval. Do you realize what a tremendous freedom that is? Have you ever pondered just how much of your personality is strangled and constrained by others' expectations? Your disapproval means nothing to me except as an object of amusement, because I realize what silly little creatures you all are.

So fuck you, I'm not going to roll over and play dead. Your condemnation may inconvenience me...or it may kill me...but it fails to discourage me. And you can put me in a cell...or in the grave...and I still won't bow down. You'll have to kill me to shut me up.

And that's really why you hate me, isn't it? That's what's at the root of it, right? All the other shit is just an excuse. You hate me because I remind you all of how thoroughly you've been tamed. Of how you willingly stood in line and begged them to remove your teeth because you got scared at how good it felt to bite things.

When the day comes that you realize I'm the only one who hasn't been lying to you, that's when I get my power.

My reputation couldn't be worse, and I couldn't be happier. Nothing you could say about me could drag me down to your level. I just scratch my head, and you all fall to the ground like dead skin flakes. You can call me a Nazi commie bitch-smackin' baby-rapin' fag-bashing faggot, and as long as I don't have to hang out with you, I'm fine. I'm not going to argue with any of the bad names you call me, but I *will* point out how your need to call people bad names hasn't evolved much since nursery school.

Because it's not about whether I deserve condemnation, it's about your sick need to condemn. It's not my opinions which are the problem, it's your superstitions. I suffer for my insights and for your delusions. I am being punished not for the implausibility of my statements, but for the imbecility of your taboos. The intensity with which you freak out over my words is evidence that I've hit a nerve. If you didn't have such guilty consciences, you'd be able to shrug and get over it.

I ain't no witch, but that doesn't matter to the witch-hunters. You still need demons and goblins, don't you? Makes you feel good to burn someone at the stake, doesn't it? Your ideas of right and wrong are primitive beyond belief. You think you're enlightened, but you still need a scapegoat. You still need someone to blame, deface, and exterminate.

What is the end result when I tell you that your little morality play is a sham?

You hand me a Devil costume and tell me to stand Stage Right.

What is the reward for pointing out that everyone's walking around carrying bucketfuls of shit?

They dump the buckets on you. They feel lighter, and you get covered in shit.

I've made a career out of guilt-tripping the guilt-trippers, since they're so often the guiltiest. People feel a need to lash out at me because I remind them of their own guilt. I complicate matters, and the simpletons don't like that. I muddy the waters. I spread the scum around. I fuck up their whole crusade. I am punished for seeing color in a black-and-white world. For seeing all the teeming microorganisms in a drop of water that you think is clear. I see goodness swirled amid the evil, and I see evil flecked within the good. I see redeeming qualities in what others have banished to hell, and I see quite a bit of wrong with the seating arrangements in heaven. I am the Galileo of Guilt. The Copernicus of Conscience. Others give you a road map; I give you a globe.

It would take only a few softly spoken words of mine to make Devil horns grow from every one of your heads, but I'm too nice to do that.

The more you know me, the more you realize how exceedingly nice I am.

The nicest guy on earth.

A friend calls me The Iron Marshmallow—I'm simultaneously the meanest bastard and the goo-goo-gushiest fella on the planet.

Unless provoked, I'm a very polite man.

I'm never rude to people unless they're first rude to me. I always let 'em make the first move.

I never attack or criticize someone out of envy.

I've never joined a crowd in persecuting someone.

I never try to get someone else in trouble.

I don't lie about other people or spread false rumors about them.

I don't use people or rip them off.

I never condemn anyone for something I do myself.

I never denounce the morality of someone's actions, only the imbecility of their logic.

I don't go where I'm not wanted and I don't go half of the places where I'm wanted.

I'm a good kisser.

I love puppy dogs and cute wittle putty-tats.

And most importantly, I don't pretend I'm good. I'm too moral to act as if I'm moral.

Because of all this, I daresay I am a more saintly son-of-a-gun than any of you on the jury.

For my transgressions, I've been punished severely. For my virtues, I've been punished even worse.

Don't think I can't feel pain. Don't think I haven't cried. And don't think it's done me a damn bit of good.

My big blunders have all been matters of conscience—not that I transgressed it, but that I *had* one. If I could have an operation to remove my conscience, I'd surely do it. The problem is that every time I kill my soul, it grows back.

My father always told me I was smart enough to be anything I wanted. Problem is, I wanted to be Satan.

Am I evil?

On occasion.

Am I evil?

Not nearly enough.

Am I evil?

No, but I'm learning.

True evil pretends that it's good. So no, I'm not evil.

My unique curse is that I'm perceived as a sadist (without enjoying any of the perks that go along with it) while suffering like a masochist (without getting any credit for it).

Behold my miraculous ability to redeem others by absorbing guilt from them. I take the fall because you're all too weak to do it. I get into trouble so you don't have to. Never doubt that there's compassion for you in the way I fashion myself into an unsympathetic character. My guilt comes from an abiding conviction that I am far superior to the vast mass of humanity, that I stick out too much and shine too brightly, and so I get myself into trouble to shoulder *your* sense of inferiority and to ease *your* burden.

The villain, not the hero, is the one who makes you feel better about yourself. I understand that it's only a role, but you don't.

I am a giant drive-in movie screen onto which you project all your worst fears, and after your pitiful horror movie plays itself out, the screen remains intact and pure white. You feel better and I feel superior, and we're both OK.

But I've been too nice.

So it's no more Mr. Nice Guy.

But by calling you stupid and worthless, I suppose I am in some way asking you to dislike me. When I tell you that you're a moron, it does neither of us any good, especially when I'm right. In a perfect world, the pinheads would suffer for their stupidity; in this world, I am made to suffer for it.

When you rub up against shit, the shit is never worse for it.

You all have dull brains but very sharp teeth.

Nature exacts a heavy price for treating your inferiors as equals. 'Twas my mistake to think that logic and evidence would sway minds which show no indication of ever having been swayed by such things. I foolishly thought that I could convert the stupes. I thought I was a fecal alchemist and could turn your shit into gold. I should have just let the turds rest where they may.

You retards need to be placated with sugary lullabies and soft pajamas. Let's all sprout butterfly wings and flit around blowing soap bubbles. Let's skip through dewy meadows, sprinkling flower petals onto the fuzzy heads of happy chipmunks and li'l rainbow-striped caterpillars with smiling faces and great senses of humor. When I tell you that you're very nice and that Jesus is waiting for you in heaven with a sweet lollipop and a new pet hamster, I'm allowed to go about my business relatively unmolested. In heaven, there is no feces.

My tribulations have taught me some lessons, but probably not the ones my accusers wanted me to learn. Among these lessons:

Trust your instincts.

Raise your standards and lower your expectations.

It's always a mistake to care.

Being nice to someone is riskier than being mean.

It is a greater evil to be average than to be wicked.

If you don't take risks, you're already dead.

Stupidity is incurable, and it is often contagious.

We are all bad, especially the good among us.

You know why you did it, so don't feel guilty about it.

Stop worrying about good and bad...and start thinking about true and false.

The problem is never what you think it is.

The answer is "no."

Better a Shit Magnet than a Pity Sponge.

And most importantly:

Shit can be used as fertilizer.

In fact, I think I'm gonna grow daisies atop the shit-heap my life has become. Being joyously happy and fully human will be my way of spiting you all...and therefore being an even bigger asshole than you expected. Being happy would be the ultimate asshole move, really. I'm going to let you expect the worst of me, then I'll scare the fuck out of you by being nice. I'm gonna be so nice, it'll make your gums bleed. My big project will be in determining how not to get myself into trouble, but how to get the rest of the world into trouble. It's the world, not me, that deserves it. The world, not me, should apologize.

You are all so much more loathsome than me. Loathsome in your weakness. Loathsome in your cowardice. Loathsome in your conformity. Loathsome in your ephemerality.

You should all be ashamed of yourselves. Really. You insult me with the very idea that I need forgiveness, especially yours. I don't know why you assumed that your approval was so powerful and life-giving that I needed it. Gawsh, all my life I survived solely on your sympathy—what will I ever do without it? The idea that I need redemption is a comical one. More has been taken from me than I ever took from anyone, and you want me to top it off by wearing sackcloth and ashes? No. I don't need your approval; you need mine. Get it straight. Yes, you are all out of step but me.

I feel clean today. Very, very clean. Couldn't feel cleaner.

Today I did some spring cleaning.

I gave all your shit back to you.

Killing me won't get rid of your self-hatred. Killing me won't stop what I've set in motion. Place my head on a guillotine, and as the blade falls, I'll stick out my tongue. My head bounces down the stairs, tongue stuck out for all to see. Nyah-nyah-nyah. I'm still not sorry.

So if you want to kill me, let's get on with the festivities. But I have one last request: I want you to look in my eyes while you're doing it and admit to me that you enjoy it. Don't hide behind ideas such as "sin" and "justice." Just confess that you get a kick out of killing me, that it makes you feel more alive. That's all I ask.

Ehhh, thank you all very much, and have a nice day.

[After a brief deliberation, the jury sentenced Goad to death. The official court records make no mention of whether the jurors looked in his eyes during the execution, nor whether they enjoyed watching him die.]

⚡18⚡

Death: Yours and Mine

HAVE I TOLD you lately that you're going to die one day? I wouldn't want you to forget. Life wouldn't be worth living without that knowledge constantly plastered to your fucking forehead.

Washed away and forgotten, you will become a millimeter-thick ribbon of fossilized slate in a wall over a million miles high. Death will rape you. Death will tear up your ugly smirking stinking self. It will trap you and squash you and consume you with smothering machine-like efficiency.

As dusk falls like volcanic ash on an open field, you see Death crawling toward you from a distance, and you can't run far enough. The giant black tapeworm opens its lamprey maws and heads your way.

If you run from it, you die.

If you fight it, you die.

If you ignore it, you die.

You die, you die, you die.

Your life is an unfolding snuff film. Death is imprinted on each cell like an invisible birthmark. The death seeds sprout inside you. Like a butterfly inside a chrysalis, your skeleton hibernates, awaiting the day it's set free.

Feel your pulse and realize it will stop ticking.

Inhale deeply and count one less breath until your last.

Wave your limbs around and know that they'll be stiff one day.

One day soon, your body will rid itself of its unwanted guest. That's the ultimate betrayal, when your own body turns against you.

The first gray hair. First wrinkle. First roll of flab. The skin sags. The gums recede. The teeth fall out. The eyes glaze over. The liver quits. The bones start cracking.

And then the mind goes. Ha, ha, that's the worst part, when your brain turns to jelly. What a triumph of the will it will be when the nurses slip the adult diapers on you and spoon-feed you strained carrots and you can't remember your own name and you keep asking when the Easter Bunny's going to show up with all his nice eggs.

Bedpans and sponge baths and cold rectal thermometers. Organ transplants and oxygen tents and catheters jammed up into your kidneys. Biopsies, spinal taps, and barium enemas. Blood in the urine and a spot on the lung. It hurts, it hurts, it hurts. Fever and vomiting and drooling palsied agony and involuntary spasms and exploding aneurysms and chest-cracking heart attacks. White cells get swarmed and destroyed.

You drop like a dog being put to sleep. Like a hair falling to the floor. Like an old elephant crashing to the sawdust.

Your meaningless life flashes before your eyes, every dim ancestral impulse, your brain riffling through flash cards of tribal symbols and ancient icons, a speed-rewind of every ugly face you've ever seen.

The cord is pulled. The picture on the TV screen shrinks to a small dot and vanishes. Your pulse flatlines. Lonely pine-cleaner smells float down the hospital corridor, long shadows slash sideways across hospital walls, cracks in the walls expand, and a bloody dried cotton ball is stuffed in a steel wastebasket.

Dusty scratching sounds hiss and pop on an old record. An upright vacuum cleaner hums in an empty room. Sweet images of laughing sunshiny children are trapped and inverted onto cockroach-colored negatives. Pesticide spray falls softly on insect eggs. The cold wind gently pulls a leaf from a branch and drags it across a field, past a prairie farmhouse that sits alone at night, lights going off from each room one by one.

Dead flames consume dark forests.

Dead ocean pummels rocks into sand.

Dead winds erode canyon walls.

Dead planets circle dead sun like yawning marbles.

Your mannequin corpse, a rotting sac of oozing putrefied proteins, a bloated repellent cadaver with its stupid facial expression of permanent defeat, mocks the notion of human sanctity. You are a plaything, a piece of meat for the pervert mortician who labors over your carcass with auto-mechanic indifference, draining your stagnant blood and spiking your collapsed veins with formaldehyde, then sending you off to the junkyard, where you become manure for our precious fragile ecosystem.

You are planted back inside Mother Earth's cold clammy cunt, down inside an earth whose crust is laced with human bones, whose stratosphere is clogged with evaporated dreams. The teasing diaphanous light laughs on your tombstone, that lifeless little megalith where your relatives pull weeds and lay dying flowers and pray to a dead God who wouldn't listen to them even if he were alive, all the pathetic prayers and anemic affirmations your loved ones recite, all the limp greeting-card slogans they parrot to hide their gleeful guilt for still being alive, each wish fizzling out before it rises ten feet high.

Oh, I forgot—you're going to "heaven," right? Or to "a better place," is that it? Where IS this better place? Could you point it out on a map, please? It's in another dimension, you say? Really? How the FUCK do you know?

You don't go to a better place, you go six feet under.

The metaphysicians have it backwards. They think your "soul," meaning your consciousness, is what lives on, when that's the only part that *dies*. Your body continues to exist, however worse for wear and tear. Your body is the only part of the equation that has an afterlife.

Maybe you don't comprehend what the word "die" means. I'm guessing you don't know what is meant by "lifeless." You're so sure there's a better world after this one, but I don't see you rushing to get there. If you're so certain that you're headed for Elysian Fields, what stops you from killing yourself? Why are you stalling, kid? Why are you postponing the big payoff? If you think you have a soul, why don't I just shoot you in the head so we can test your charming little theory?

The reason you cling to life is because every cell in your body knows the meaning of death.

All of humanity forms a straight line, cradle to grave, toward decomposition and dissolution. Entropy. Things break. Pale Death comes and wins.

How many millennia have we been waiting for a soul—just one—to return from the dead? Since no one has ever come back from the grave, I'm going to take a wild guess and presume that they don't.

The ego doesn't want to hear that it won't last forever. It sees death as a problem. But death sees ego as a problem, and that's why death has killed every ego that ever existed.

Depressing? Death is only depressing to those who find some hope in life. Death only has a sting if you think life means something. But if you don't, you aren't empty.

You're free.

Free from worry.

Free from obligation.

Free from disappointment.

Free to paint reality whatever colors you wish. The colors will all fade eventually, anyway. And once they've faded, you're free to see things clearly again.

When all your dreams are smashed, finally you can see things as they are. Finally comes perception as pure and fast as light. An open endless vacuum stands between you and your own demise. A free-fall into eternity.

Nothing lasts longer than eternal humming blackness. Imagine the midnight sky without any moon or stars. It isn't too far off in your future. This planet can't last forever. We've been pretty lucky slaloming around asteroids. And when that ultra-speedy chunk of star candy finally wallops this orb into a shapeless mass of super-heated vapors, all traces of human existence will be wiped away like tears on a handkerchief. Gone. Everything you ever held dear—gone.

You become space dust, interplanetary waste, a dependent, enslaved, boring micron raped of personality, just microparticles of what used to be a soul now littered into the dark, endless firmament.

Time, the great devourer. Time's mortar and pestle will grind you down. The four seasons follow one another in a seamless loop, softly, brutally wiping you away. One grain in the hourglass. One tick of the wristwatch. One fleck of spent gunpowder smudged along eternity's gaping shotgun barrel. A jerk of the seismograph, that's all you get. A jagged blip on an endless sheet of blank paper.

No angels. No harps. No warm white light. No marshmallowy clouds. No white silk gowns. No gold-paved streets. No annoying choirs. No heavenly father to come and suck you up into his frosty-haired bosom.

No salvation. No forgiveness. No redemption, rebirth, or regeneration. No galloping into the sunset.

Just erasure.

Neutered existence. Antimatter's complete ascendance. Subject becomes object. The cosmic insult of eternal nothingness. Identity wipeout. No ears. No eyes. No you. Death is the victory of everything that isn't you.

There is no fate worse than death. There is no fate other than death. There is no heaven. Everyone goes to hell.

You can't kill death. It is the unifying principle, the vital force, the only constant factor, the only thing that's truly alive. Death is undefeated. Death is God.

What a black comedy, this little divine flea circus, this ant farm of the creator. What a prank God plays on us. God laughs at all ideas of morality. Life is a joke that God tells over and over again, laughing harder each time.

God is not your friend. God does not love you. God isn't here to help you. God is hostile to your interests. God will murder you. God wills you into existence just to tease you, and then he erases you from the blackboard. You are God's pornography, his objectified pleasure.

The only person I ever loved died a few months ago, passing away anonymously in a halfway house, heavily sedated, shriveled and gray like a senior citizen, no friends, family, or pets by her side.

We never made peace with one another.

"Life is torture," she said to a mutual acquaintance near the end, and it's hard to argue with her on that account.

About three years ago while she was undergoing chemotherapy, she told me she dreamed that she was standing on a precipice, looking over at another cliff where cemetery workers were throwing bodies into the chasm between the two cliffs. She couldn't see the bodies as they hit the ground, but she could hear the thumps as they landed.

She's alive only in my dreams. The other night I saw her face, the same dark sadness in her eyes, the same confused purposelessness. She had wished for death all her life, up until the point where it appeared that her wish was being granted, and then she groped for the eternal life which has such a desperate appeal for the dying.

"Better safe than sorry," she always used to tell me, and she wound up sorry anyway. She played life safely, and to what end? Death didn't care. Death came and swallowed her alive. It gulped her down like a bon-bon and kept moving. For a dozen years I could pry nothing more out of the girl than a vague wish for security, yet death came and trampled her.

And me, I haven't been feeling so well myself lately.

I can feel Death passing through me tonight while everyone else sleeps. Wraithlike, Death embraces me, whispering in my ear that my number is soon up. For years now, long before I started writing this book, I've been beset with a profound morbidity, wading through a hall of mirrors where every mirror reflects a skull face. I can't shake the death vibe. It's so hard to walk with one foot in the grave. I'm spooked, punch-drunk on death, a black angel banished to the shadowlands. I came so close to death during all this, it's as if I've been stained by it. As if I've inhaled death. My lungs are clogged with death spores like microscopic burrs, my blood speckled with little black death chips, each sperm a black-hooded executioner.

And oh, how dry the skin on my hands is getting.

I remember dad's flesh all strung tight and strapped across his bones from the cancer, dad humbled and scrawny and hunched-over like a rejected chicken embryo, eyes squinted with pain, coughing, sallow, writhing, wrecked, humiliated, leveled, mocked by the death which had spread through his body like black ink in a glass of water.

And I remember the look on his face as if he'd been cheated, an expression that said his life was a long joke and his corpse would be the punchline:

This is how it ends? This is what I worked for? This is why I fought in the war and paid my taxes?

I ain't going out like daddy did, I can tell you that much. My life may have started with his ejaculatory whimper, but bet all your money that it will go out with a bang. Wide, wide, I open my eyes, straining to glimpse every hue in this Technicolor disaster awaiting me. I came in kicking and screaming, and I'll go out the same way. I'll be plenty relaxed when I'm dead. But until then, I'm going to keep bringing trouble.

I've yet to do everything I want to do, but I'll die trying. This isn't the time or place to reveal my plans. I have a few projects I'm working on, and that's all I can tell you right now.

Somebody will read these words after I'm dead. Maybe it's you. I resurrect myself inside your mind. Writing is the only way I know to stay alive a little while longer. Not forever, mind you—that's impossible, but just a touch longer than they had planned. It's like throwing the car keys in the trunk while it's closing. Or like picking the Grim Reaper's nose while he's carting me away.

Indisputable proof of life's worthlessness is that it always ends. But that shouldn't stop you from whistling "Dixie" as they march you to the ovens.

At the first mention of your terminal diagnosis, I want you to think about me.

As you close your eyes and sink into the drain, I want you to think about me.

Life grows short. Have you done everything you wanted to do, or have you played it safe?

Your entire life is only a dress rehearsal for those terrible last moments when you pass judgment on yourself. In the final seconds before the lights blow out, only you will know whether you've cheated yourself.

Death will approach you. It will ask you if you're ready, and before you can answer, it will take you.

There is no sacrilege you can commit which is worse than what Death will do to you.

So burn as bright and hot as you can, because they're coming to snuff you.

NOTICE

After seeing the printer's bluelines of *Shit Magnet*, author Jim Goad objected to two of the three books we chose to list on the Feral House ad page.

The final page of every book Feral House publishes promotes the products of the company, and its content is created by Feral House's publisher, and not the author of said book.

Because, dear reader, we wish to pacify Mr. Goad, you get to read this announcement instead of seeing book covers and review blurbs.

If you wish to receive a full catalogue of publications, send us a self-addressed envelope to the address below. Or go to the Feral House website at www.feralhouse.com.

Thank you.

Feral House
PO Box 13067
Los Angeles, CA 90013